Baptist Faith in Action

Baptist Faith in Action

The Private Writings of Maria Baker Taylor, 1813–1895

KATHRYN CARLISLE SCHWARTZ

University of South Carolina Press

© 2003 University of South Carolina

Published in Columbia, South Carolina, by the
University of South Carolina Press

Manufactured in the United States of America

07 06 05 04 03   5 4 3 2 1

Library of Congress Cataloging-in-Publication Data

Schwartz, Kathryn Carlisle, 1926–
    Baptist faith in action : the private writings of Maria Baker Taylor, 1813–1895 /
Kathryn Carlisle Schwartz.
        p. cm.
    Includes bibliographical references and index.
    ISBN 1-57003-497-4 (cloth : alk. paper)
    1. Taylor, Maria Baker, 1813–1895. 2. Plantation owners' spouses—Southern States—
Biography. 3. Baptists—Southern States—Biography. I. Title.
    BX6495.T396 S39 2003
    286'.1'092—dc21

To all of Maria's living descendants, especially her great-great-granddaughters Angela, Isabel, and Julia and her great-great-great-granddaughters Serena and Alma, that they may understand this part of where they came from

Contents

Illustrations

Acknowledgments

I am indebted to everyone who has contributed to this study of Maria Baker Taylor, especially those named below.

Although Maria Baker Taylor was my great-grandmother, I learned of the existence of her personal papers only thirteen years ago and quite by coincidence. The initial discovery made, I was then granted access to the mass of family documents that inspired the present volume thanks to the generosity of long-lost second cousins: William Furman Wallace and Dorothea Lee Wallace, descendants of Maria's daughter Dore; and Paul John Weiss Jr., descendant of Maria's daughter Mary, and his wife, Barbara Barnett Weiss. Cousin-in-law Sidney Ford Tatom worked with me in sorting the Wallace Collection and made available another diary.

More-distant cousins also kindly contributed. Thomas deSaussure Furman, a descendant of Maria's eldest brother, provided me with his genealogical record of the Furman/Baker family, the unpublished memoir of James Lyons Furman, information about the South Carolina school that Maria's daughters attended, and family photos. Evelyn Gaillard Rhame, a descendant of Maria's sister, pinpointed the location of Oak Grove, Maria's girlhood home, sent me the record of the archaeological excavation of the site of the first school Maria attended, and added to my collection of family photos.

Two colleagues at Ohio Wesleyan University gave welcome assistance. Uelle Lewes of the English Department followed the project from its inception, making substantive and editorial suggestions at all stages, and Deborah van Broekhoven of the History Department discussed methodological and editorial choices with me from the perspective of the professional historian. Ohio Wesleyan University itself supported my project with two grants for archival research. The cooperative and efficient librarians at the institutions where I carried on most of that research included Lisa Pruitt, curator of special collections at Furman University; Bill Sumners, director of the Southern Baptist Historical Library and Archives; and William Esmonde Howell, archivist of the Sumter County (S.C.) Historical Society.

I am also grateful to Alexander Moore, South Carolina historian who, from his first encounter with the manuscript, immediately recognized the value of the material and understood the reasons for my way of treating it. He then made valuable suggestions for better realizing my aims and provided a number of specific leads for further research.

Finally, I thank my husband, Paul Schwartz, for his advice, assistance, and patience at all stages of this study.

Editorial Notes

A few comments concerning editorial choices that affect the whole volume may be helpful.

Repetition of information among sections. Because the volume has such a large cast of characters, I have repeated some information such as relationships, ages, and dates from one section to the next. The family charts at the beginning of the volume might still be useful for reference.

Mechanics in the diary and letter excerpts. To avoid annoying clutter, I have not employed signals to distinguish partial from complete entries or to indicate the position of the omissions in the partial entries. When Maria's references to the topic at hand consist of only a few words per entry, I have tied these snippets together in an editorial narrative to avoid the distracting interruptions of the diary format. This situation arises in a few parts of the education topics. I have faithfully reproduced the spelling in the primary documents and added commas and paragraphing where needed for immediate intelligibility.

Genealogical information. I have collated five genealogical sources, which contain considerable corroborative overlap; thus I do not identify a specific source for a specific fact. The sources appear in the bibliography: TdeS Furman, Wallace, and Weiss under "Unpublished Genealogical and Biographical Sources"; Haynsworth and Virkus under "Books." The "Family Connections" charts provide a quick overview of the principal players.

The family photographs. I was able to locate three photographs of Maria, one of her husband, photos of all of Maria's children who survived childhood, and photos of four of their spouses. In addition to their names and life spans, the subjects are identified by the names Maria habitually uses for them and by their relationship to her. For the few cases in which the photos are dated or their dates can be closely assigned from evidence in the diaries, I have given the photo a date and the subject an age. Otherwise, approximate dates and ages can be estimated from the life spans of the subjects and their appearance. On this basis, I am certain that all of the photos were taken during Maria's lifetime and represent her family members as she saw and knew them at some point in her long life.

Introduction

Maria Baker Taylor (1813–95) was a Southern Baptist woman of the planter class who was known to few outside her extended family and immediate community. Nevertheless, many aspects of her long life, from girlhood on a South Carolina plantation to old age in a small Florida town, can be reconstructed through documents that total more than one-half million words. This mass of material consists primarily of Maria's diaries, letters, essays, and poems, and includes a variety of supplementary documents. From these primary sources there gradually emerges a portrait of a nineteenth-century woman who accepted the conventional social roles and norms of her milieu. But she was also a woman who brought striking determination and thoughtfulness to fulfilling herself within those confines.

The Subject

Despite her witness to many facets of the extraordinary changes in the American scene during her long life of eighty-two years, Maria Baker Taylor never wavered from a set of beliefs and an attitude toward life that were established in her youth through her family background. Conservative factors in her wider environment later confirmed this mind-set. For example, rather than modify their proslavery views, which Maria's maternal grandfather Richard Furman (1755–1825) had been prominent in formulating, Southern Baptists split from the national church in 1845; and even after the Civil War the South continued in an agrarian social order that in many ways remained unchanged from the pattern Maria had been born into decades earlier.

More specifically, Maria Baker Taylor can be described as a fervent Baptist, wife, mother of thirteen children, educator of her children and grandchildren, plantation mistress, church worker, voracious reader, and dedicated diarist of her daily life and thoughts. Of all of these characteristics, Maria's Baptist faith was paramount, for it controlled and resonated in everything she did and thought. As she wrote in her diary entry of 8 January 1875, "Religion should be carried into the minutest affairs of everyday life." Her self-identity was most powerfully based on her faith, with her family as her chief medium for manifesting that faith. For Maria the purpose of life was to gain the salvation of her immortal soul by discovering and submitting herself to God's will and to guide her family in the same course. Maria's sense of herself as her husband's spiritual equal stemmed from her Baptist tradition, and religion was also at the center of the education she gave her children, in both her own home instruction and her choice of schools. Her views on slavery and her treatment of servants were similarly grounded in her Southern Baptist beliefs.

Maria's faith also impelled her to undertake a wide variety of religious reading. Besides daily immersion in the scriptures, Maria read tracts, collections of sermons, commentaries on the Bible, histories of religion, biographies of religious figures, and weekly religious newspapers of several denominations. She investigated Swedenborg and the Qur'an, Catholic doctrine and Jewish ceremonies. Thus while her faith was simple and unquestioning, she was far from parochial in her intellectual outlook on religion. As for Maria's writing, most of her poems and short prose pieces are in a religious vein, and her diaries and letters frequently attest to an engaged religious consciousness.

Although she was anti-Catholic on a basic doctrinal level and disagreed with other Protestants over specifics such as infant baptism, on a personal level Maria claimed to "have no feeling of bigotry that I am aware of, as I have Methodists, Presbyterians & Baptists in my family, & have had a Catholic, & never had a religious quarrel, & believing as I do with Cowper[1] 'that Religion should extinguish strife,' I hope I never will."

Many of Maria's ancestors on both sides had arrived in America by the end of the seventeenth century. On her mother's side, her earliest immigrant ancestor, John Furman, was a Puritan who came to

Massachusetts with Winthrop's fleet in 1631. Wood Furman, fifth-generation American and the first Furman in South Carolina, located in Sumter District with his family in 1756. His wife, Rachel Brodhead, was descended from English and Dutch immigrants who had settled near the present-day Hudson River town of Kingston, New York, in the 1660s. Wood and Rachel's son Richard Furman, mentioned above, married Elizabeth Haynsworth, descended from a seventeenth-century English immigrant to Virginia and a Swiss family that arrived in South Carolina in 1734.

On her father's side, the Bakers, Maria appears to have been of English descent only. Her father's great-great-grandfather arrived in South Carolina from Yorkshire in the 1680s, and the known names of the women who married into the Baker family are all English. Maria, then, was the descendant of long-established American families.

Maria's life falls naturally into four periods of roughly twenty years each, and she spent each period in a distinct locale. From her birth on 5 December 1813 until her marriage at age twenty, she lived in Sumter District, South Carolina, on the plantation of her parents, Thomas and Rachel Furman Baker. In early adulthood, ages twenty through thirty-nine, she lived in Beaufort District, South Carolina, on the plantation of her husband, John Morgandollar Taylor. Here eleven of her children were born.

In middle age, thirty-nine through sixty-two years, she lived on her husband's (and later her own) plantation in Marion County, Florida. Here her two youngest children were born and her husband died. After struggling with the plantation for a few years after his death, Maria moved to Gainesville, Florida, and spent her remaining years, ages sixty-two to eighty-two, residing in turn with several of her children who had settled there. She died in December 1895.

Maria was economically privileged from birth. Her father owned a 3,000-acre plantation. According to U.S. Census reports, he held forty slaves in 1820 and sixty-five slaves in 1830, figures that locate the Baker family well within the planter class. Of course, factors other than economic level also contribute to the concept of class, perhaps most powerfully family lifestyle and aspirations. Maria's milieu in this sense contrasted with the sentimental popular image of the southern planter class—the high-living, high-toned chivalric gentleman, and the charming, coquettish southern belle—as well as with an actual group like the Sea Island planters of Beaufort District, South Carolina (where Maria lived in the early years of her marriage), whose main aspirations consisted of competitive conspicuous consumption.[2]

Maria's immediate cultural locale might be termed the evangelical planter class, for, in comparison to the above images, family documents suggest that it was a sober-minded group in its focus on religious and family duty and its disapproval of worldly vanities. Although there had been pockets of wealthy Baptist planters in South Carolina since the eighteenth century,[3] the merging of planter status with Baptist discipline was somewhat unusual at a time when the Baptist denomination was made up largely of blacks and the poorer whites. In the Bakers' case, the merging can be ascribed at least partly to Maria's grandfather Richard Furman, who by 1814 was the most important Baptist in America[4] and who evangelized extensively among rich and poor in South Carolina.

Maria remained in the planter class after her marriage, the figures for her husband's plantations in South Carolina and Florida being comparable to those of her father's plantation. The same strong evangelical element surrounded her in the Beaufort District area she and her husband first lived in, but that influence was considerably diluted in the frontier area of their Florida plantation. After the Civil War, the Florida plantation lost much of its value because of crop failures and labor problems, but Maria derived a little income from it even after she moved into town.

The degree to which Maria depended financially on her children during the final phase of her life is not entirely clear. She made gifts of parcels of the plantation land to several of them, so they had some material obligation to her on that account. Also, her children paid Maria tuition for the family school she conducted for her grandchildren, and services that were less quantifiable frequently were exchanged within the family.

Provenance of the Primary Sources

Most of the primary documents were discovered in five collections, two of them privately held by Maria's descendants and three located in Baptist institutions.

The Wallace Collection in Gainesville, Florida, contains thirteen of Maria's diaries, a portfolio of her miscellaneous writings, letters written by Maria and other family members, a genealogy, photographs, and legal documents. The Weiss Collection in Greensboro, North Carolina, contains nine more of Maria's diaries, assorted other papers of Maria, photographs, a genealogy, and diaries of Maria's daughter Mary Louise and Mary's husband Thomas Creyon Bauskett.

The Furman Family Papers in the Southern Baptist Collection at Furman University in Greenville, South Carolina, yielded seventy letters written by Maria over a sixty-year period to her uncle James Clement Furman and his sister Ann Eliza Furman, as well as thirty-five letters written by other members of the Furman family that pertain to Maria and her family. The newspaper archives of the Southern Baptist Historical Commission in Nashville, Tennessee, and the Southern Baptist Theological Seminary in Louisville, Kentucky, yielded sixteen of the poems and prose pieces Maria published in Baptist newspapers in the 1870s and 1880s.

Except for the newspaper pieces, an undated letter of Maria's found only in Harvey Toliver Cook's 1926 biography of James Clement Furman, and the 1867 diary found only in a typescript authorized by Maria's granddaughter Ellen Wallace, all of the above documents have survived in original manuscript form. This material, obviously rich in variety and chronological range, totals about 650,000 words.[5]

Description of the Primary Sources

A major feature of Maria's religious consciousness was the familiar Christian "duty of self examination," as she put it. This awareness of who she is and how she wishes to project herself comes out most clearly in the letters and miscellaneous writings, but it also appears in small instances in the diaries.

Twenty-two extant diaries, distributed over the years 1857 through 1895,[6] can be most generally described as logs of daily activities from which emerges a picture of a way of life. The majority of the diary entries fall between 60 and 150 words, and for the most part the entries are written in short simple sentences. However, the diaries open and close with prayers that reveal Maria's control of a more complex style, and at the end of many of the diaries she wrote flowing narrative summaries and meditative comments on the year's major events. Unlike some of her diary-writing contemporaries, Maria did not address her diary as a trusted confidante or otherwise personify it,[7] and expressions of emotion, interpretations of events, or judgments on other people are for the most part restrained, brief, and scattered. Nevertheless, readers can easily fathom Maria's attitudes, concerns, and values.

The diaries reveal that Maria strove for tranquil self-possession in the face of difficulties and for order in the conduct of practical affairs. She apparently expected the same from her husband; her main criticisms of him are for depression, irritability, and lack of system. Although occasionally hinted at, details of unpleasant family scenes and explicit negative judgments of family members are largely missing from the diaries, no doubt from Maria's desire not to memorialize emotional wounds and from her sense of what was unworthy of a Christian to dwell on. While Maria may mention "a foolish quarrel" among family members, she rarely names the people or tells the substance of the friction, thus minimizing it while admitting its existence.[8] In a few cases in which an interesting situation has been building up over several entries and seems headed for a showdown— the bad influence of a future son-in-law on her boys, family conflict over the disciplining of a servant—two or three entries have been removed and no more is heard of the affair. But perhaps someone other than Maria did the censoring.

As for her motives in diary-writing, if Maria had had any thought of publication for her diaries, there would surely be many more developed and polished entries that were written in a manner comparable to her sophisticated letter-writing style. But of course she did have audiences, herself for one. Parts of some entries are practical notations for future reference, for example, when the beans were planted or a servant assigned a task. On a higher plane, Maria occasionally mentions an evening spent reading over her old diaries, an exercise that must have developed and confirmed her sense of self-identity. She also read diary passages aloud to family members, rehearsing the past and cementing family ties. Occasionally she read passages to close friends when they faced problems similar to those she had recorded, for example, the death of a child.

Maria clearly expected her children to have access to her diaries after she died, for she did not destroy them when she was obviously failing, and one daughter claimed that Maria had promised them all to her. A few of Maria's comments seem concerned to project a certain image of herself to a potential family reader. For example, writing on the Fourth of July 1873, Maria makes clear that she is not the kind of person who enjoys vulgar entertainments when she distances herself from the spectacle of boys climbing a greasy pole "for the $15.00 on top" by calling it "a semi-barbaric practice." Two days later, she examines why she took communion from a clergyman of a denomination (Presbyterian) that practiced infant baptism, a sacrament disapproved of by Baptists. And some years later, on her only trip to New York City, she comments about seeing a play, "I was somewhat amused. I went to the theater with an object & not to spend money foolishly" (20 August 1875).

Maria kept up a voluminous correspondence with immediate family members away from home and with South Carolina relatives and friends. Especially after the move to Florida, Maria felt isolated from her South Carolina connections and yearned for communication with them, a feeling she had in common with the many nineteenth-century American women who resettled in areas far from their original homes. The bulk of her extant letters were written to Ann Eliza Furman and James Clement Furman, her mother's much younger half-sister and half-brother. Maria's explicit aim was to write in such a way that these South Carolina relatives would be enticed to reply. For example, in an 1853 letter to James, she speaks of "my wish to write you a long letter which I was desirous should be very interesting" in response to his "kind and prompt answer to my last." She also wanted to exchange ideas with James and Ann, whom she had always admired as persons of superior intellect and refinement. In addition to the usual family news, Maria wrote on educational, religious, political, and literary topics, and about Florida property.

Maria's letter-writing vocabulary is sophisticated, complex syntactic structures are handled with authority, and graceful or pointed turns of phrase are not uncommon. The tone in the letters is alternately serious and sprightly, objective and affectionate. Maria can suggest criticism through a tone of wry amusement, as when she writes to Ann Furman that her daughter Anne's fiancé has given Anne "a photograph album with his own phiz adorning it" and sums up the couple's relationship as "she loves, & he loves, & she has a good deal to love, for he weighs over 200!" (10 February 1874). Some idea of the tone Maria liked to see in a letter can be derived from comments on her children's letters. After thanking a daughter for writing, Maria says forthrightly, "I was disappointed that you did not have it a little more of a 'Dore Taylor letter,'" evidently finding it lacking in personal voice; and on an approving note, she comments on some correspondence between a son and a daughter that it is "characterized by affection and delicacy of sentiment."

Maria clearly aspired to a modest degree of acknowledgment as a writer from her personal circle and religious community. Throughout her life she kept a manuscript portfolio of her writings from which she read to family and friends, and she published pieces in community and regional Baptist newspapers. Revisions in some of her manuscripts, comments in her diaries, and letters asking advice from her college-professor son-in-law, indicate that Maria worked thoughtfully at her craft.

Many of Maria's poems are of a domestic nature, commemorating family birthdays and deaths or meditating on the state of her children's souls. Other pieces are more generally devotional, and a few can be described as theological. Maria composed a long epic poem about the family's move to Florida, and other verses include a political campaign song, an attack on barrooms, and praise of a piano. The miscellaneous prose writings include a defense of slavery, a reminiscence of her girlhood, advice to children, obituaries of friends and relatives, newspaper travel letters, and brief religious and didactic articles. Some of the latter were solicited by a friend who was an editor for several Baptist newspapers, and he paid her a little something for them.

Presentation of the Primary Sources

Each set of women's private writings presents its own characteristics that require unique solutions to render them accessible to the reading public. The most basic editorial task presented by the Maria Baker Taylor material was reducing it to produce a volume of sensible size given the subject. The judgment call here was to eliminate about nine-tenths of the available mass. At the same time, it was essential to preserve the features of the primary material that make it a distinctive record of a nineteenth-century woman's private life. These features were primarily the chronological range of the material, which represents all phases of Maria's long life, and the diversity of the primary sources, which include not only the various types of Maria's writings but also letters and diaries from other hands, legal documents, and obscure published sources. On the substantive level, the most challenging task was of course to select the one-tenth of the material that would faithfully project Maria's life course, mind-set, and central concerns, and to arrange the selections in a manner that would make them immediately intelligible to the reader.

After long and thorough familiarity with the initially unwieldy set of documents, I became convinced that an organic basic structure was inherent in the material, namely, a structure that integrated two large-scale features of the documents, Maria's life phases and her central concerns. Thus the four parts of the volume correspond with the four twenty-year periods produced by the fortuitous coinciding of natural life phases with the changes in Maria's place of residence noted above. During these periods, a relatively small number of central concerns dominated Maria's consciousness and activities. These concerns for the most part remained constant throughout her adult life, although their manifestation naturally changed somewhat with her age and circumstances. The topics, or chapters, within each part, then, represent Maria's central concerns for that period, and each topic, illustrated with the most pertinent material from the primary documents, is taken through its own chronology. The topics themselves are arranged within the sections as chronologically as their material allows; that is, there is occasionally some necessary chronological overlap among topics. An introduction and conclusion for each part provide useful orientation and draw on material not elsewhere exploited.[9] In the epilogue I present my assessment of the meaning of Maria's life, aided by others who knew her well.

Two considerations about the structure just described should be noted. In the first part, which deals with Maria's girlhood, most of the documents are from hands other than Maria's and therefore the identified concerns are not expressed by Maria herself. However, the topics represent concerns crucial to any young person, and the material naturally sorts itself out accordingly. The third part, which covers Maria's middle years, is longer than the other three parts combined. This length reflects both the richness of the material for that period and the need to adequately illustrate the radical changes in circumstance, but not locale, wrought by the Civil War.

As for the details of presentation within each chapter, the diary and letter excerpts are for the most part confined to the topic at hand, but occasional fuller excerpts suggest the context of daily living in which the topic plays out. However, some parts of a few topics require a somewhat different treatment to be easily grasped; reasons for such differences are explained locally. In all cases, the nature of the sources and the presentation that renders them most readable take precedence over an artificial uniformity.

Once selected and arranged as described above, the primary documents required editorial intervention to provide sufficient continuity and context to render them readily intelligible, given their variety, large cast of characters, changing locales, and chronological range and gaps. As part of this editorial intervention, information is provided about such things as Maria's family milieu, the places in which she lived, the schools she sent her children to, and other conditions that most closely pressed upon her. While this necessary intervention forms a narrative of sorts that may occasionally bear a superficial resemblance to a standard biography, the product remains a documentary edition: the quantity of primary material greatly outweighs the commentary, and the interpretation of the documents is left to the reader. The voice of Maria Baker Taylor holds center stage.

The Value of the Study

The value of the private writings of obscure persons such as Maria is frequently addressed by scholars in the field. Individual scholars bring out different facets, and it is illuminating to touch on a few of these. Judy Nolte Lensink cites Franz Boas's[10] assertion that "each person is the locus of culture" to suggest that diaries of unknown women are valuable ethnographic records because they preserve the multiplicity of perspectives lost in the drive to generalize and abstract. Elizabeth Hampsten stresses that "usually the quest is for a sense of presence" that is "rooted in the concrete and particular," while Virginia Beauchamp reminds us that, throughout American history, "people have gone about their daily lives in wholly personal ways" and that women's private writings can feed our insatiable desire to know what those ways were. Robert Manson Myers speaks simply of the importance of "the records of ordinary people leading ordinary lives and facing ordinary problems." In a different vein, Minrose C. Gwin sees in women's private writings "the textual production of history as a domestic subject," a new field of inquiry, and Elizabeth Fox-Genovese's finding that the history of southern women is still inadequate implies the importance of private writings in increasing the body of evidence.[11]

Of course, scholars will quickly see that Maria Baker Taylor could be treated in terms of any number of already established nineteenth-century frameworks: plantation life, southern evangelicals, education of children, women's kinship networks, prescriptive models of womanhood, private writings of other obscure persons, theory and stylistic analysis of women's private writings, the grief process in women's diaries, ordinary people's perceptions of crucial historical events, and so on. Scholars working in these and similar specialities may find these documents, here put into public circulation for the first time, to be useful resources. General readers too may find material they can apply to their perspectives; for example, Baptists can witness the workings of their faith, southerners may engage more intimately with their past way of life, and women might ponder whether what now seems an archaic female role has anything to recommend it.

For academic and general readers, value in all of these senses inheres in the private writings of Maria Baker Taylor and the associated documents. In addition, three specific features of the MBT material are of special value, for they are not often found in similar studies: the documents access in some degree all the phases of the long life of an obscure nineteenth-century woman; they give a full picture of old age at a time when old age was much less frequently attained than at present; and they offer insight into a Baptist planter sensibility. But I hope that, most importantly, whoever takes up this volume for whatever reason will come away with a sense of what it was like to be Maria Baker Taylor.

Family Connections

Furman Descent of Maria Baker Taylor

Wood Furman (1712–83)
m 1742 Rachel Brodhead (1712–94)

> Richard Furman (1755–1825)
> *m* (1st) 1774 Elizabeth Haynsworth (1755–87)
>
>> Rachel Furman (1777–1848)
>> *m* 1796 Thomas Baker (1772–1842)
>>
>>> Maria Baker
>>> *m* 1834 John Morgandollar Taylor

ॐ

Issue of Richard Furman's Second Marriage Mentioned in MBT Documents

Richard Furman
m (2nd) 1789 Dorothea Burn

> Samuel Furman (1792–1877)
> *m* Eliza Scrimzeour (see JMT descent below)
>
> Josiah Furman (1795–?)
> Maria Dorothea Furman (1799–1870)
> Henry Hart Furman (1801–46)

Issue of Richard Furman's Second Marriage
Mentioned in MBT Documents *continued*

Sarah Susannah Furman (1804–36)
James Clement Furman (1809–91)
Ann Eliza Furman (1812–97)

ॐ

Descent of John Morgandollar Taylor

John Morgandollar (1751–1806)
m 1774 Elizabeth Strobel (1746–1809)

Mary Morgandollar (1774–1842) *first marriage*
m (**1st**) James Scrimzeour

Eliza Scrimzeour
m Samuel Furman (see RF list above)

Mary Furman (b 1815)

Mary Morgandollar *second marriage*
m (**2nd**) 1808 John Taylor (1762–1825)

John Morgandollar Taylor
m Maria Baker

ॐ

Issue of Maria Baker Taylor (1813–95)
and John Morgandollar Taylor (1809–72)

Caroline Taylor (1835–98)
m 1858 James Baird Dawkins (1819–83)

Elizabeth Taylor (1836–41)

Mary Louise Taylor (1837–1905)
m (**1st**) 1857 Thomas Creyon Bauskett (1829–68)
m (**2nd**) 1870 Frederick William Ansley

Issue of Maria Baker Taylor (1813–95)
and John Morgandollar Taylor (1809–72) *continued*

Thomas Baker Taylor (1839–41)

Lydia Taylor (1840–1920?)
m 1869 Edward Payson Crane (1832–1905)

John Morgandollar Taylor Jr. (1842–1904)
m 1864 Curran Broome (1844–1933)

Susan Taylor (1844–1895)
m 1883 John William Nott Beard (1842–99)

William Baker Taylor (1845–64)

Richard Furman Baker Taylor (1847–1931)
m 1876 Kate Ansley

Robert Fenwick Taylor (1849–1928)
m 1872 Amelia Evans Haile (1850–1902)

Maria Dorothea Taylor (1850–1919)
m 1874 William Christian Wallace (1832–1902)

Jane Thomasa Taylor (1854–64)

Anne Baker Taylor (1856–89)
m 1874 Julius Addison Carlisle (1846–1915)

ꝏ

Grandchildren Taught by MBT (birth year following name)

John Taylor

Willie / 1869
Nettie / 1872
Gilbert / 1879

Fen Taylor

Serena (Ena) / 1878
Carl / 1882

Grandchildren Taught by MBT
(birth year following name) *continued*

Dore Wallace

Richie / 1880
Ellen / 1883
Harney / 1888

Anne Carlisle

Millie / 1875
Carrie / 1877
Kitty / 1878
Tommy / 1881
Maria / 1883
John / 1887

One

GIRLHOOD IN SUMTER DISTRICT,
SOUTH CAROLINA, 1813–34

Introduction

Christened Sarah Maria but always called by her second name, Maria Baker[1] was the beneficiary of a stable and prosperous family setting. The immediate family circle consisted of her parents, Thomas Baker (1772–1842) and Rachel Furman Baker (1777–1848), and their five children. Maria, the middle child, had two older brothers and a younger brother and sister; after the oldest brother's early death, his widow and daughter joined the household, becoming in effect Maria's older sister and a second younger sister.

Several years before Maria was born on 5 December 1813, her parents had moved from Charleston to Sumter District, Thomas having purchased a plantation in the area known as the High Hills of Santee. This was familiar territory to Rachel, who had been born in "the Hills" and reared there until her father, Richard Furman, accepted the pastorate of the First Baptist Church in Charleston when Rachel was ten. Thomas, the fourth generation in a line of Charleston merchants, appears to have been the first planter in his family.

The 1825 *Mills Atlas* marks the Bakers' plantation house, Oak Grove, at about six miles north-northeast of Stateburg and ten miles northwest of Sumterville.[2] Their summer residence, Woodville, was nearby, as were the Woodville Academy, cofounded by Thomas Baker for the education of the neighborhood children,[3] and the Furman Theological Institution. The 3,000-acre plantation itself, called Bradleys, was a mile or so away on the Wateree River. The Bakers attended the High Hills Baptist Church, where Rachel's father had been converted from the Anglican faith in 1774.

Maria's writings from this period, consisting of her school papers and one letter, are supplemented by contemporary letters of family members and by reminiscences written much later by Maria and other people who knew the Bakers at the time. Because so much of the material that provides glimpses of Maria and her girlhood milieu comes from correspondence of Furman family members, it will be useful to identify her six Furman half-uncles and half-aunts (much younger half-siblings of her mother) whose documents are drawn on or who are referred to in this section.

Samuel Furman was a Baptist clergyman, married to Eliza Scrimzeour, the half-sister of Maria's future husband; Samuel and Eliza lived at various times in Beaufort and Sumter Districts. Henry Furman was a Charleston merchant and Maria's father's cotton agent. James Clement Furman, only four years older than Maria, was also a Baptist clergyman. When Maria was in her teens, James was something of a youthful prodigy as a preacher. Maria Dorothea, Sara Susannah (Susan), and Ann Eliza Furman lived together in Charleston and also for extended periods in Sumter District. Ann, the youngest, was only a year older than Maria. Also mentioned is Wood Furman II, Rachel Baker's only full sibling, a schoolmaster. Members of the Baker/Furman clan, most of whom were intensely pious Baptists, exchanged constant visits and correspondence in the triangle of Sumter District, Charleston, and Beaufort District.

ONE

Family and Formative Background

Impressions of Maria's parents and her family background emerge from passages in a wide range of documents: family letters from 1793, 1799, 1829, 1832, 1833, and 1836; and reminiscences from 1875, 1881, and 1882.

The religious commitment Rachel Furman Baker passed on to Maria may be inferred from two documents. First, Rachel's Baptist education and youthful piety are apparent in a letter she wrote from Charleston at the age of sixteen to her father's mother. Rachel Jr. had apparently just made her own profession of faith.

17 August 1793. Rachel Furman to Rachel Brodhead Furman
[XX=tear in ms]

Dear Grandmama

I embrace this oppertunity to inform you that we are tolerable XX through mercy at present and hope you all are the same Through grace I have [been] inabled to take on me the profession of Christ tho' unworthy of it I find his ways to be ways of pleasantness and all his paths peace. I long to see you all very much but don't know when I shall. Do Grandmama come down to see us if you can. I must now conclude, beging your prayers at a throne of grace that I may be enabled to grow in grace and in the knowledge of Christ XX I have put my hand to the gospel plough. I may not look back again to the world and the things thereof. Give my kind

love to Uncle, Aunt and all my relations. I remain Dear Grandmama

Your loving granddaughter R Furman

An example of Rachel's religious activity as an adult can be seen in an
incident of 1824 described in a letter written by Mrs. V. A. Scarsboro
to James Clement Furman about 1881:

> If I live till the 27th of next November, it will be 57 years since
> I was assembled in the vestry room, belonging to the Baptist
> Church at the High Hills of Santee and your dear sister of very
> precious memory, Mrs Rachel Baker, was there in preparing me
> for the baptismal waters, administered by dear brother Hartwell.
> She, at the time, stated how fervently and earnestly and sincerely
> she had with three other females prayed for a revival of religion in
> that church and before the close of the year, one hundred persons
> were baptised and added to the church.[1]

Richard Furman must have thought well of his daughter's intelligence and practical ability, because he named her, along with three of
his sons, as co-executor of his will although he had a number of other
sons. Much earlier, in a letter of 4 March 1799 to his sister, Richard
had noted that Rachel at age twenty-two "enjoys the proper Encriese
of her rational Powers," a comment suggesting that the women of the
family were expected to be persons of intellectual capacity.

Thomas Baker, called "Captain" from his service in the U.S.
Army Corps of Engineers during the War of 1812, had a local reputation as architect, surveyor, and exacting businessman, the latter a
trait derived from his merchant family background. Other traits and
interests are evident in these two passages.

10 April 1829. Henry Hart Furman to James Clement Furman

> I also understand that Capt Baker has been planting the sugar
> cane. It is worthy of an experiment and I hope it may realize the
> most sanguine expectations. I will thank you to tell Capt Baker
> that Col Johnson's foreman informs me that a northern mile has
> come out similar to his own, with but a slight variation.

8 October 1832. Maria Dorothea Furman to Henrietta Dargan Furman

Capt Baker has offered any or all of the students [at the Furman Theological Institution] the means of going to Sumterville if they will vote with him. He seems to entertain no doubt of the success of our ticket.[2]

In a long letter in which he explains the architectural plans that James Clement Furman had asked him to draw up for a Baptist church, Thomas reveals attitudes on race and Catholicism, which Maria absorbed.

28 October 1836. Thomas Baker to James Clement Furman

I have drawn a font in the church, which ought not to be dispensed with in any Baptist church. The well to supply it with water may be placed in the [?] under the portico and a trough to carry the water may pass through the building under the pulpit to this font. Supposing that it would not be so pleasant to have the white & colored persons all entering the church through one door, I have designed two side doors[3] leading from the recess under the portico into the lobbies. . . . I have just been requested to draw a plan of a catholic church to be erected somewhere near the Borough. I excused myself by observing that I was just then ingaged in drawing the plan of a Christian church[4]—but I suppose I shall have to do or give offence to some of my neighbors.

As for the two doors, one wonders through which door Thomas would have had people like the Ellisons enter. Members of the William Ellison family, fellow parishioners of Thomas Baker at the High Hills Baptist Church, were free blacks, one of whom owned twelve and another thirty slaves,[5] and other free blacks also attended the church.[6]

From a remove of forty years, Maria herself gives a glimpse of her life at Oak Grove in one of the "Grandmother's Letters" she was writing in the 1870s. Letter No. 3 presents a lightly fictionalized account of her girlhood home; Maria's sister Mary Louise becomes "Aunt Louise," and the letter-writer persona is a granddaughter telling her grandmother about her visit to the grandmother's child-hood home. The formative influences of the rural social life and the seminary atmosphere are apparent.

Aunt Louise says this neighborhood was a gay place when you were a young lady & lived here; that it was then a summer resort, for health & pleasure, & that your father's house was scarcely ever free from company of the young & old. Evening parties were frequent, & gotten up without any effort, & delightful weekly riding parties on horseback, when gentlemen would come for forty miles, to join them; I think they must have had some other attraction & object in view, than the ride, as there were, of course, no Rail Roads in South Carolina then, & I think she built the first in the United States.

The Furman Theological Seminary, a Baptist Institution, was within walking distance of you, situated on a beautiful Hill, to which your riding parties attached the sobriquet of "Paradise regained," Aunt Louise informs me. From the number of intelligent students, who were members of the Institution, it must have been very pleasant to attend their debating society, the Lyceum, & the preaching at the Chapel, which must certainly have had the charm of variety.[7]

The country religious revival meetings Maria attended were another formative influence. Maria wrote an account of one such meeting in response to a request she received some fifty years after the event.

14 September 1882. Maria Baker Taylor to Ann Eliza Furman

I had a postal from Uncle James [Clement Furman] a few evenings ago, asking me if I remembered any incidents of the Edgefield meetings we attended, between 1831 & 33. He & I went together in a gig or buggy, & Mr Hartwell & Miss E Brodie accompanied us. The meetings before we went, had been so interesting & successful in the conversion of souls, that they had sent for help.

The meeting Maria chose to describe occurred in 1831, when James was twenty-one and Maria seventeen.

1882. Maria Baker Taylor in response to James Clement Furman's request[8]

I had a charming time going into the midst of a remarkable revival and participating in the benefits of the meeting . . . The whole country was ablaze with the wonderful conversions and marvellous work of God's Spirit. The country churches that had caught the flame and imbibed the spirit desired preaching. To one of these about six miles from the town my uncle was sent and asked me to accompany him. . . . The youthful preacher with deep solemnity invited his many listeners to "come and see." They did so with open ears, eyes and mouths, and if they did not it was not the fault of the divinely gifted speaker or the Spirit of Power who inspired him.

The two brethren in the pulpit found it impossible to keep their seats, and, leaning near his side, one would continually nod his approbation, while the other occasionally ejaculated, "That's it, that's it." The occupants of the galleries and stairs went on like Methodists in their utterances of feelings and approval.

What a harvest of souls there was to that sermon! When it was ended the space between the pulpit and the aisles was crowded with weeping and praying mourners—old grey-headed men, young men, and maidens, and stout-hearted infidels who had persistently and prominently with loud mouths resisted all the previous administrations of divine truth.

One of them who had been the subject of conversation at our meals, swung himself from the gallery, the stairway being crowded, his friends all around uttering exclamations of surprise and delight. I could not help it and laughed out and cried, and thought I never would say a word against the holy laugh again.

In addition to the joyful side of the religious atmosphere Maria grew up in, the child herself had a sunny temperament, for "laughing like Maria Baker" was a family saying, and accounts of the brother closest to her in age and companionship portray an amusing, spirited youth.[9] The social values and tone cultivated in the wider family circle are seen in an 1833 exchange of letters between Ann and Maria Furman regarding Maria Baker's hurt feelings.

4 July 1833. Ann Eliza Furman to Maria Dorothea Furman in Stateburg

I am afraid that Maria [Baker] is seriously hurt with me, & I must acknowledge, that she has to all appearances much cause to be so. Do tell her for me, that because I have not written she must not suppose that I have forgotten her; or that I feel the less obliged to her for the pleasure which her kind and interesting letters afforded me. I suppose that I must not expect her forgiveness until she becomes a housekeeper, & has learnt by experience, how difficult it is to find time for epistolary correspondence. Tell Maria that should she accompany you down in the winter which she certainly must do, I hope to have a fine supply of sweetmeats to regale her on; & that I shall have a special regard to her in making them.

[?] July 1833. Maria Dorothea Furman to Ann Eliza Furman

Maria was I believe somewhat disposed to be hurt at your silence, but she says that the news of the sweetmeats has quite reconciled her. Cousin Lydia[10] asks if you have forgotten that she has a mouth too, which relishes good things as well as any other person's.

30 July 1833. Ann Eliza Furman to Maria Dorothea Furman

Tell Cousin Lydia, that I was far from forgetting her, I only mentioned to Maria what my designs were with regard to the sweetmeats, in order to appease her wrath, & I am happy to hear that it has produced that effect. The idea that my dear Cousin will partake of them with me, will greatly enhance the pleasure of making them.

TWO

Schooling

Maria's school experiences can be partially reconstructed from her school papers, a memoir of 1905, and family letters of 1829, 1832, and 1833.

Maria's only mention of her first school is the brief comment, "I was first initiated into school life at Woodville," found in a diary entry when at the age of sixty-two she was revisiting Oak Grove and walked over to the school site. James Lyons Furman, a first cousin of Maria's who also attended the school, gives more information in an unpublished memoir written in 1905. The Woodville Academy, founded in 1817 by Thomas Baker and his neighbors for the education of their children,[1] was housed in a fifteen-by-thirty-foot log cabin especially erected for the purpose. Maria's uncle Wood Furman II, a 1799 honors graduate of Rhode Island College, a Baptist institution in Providence,[2] was engaged as teacher. The curriculum included reading, grammar, spelling, geography, history, arithmetic, and Latin.[3]

Among the sixty-three sheets of Maria's school papers, three undated sheets in a childish scrawl and with childish misspellings may be presumed to date from her Woodville Academy days. The content suggests that another significant feature of the curriculum was instilling social, moral. and religious values. Some samples follow.

> Be industrious, be economical, shun avarice; determine to be
> useful.
> Never complain of unavoidable calamities.

It is not honarble to dispute about trifles.

You must not try to deceive your playmates.

Never quarel with your playmates.

Little girl and boys must not be fretful.

Idle children neglect there books while young and thus reject their advantages.

There are many ocasions in life in which silence and simplicity are true wisdom.

Vain persons are fond of the allurementt of dress.

If sinners intice thee, consent thou not, but withdraw from their company.

No pleasure is equal to that of a quiet conscience.

Before you retire at night or rise in the morning, give thanks to God for his mercies and implore the continuance of his protection.

Guard well thy thoughts, thy thoughts are heard in heaven.

The death bed is a detector of the heart.

The Academy also had good advice for the writer.

> A tale should be judicious, clear, succinct,
> the language plain, and in cedence⁴ well linked,
> tell not as new, what everybody knows,
> and new or old hasten to a close.

Several letters show Maria attending school in Charleston early in 1829, soon after her fifteenth birthday; this was probably the beginning of her schooling away from home. Nothing is known of the institution beyond the information in the letters; it was doubtless one of the many proprietary schools in Charleston at the time.⁵

In Charleston, Maria lived with her mother's bachelor half-brother Henry Hart Furman, a merchant who served as her father's cotton agent. At Henry's house, Maria found an atmosphere as strongly Baptist as that at Oak Grove, and looking back some ten years later, she pronounced him a person of "pure & refined feelings."⁶ The cast of mind of this relative, and hence his *in loco parentis* influence on Maria, can be sensed from three documents. In the first, a paragraph in her Charleston school papers that Maria attributes to Henry, he reflects on the human condition.

The essence of the gospel is universal love, and in the admission of this principle, we are to admit of no distinction among our fellow men, we are required to love our neighbor as ourselves. Did the gospel have its proper influence there would not be a state of enmity existing in our world: but such is our present constitution, that we cannot act in full accordance with the gospel requisition; we cannot now, in the strict sense of the word, love our enemies as we do our friends. Henry Furman

In the second document, Henry expresses views that were stricter than the general Southern Baptist toleration of moderate drinking.[7]

22 June 1832. Henry Hart Furman to James Clement Furman

I send you two copies of a national circular on Temperance, which I think well deserving the attention of every individual. I believe we cannot estimate fully the ill effects resulting to individuals and society from the use, and what too is termed the moderate use, of alcoholic liquors, and every one who feels an interest in the happiness of society [should] lend his aid in putting down so pernicious a practice. I would be pleased if you would let our friends generally have the perusal of these pieces, Bro Wood, Bro Samuel, Capt Baker etc.[8] It is a matter that ought to have attention. Is there a Temperance Society in the neighbourhood? If not I would advise you to endeavor to get up one.

In another letter, Henry refers specifically to Maria's education.

20 February 1829. Henry Hart Furman to James Clement Furman

I scarcely know what to say in relation to Capt. Baker's inquiries respecting Maria's progress and Miss B's qualifications. I have not thought from what I have seen of Miss B[9] that her qualifications were sufficiently ample to enable her to discharge properly the high and important duties which belong to the station which she at present fills, but this may be an erroneous opinion, and I would rather withhold it, and let her qualifications be attested by the proficiency of her pupils. With respect to Maria's economy I have no reason to complain, and I do not think her father will find her wanting in that particular.

A letter of Thomas Baker's gives more information about Maria's schooling and illustrates Thomas's own continuing education of his daughter. Decades later, Maria made a gift of the letter to one of her daughters, writing on the envelope, "Valuable as an example of the education and style of expression of those days."

5 March 1829. Thomas Baker to Maria Baker (complete letter)

My Dear Daughter

Your favor of the 5th instant[10] came to hand in due course some ten or twelve days since, as also a letter to your sister Lydia,[11] and within a day or two one to your Brother; yours of the 5th I would have answered immediately, but as I have been much engaged in preparing the buildings which are necessary for the accomodation and comfort of your aunts previous to them going to house keeping I deferred doing so with the hope that others of the family who have much leisure would write and inform you of all that was passing here that could at all be interesting to you.

The information contained in the letters you have written afforded us much pleasure, there was a struggle among the members of the family who should first read them contending, that though they were directed to a particular person they were intended for the whole to peruse & after they were read by one to every member, then there was a dispute as to what was said and the manner in which it was said, all appeared to regret that you had communicated so little & that you had not been more minute.[12]

I was particularly pleased to learn that Caroline and yourself were examined and found sufficiently advanced in your study to enter the senior class, tho I do not think from my knowledge of the proficiency of either of you that it argues much in favor of the standing of that class. However even I shall suspend my opinion until I see more of your letters & your return home.

By the return of Jno. Haynsworth jun. I received a short note from Miss Brainard, encouraging me to hope that my wishes and expectations as regards your improvement will be realized. Your mother and myself were much gratified to hear of the attention that was shown you by our friends, & we trust & hope that your conduct will allways be such as to claim their regard and respect.

When you write to any of us you should be careful to mention the health of Caroline & Elizabeth, for their parents are particular in their inquiry whether we have received letters and what was said of their daughters, & I dislike to answer that you said nothing of them.

I expected to receive a letter from you by the return of the doctor but was disappointed, he had a dreadful time of it coming up, having to spend one very cold rainy night in the swamp between the lakes, the water being too high to ford & the ferry man not being in place to take him over. He told me of some wonderful things that were told his daughters by a fortune teller who he says is in great repute with the ladies in Charleston, I think in this you will show some superiority to the ladies of Charleston, if you will treat what you may hear on the subject with that indifference that every thing of the sort merits. I hope that no persuasion will induce you to visit this good woman let her merits be what they may.

It is possible that about the latter end of next week I may have everything in that state, that your aunts may go to house keeping on the week following, they have been gardening for some time past & are now collecting a stock of fowls, your sister Lydia has also had a fowl house built & intends trying her luck at the business. The family enjoy their usual health. Your Mother & also the children join me in affectionate remembrance to you, your aunts also asking to be remembered. I have written in much haste, shall therefore conclude by subscribing myself your

Affectionate Father Thos Baker

Exactly how long Maria attended school in Charleston is unknown. However, most of her school papers are dated 1830 and 1831, so she was formally educated at least into her eighteenth year. These papers contain copies in an elegant hand of a piece by Hannah More (1745–1833)[13] on female accomplishment and poems by Oliver Goldsmith (1728–74), Lord Byron (1788–1824), and Thomas Moore (1779–1852), luminaries who were extremely popular at the time. There are also rather inane tales of lords and ladies and peasants probably written by young Maria herself, and in contrast, detailed instructions for prayer, excerpts from scripture and the writings of divines, Maria's own religious meditations, and maxims based on religious precept. The devotional material forms the largest part of the collection, not surprising since the typical curriculum in southern girls' schools at the time emphasized the Bible, biblical history, and theology.[14] Thus Maria was continuing the heavily moral and religious education begun at Woodville.

Although she seldom names sources, Maria tacitly attributes some passages by enclosing them in quotation marks, others she claims as her own thoughts by signing them, and some items, mostly aphorisms, are unmarked. Several samples of the devotional material— the first three claimed by Maria herself, the others not attributed —illustrate the typical topics.

> "And one cried to another, and said, Holy, holy, holy is the Lord of Hosts, the whole earth is full of his glory—He is of purer eyes than to behold evil; and cannot look on iniquity—a God of truth without iniquity, just and right is he." Old Testament. Would that I could feel such a sense of the Majesty and holiness of God, as these words are calculated to convey to the heart. I feel that I have not yet accepted Christ as my Savior my Mediator. Send down thy Spirit into my heart. Do I really desire it, O my Father? If I do not, wilt thou, Heavenly Father fill my heart with those desires; wilt thou teach me to adore thee and make me to acknowledge thee my Master? SM Baker

> We should avoid ostentation, and when we pray enter into some secret place, where we could unseen, unheard, and undisturbed be enabled to pray with a holy freedom of soul. Doing this will show that our prayers are the emotions of a pious and sincere heart. Remember that the Lord will reward thee openly—"The life of prayer consists in lifting up the soul to God." SM Baker

> "He went about doing good." Let us imitate his bright example and prove ourselves worthy of being called Christians. Let us not be disconcerted, when we behold his perfection, and say we can never attain it. Nothing is too hard for the Lord, and we may say with St. Paul, "do all things, through Christ which strengtheneth us." SM Baker

"Plato, though a pagan, gives a good lesson to Christians, teaching them what they ought to beg of God in prayer. It was a petition of his, 'O God, give me things good for me though I should not ask them, and keep from me things hurtful, tho' I should pray for them.'"

"Self Love; It is that which is the conductor of all our errors, which corrupts our judgement, darkens our understanding, and in short disguises truth so much that we cannot percieve it."

"He who is in pain at the thought of death, will be in dispair at the hour of it. The best school for a good life, is the frequent meditation upon a happy death. The serious thoughts of eternity prompt a man to make good use of his time, and in a great measure remove the sting of death."

The maxims form another category of the school papers. In later life, Maria regarded maxims as "terse expressions of truths, important for us to know, remember, and energize." Hence aphorisms such as these did not become tiresome commonplaces for her but remained guides to the conduct of life.

Deligence, industry, and proper improvement of time, are material duties of the young.

The acquisition of knowledge is one of the most honourable occupations of youth.

Whatever useful or engaging endowments we possess, virtue is requisite, in order to their shining with proper lustre.

True happiness is of a retired nature and an enemy to pomp and noise.

To maintain a steady and unbroken mind amidst all the show of the world, marks a great and noble spirit.

Let usefuless and beneficences not ostentation and vanity, direct the train of your persuit.

The love of the world can never be too much restrained; if the love of God has any bounds 'tis imperfect.

He who spends too much upon his pleasures, commonly leaves himself too scanty an allowance for his necessities.

Religion forbids us nothing but what corrupts the purity of our minds, and breaks the force and vigour of them.

A final sample from Maria's school papers is probably as close as her school came to sex education.

> A traveller, if he chance to stray,
> May find again the once lost way,
> Polluted streams again run pure,
> And deepest wounds admit a cure,
> But woman no redemption knows;
> The wounds of honour never close.

Clearly, Maria's Charleston school placed heavy emphasis on forming mind, character, and writing style through copying and imitating models, an effective system inasmuch as the principles so inculcated remained with Maria for the rest of her life.

When Maria was nineteen and her schooling completed, one member of the Furman clan commented on Maria's religious development, the major purpose of her education. The writer uses the terms "impressed" and "impression" in the special Baptist sense of "an idea proposed to the mind through the agency of the Holy Spirit."[15]

5 March 1833. Sara Susannah Furman to Henrietta Dargan Furman

Maria Baker is I hope seriously impressed. She certainly manifests far greater interest in religious matters than she has ever done before, but as these impressions with young persons too often prove evanescent it would perhaps be best to say but little about them until they assume a decided character.

THREE

Suitors and Wedding

Judging from the "Grandmother's Letter" cited earlier, Maria had many opportunities to meet eligible young men at Oak Grove, and she had other opportunities through her extended family. Family letters of 1830, 1833, and 1834; a book inscription of 1833; an 1875 biography; and an 1884 memoir shed a little light on Maria's affairs of the heart. As in her education, religion played a large role.

A letter written when Maria was sixteen mentions a student at the nearby Furman Theological Institution who may have been Maria's first suitor.

4 September 1830. Sara Susannah Furman to Maria Dorothea Furman

> Mr Barns has offered himself to the missionary board with a view to Burmah. You never saw any one rise as he has done in the good opinion of the family at Oak grove. It is currently reputed that he is very attentive to Maria Baker but whether he is or not I cannot tell tho he certainly visits the Capt's very constantly and is I think pleased with M, but respecting the nature of her feelings towards him I am quite ignorant.

The next mention of a suitor is found in an 1884 memoir by J. Marion Sims, a friend of Maria's brother Richard from the South Carolina College. Sims recounts the relationship that developed in the summer of 1832 between Maria and James Henley Thornwell (1812–62), a classmate ('31) of Richard's at the South Carolina

College. Richard had invited Thornwell for a summer visit at Oak Grove.

> Dick had a sister, a beautiful and accomplished young woman. Thornwell fell in love with her, and wanted to marry her. She was a rigid member of the Presbyterian Church[1] and they talked a good deal about religion, and he professed to be inquiring the way of salvation. . . . some persons had given him one book on the subject, and some another, for him to read. He read and studied them all, and at last he was as far from the convincing evidence as ever.
>
> Then this beautiful woman told him if he would take the ordinary Confession of Faith, and study that, she thought that there he would see the truth. He did so, and he rose from its perusal a converted man; and from that time he determined to give himself to the Church. . . . But, what is strange, Miss Baker did not marry him. I do not know that I could blame her; for physically he was nothing, though intellectually he was a giant.[2]

This decision on the part of a girl of eighteen years appears less strange considering Thornwell's appearance at this time as described by his 1875 biographer: "very short in stature . . . very lean in flesh, with a skin the color of old parchment, his hands and face thickly studded with black freckles, and an eye rendered dull in repose by a drooping lid,"[3] and Sims's description of "a dirty-looking, malarial-looking boy" is in the same vein. Nevertheless, Thomas Baker was right when he predicted at the time that Thornwell "would be a distinguished man." Thornwell became "the South's most sophisticated Evangelical theorist" on the subject of slavery,[4] and "the most intellectually powerful of the southern divines."[5]

Maria must have known of her future husband John Morgandollar Taylor (1809–72) since childhood, for in 1814 her half-uncle Samuel Furman, a Baptist clergyman, had married John's older half-sister Eliza Scrimzeour. Eliza and Samuel lived near Coosawhatchie in Beaufort District, the home ground of the Morgandollar/Taylor family group, but from 1831 through 1834 they located near the Bakers in the High Hills area, where Samuel taught at the Furman Theological Institution. Members of the Furman clan, including the patriarch Richard, had long been acquainted with members of the Morgandollar/Taylor clan, many of whom were Baptists.

Only a single scrap of Maria and John's courtship correspondence has survived, an undated note in John's hand, which apparently accompanied a gift:

> This is Cupid. You must keep him safely until I come up, when I shall have to demand his lordship of you. Let me again entreat you by "love" to write oftener than you do and send to the [post] office as often & shall often find a letter from him who only cares to live, that he may live for Maria. Your own Jno M

The first dated record of John and Maria's acquaintance is the inscription "Maria S. Baker from John M. Taylor, Jan 1833" found in one volume of a two-volume set of the works of the English poet Felicia Hemans (1793–1835). At that time, Maria had just turned nineteen and John was twenty-three. They must have known each other for a while for him to be giving her this significant gift. Later that year Maria Furman had some comments on the progress of the courtship, writing from Sumter District where she and her sister Susan were living near the Bakers. John's mother had come to visit her daughter Eliza Furman.

[?] July 1833. Maria Dorothea Furman to Ann Eliza Furman

> It is nearly four weeks since Mrs Taylor has been with Eliza. John accompanied her but returned to the low country before we arrived. Capt Baker's family were quite pleased with him, and from hints thrown out, I am inclined to think he is not a little pleased with Maria; he was charmed with the Hills.

27 July 1833. Maria Dorothea Furman to Ann Eliza Furman

> John Taylor is to be here in a day or two; from hints thrown out by his Mother & Sister, I strongly suspect him to be seriously an admirer of Maria. She has made him a very handsome guard, it is the property of the society [unknown] but he requested her particularly to make it.

A little later Maria Furman provides glimpses of John's upbringing as she and her sister Susan plan a trip to visit their brother James and his wife.

8 August 1833. Maria Dorothea Furman to Ann Eliza Furman

John Taylor who is now here, has very politely, and kindly offered his services to accompany us to Greenville [South Carolina]; having the prospect of an escort, is one great impediment removed out of the way of our travelling, as it would be highly improper as well as extremely unpleasant to undertake any thing like a journey without the protection of a gentleman.

28 August 1833. Maria Dorothea Furman to Ann Eliza Furman

It is altogether impossible for us even to go a few miles without a gentleman, strangers as we are to the country, and entirely ignorant of the roads. So that without the politeness, and attentions of John, we should have been obliged to remain stationary.

The final prenuptial document is the earliest extant letter from Maria's own hand. As she invites James Clement Furman and his wife Harriet to her wedding, Maria reveals an interesting attitude toward these newlyweds.

3 March 1834. Maria Baker to Harriet Davis Furman

It is scarcely a year ago, my dear Harriet, since I received a formal invitation to visit Fairfield for the special purpose of seeing yourself & my <u>very</u> dear Uncle publicly avow your matreal [matrimonial] faith & attachment; & <u>I now</u> write to request that both Uncle James & yourself will visit Oak Grove a few days previous to the 27th of March for the purpose of being present on the evening of that day to witness a similar avowal on my part & ———'s; but I deem it unnecessary, my dear Harriet, to make further explanations, as I am aware that you are acquainted with the engagement existing between a <u>certain</u> individual & myself.

Now Harriet I hope that neither Uncle James or yourself from <u>sad experience</u> feel inclined to advise me against changing my state of "Single Blessedness"? If so, I shall feel strongly inclined to act upon your advice, as to all appearance, you bade fair to make a <u>very</u> happy couple.

I was pleased to learn that you were pleasantly situated in Mrs Williams's family. I hope you will continue to like Society Hill. Remember me affectionately to Uncle James, tell him that I will be more than pleased to receive a letter from him. I do not like the idea of his bestowing <u>all</u> his love & thoughts on "Harriet."

I will be deeply & truly disappointed, my dear H, if both Uncle James & yourself do not attend to my solicitations for the pleasure of your company at the time requested. His friends are all anxious to see & welcome you here, & among them all you will not find one, with warmer or more affectionate feelings towards you than your "dutch niece."[6]

Now, I hope my dear Harriet you will not think this short epistle unworthy of an answer, for I assure you it should be longer, did I have time to render it so. You will not, I <u>presume</u>, expect a more <u>formal</u> invitation than the one herein given. Excuse the brevity of this letter, if you please, & believe me, my dear Aunt, as I am, your sincere friend & affectionate niece. Maria S Baker.

The young Furmans had apparently already discussed attending the wedding.

5 March 1834. James Clement Furman to Harriet Davis Furman

From her letters I judge Maria will be very much disappointed if you do not attend her wedding. She is truly attached to you, your surmises to the contrary notwithstanding. If you can attend, I think we must go. Indeed I believe I am the choice of both parties as the performer of ceremonies.

Whether James and Harriet attended or James officiated is unknown. Maria and John were married on 27 March 1834 at Oak Grove. All that is known of the wedding gifts is that Maria's china came from France and that her father gave her at least two slaves.[7] A few weeks after the wedding and the young couple's departure for John's plantation, a family member commented on Maria's future.

20 April 1834. Ann Eliza Furman to Maria Dorothea Furman

Sister [Rachel Baker] received a long letter from Maria the other day. She appears very much delighted with her new situation. I have no doubt that M will make friends of all who become acquainted with her.

Conclusion

Maria Baker was born and bred to several kinds of privilege. Her parents were people of fairly large means based on land ownership who were able to provide her with a varied experience of both rural and city life. Maria also had the security of a stable immediate family and a large extended family that maintained close ties and had prestigious standing in the religious life of the state. As the middle child of a sibling group spread out over twenty years, including "sisters" from her deceased brother's family, Maria was enriched by both brothers and sisters older and younger than herself.

Another advantage was her structured upbringing. Thomas and Rachel Baker were mature people in their late thirties when Maria was born; they knew who they were and what they wanted their daughter to be. Although they regulated their family under a rigorous Baptist discipline, the atmosphere was far from grim. Maria's family valued education, not as social adornment for an upper-class woman, but as training for the moral conduct of life and the salvation of the soul.

Thus Maria entered her marriage as a person brought up to be strong in her own principles. The instruction she received on the relation of the sexes may be inferred from passages from sermons delivered by a Baptist preacher, Rufus William Bailey, in nearby Sumterville in the early 1830s and published in 1837 as *The Family Preacher.* The Baker family, constantly seeking good preaching, no doubt attended Bailey's sermons, and Maria's sister-in-law Lydia Dick Baker gave her a copy of the published version.[1] Rufus William Bailey writes:

The distinctions of sex relate only to time, and will end with it. In eternity, each soul will be exhibited in its moral character, and holiness will form the only ground of difference or superiority.

There [woman] stands, a burning intelligence of the same immortal, inextinguishable fire, sent to mingle her light and heat with his.

[The wife] cannot submit to [the husband] her moral reasonings and decisions. Her separate mental operations must proceed. . . . She may not be required on any subject to render a slavish submission.

Remember [the forceful influence of] the mother of the Gracci and of Coriolanus, the wives of Tarquinus Collatinus and of Pilate.

The Gospel elevates [women] to an equality with the other sex, and honours them. It teaches that there exists in both the same moral character and accountability, the same foundation for intellectual and moral improvement, and the same capacity for religious enjoyment.[2]

As she entered the married state, teachings such as these must have given Maria Baker a sturdy sense of herself as John Taylor's equal in the essentials of mind and soul, however different her social and biological roles would be from those of her husband.

Two

EARLY ADULT YEARS IN BEAUFORT
DISTRICT, SOUTH CAROLINA, 1834–53

Introduction

From their marriage in March 1834 until they moved to Florida early in 1853, Maria Baker Taylor and John Morgandollar Taylor lived in the Pipe Creek area of upper St. Peter's Parish, Beaufort District, South Carolina, in the southeast coastal region of the state. At the turn of the century, the upper parish had been a frontier of subsistence farming and livestock operations, but by the time John and Maria set up for themselves, a sizeable community of substantial planters had emerged. This regional trend of increasing prosperity continued throughout the Taylors' years there.[1]

John's family was well established in Beaufort District at the time of his marriage to Maria. John's maternal grandfather, John Morgandollar, was the son of German immigrants from Württemberg. Born in South Carolina in 1751, Morgandollar served under Francis Marion in the American Revolution[2] and by 1790 owned a plantation of several hundred acres and twenty-five slaves (U.S. Census). His daughter Mary was a widow when she married John's father, John Taylor, who at age thirty-six had emigrated with four brothers from Newcastle, England, to South Carolina in 1798. Both of John's parents had owned land in the Coosawhatchie area before their marriage in 1808, and later as a widow his mother worked a large plantation with seventy-three slaves (1830 U.S. Census). John's Morgandollar aunts and his Taylor sisters had married into well-off neighboring families (Wallace, Maner, Lawton, Nicholes), and his uncle Henry Taylor was a wealthy rice planter in lower St. Peter's.[3] Thus in marrying John, Maria became a member of another large and prosperous family group that was already linked to the Fur-man/Baker clan through the marriage of John's half-sister and Maria's half-uncle.

Myrtle Hill, John and Maria's plantation in Beaufort District, con-sisted of 3,200 acres valued at $11,000. Their slaves numbered forty-three in 1840, sixty-eight in 1850 (U.S. Censuses), the increase probably equally due to inheritance from John's mother and the growing pros-perity of the parish. These figures place the Taylors in the upper quarter of the slaveholders in the upper parish, but not among the great planters such as John Seth Maner, husband of John's aunt Catherine Morgandollar, who by 1840 was the largest slaveholder in the parish with 315 slaves.[4] Although no legal description of the Tay-lors' property remains, the site can be located fairly closely. Their mail was variously addressed to Pipe Creek, Lawtonville, and several landings along the Savannah River (the boundary between South Carolina and Georgia). A Civil War map shows Pipe Creek begin-ning west-northwest of Lawtonville and flowing into the Savannah.[5] Of Lawtonville only the old cemetery remains, about a mile west of present-day Estill. In modern terms, then, the plantation was about fifty miles upriver from Savannah and between the river and Estill.[6] None of the MBT documents describe the Taylors' crops, but like most upper St. Peter's plantations of the time, Myrtle Hill was no doubt a multicrop operation, with sweet potatoes and corn being more important than the short-staple cotton grown in the area.[7]

Similarly, the MBT documents are silent about the land and neighborhood. However, former-slave narratives collected by Fed-eral Writers' Project interviewers in 1937 give glimpses of antebel-lum times in the Pipe Creek region and also mention some of the related families discussed above as well as other families Maria speaks of in her diaries and correspondence.[8] Phoebe Faucette, one of the interviewers, describes the area she entered to meet with former slave George Anne Butler, who was born about 1860: "Nature has done her best in producing beautiful evergreen trees of immense size and much luxuriant shrubbery of many kinds. Live oaks, magnolias, yellow pines, and many evergreen shrubs keep the woods green even in winter, a fascinating wilderness to hunters and nature lovers." George Anne herself says, "Cotton was de thing 'way back yonder.

An' right 'long dis road dey'd haul it. Haul it to Cohen's Bluff! Haul it to Matthews Bluff! Haul it to Parichucla [Pallichicola]! . . . In dem days it was de ships dat carried it to Savannah."[9]

Former slave Isaiah Butler, born about 1856, mentions the Maners, Wallaces, Lawtons, and Bosticks and then describes the Bostick place, which was very close to Myrtle Hill: "Back in dem times dey cultivated rice. Had mules to cultivate it! But cotton and corn was what dey planted most of all; 4,000 acres I think dey tell me was on dis place. . . . Ole Mr Ben Bostick[10] used to bring clothes an' shoes to us and see dat we was well cared for."[11] And Daphney Wright, born about 1831 (claiming to be 106 in 1937), after mentioning the "big handsome houses" owned by the Taylors' friends and relatives in the Pipe Creek area, the Lawtons and Maners, tells about the abundance of fish and shellfish in the nearby Savannah River: "When de stars would come out dere over de water it wuz a beautiful sight. . . . Sometimes my father would go out in de night an' catch de fish with a seine. He's come back with a bushel of fish most anytime. . . . Dey have de mullets, an' de oysters, an' de crabs, an' dese little clams. Dey have oyster-stew. Dey have roast oysters, den de raw oysters. An dey have de fried oysters. Dat sure is good."[12] Oysters remained one of Maria's lifelong favorite foods.

A glimpse of what the houses in the area were like is given by Henry Pristell, born about 1854, a slave on the plantation of John Taylor's sister Anne Mary and her husband, Samuel Baker Wallace, near Lawtonville. After mentioning cows, hogs, turkeys, ducks, geese, and chickens on the place, Henry says of the Wallace house: "Dat been a fine place. Oh, yes ma'am. De house was built up high off the ground, as high as de top of dat room dere. . . . De kitchen was off from de house. It had a big fireplace in it. Didn't have no stove. . . . Had a loom in it an' a spinnin' wheel. I seen dem a many a time spinnin' an' weavin'."[13] Pleasant, even idyllic, as the setting appears from all of these accounts, fevers and other illnesses frequently swept the region, debilitating and carrying off young and old, black and white, alike.

Baptist church life was firmly established in the area, and the young Taylors were active members of two well-attended country congregations: first at Lawtonville, where the Pipe Creek Baptist

Church, founded in 1775, had moved in 1826;[14] and then at Robertville, where the Black Swamp Baptist Church had received fund-raising visits from Maria's grandfather in the late 1780s.

At Myrtle Hill, John and Maria Taylor became the parents of six daughters and five sons, all but two of whom survived to adulthood, and they took their place on the generational front line with the deaths of their remaining parents, Thomas Baker, Rachel Furman Baker, and Mary Morgandollar Taylor.

ONE

Education of the Children

In letters dated 1846, 1847, 1849, 1850, and 1852, and a poem from 1847, Maria expresses great concern for the education of Caroline, her oldest child, and relays a bit of information about educating her younger children. At age eleven, Caroline was sent to the Limestone Springs Female High School, located in the rolling hills of the Piedmont section of South Carolina, more than 200 miles diagonally across the state from her home in Beaufort District. Sending such a young child so far away indicates that the Taylors took the education of their daughters seriously and that they wanted their children to receive a Baptist education.[1]

Limestone Springs was founded in 1845 by two Baptist clergymen, Thomas Curtis LL.D. and his son William Curtis, who were born and educated in England. The Curtises bought a failed resort hotel and 300 acres of land near Gaffney, South Carolina, to house their school. An account based on the school catalog of 1846, when Caroline Taylor entered, describes the imposing premises:

> The hotel building was two hundred seventy-four feet long, forty feet wide, having a large dining hall in one end and corresponding drawing rooms in the opposite wing, with small parlours for families. It contained over one hundred rooms and every office necessary to a large establishment. The walls of the main brick building were twenty-seven inches thick. The spacious grounds were laid out in circling walks and broad driveways. Money had been spent

lavishly and artistic skill had been employed in making it a place of striking beauty.[2]

Thomas Curtis himself expressed his educational ambitions in a letter of 19 April 1847 inviting John C. Calhoun to attend the June commencement at which the governor of South Carolina would speak: "We wish to exhibit a species of Female College in S. Carolina . . . that shall compete, for advantages, with any of the Northern Schools, and fairly settle the preference of the State for educating its own daughters."[3] Several other girls from the Taylors' neighborhood were also sent to Limestone, which had 104 pupils when Caroline entered in 1846.

Caroline first had to be outfitted, and Maria solicited the "taste and judgement" of her aunts in Charleston in "selecting articles for Caroline." The shopping list Maria sent includes a total of 55 yards of calico, linen, flannel, and silk, and a $6 bonnet trimmed in blue (6 April 1846 letter to Ann Furman). Caroline entered school on 1 June, and in a long letter a few months later, Maria writes about Dr Curtis's methods and views and Caroline's progress:

17 September 1846. Maria Baker Taylor to Ann Eliza Furman

Caroline will be delighted to receive a letter from you and I will thank you to write to her, as I think it will act as a stimulus for her friends to appear interested in her improvement. You need not fear any "piercing" glances from Dr Curtis will be directed to your letter. The old Doctor was interrogated, I understand, by one of his patrons, as to this same matter, the examination of the young ladies' letters, those they wrote and received; the old gentleman appeared to be horrified; and disclaimed all intentions to submit even to the suspicion of so "ungentlemanly an act."

Caroline continues much pleased with the school, she has recently had the mumps, but I hope it was not an aggravated case, as I understand that she has entirely recovered and resumed her studies.

It affords me much gratification to find that the young ladies from this neighbourhood write such favourable accounts of Caroline to their parents and friends; I suppose I may be allowed (without the suspicion of vanity) to give you some of the extracts from their letters, which please me most. Mary N——— writes "Caroline Taylor is decidedly the most liberal girl in school, she takes after her father." Don't you think I should feel a little cut? "Mrs Curtis and Mrs Carr (the housekeeper) say that Cornelia Willingham, Caroline Taylor & the Miss Nicholes keep the neatest rooms, of any girls in the school." "Caroline Taylor, CW & myself rise every morning an hour before any one else in the house to practice music."

Dr Curtis writes "your daughter is making steady progress in her studies; she interests us much." Miss Willingham writes "I love Caroline Taylor dearly, she is a sweet, amiable girl, and a great favourite with all the teachers." Miss Lawton writes that Caroline has been put in a class with them in french although they have been studying it all the winter & that the french teacher says that she excels in pronouncing it, but they seem to imply that she is only in a class with them from being a favourite with the teacher as they have been studying it for nearly a year.

Dr Curtis had an examination in July, at which time he was much pleased with the manner in which his scholars acquited themselves, and said he felt quite proud of them. Mr Poinsett, former secretary to the navy, was present, but as he did not feel well enough to deliver an address, he wrote the young ladies a letter, which Dr Curtis made the second class answer. Major Herrys of Spartanburg, delivered a very handsome address on the importance of female education.

They were three days in examining the school, and had considerable pomp and display in so doing. The old Doctor has an idea of showing us a little of how the English do these things. He has had several Tableaux, performed by the scholars, in which Mr Curtis and himself took part. Caroline acted in two, once as an infant, being the smallest girl in school, and once as a school-girl standing by the side of her mistress.

As the letter continues, Maria discusses the morality of dancing, a worldly amusement that was being heavily criticized in the evangelical press at the time. Because she was an inveterate reader of religious newspapers, Maria must have felt that she was weighing in on the minority side of an important current controversy, hence the length and eloquence of her defense of Dr. Curtis's enlightened views:

> I differ with you, in not regreting, as you do, that Dr Curtis countenances dancing, only as an amusement for young people; to be enjoyed with moderation, and never entered into except on particular and specified occasions; and this objection you say arises from the fact that the amusement has been much abused.
>
> I may be wrong, but I rejoice that a man with learning, piety, knowledge, and one in a situation to extend his influence, has thus attacked the prejudices of the age: for that it is a prejudice I have ever felt convinced, from the lame reasons always urged against by its opponents (I do not count you one of its opposers, for I know your real sentiments on the subject). And I think the views he gives his pupils respecting it will do more to put down its abuses, than all the opposition they meet with at home for using it in any form or at any time, could ever do.
>
> Religion is of heavenly origin. Superstition is of the earthly. Holy courage is for the resistance of vice, evil, sin, & unhallowed thoughts; it is the offspring of Heaven. Prejudice, and bigotry are the offspring of the evil one: they hurry us into error; that [holy courage] nerves us for all that is good.

Maria couches her final remarks in a sentence that demonstrates the effectiveness of one facet of her own education: although formally schooled only to the age of seventeen or eighteen, she had absorbed the demanding syntax of the elevated sermon style:[4]

> Could you see Dr Curtis, as he has been represented to me, in the Sunday school, or the chapel pulpit, making earnest appeals to the girls, to seek the Lord early, when he will be found; to seek first the kingdom of God and his righteousness; and representing the fearful danger of procrastination, and the great delight and happiness to be experienced in keeping his commandments; the great injustice they do themselves in delaying to enter into so pleasant a service for youth, and securing for themselves a good hope, or an

abundant entrance into that heavenly inheritance of light, life, & love; the gift, and purchase of Christ; you would if possible, be more fully persuaded than ever, that religion was the one thing needful in his opinion.

After this spirited defense of Dr. Curtis, Maria developed some reservations over the following year:

27 October 1846. Maria Baker Taylor to Ann Eliza Furman

Caroline is still much pleased with her school but has written such an earnest appeal to her father to bring her home during vacation, that he cannot withstand the temptation to do so, and we expect her the last of November. I am rather opposed to sending her back before next May or June, but at present he thinks of returning with her this February, when the school again commences.

I do not think she has improved much either in her hand writing or diction, but, as her class does not write compositions, I suppose this is not much to be wondered at. As you have expressed considerable interest in Caroline, and I know feel a good deal in Dr Curtis' school, I send you a letter from Mr William Curtis, and two from Caroline, one of her first and her last. She apologizes for placing her words so far apart, by saying she has to write her french exercises off in that way and has got in the habit of it.

17 September 1847. Maria Baker Taylor to Ann Eliza Furman

Caroline is still at Limestone we expect to bring her home the last of Oct and I have an idea of keeping her here until June, as I am reluctant to have her so much from me at so early an age [twelve].

Mary and Lydia[5] are going to school to Miss Hyginbottom, a teacher employed by Mrs U Robert in her family—the house she teaches in is in sight of ours and the children return to each meal.

In addition to the formal schooling at Limestone, Caroline received moral and religious instruction from her mother.

To my daughter Caroline on her 12th birthday
[13 February 1847]

Just entered on your teens,[6] dear girl, today,
I think of thee, to thee a word would say.
You number twice six years, or three times four,
Oh, may you live to number many more.
What are your wishes now? Say what will please,
A box of good things, candies, cakes, or books?
With play or study, are you most at ease?
To what the most attentive, mind, or looks?

Neatness is pleasant if the mind & heart
Are well reflected through th' exterior part.
But if neglected, they are left to chance,
Minor attractions, these defects enhance.
Be neat in person, but be pure in heart,
Courteous in manners, ruled by love, not art.
In conversation chaste, in spirit meek,
Thy wisdom & thy strength from Jesus seek.

For He alone true wisdom can impart
To check the follies of thy childlike heart;
He will to thee sufficient strength supply
To shun the temptor & from guilt to fly.
Be wise, dear girl, nor let the ungodly lead
Thy youthful steps in danger's part to tread.
Sinners entice. Oh, stand not in their way.
Study God's word, oft meditate & pray.

Letters that Maria wrote between 1849 and 1852 to her uncle
James Clement Furman, by then a professor at Furman University,
show the end of the connection with Limestone. In 1849, Caroline
had already been at the school for three years.

27 August 1849. Maria Baker Taylor to James Clement Furman

Caroline writes me word that her health is not good. She is frequently sick at Limestone. I am in hopes from the style of her last

letters that she is not indifferent to the subject of religion, although being a reserved child she does not exactly tell me so. Would it be asking too great a favour of you my [dear uncle, to][7] beg you to write to her? I think a letter [from you on the] subject of religion might do her good, as she has the highest respect and affection for you. [She will remain] at Limestone until the last of October.

Caroline stayed home until April, when she returned to Limestone with her sister Mary, age twelve, probably Mary's first attendance at the school. A few months after the birth of her daughter Maria Dorothea, Maria reports on the children's education:

4 September 1850. Maria Baker Taylor to James Clement Furman

> As soon as I recovered, and even before, I had to be busily engaged in assisting Mary and Caroline to get ready for school, and when they got off here came all the summer clothes for Mr T & all the little fry to be made up in a hurry, and then teaching them all myself from Lyd [ten] with her Grammar down to Fenwick [1 ½] with his ABC of which he only knows one or two. Richard [three] knows all of his and is trying to spell b-a. I gave Cousin Peony Caroline's last letter to me on the state of her mind to read when she was here last; she remarked to me, when she had finished reading it, "Why Cousin Maria she writes like an experienced Christian, I am sure it must be truly gratifying to you to receive such a letter from her." She said this with much feeling.

By the fall of 1851, Caroline and Mary had left Limestone for good, and on an unfortunate note.

6 September 1852. Maria Baker Taylor to James Clement Furman

> Mr Taylor begs me to say to you that when he was leaving Limestone last fall with the girls Mr W Curtis promised to get a letter of dismission[8] from his church for Caroline at the first church meeting and send on to her; since that time Mr Taylor has written for it twice and Caroline twice, and no notice has been taken of either of the letters. Caroline is still without a letter. Caroline's last to Mr Curtis has been written rather more than a month

ago—iron and steam [the railroad] have given him the most abundant time to answer.

What step would you advise us next to take? Caroline says he is generally dilatory in such matters but it is very nearly a year now since she left there and he promised Mr Taylor then to send it on after the first church meeting. Mr Taylor appears anxious to get your advice and asks me to write for it. Caroline's letters to Mr Curtis have been respectful and even affectionate, as she entertains high regard for him; and if they are personally offended with us for not continuing Mary at their school or for discouraging the attentions of "Henri" [unknown]—I do not think they should carry it into church matters, and, I hope better things of them than to suppose they would.

Caroline had attended Limestone for five years (1846–51), from ages eleven through sixteen, and Mary probably attended for two years.

TWO

Church Life

The Baptist church in its temporal and spiritual manifestations had a central place in Maria's life during her young adulthood in Beaufort District, as it did for many residents of upper St. Peter's Parish, which was "one of the wellsprings of the Southern Baptist movement" as a whole.[1] A variety of church-related situations are described in letters written by Maria and other family members in 1836, 1846, and 1848–50.

The first situation does not involve Maria or John Taylor directly, but is of interest because the neighboring Samuel Furman family was related to both Maria and John, and their daughter Mary was close in age to Maria. Also, the situation reveals more of the Baptist attitudes that were part of Maria's milieu. Samuel and Eliza, taking some of their children with them, had gone to Scotland in an attempt to have their son Richard recognized as heir to the Scrimzeour estates, Eliza's father James Scrimzeour (John's mother's first husband) having been the heir to the earldom. Writing to his sister, Josiah Furman, Samuel's brother and fellow Baptist clergyman, expresses his disapproval of Mary's sumptuary extravagance and her father's failure to control her.

10 June 1836. Josiah B. Furman to Maria Dorothea Furman

Even if it [the estate] should be considerable, the disposition for extravagance in a certain quarter may perhaps render it no blessing. I have been informed that Mary's fashionable & expensive dressing is a theme for conversation over the country. I refer particularly to her extravagance in this respect during the last winter in Charleston.

I felt very much mortified & distressed at it, for I knew that objection had been made to Saml on that account while he was in the [Furman Theological] Institution before, & that it would be regarded as an insuperable objection to his appointment again. Besides it is painful & humiliating to have the vanity of one's family (of the lowest kind too, that of dress), made the subject of comment in the whole country. I hope & pray that God may bring Mary to a right view of things, & to that sobriety of conduct & dress, the invariable accompaniments of a well regulated mind. If what is reported of her extravagance last winter be true, I shall be constrained to abandon all the hope I had entertained of her amendment. I fear that this disposition will lead to still more dazzling displays in Great Britain, & feel mortified at the sort of introduction it will afford to the public there of an American Clergyman's family.

It is possible you may now be at Captn Baker's[2] but being anxious to write to you, & in the hope that a letter from me will have the effect of drawing one from yourself or Ann the sooner,[3] I felt it proper to drop you a line, directed to Charleston, as it can be forwarded from thence.

Josiah was reflecting the Baptist position on dress stated by the Charleston Baptist Association in 1788: "both extravagance and neglect should be carefully avoided."[4] However, judging from the shopping list Maria sent to the Furman sisters when she was outfitting her daughter for school in 1846,[5] the Baptist standard was far from austere, so Mary's display must have been "dazzling" indeed.

In a second church-related situation, Maria herself trains an observant eye on the clergy at an ecumenical revival meeting. Her remarks about her own pastor, the Reverend Isaac Nicholes, are in the vein of a later description of him as "unassuming, humble." He seems to have been overendowed with these qualities for Maria's taste in clergymen.[6]

24 August 1846. Maria Baker Taylor to Ann Eliza Furman

We had a very interesting meeting at the Lawtonville church, of which Mr [Isaac] Nicholes is pastor, commenced on the 31st of July and continued for twelve days, which resulted in a very pleasing revival, which was much required among us. Mssrs Rambaut, Sweat, Stokes (a methodist) and Gallaway (a presbyterian) were Mr Nicholes' assistants. I never enjoyed a meeting more, or felt more sensibly the Divine presence. Old Christians were melted down, and settled differences among them, which were threatening to break up our church; their intercourse seems now to be a feast of love.

Mr Rambaut[7] was eloquent and soul stirring, Mr Sweat[8] full of zeal and prayer, Mr Stokes solemn and orderly, Mr Gallaway's unfortunate manner & delivery was overlooked in the depth of feeling he displayed, and the good matter of his discourses. He frequently sobbed aloud during the whole time of prayer and responded, but rather more mildly than a methodist; as for Isaac [Nicholes], he actually dug out hidden treasures, that I never dreamed he was in possession of. Two of his children were among the converts,[9] and cousin Tom Nicholes's widow likewise.

Yes, our friend [Reverend Isaac Nicholes] has truly been at last spurred into action, and it has proved to be wise action too, which I hope will yet result in bringing many to righteousness. Eight persons have already been baptised, the subjects of conversion during the meeting; and many more appear to be cut to the heart.

The emotionalism of this event was typical of rural revival meetings and a reminder that even most of the well-to-do people of the area were only a generation removed from frontier life.[10]

In a third church-related situation, Maria employs both temporal and spiritual methods as a fund-raiser for the Lawtonville church. In 1844, as secretary of the Female Missionary Society, Maria had turned in $92.50 to Reverend Nicholes,[11] perhaps the standard by which she was measuring her lack of success in the following 1848 letter. "Mr Fuller" is Richard Fuller (1804–76), a native of the town of Beaufort, South Carolina, and an eminent Baptist minister. Fuller was a formidable figure for Maria to be criticizing. Born to a prosperous and cultivated family and educated at Harvard College, Fuller was a lawyer specializing in criminal law when he was "born again" and ordained a Baptist minister in 1832. In the years up to Maria's letter below, he had become the most sought-after preacher in Beaufort District, the founder of plantation "preaching stations" for slaves, a nationally known polemicist on the slavery issue, and a skilled fundraiser. He had left his pastorate in Beaufort for one in Baltimore in 1847,[12] a year before Maria wrote the following letter. The Taylors must have known Fuller for a long time.

Maria's rhetoric in the letter injects theological implications into what is essentially a matter of money:[13]

29 September 1848. Maria Baker Taylor to Ann Eliza Furman

But to the matter in question, namely, funds for the Church; unfortunately for my credit with you, Mr Fuller entered this field some time ago, and "threw his filarity" so completely around the good people of this region, that I have not the least particle of <u>faith</u> to approach them for even a <u>mite</u>. He made them roll out <u>dollars</u> where I could not even look for <u>cents</u>, for that same Charleston church, using among his many other arguments the one you applied to me; seasoning his sound reasons so with flattery that they were readily swallowed. Even Mr Taylor subscribed him fifty dollars, which at this distance from the interesting question, I feel to be quite enough for our means.

We are extremely anxious to put up a new church at Lawtonville,[14] spoke of it more than a year ago; for repairing the old one, on my subscription paper, I had nearly or quite two hundred dollars, from one mornings effort, by getting my "good man" to put down his name at the head for what he considered liberal, but upon consideration we thought the old one not worth repairing, and upon consulting found some opposed to building a new one.

I thought of my dear mother's good old plan of prayer, & of her favourite lines respecting it "Prayer makes the darkened cloud withdraw" etc and as the ladies were the principal suggesters of the new building we concluded to wait quietly awhile, and pray down opposition by beseeching God to bestow upon us all more inward grace and zeal for his cause.

Several months ago a proposition came from the gentleman most opposed, that we put up a new church at Lawtonville; well, my heart was glad, & I hope I did not fail to bless God and take courage; thinking (perhaps in the pride of my heart) now I will have my subscription paper and persuade Mr Taylor to cap the list with four or five hundred dollars[15] & then go to several others of the same means, get them to subscribe equally; give fifty myself[16] & follow up some of our zealous sisters for the same, & thus get myself about half the amount necessary for the church.

But, Alas! for my plans! Mr Taylor's crop is a failure, and we will not make more than enough to bear family expenses & support the negroes. But my great consolation is that man's plans are not the best. "Tis not in man that walketh to direct his steps," surely not to direct them aright. And I trust that God has the plans for the accomplishment of our object all laid in wisdom, and that in due time it will be fulfiled.

I feel very certain of one thing, that my pride does not need the least particle of feeding, but on the contrary much mortification, & I fear it is equally certain that I would never take the knife in my own hands for my own cure, therefore I will try to bless God more for all the times past wherein he hath done it for me, & not fear so much for the future, but feel as dependent & confiding as the little sparrows, who all receive their food in due time.

Several instances of church politics are revealed in letters of 1849 and 1850. In the first, John Taylor appeals to James Clement Furman for help in an emergency. The villains of the piece, "Whitaker" and "Wm S"/ "Lawton," were sons-in-law of Samuel and Eliza Furman. Daniel K. Whitaker, a New Orleans literary man, was the second husband of their daughter Mary (of extravagant dress), and William S. Lawton was the first husband of their daughter Dorothea. "Your late venerated father" is of course Richard Furman, the eminent Baptist divine and Maria's grandfather. It may be assumed that John consulted Maria about writing the letter.

3 June 1849. John Morgandollar Taylor to James Clement Furman

I do not wish to seem obtrusive or officious in a matter which concerns me remotely, but after observing as I have recently done, the extreme repugnance which is felt on the part of the immediate family[17] of your late venerated father, & the general indignation felt on the part of his freinds, at the very idea of having the life of such a man written by Mr Whitaker, I should feel myself to blame, to be silent.

On my way to town I heard ministers condemn the project, on my return the scheme was severely animadverted upon. Hearing & seeing the whole matter so much regretted, I took the liberty to represent the feelings of the family & freinds to a particular freind of mine,[18] who upon mature deliberation expressed the opinion, that the only way to forestall Whitaker, was <u>at once</u> to notify the public that the family were about to commit the papers of your Father to some eminent divine of our denomination, Dr Curtis for instance, with the view to have his life given to the world.

My freind is a man of great sagacity & tried sincerity. He thinks such a course would bar Whitaker, even supposing the person you select to write would decline to do so, it would bar him, by creating suspicion in the public mind as to himself, his capacity etc & would effectually put down the cry of persecution he might raise, were any direct means resorted to to stop him. I will suggest that any steps you may deem necessary to be taken to stop him, should be promptly taken. He is very busy in getting subscribers & I learn has a sufficient number on his list to secure the publication. The work is evidently called for & expected by the public, & Whitaker I fear is more after the profit, than the truthfulness of the history.

When I reached church yesterday I found him there with his freind Wm S. As soon as services were over I stated to sundry individuals the opposition of the family, all of them regretted they had not known it earlier, they had subscribed for the work, as one they had long wanted, & looked for, & supposed they were about to secure one sanctioned by the entire family. This feeling I opine, is universal, hence my estimate of the merit of the advice of my freinds, as given above.

I put myself in Whitaker's way yesterday at church hoping he would push the subscription list at me as he was doing at others, that I might have an opportunity to cut him, but he & Lawton were too smart for that. I could not conceal the indignation I felt, that two such fellows, were there making capital of such a man as Dr Furman. I have let it be known far & near, that the family disapprove of the work.

This information will deter some from subscribing, but I cannot keep pace with Mr Whitakers activity. I will only add that I entirely concur in the opinion expressed by my freinds, that the most certain bar, to the forthcoming work from Whitaker, is to promise & give one to the public, under the direction of the immediate family.

I have only suggested Dr Curtis name,[19] because none other more competent to the work has been suggested to my mind.

One gentleman (Mr Rhodes) to whom I spoke yesterday, said the work was called for & expected. I only mention this to shew you how the public generally feel on the subject. I also found that it was generally supposed the work was to be under the direction & with the sanction of the family.

Leaving the whole matter with you I am Dear Sir, Yours most respectfully Jno M Taylor

The projected biography never appeared.

Maria's own correspondence also deals with instances of church politicking. In a letter of "unconscionable length" Maria first explains to James Furman why she and John left the Lawtonville Baptist Church and joined the church in Robertville, a few miles away. "Mr Rambaut" is Thomas Rambaut (1819–90), a native of Ireland who had been converted by Richard Fuller in Beaufort and whose first ministry was in Robertville, 1843–48. Maria had written to Ann Furman in 1846 that Rambaut was "a particular favorite of Mr Taylor's and mine." By the date of the letter, Rambaut had moved on to the First Baptist Church of Savannah.[20]

4 September 1850. Maria Baker Taylor to James Clement Furman

We have got a very clever looking church put up at Lawtonville,[21] but they have added to their other irregularities, a Resolution on their books prohibiting Mr Rambaut from the use of their pulpit, and making it actionable for any one to invite him to preach there. We of course could not stand this resolution and got our letters. I have never communed there since it was passed. If a minister cannot <u>reprove rebuke exhort</u> without submitting himself to censure I can't tell what the Baptist churches are coming to. I'm sure they did not so learn from Christ, & I cannot willingly encourage in any way what is so contrary to his doctrine.

As the letter continues, Maria explains the situation in the Taylors' new church in Robertville, where Rambaut had been replaced by Dr. Joseph Thomas Robert:

The congregation began to set themselves to work how to get rid of him [Dr. Robert],[22] even some of his own relations are dissatisfied with him. I attended the church the Sabbath before the election [for pastor]. We are always greeted there in the most affectionate and welcome manner. Aunt Kitsey[23] as soon as our salutations were over said, "Do you think we could get your Uncle James?" I told her that candidly I did not think they could, "well she says I was afraid so from what you told me before and it will be best for us all to be united on some one, for really Dr Robert is preaching the congregation away."

Later in the letter Maria relates a talk she had with Mr. Ben Buckner, the clerk of the church. The "Mr Bostick" who plays the determining role in the deliberations is Benjamin Bostick. He was one of the great planters in the whole area and "the richest man in the congregation, [who] paid the highest pew rent, and topped every subscription raised during his years in office" as deacon.[24]

The conversation then turned upon the Pastor, the great dissatisfaction their [*sic*] was with Dr Robert. Mr Buckner said the church was fast going to pieces under his administration, that only 2 thirds of the members present at the election voted for him and that some staid away to keep from voting for him or giving offence, a good many persons had given up their pews and some families reduced the number of them, the young people had left off going to church, and all together he said there was a sad state of affairs. Mr Taylor told him the church was well able to give a fine salary and get a first rate minister. The difficulties of selecting a pastor was next spoken of and then when selected of getting him. . . . I answered that it would be best for us to be united in our votes & increase the salary so as to get such a preacher as Robertville ought to have for we ought not willingly to ask such a one there with the present salary. Mr Bostick said he would get up single handed & oppose Dr Robert if he was elected. Mrs Bostick[25] agreed with me in thinking the salary should be increased, the old gentleman did not say anything to it, but Mr Taylor seems to think he will pay more to get a pastor he likes.

On Saturday last the election came on. I did not go down myself but Mr Taylor did, he dined with Mr Bostwick [same as Bostick] on Friday and spent the night at Uncle Maner's. He says he was assailed on all sides with the inquiry "do you think there is any possibility of getting Mr Furman?" He told them he thought not, the Miss Buckners, Aunt Kitsey, Ben Buckner & Mr Bostwick all wished to vote for you but Mr Taylor told them he feared it would be useless and after finding no encouragement for their hopes of getting you they went into the election. Dr Robert got 10 votes, 13 against him, another balloting gave him 7 votes some of them sent, the 3rd & last balloting gave him four votes the other votes scattering. No pastor elected, Mr Fury having the majority, they agreed to reconsider the subject and enter into another election on the Friday before the 4th Sunday in October. . . .

If I thought their was any hopes of your being induced to come how gladly would I welcome you in our midst, & Mr Taylor says he would willingly put down $150 for his subscription, if it would aid in securing for you a salary which you should have, if you would come. He thinks if you could be induced to take charge of the Church, that you would assist or be the means of building up one of the most flourishing country churches in the denomination.

The Robertville church, known as the Black Swamp Church, was already by far the most flourishing Baptist church in the Carolina lowcountry. The congregation at this time has been described as "a refined, intelligent, and wealthy people, many of them noted for their deep, simple piety and their large hearted liberality,"[26] and as a show-case for the whole Baptist denomination. For a Baptist country church, the wealth was unusual: of the twenty-one contributors to the minis-ter's salary in 1848, fourteen owned more than twenty-five slaves, and five owned more than one hundred slaves. Entering the congregation in 1850, the Taylors with their sixty-eight slaves would have fallen toward the middle of this range. However, judging from the number of contributors and Maria's tally of the ballots, the white membership was quite small, although there were noncontributing white mem-bers. On the other hand, black members at Baptist country churches usually outnumbered whites by two or three times,[27] and nonmem-bers regularly attending services have been estimated as being any-where from three to six times more numerous than the members (defined as converted adults, white and black). Thus, of its kind, the Robertville situation had much to offer a minister in terms of both existing advantages and future possibilities.

James Clement Furman at age forty-one was now senior professor (out of three) at the Furman Theological Institution in Winnsboro, having entered academic life after sixteen years of serving parishes. An observer of the institution described James about this time.

> The Rev. J. C. Furman in form and appearance is not very digni-fied or graceful. As regards to features you would not say that there is anything very regal looking in the nose but about the mouth and eye and forehead you discern the scholar and the Christian, more of the latter than the former. The whole counte-nance displays as much meekness and humility as you will find in any human being. As a writer he is gifted with a clear, logical, comprehensive mind. As an orator he is fluent, solid as regards to matter and in manner exceedingly mild and persuasive. He is never truly eloquent except when on the prophetic.[28]

In addition to his professorial duties, James was in the midst of moving the institution to Greenville and raising money for the college that the Baptist Convention hoped to establish there. He did not come to Robertville.

THREE

Family Deaths

During their years at Myrtle Hill, Maria and John lost several family members: two young children, John's mother, and both of Maria's parents. In addition to the individual traumas of these events, Maria must have had a general sense of ground-shifting as she and John became the older generation and experienced the ultimate sorrow of parenthood. Letters of 1841, 1843, and 1848, an obituary of 1842, a poem of 1847, and retrospective poems from 1872 and 1893 reveal Maria's responses to her losses.

Elizabeth and Thomas, Maria and John's second and fourth children, died sometime between April 1841 and December 1842.[1] The deaths evidently occurred in rapid succession, for in Maria's 1872 poem "Home Memories: Attracting Heavenward," which goes chronologically through the family necrology, she writes of them: "Next came our own lov'd ones, two at one stroke, / Belov'd and loving!" and in an 1893 poem she states that they were buried in one grave. Ironically, Maria had written about the good health of the family shortly before Elizabeth and Thomas died.

20 April 1841. Maria Baker Taylor to James Clement Furman

> A kind & merciful God saw fit to preserve them [her children Caroline, Elizabeth, Mary, Thomas, Lydia] during the last trying year, when we were surrounded by sickness & death. You have no doubt heard of how many in our neighbourhood were victims to the prevailing fever; in many instances two or three children were taken from one family.

Our family was almost the only one in the neighbourhood who enjoyed any thing like health, & I was often led to inquire why is this? I was afraid to consider it as a matter of peculiar favour with God, for I knew that I deserved much more of His wrath than many who were affected, & the scriptures assured me that "whom the Lord loveth he chastiseth and scourgeth every son whom he receiveth." Then why should I shrink from his scourging hand or exult that I was chastised not, except through the chastisement of others?

"In the day of prosperity rejoice, in the day of adversity consider," was a text I frequently thought on, & felt that both items involved frames of mind I should indulge under the dispensations of Providence. I humbly hope that the author of all mercy did not send leanness into our souls, but filled us in a good degree with gratitude & love to Him.

We anticipate another trying season this summer, may the Lord prepare us for His will, and give us that love for Him and childlike spirit which will make His will ours.

Maria commemorated Elizabeth and Thomas in a poem dated May 1847, at least five years after their deaths. The tone of the poem is the only indication that Maria was eventually able to make God's will her own. Although conventional, the piece has a simple dignity. The "babes" appear only in the last line.

To the Yellow Jessamine

My pretty graceful hanging vine,
Sweet, lovely yellow jessamine.
Joyous I greet my favourite flower,
In clustering bloom upon yon bow'r.

Ah! why so short must be thy stay!
So much admir'd why haste away?
With all thy beauty, perfume rare
I count thee, mongst the fairest, fair.

The mock-bird midst thy deep green leaves
Now ope's his throat, his bosom heaves,
And warbling rich and varied song
Invites thee too, thy stay prolong.

My favourite bird, my favourite flower!
Ye 'mind me of the happy hour,
When those were here, who now are flown
Like ye they hasted to be gone.

So fair, they would not long remain
Lest earth should their pure spirits stain
Early winged their flight to heaven
Where deathless flowers to babes are given.

Maria was about twenty-eight when she lost these children and thirty-three when she wrote the poem.

A clipping of an undated and unsigned newspaper obituary states that Maria's mother-in-law, Mary Morgandollar Taylor, died in her sixty-ninth year in St. Peter's Parish, Beaufort District, South Carolina. Because Mary was born in 1774, her death can be placed sometime in 1842. It was probably Maria who wrote the obituary; the details of the deathbed strongly suggest an eyewitness family member as the writer, and the eulogist clearly knew Mary well. Also, an obituary that was definitely written by Maria for another Beaufort District coreligionist is in much the same rhetorical and syntactic style. But whoever wrote it, the obituary sets forth Christian traits the St. Peter's Baptists admired:

In early life Mrs. Taylor became a member of the Euhaw Baptist Church,[2] and up to the time of her decease was regarded by all who knew her as a consistent and exemplary Christian. Humility, benevolence, and cheerfulness were in remarkable degree her characteristics. Ever esteeming others better than herself, their excellences were her subjects of complacency or admiration, her own, of rigid scrutiny.

In the duty of self-examination she was often engaged. To the best, which not only the word of God, but the writings of profound thinkers afford, her experiences were submitted. "Edwards on the Affections" she alluded to as having aided her during this trial of her faith. Of that faith, in consequence, if through life she lamented the feebleness, she was yet convinced of the reality.

Nor was this conviction shaken on the approach of death. She then intimated her cordial acquiescence to the Divine appointments; assured her weeping relatives that she was not afraid to die; declared that "Christ was precious to her; that to Him she would trust, and dying, clasp Him to her breast, the antidote of death." The words recorded in the 14th chap. of John, of Him whom she had as yet seen through a glass darkly, but whom she was now immediately to behold in his glory, read at her request when she could with difficulty articulate, were the last to which her departing spirit listened on earth. Quietly she went down into the dark valley, cheerful with the light of hope.

Thomas Baker died on 20 December 1842, shortly after his seventieth birthday. No writing of Maria's about her father's death has survived from that time, but a letter her sister wrote the following year expresses what were likely to have been Maria's feelings as well. Maria was visiting Mary at the Bakers' old summer home when Mary (age twenty-two) wrote the letter, and it would have been only natural for the sisters to discuss their feelings.

15 September 1843. Mary Louise Baker to Maria Dorothea Furman

I owe Aunt Ann[3] an apology for not answering her kind and sympathizing letter after the death of my dear father, my distress at that time was such that I could not bear to dwell upon the subject, active employment was the only thing that relieved my mind, and [kept] me from sinking into dispair. Words cannot express my feelings when I think of our loss, nor can I say any thing to the praise of my father to those who knew him.

Life has lost half its charmes to me since his death, my evry wish my evry desire was to please him and to merit his approbation. I now find it a great source of gratification to act in the way that I think he would most approve, and to let those principles actuate me which he laboured hard to impress upon my mind and seemed more than anxious that I should fully appreciate. When I think of all the valued lessons, which he taught, both by example and precept, my heart swells with greateful emotions to him who is the giver of all earthly good, that he blest me with such a parent, and [desires] are created within that I might know and do his will more perfectly.

Thirty years after Thomas Baker's death, Maria wrote of him in two stanzas of her "Home Memories" poem. The conventional love-poem imagery of tree and vine is striking in a father-daughter context, even though the entwining entities are immortal souls.

> I lov'd—I lov'd him—no words can express—
> I felt that he lov'd me not any less—
> My soul, with his soul, did as closely entwine;
> As yon oak and ivy—one tree or one vine!

Thomas bequeathed to his wife, Rachel, his summer residence Woodville with its attached ten acres and the eight negroes who belonged to the place. He then divided the remainder of his real and personal property equally among his four children, with the proviso that the value of the negroes he had given Richard and Maria upon their marriages be deducted from their part of the estate. The only recorded evidence of the value of Maria's inheritance shows that in 1851 she sold her one-fifth share in 1,000 acres in Sumter District to her brother Thomas McDonald Baker for $1,000.[4] Maria was twenty-nine when her father died.

Maria's mother died at Woodville on 12 January 1848 at the age of seventy. In reply to a consolatory letter, Maria reflected on what Rachel meant to her.

14 February 1848. Maria Baker Taylor to Ann Eliza Furman

Circumscribed indeed was the circle of those who felt solicitude in my welfare; who cared for my soul. The blank which has recently been made in it can never again be filled except by the cherished memory of departed love & departed worth.

I have felt the want of my dear Mother's society, the want of her advice and of her experience, patience and tenderness for a long time [since her marriage in 1834]. I fear I shall now feel the absence of her watchfulness and prayers not only for myself but for all I love. "Ye are the salt of the earth" could verily be addressed to her. I trust that daily realizing the necessity of obedience to the command "have <u>salt</u> within yourselves," will urge me on to emulate her bright example of faith and patience, to add grace to grace "walking in all the commandments and ordinances of the Lord blameless" even as she did.

I have often thought of and wondered at the ease with which my dear Mother performed duties I find so difficult. The secret was that in "jehovah she found righteousness and strength" by feeding <u>daily</u> on the "hidden manna." And if "faith and patience inherit the promises" how rich will be her portion.

"Our blessings brighten as they take their flight." So is it with the blessing I enjoyed in my <u>Christian</u> Mother. When I contemplate her character I feel assured that had she preceded St Paul he would have enrolled her name amongst his host of worthies! Like himself, she had learned in every situation to be content, like him she "counted all things but loss for the excellency of the knowledge of Christ."

But my dear Aunt, although you knew her too well not to know her virtues and deep piety yet you will still allow me the melancholy pleasure of dwelling upon them, particularly to one, who I know will appreciate my feelings. Oh that our last end may be like hers. She looked, longed for, and loved the appearing of her Righteous Judge and henceforth there is a crown of life laid up for her.

She was perfectly conscious of the near approach of death, but he had lost his sting and she bade him welcome; her favourite passage of scripture during her illness was the latter part of the 11th chap of Math. "Come unto me all ye that labour."

This tribute sums up a legacy of Christian faith and action that is later reflected in Maria's own life. As for a worldly legacy, Rachel bequeathed to Maria two slaves, Candace and Dick, and a chest of drawers.[5] Maria was thirty-four when her mother died.

FOUR

Wife and Husband

The foundational fact of Maria's life during these years in Beaufort District was her marriage to John. One indication of how Maria construed her wifely duties can be seen in her handwritten copy of the essay "Female Accomplishment" by Hannah Moore, dating from her school days. The essay ends: "When a man of sense comes to marry, it is a companion whom he wants . . . a being who can comfort and counsel him; who can reason, and reflect and feel, and judge and discourse, and discriminate, one who can assist him in his affairs, lighten his cares, soothe his sorrows, purify his joys, strengthen his principles and educate his children."

Another indication of her expectations of marriage is the evangelical teaching of the time that husbands and wives should nurture each other's personal holiness and gently correct each other's moral lapses. A common lapse in slaveholder marriages was the husband's sexual relations with slaves, a practice that some southern white women expressed great bitterness about in their private writings.[1] However, in her extant writings Maria never mentions or even hints at the subject in regard to her own or anybody else's marriage.

In letters from 1841, 1845, 1851, and 1852, several kinds of interactions between Maria and John appear, as well as glimpses of John's personality. Also, a discrete set of documents, dated 1841–45 and consisting of letters, accountings, and a legal opinion, deals with the estate of John's uncle.[2] Some of the letters are copies in Maria's hand of letters John wrote, so Maria was well acquainted with this episode.

Taken as a whole, these documents reveal a significant and tangled situation the young couple had to deal with and further illustrate personal qualities.

John's uncle Henry Taylor, one of the wealthiest rice planters of Beaufort District, died in January 1841, leaving a wife and young child along with property in South Carolina, Georgia, and England, with the greater part of the assets lying in South Carolina. Henry's will named John Taylor and John P. Williamson of Savannah as executors.[3] John was thus faced with what could turn out to be a heavy and perhaps even perilous responsibility for a thirty-two-year-old husband and father of moderate means.

In a legal opinion solicited by John, William Ferguson Colcock, a prominent Beaufort lawyer and politician,[4] outlines the essentials of the situation: "Mr Williamson has proved the will and qualified as executor in Georgia, but declines to qualify in South Carolina. Mr Taylor has proved the will and qualified in South Carolina, but by the laws of Georgia cannot act as executor in that state, as none but a citizen of that commonwealth . . . can exercise that office." Colcock goes on to explain that the will instructs the executors to sell within two years all real and personal assets except bank stock and to apply the proceeds to purchase of bank or other stock "as they may think most advantageous to my heirs."

Colcock then addresses John's two specific inquiries. First, "Mr Taylor desires to know if he should sell this property as directed by the foregoing clause of the will & pay over the proceeds to Mr Williamson of Georgia to be invested in bank or other stock in Savannah, would he be exonerated from all further responsibility in case of loss or mismanagement of the funds by Mr Williamson." Colcock explains John's main motivation to wind up the business quickly: the young age of Henry's child could involve him in a protracted responsibility. On this whole issue, Colcock gives the opinion that John's goal could be reached through the proper court proceedings.

Colcock proceeds to address John's second inquiry: "Mr Taylor desires to know whether it will be necessary for him to continue to act as executor after paying over all the funds, which may come to his

hands, to his co-executor in Savannah in case he is allowed to do so."
Colcock replies by stating that "an executor who once qualifies & acts
cannot renounce his office, nor can the court release him. But . . . an
exor is not liable for the devastavit[5] of his co-exor, provided he has not
intentionally or otherwise contributed to it. Mr Taylor would only
have to be careful not to concur in Mr Williamson's acts, nor in any
manner contribute to his management of the estate in order to save
himself harmless."

John had already communicated his apprehensions to Williamson,
thus beginning a prickly relationship between the two executors.

9 March 1841. John Morgandollar Taylor to John P. Williamson

I regret to collect from the tenor of yours of the 31st ult [Feb-
ruary] that your feelings have been wounded by my several letters.
I disclaim any intention of offence and am sorry that you have so
construed my communications. I am and always have been averse
to joint action on business of importance hence my unwillingness
to have any connection with the Est of my uncle in the event of
your acting in this state. I regret that my counsel led me into an
error by his off hand opinion, that your being a witness should dis-
qualify you for the office of exor, his written opinion differs & I
transcribe it for your satisfaction.

Maria explains John's decision on going through with the executor-
ship after receiving Colcock's opinion. Considering the legal com-
plexities, the cautiousness that Maria attributes to John is appropriate
in spite of Colcock's reassurances that he could come out unscathed.

April 1841. Maria Baker Taylor to James Clement Furman

Mr Taylor is now on a visit to Savannah; his late Uncle Mr H
Taylor left him, together with Mr J Williamson of Savannah,
Executor of his estate. Mr Taylor will decline acting, contrary to
the advice of all his friends, because he does not wish to become
responsible for the acts of his coexecutor who he understands has
all of his property covered. If his fund of cautiousness was not
quite so large, he might benefit himself considerably by acting, as

the estate is quite a large one.[6] I have heard it remarked that no partnership was safe, except that entered in by marriage, & I partly believe it, therefore I am glad that "my gude man" has declined having anyone else than myself to contend with.

Apparently, Williamson decided to qualify in South Carolina as well as in Georgia, and John was largely out of the picture during 1842. However, that situation changed. In a curt note dated 4 January 1843, Williamson's attorneys, McAllister and Cohen of Savannah, informed John of Williamson's death and advised John "to proceed forthwith to Mr Colcock's residence. . . . It is now necessary for you to qualify as Exor. of the estate of Taylor." John was now sole executor. His duties over the next two years occasioned trips to Savannah, Charleston, and Henry's plantation, Laurel Hill, as well as dealing with such diverse matters as rice mill repairs, the fate of an elderly runaway slave, rice sale accountings, illegal building on Laurel Hill land, and bills incurred by Williamson on behalf of the estate.

As the tone of the next letter makes plain, John was feeling the pressures of his position. He writes in response to a request to pay a lawyer's bill of $500 incurred by Williamson:

28 February 1844. John Morgandollar Taylor to Solomon Cohen

> Your letter of the 20th inst. to Mr Colcock was yesterday handed to me, but without definite advice as to my course of action on the subject of it, being thrown there on my own resources, I must, as painful as it is to me, decline to act in this matter, as I have in all others of the same nature. I even do not expect to perform Mr Jno. P. Williamsons contract with Mssrs Terville & Colcock but must be considered as beginning "de novo" with them. Mr Jno. Williamson [son] must act as he pleases. He has performed all the other contracts of his father without my interference in any way & can you say why not do likewise in this? I trust you will not deem me captious, or disposed to give offence, nothing is farther from my mind, but I am placed in a most delicate situation, wishing to do right, yet acting under the impulse of the first law of nature, self-preservation.

The last rice accountings are dated 24 February 1845, so presumably John managed to be released as executor shortly thereafter.[7] Although John and Maria were no doubt greatly relieved to be rid of the responsibility, the whole experience must have furthered their practical education in property management and legalities.

The nature of John's operation mentioned in the next letter is unknown. Considering that Maria had five small children to care for at home, it is not surprising that she was not in Charleston with her sick husband.

28 April 1845. John Morgandollar Taylor to Maria Baker Taylor

My Beloved Wife, I thank God that I am able to write you this one more letter. I do it however lying upon my back with a board across my knees for a desk. My sufferings have been & are still great & worse than all no soothing hands of dear companion & freind to smooth the sea of pain. But I trust that god is with me, & I know that he is the best of all freinds, & the only one able to raise me up. I am happy to say to you that the fever has not raged as high as I had feared tho the inflamation has run high and I am suffering this evening from intense pain in my back.

It is very certain that I shall not be able to stir this week. I hope to be able to do so the next. At all events, do send the Barouche to Parachuckla on Wednesday next, the 6th of May, for me, the Ivanhoe leaves Sat the evening before & if possible I will leave here on this day week so as to take her up. If however I do not go then you must not be uneasy as I may be too sore to travel & not out of danger.

The Surgeon thinks I am far better than he expected & says I will soon be well. He says he never saw a person stand an operation better, few so well. If I ever reach home I shall have some fancey tales to tell you. In the mean time remember me at a throne of grace. Kiss all my dear children for me & believe me now as ever your sincerely affectionate Husband.

In the next letter, Maria dispatches John's business affairs in his absence in a manner suggesting that she is her husband's de facto business partner, as was the case with many planter couples.[8]

26 February 1850. Maria Baker Taylor to John Morgandollar Taylor

I sent you two letters which have come here since you left, and which it may be necessary, or well, for you to see before you arrange your money matters in Savannah. I wish you could answer Mr Curtis[9] letter favourably. I wrote immediately to him & informed him that you had left the day before its reception and would be absent some time & that if Dr Nott could conveniently hold on to the house until your return I would be glad if he would persuade him to do so, as you would then be able to answer his proposition for yourself. TW's[10] letter has likewise some things which may immediately require your attention.

Did you get the 2 boxes of soap, the indelible ink & the shoes for the children? If not please do not forget them at this time, & lest your list is lost I send another. For Caroline 1 pr thick soled coarse Bootes & 1 pr dress shoes between No 2½ and No 3. 1 pr dress shoes not Bootes for Mary fully No 3. 1 pr of very coarse Booties like the Servants No 2½ for Lydia. 1 pr of nice small shoes for Richard to fit the enclosed measure. 2 boxes of old turpentine soap. 1 viol of indelible ink. The beet seed has not yet come.

Conjugal helpfulness and devotion are especially apparent as John writes aboard ship en route to Florida to prepare for the family's move there.[11]

25 November 1851. John Morgandollar Taylor to Maria Baker Taylor

My Dear Wife, I was so unwell & so fatigued when I reached Savannah, & had so much to do this morning that I could not find time to write to you. I hardly had time to reach the boat, as she was about to put off from the wharf. Yesterday was a holiday in Sav, & consequently I had to do what had to be done this morning— hence my great hurry. By pushing very hard, I found time to purchase the articles you wanted, & to get Behn[12] to purchase the butter chair & washstand. They will be shipped by the DeKalb tomorrow morning & I hope you will receive them in good time & in good order.

I will write to Levy[13] as soon as I have finished this. My cold is better, & now my dear that I am nearly well, I am [?] for you & the dear chicks, expecting that you too will have to pass through the same ordeal [in making the trip to Florida]. I trust that none of you may suffer as I have done, which has been more, than I have confessed to.

May the Lord bless & keep you all during my absence which shall be for as short a time as possible. Write to me at Ocala [Florida] & meet me with a letter at Savannah & let me know what you may want from there so that I can get it for you. Write to Jackson & say unless he reaches Ocala by the 12th or 14th Dec, I shall leave there for home. How much I wish to see you. I think I shall be more considerate for the rest of my life. Kiss all the dear children for me & believe me my wife

Your Sincerely devoted Husband Jno M Taylor

While John was still in Florida, Maria handled business correspondence concerning property he was buying there.

4 February 1852. Maria Baker Taylor to John Morgandollar Taylor

Necessity seems to call me to dictate the matter of fact affairs of this life, which we must admit it is our duty <u>faithfully</u> to perform, and which I contend we can only do under a proper and constant sense of the <u>divine government</u>.

I received yesterday by mail a package from Mr Colcock,[14] containing a patent issued in your favour on Military Bounty Land Warrant No 28575 with the enclosed notice around it, signed by Butterfield; also the receipt for $100/2 from Halliday, being in full for the South half of the South East quarter Section No. thirty five in Township No. fifteen South of Range No. twenty one East containing eighty acres and ten hundredths at $1.25 per acre. I am this particular that you may be at no loss.

I am almost afraid to send the papers by mail, as I know the patent and receipt are both valuable papers. I will send them to you by Mr Martin,[15] if you wish it and write me in time; he goes in a fortnight. The Patent is signed by Millard Fillmore,[16] Alex

McCormick Assit Secy & Jos S. Wilson, acting Recorder of the General Land Office, and, as a matter of course, the Eagle with outspread wings protects it.

I went round to Mr Martin's this morning, thinking it probable that he would go to Florida next week; I did not see him, but Mrs Martin informed me that he was just from Savannah and had a letter for me from you, and that he did not expect to go to Florida in less than a fortnight. I had carried the package from Mr Colcock with me, but determined not to wait so long in sending it to you, as the letter might be of service to you in your disposal of your business, and as the mail goes from Peples' this evening, I concluded to write to you, & copy verbatim Mr Colcock's letter.

For all her efficiency, Maria was careful to make clear that she was serving John's interests and God's will.

FIVE

Slavery and Plantation Affairs

In none of the several hundred thousand words of Maria's extant writings is there any clear indication that at any time in her long life she thought slavery was wrong in principle. On the practical level, Maria of course understood that slavery was the basis of her socio-economic class and of her relative personal freedom from domestic drudgery.

From her immediate environment, Maria was familiar with a wide variety of practices and views concerning black people. She had encountered the well-to-do free black Ellison family in her girlhood church, and now in upper St. Peter's Parish she lived in a small area that had by far the largest number of free black farm families in all of Beaufort District, a situation that may have been related to the vigorous outreach of local Baptist missionaries to black people.[1] Among her neighbors, treatment of slaves varied plantation by plantation. For example, one slaveholder refused to break up slave families through sale, while another whipped a slave to death;[2] and Maria mentions in letters below an abolitionist pastor and an abolitionist family in the two upper St. Peter's churches the Taylors attended.

However, two Baptist documents that Maria was surely acquainted with suggest that her Baptist faith was the most powerful determinant of her intellectual views on slavery and her treatment of her enslaved servants. Selections from these two documents are followed by writings from Maria's own hand; in letters from 1846, 1847, 1848, and 1850, she discusses situations concerning the plantation, the black workforce, and abolitionist neighbors.

The first of the Baptist documents is a letter written by Maria's grandfather Richard Furman to the governor of South Carolina in Furman's capacity as president of the South Carolina Baptist State Convention. Dated 24 December 1822 and published in 1823, the document had a wide circulation in both South and North, and was a significant early statement of the emerging argument that slavery was a positive good.[3]

Richard Furman sets forth a closely reasoned argument based on both the Old and New Testaments. He asserts that "the right of holding slaves is clearly established in the Holy Scriptures, both by precept and example." He points out that when masters and slaves were received into the primitive Christian church "while it was yet under the ministry of the inspired Apostles their relationship, as masters and slaves, was not dissolved. Their respective duties are strictly enjoined. The masters are not required to emancipate their slaves; but to give them the things that are just and equal, forbearing threatening; and to remember, they also have a master in Heaven." Furman continues, "In proving this subject justifiable by Scriptural authority, its morality is also proved; for the Divine Law never sanctions immoral actions." He then explains:

> As for the Golden Rule, it should never be urged against that order of things, which the Divine government has established; nor do our desires become a standard to us, under this rule, unless they have a due regard to justice, propriety and the general good. . . . If the holding of slaves is lawful, or according to the Scriptures; then this Scriptural rule can be considered as requiring no more of the master, in respect of justice (whatever it may do in point of generosity) than what he, if a slave, could, consistently wish to be done to himself, while the relationship between master and servant should be still continued. . . . A bondservant may be treated with justice and humanity as a servant.

Furman also urges the religious education of slaves, for "though they are slaves, they are also men; and are with ourselves accountable creatures, having immortal souls, and being destined to future eternal reward."[4]

The second document is a collection of sermons, *The Family Preacher*, by William Rufus Bailey, first preached in the Baptist Church in Sumterville, South Carolina, and published in 1837.[5] The seventh and eighth discourses are on the duties of masters and servants. Like Furman, Bailey accepts slavery as God's will. God ordained the obvious differences in the natural capacities of human beings, and these have resulted in unequal social arrangements that are not challenged in the Bible. The superiority of masters is neither a crime nor a merit, but is a responsibility. Bailey defines the duties of masters on the basis of Colossians 4:1: "Masters, give unto your servants that which is just and equal, knowing that ye also have a Master in heaven." He interprets justice and equity as fairness under the circumstances of the case, that is, slavery. The labor of servants is rendered by divine constitution, and in return masters must supply their essential wants in regular returns to their labor.

More specifically, masters must supply food, clothing, domestic comforts, and time for sleep, recreation, and social intercourse, all of these things in sufficient measure to assure long life, health, cheerfulness, and productive labor. While insisting on "industrious and economic habits," the master must have "a reasonable regard for the strength of the labourer." In personal address, the master must never use "opprobrious, intemperate, profane, or abusive language," always remembering that "although his inferiors, his servants are men. They are intellectual, moral, immortal. They walk erect, and they can never forget to honour themselves as belonging to the race, who were created in the image of God."

Thus the master has the duty of the "moral and religious improvement" of his servants, by exerting a "salutary moral influence" in his own life and by seeing that the servants have religious instruction within the family and in public worship. In personal attitude and management, the master owes "a conciliating and kind manner, suitable indulgence, and good advice . . . lenity towards their faults, wholesome restraints and discipline."

The main duty of servants is obedience, for by obeying the master, the servant obeys God and partakes of "the grand harmony of divine wisdom in the domestic economy." The servant has the duty to show reasons when he believes the master wrong, but he may not resist the master's orders. If the master "abuses his power, he must answer for it," not to his servants but to their common master in heaven. In addition, the servant has the duties of fidelity, truth-telling, and honesty in handling property.

Such was the Baptist theory of slavery that Maria was brought up with.

In the earliest of Maria's 1846–50 letters, there are two plantation-related discussions: John Taylor's desire to move out of Beaufort District and his selling "a negro man." Maria then uses the term "servant" rather than "slave," a term that appears nowhere in her writings.[6] The "roguish tricks" are not specified, but at the time "rogue" was a common term for "thief," and Maria uses it elsewhere with this meaning. Prime field hands brought an average of $550 in Charleston in 1845,[7] so the skilled slave Maria describes would probably have brought at least as much. With such a sum, John could have paid for about one hundred acres of the Florida land he was soon to buy.

18 March 1846. Maria Baker Taylor to Ann Eliza Furman

> Mr Taylor and Tom[8] have returned from their peregrinations in Florida and Georgia. They arrived on the 15th instant, having been absent from here nearly a month, and after having seen some very fine lands, that have increased their anxiety to move. I think it more than probable that Mr Taylor will purchase in the neighbourhood that S Sufman is living in, as he liked the land in that neighbourhood, which Mr McDonald had for sale, more than any other he had seen. The land rich, church within reach, a market and oysters convenient; and by making a small purchase about five miles from the plantation, we may have a healthy permanent residence near a school and very good society.
>
> Mr T expects to sell while in Charleston a negro man, whom I have had in the house ever since I began housekeeping until last fall, when we caught him in so many roguish tricks, as to make it necessary to turn him in the field. He promised his master faithfully then, if he would not sell him that he would try and amend

his ways, but having been guilty again recently of some of his old pranks we have determined to sell him. I regret his behavior, as he is a servant I am quite partial to, a complete house servant, very capable and active, and with a turn for carpenter's work, & various other things required about a "domestic," which we do not always meet with united in one.

A few months later, John Taylor made a land purchase in Georgia.

17 September 1846. Maria Baker Taylor to Ann Eliza Furman

Mr Taylor was so much pleased with Glynn[9] that he has purchased a plantation out there, which he regards as quite a bargain at five thousand dollars; and we are to remove there, if no unforeseen accident occurs, this winter twelve month. He enumerates a great many advantages we are to have in the way of abundance and fine living, when we get out there, and then promises that nothing in the way of religion, health, morals or society will I find inferior to that I here enjoy; he seems very much disappointed that notwithstanding my willingness to go, I am not in ecstacies at the thoughts of a removal. When we get there, should that time ever arrive, I will give you a full & unreserved discription.

For whatever reason, the time for Glynn never arrived, and John's next land purchases tied the Taylors more firmly to Myrtle Hill:

17 September 1847. Maria Baker Taylor to Ann Eliza Furman

I suppose you have learnt ere this that Mr Taylor has made a purchase of his Mother's old place adjoining the one we live at? with an additional tract that Tom Wallace purchased from Solomons for $1000, Mr Taylor gave $2888.00 for the two tracts united. I suppose we are now fixed here permanently a time, but I hope the time is not far distant when we will be able to get a summer place in some healthier region, where I can enjoy more peace of mind during what is termed the sickly season.[10]

However, a year later the projected move was again a lively issue.

29 September 1848. Maria Baker Taylor to Ann Eliza Furman

Mr Taylor's crop is a failure, and we will not make more than enough to bear family expenses & support the negroes. My own health has been bad all the summer, I was afraid at one time that I should have to leave home. Mr Taylor is now offering his plantation & negroes for sale, in order to leave the low country & look for a more healthy region, & where we can enjoy advantages for the education of our children which we cannot obtain about here.

In the next letter, no reason is stated for selling the eleven servants, who were apparently well thought of. However, the context of the other letters suggests several possibilities: the Taylors needed money due to crop failures; they were cutting back on the workforce as plans for moving became firmer; they were raising money to buy land in Florida. The immediate situation in the letter is that John was on his way to Florida when the man who was purchasing the slaves arrived earlier than expected. Maria then had to see the distasteful business through on her own.

It is curious that Maria mentions Brisbane in a letter dealing with selling slaves. Reverend William Henry Brisbane (1803–78) was pastor at the Pipe Creek church when the Taylors began attending in 1834. A prosperous slaveholder, in 1835 he turned against slavery, sold most of his slaves to his brother-in-law, and moved to Ohio. In 1840 he bought back his slaves at $200 above market price, moved them to Ohio, freed them, and set them up in life. He soon became one of the foremost early abolitionists on the national scene. The tenor of his views can be seen in his 1846 phrase, "the barbarian lynch-law spirit of the South."[11] The publication and documents he sent to John Taylor were most likely on the slavery issue. Perhaps he did not consider John as one of the barbarians.

26 February 1850. Maria Baker Taylor to John Morgandollar Taylor (complete)

My dear Husband, I received this morning your short letter of the 14th instant, sent by the steamer via Savannah.

Mr Lufburrow[12] arrived here on Saturday most unexpectedly to me, I was astonished almost shocked when he mentioned his name, having no anticipation of such a "Suddenty." I suppose the old gentleman will tell you of all his difficulties in getting here and then back to Savannah, he will leave the neighbourhood on the DeKalb tomorrow, his wagon is to meet yours at the Sister's Ferry on Friday for the negroes.

The old gentleman seems well satisfied with his bargain, but expressed some regret that there were so many small ones; I told him if there had been more workers he could not have begun to get them so cheap & that I thought he had quite a bargain even at $400 all round, & you had sacrificed their value in taking off $200 from [the price of] the children. I think you ought to have asked at least $4400 for the 11.

It has been a great trial to me to have this business to attend to in your absence, but I suppose as you have known them so much longer than I have you would have felt it more. If your feelings are spared I rest satisfied.

Mr Lufburrow appears to be a very upright man, I like him. He went to Robert Lawton's yesterday, is now there; they both called here this morning Mr Lawton will send him to the River tomorrow. I suppose hearing of the price RLL paid for negroes where I understand at least half of them are small will convince him that you have been at least fair.

I told him how much we thought of Juss and that your only objection to him was that he was too lenient & would rather assist the workers than resort to strictness, he seemed to regard that as rather in his favour as he would have too few under him to be strictly a driver.[13] Betty he wants as a cook, which kind of work she always seems to like better than any other, I think too it will agree better with her than sewing.

Brisbane has sent you another "Crisis" full of the South Carolinian & Brutus documents. Rachel[14] has a fine son which I believe she calls Juss or Jesse. We have all continued well, 6 or 7 negroes have been lying up for little or nothing. Logan Wallace says Sam is bad off, & from what I can learn he is affected in the same way

his father Dublin was. You had best get a truss for him at once
before he gets worse.

I gave Juss my due bill for twenty dollars, which Mr Lufburrow promises to pay him & settle with you for, I suppose you will
honour it as a matter of course, it is the price of his hogs & some
other little matters that I got him to prevent his sacrificing them.[15]
In addition to it I made both Betty & himself a present of five dollars a piece in cash & gave Aggy some change.

We all long to see you. The children have all been asleep some
time. I trust the Lord is with us in all our ways guiding us for
good, Oh that he would give us hearts to love & praise him, Wisdom, grace & strength to know & obey him. Accept much love
from your ever affectionate wife Maria B. Taylor

PS. You had best get your summer clothes at once. 3 yds of cloth
in three pieces for pantaloons, 2 coats & 2 vests may answer for you
with summer hat. Get a summer hat a piece for the three boys. Mr
Lufburrow gave me no paper except a reciept for the negroes &
a promise to settle with you on your return. No price mentioned
in it.

As the decision to leave South Carolina drew nearer, Maria
expressed mixed feelings. Of the persons she mentions in the next letter, Edmund Martin, in whose judgment Maria expresses such confidence, was in 1850 the largest of the great planters in upper St. Peter's
in terms of the number of his slaves (249), as well as a family connection, his wife being a sister-in-law of John's aunt.[16] The Robert family, of nearby Robertville, included Baptist preachers and teachers,
among them the incumbent preacher of the Taylors' church, Joseph
Thomas Robert.

5 March 1850. Maria Baker Taylor to James Clement Furman

Mr Taylor left for Florida the morning of the same day your
letter was received, he therefore did not read your messages to him
about that goodly land, and the effects of its sugar cane upon both
lean and fat. As he has no teeth to eat it and I very little disposition to do so, I suppose we can have nothing to fear except from
the climate.

I cannot say that I think with you that "Candling" under all circumstances is improper. "A continual dropping"[17] can certainly result in nothing good, but the "Lords of creation" with all their perfections sometimes need a quick & short currying, it sometimes has a fine effect, although in this matter [the projected move] I feel its importance too much as bearing both on the temporal and eternal interests of ourselves & children, to waste many words in idle talk about it, either in opposing or encouraging Mr Taylor's determination to move if practicable.

I have this confidence in God, that unless he goes with us we will not go, and unless he stays with us he will not permit us to remain here; then whether we go or stay I feel assured we act under his guidance. Mr Taylor writes me that he is more and more pleased with Florida and encouraged to purchase; the lands are from five to six dollars an acre in Marion [County] where he last wrote from. Mr Edmund Martin went out in company with him. You know that he is a gentleman of fine judgements & quick discrimination, particularly where money making and comfort are concerned. Advantages and disadvantages will not escape his observing eye. He and Mr Taylor intend purchasing near each other if pleased, and as two heads are better than one, wisdom being found in counsel I trust they will make a wise choice.

The information you obtained respecting Mr John Robert's family is correct; they are all, with the exception of Lawrence (whose better half was against it) going to Ohio, many persons say to turn ——— but I will not judge them. If they are tinctured with the unholy leaven of Abolitionism the sooner they go the better; "the thieves that would break through and steal from without," are preferable to the moth that would corrupt and consume us within"; I think, when they <u>can even now</u> bring their fanatical principles to bear upon our southern churches in influencing their decisions and actions it is impossible for us to apprehend worse consequences than may ensue.

When I read the first five verses of the vi chap of Paul's first epistle to Timothy[18] I feel like declaring war against the whole fraternity of Abo's and would feel almost sorry to learn that our

Representatives had hearkened to any thing like a compromise with the North. Old Harry Clay must be driveling in Washington in supposing that the South is ready to listen to his efforts at compromise. I think his compromise with the tariff and his letter written privately and since brought to light, stating his reasons for offering the resolutions, ought to be sufficient to keep Southern eyes open to him. I am sorry to say it, but I have no faith in the old gentleman.

Maria's reference here is to Henry Clay (1777–1852), famed legislator from Kentucky known as the Great Compromiser, and to the resolutions he had offered to Congress on several slavery issues a few weeks before Maria wrote the above letter. Her reference to "his letter" is probably to a letter favoring gradual emancipation that Clay addressed to a friend in February 1849 but that he always intended for publication. Thus Maria's insinuation that the publication of the letter constituted some sort of exposé of Clay is unwarranted and further indicative of her extreme hostility to his spirit of compromise.

After invoking the religious and political realms on the issue in the foregoing letter, Maria acknowledges a few months later that slavery is also a gritty question of who has to do the dirty work.

4 September 1850. Maria Baker Taylor to James Clement Furman

> We had understood that Old Mr John Robert had become quite disgusted with Ohio. . . . Mrs R did not like the wash tub so well, nor did Julianna the cookpot and so they determined to come back bag & baggage and content themselves for life (if they can) in Carolina. The Robertvilleans began to think the Dr,[19] who thought of going to Ohio in the fall, was a fixture upon them. And began to set themselves to work how to get rid of him, even some of his own relations are dissatisfied with him. Mrs R is an avowed Abolitionist, the Doctor is suspected, though I think unjustly, on the subject.

Perhaps one of the factors that motivated the Taylors' move to Florida was what they perceived as an increasingly unsettled atmosphere concerning slavery in upper St. Peter's Parish.

Conclusion

During her years in Beaufort District, from age twenty through age thirty-nine, Maria Baker Taylor developed into a capable mature woman, evident in her roles as wife, mother, plantation mistress, and community member. Her Baptist faith was basic to all of the central concerns of her young adulthood. She wanted a Baptist education for her children, she was active in Baptist church life, her reactions to family deaths were governed by her religious beliefs, her relationship with her husband was grounded in their mutual faith, her views of slavery were based on Baptist theory, and she had the abiding sense that God was present in even the most practical of life's affairs.

Toward the end of these years, the Taylors determined to make a radical change in their lives. As early as 1846 John had been contemplating leaving South Carolina, in that year purchasing a plantation in Georgia but then deciding not to relocate there. Why the Taylors finally bought Florida property and then actually followed through with the move may be inferred from reports extolling the benefits of various areas of Florida that had been circulating for almost a decade.

For example, a close political ally of U.S. Senator for South Carolina John C. Calhoun wrote to a newspaper editor friend in June 1842: "I want to see you and talk about Florida. I wish you could devote six weeks between this & November in going to St. Lucie or Fort Lauderdale on the eastern coast of the Peninsula. . . . The land is as good as it can be, the water fine, high pine hills to within two miles of the coast, the climate Arcadian—Oranges Bananas Coca nuts & other tropical fruits in abundance & all cheap as dirt. . . . 2

Thousand dollars each would buy us a Dukedom."[1] And the writer urged again in December: "I want to move to Florida & want you to go with me. Land can be had there now at from 25 cts to Government price, of the best quality & on the sea coast. I have much information in relation to it."[2] Others spoke of the "vast and incalculable" commercial and naval advantages to be realized from improving Florida's harbors and waterways, which would also stimulate agriculture by bringing into the market "the immense quantity of land now lying dormant."[3] All that was needed for great material prosperity was for the people of Florida to "push for a developement of the resources they possess."[4]

With such promising land, potential migrants to Florida would not need to worry about the condition of their black workforce either. In 1844 Calhoun himself wrote glowingly about the mental and physical health of slaves in Florida, citing figures from the 1840 census: "Taking the two extremes of North and South, in the State of Maine the number of negroes returned as deaf and dumb, blind, insane and idiots . . . is one out of every twelve, and in Florida, by the same returns, is one out of every eleven hundred and five; or ninety-two to one in favor of the slaves of Florida."[5] Politically too, South Carolinians would find Florida attractive. James E. Broome, the first governor of the new state and a native of South Carolina, wrote to John C. Calhoun in 1845 on the hugely important tariff question, "I feel assured that when ground is to be taken, South Carolina will lead, and I wish Florida committed to follow and when committed I desire that there shall be no mistake in the position she assumes."[6]

The gradual accumulation of such views would eventually persuade a South Carolina family contemplating a move to consider Florida, that tropical paradise just waiting to be exploited (and cheap at that). John Taylor, then, made at least two trips to Florida, one in February–March 1850 and another beginning in November 1851 and extending into February 1852, making land purchases in 1850 and 1852.

Having purchased Florida property in Marion County, the Taylors would have been reassured to go through with the relocation this time (unlike their decision respecting Georgia). An early 1851 South

Carolina newspaper report on the 1850 Florida crops stated that "the high price of Cotton has fully remunerated our planters, and their affairs are generally in a prosperous condition," while tobacco, "a leading article with the planters of Marion and Alachua counties. . . has thus far proved exceedingly profitable." Sugar cane would have done well if not injured by an unusual "cold turn," but the extensivly grown arrow root had been a highly successful crop, with plans made for processing it in Marion County. As the Florida reporter concluded, "our planters have great cause of satisfaction with the result of their crops, and we learn there is considerable migration to the State the present season."[7]

The Taylors would also have been reassured about having a market for their Florida crops in their native state. A Charleston newspaper in early 1852, commenting on a new ship just arrived from Palatka, Florida, via Savannah and Beaufort, listed its cargo as "cotton, sugar, hides, arrow-root, oranges, moss and syrup," gave the impressive 1850 census figures for the leading Florida crops, and adjured the Charleston merchants, "with the energy and spirit that has ever characterized them," to turn their attention to the Florida trade.[8]

A long article that appeared in at least two South Carolina newspapers in mid-1852 would have brought reassurances about Florida at a time close to the Taylors' move there. The article, in the form of a letter from Florida, after extolling the salubrious climate in a lyrical vein ("the sea breezes modifying the searching vertical rays of the sun, and wafting away the approaching northern frost"), proceeds to discuss the "extraordinay crops" of cotton, sugar, tobacco, and corn being produced on the former Indian and Spanish lands. The writer then singles out Marion County, "quite thickly settled up by planters from South Carolina . . . where you will see the land in a high state of cultivation, her citizens all satisfied with their new homes, and the country prosperous." Ocala, the county seat, he praises as "a flourishing little town . . . with seven stores, a good church, a fine court house, and an academy, just finished . . . and among her citizens you will find as much intelligence, politeness, and hospitality, as in any other town of her sister States."[9]

But by now Maria had already seen some of this for herself, having made her own exploratory trip to Florida. Apparently liking what she saw and in anticipation of the move, Maria wrote a long poem that she dated April 1852 and called "Ode to the St Johns River," with the notation "When visiting Florida for the first time." The poem concludes with a transcendent vision of her new home.

> Roll on Majestic River, swiftly roll,
> Bearing great gospel truth to fallen man.[10]
> Bear me too, on to my new home untried.
> Upon thy lovely banks may cities rise,
> And groves of orange, citron, lemon grow.
> And here may strangers find a peaceful home,
> Where health & joy may crown the passing hours.
> And may the spreading branches of the trees
> With beauty ever green shade sacred spots
> Where prayer & praise ascend, & gospel truths
> In purity proclaimed, convert the soul,
> And lead it up to Him, whose love abounds
> In all His gifts to men, in this dear land.

In January 1853, after nineteen years of married life in Beaufort District, South Carolina, John and Maria Taylor and their nine surviving children—Caroline, Mary, Lydia, John, Susan, William, Richard, Fenwick, Dora—emigrated south to become one of the pioneering families of Marion County, Florida. The number of slaves they took with them is unknown, but certainly enough to begin work on the "new home" immediately upon arrival. Maria makes no mention of these enslaved people in her vision of the "dear land." The prospect probably looked very different to these travelers.

Outline of South Carolina, marking locales associated with
Maria Baker Taylor, 1813–52

1. Oak Grove, Baker Plantation, Sumter District, 1813–1834
2. Charleston, School, 1830–1831
3. Myrtle Hill, Taylor Plantation, Beaufort District, 1834–1853
4. Limestone Springs, Gaffney, Taylor daughters' school, 1846–1852
5. Savannah, Georgia, plantation business center

Osceola Plantation House in Marion County, Florida. Taylor residence 1853–76. Photo taken 1873

Maria Baker Taylor
(1813–95) in midlife

Maria Baker Taylor
(1813–95) in old age

Four generations: Maria
Baker Taylor with daughter
Mary Ansley, granddaughter
Caroline Bauskett Kraetzer,
great-granddaughters Mary
and Katherine Kraetzer (children b. 1882, 1884)

John Morgandollar Taylor Sr. (1809–72), MBT's husband

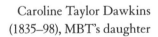

Caroline Taylor Dawkins (1835–98), MBT's daughter

Mary Louise Taylor Bauskett
Ansley (1837–1905), MBT's
daughter

Thomas Creyon Baus-
kett (1829–68), MBT's
son-in-law (Mary Louise
Taylor's first husband)

Lydia Taylor Crane
(1840–ca. 1920), MBT's
daughter

Edward Payson Crane
(1832–1905), MBT's son-
in-law (Lydia Taylor's
husband)

John Morgandollar Taylor Jr.,
"Johnny," (1842–1904), MBT's son

Curran Broome Taylor
(1844–1933), MBT's daugh-
ter-in-law (J. M. Taylor Jr.'s
wife)

Susan Taylor Beard (1844–95),
MBT's daughter

William Baker Taylor,
(1845–64), MBT's son. Photo
taken 1863, at age 18

Richard Furman Baker Taylor
(1847–1931), MBT's son. Photo
taken 1866, at age 18

Robert Fenwick Taylor,
"Fen," (1849–1928),
MBT's son

Maria Dorothea Taylor Wallace, "Dore" or "Dora," (1850–1919), MBT's daughter

Anne Baker Taylor Carlisle, "Nan," (1856–89), MBT's daughter

Julius Addison Carlisle (1846–1915), MBT's son-in-law (Anne Taylor's husband)

Maria Taylor Carlisle (1883–1933), MBT's granddaughter. Photo taken 1889, at age 6

Three

MIDLIFE YEARS IN MARION
COUNTY, FLORIDA, 1853–75

Introduction

In January 1853 the Taylors moved from Beaufort District, South Carolina, to Marion County, Florida, which had become a state only eight years before. The county had been named for Francis Marion, the South Carolina Revolutionary War hero, and the Taylors were part of a large ongoing South Carolina migration to Florida. The plantation, or cotton, belt of middle Florida, originally the prosperous north-border counties between the Apalachicola and Suwannee Rivers, was first settled by relatively wealthy emigrants from slave states who brought their way of life with them. As they prospered, they encouraged similar immigrants to join them. During the 1840s and 1850s this influx extended the middle Florida plantation belt southward into Alachua and Marion Counties.[1] More specifically, Marion County came to be dominated by South Carolinians during the 1850s,[2] in effect creating a "little South Carolina." Surrounded by such neighbors and with cotton prices at record highs,[3] the Taylors must have looked forward to a congenial and prosperous future.

By the middle of 1853 the Taylor family was well settled on the new plantation, named Osceola after the famed Indian chief (ca. 1800–38), the site of whose original camp was nearby.[4] Maria lived at Osceola for the next twenty-two years, a period similar to her Myrtle Hill years in both length and basic concerns. However, there are many more documents for Maria's midlife phase than for the earlier phases, most notably the diaries that begin in 1857. Also, a number of Maria's letters to Ann and James Furman fall in this period, and documents from other hands further enrich the sources.

Before turning to the concerns that absorbed Maria in her middle years, information about two underlying factors that determined those concerns will be presented: Maria's childbearing and features of the setting she now found herself in.

Maria's persistent concern with education was of course the principal consequence of her twenty-two years of childbearing, a taxing phase that continued and concluded at Osceola with the births of two more daughters in 1854 and 1856. Short and stocky in build, Maria appears to have emerged from these reproductive years in decent physical condition. Nothing of her intimate experience of pregnancy and childbirth appears in her writings, but a review of family vital statistics brings out some elements of this consuming biological activity.

Maria's first child was born thirteen months after her wedding, and by age thirty-six she had borne eleven children in a little over fifteen years at intervals ranging from thirteen to twenty-five months. The two intervals between the last three of these children had been only fourteen and thirteen months, and Maria may well have found the quickened pace of childbearing as she grew older an alarming development that required control. At any rate, an unusual hiatus of more than four years ensued before the twelfth child was born. Given Maria's record of successful births, this respite may have represented a deliberate choice, for during this time the Taylors were planning their move to Florida, transporting a large household and workforce, and relocating in pioneer territory, activities that were demanding enough without pregnancy. Given the times, abstinence would have been their only certain recourse.[5]

When Maria again became pregnant after settling in Florida, she was forty years old. The interval between her last two children was then less than fourteen months, with her thirteenth child, Anne, arriving a month after Maria turned forty-two, a figure somewhat above the average age of 38.7 years for the birth of the last child among southern antebellum women.[6] The pattern of a rapid succession of births was reasserting itself, and Maria can hardly have looked forward to a continuation even if her attitude then had been the familiar one she expressed in her old age, that her children were gifts of God.

Maria's coded references (OT on M)[7] in the 1857 and 1858 diaries indicate that at age 43–44 she was still having regular menstrual periods at 25–28-day intervals. In spite of this continued vulnerability, she somehow avoided pregnancy after Anne's birth, through abstinence or perhaps through prolonged breast-feeding, which Southern women may have (correctly) understood to ward off conception for about two years.[8] In the diary entry for 13 March 1858, when her youngest child was more than two years old, Maria writes "Commenced weaning Anne," and on 29 April she adds the pointed statement, "I had a conversation of some importance with Mr T concerning some of our household arrangements." Apparently Maria had preventively nursed Anne as long as she deemed appropriate and then claimed a separate room, thus in effect declaring an end to childbearing.

Thirty-nine years elapsed between the conception of Maria's eldest child and her youngest child's high-school graduation. Her oldest and youngest children were twenty-one years apart, and her second daughter had already started her family when Maria left the marital bed. Such generational overlaps were of course common in a time of large families and could have beneficial effects in holding a family together;[9] for example, even after her marriage Maria's oldest daughter often acted in a maternal role to the three youngest girls.

In addition to Maria's concerns about her children, during her midlife years she also dealt with moving to a new home. On his trips to Florida in 1850 and 1852, Maria's husband had purchased several adjacent parcels of land in Marion County. The property was located about four miles southwest of Ocala, a village of a few hundred people. Except for 80 acres of military bounty lands purchased at $1.25 per acre, John Taylor paid $5.00 and $5.50 per acre, the same price Maria had received for her land in Sumter District in 1851. All told, John paid about $6,450 for about 1,300 acres, a little over two square miles.[10] Eight years later, the 1860 census assigned a value of $16,000 to John's Florida real estate. The dwelling itself was a long two-story farm house with a roofed porch, or piazza, across the full extent of the front (see the photograph of the Osceola Plantation House, following page 79), the simple rustic building representing a style common among lesser planters.[11]

With their 1,300-acre plantation and more than sixty slaves,[12] the Taylors qualified as midrange members of the Florida plantation aristocracy, usually defined as families owning more than 1,000 acres and only seventy-seven in number as late as 1860.[13] Another indicator of status is that only 200 Florida plantations used thirty or more slaves.[14] Looked at from the other end, in the 1850s, 72 percent of rural middle Florida slaveholders held nine or fewer slaves.[15] The 1860 census gives $50,000 as the value of John Taylor's personal property, and about $35,000 of that figure probably represented his slave holdings.[16]

In a long letter she wrote a few months after the move, Maria gives a good deal of information about the new home and her hopes for it. Although she mentions "our negroes" only twice, much of what she describes of course affected black and white alike: the climate, the health conditions, the farming, and the difficulties of provisioning. The letter returns time and again to the question of health in the new country, but Maria's hopeful expressions are at odds with even the brief Florida experience she relates, for the family members are still having chills and fever. But then after so many years in the Carolina lowcountry, they no doubt already had malaria.

28 June/23 July 1853. Maria Baker Taylor to James Clement Furman

> Your kind and prompt answer to my last was most welcome, and would have been speedily replied to, if I could have followed the promptings of feeling, but other duties of a more pressing nature called for so much of my time and thoughts as to leave me not enough for the accomplishment of my wish to write you a long letter which I was desirous should be very interesting.
>
> The foregoing will be more than sufficient to prepare you for the dry epistle about to be written, with the aid of a forefinger too sore to be used in sewing the vast amount of work which has been accumulating while we were all undergoing the acclimating process. I am truly happy to say that we are all well again, and our hands & fingers have been busily employed upon summer clothing for us all. We are not yet quite through with it [becoming acclimated] but getting very comfortable.
>
> All of my family have had chill and fever without an exception. Although the attacks were pretty severe for a few hours they

were not at all alarming and seldom kept the patient in bed for a day, yet they kept me in dread that their continuance would end in ill health. Caroline's appearance[17] was such after several attacks that we thought something of allowing her to return to Carolina with Mr Richard Davant. I never felt better in my life than I am doing now, I have not had the fever since the first week in May.

[23 July continuation] More than half a years adventures and experience in a new country is not easily narrated. When I have the happiness of seeing you, I will have a great many things to tell & will read you my diary, which goes to show upon comparison with last years that we have not had more sickness here than we had in Carolina last year up to this time.

The climate is truly delightful; we have refreshing breezes here at all times, both from the Gulf & the Atlantic. Mr Taylor keeps a diary of the weather; about three or four days the thermometer has reached ninety-two in our passage never higher. It ranges through the day from 74 to 86. Until the last of June we slept under a blanket every night.

We are now having the tropical rains. It rained fifteen days in June & we have only had nine dry days this month; but it is not like a rainy season in Carolina; there everything gets mouldy & looks gloomy during a rainy spell. Here we have bright sunshiny mornings & a brisk heavy shower sometime between 2 o'clock & sundown, when the sun comes out gloriously, the earth soon is dry enough for a walk, & we have beautiful clear moonlight nights of the brightest kind, succeeding such days, never too warm to sleep well. And then at this place we have no mosquitoes; I have not seen or felt more than five since we moved here.

Mr Taylor is delighted with it as a farming country; he finds the lands very easy to cultivate, the growth luxurient & bearing well. He says I must tell you he never had such a crop in his life, as he has now of everything, and if the caterpillar, bug, or storm or some other unforseen evil does not come upon it he will make more cotton than he can possibly pick & a superabundance of provisions. His entire cotton crop is blackseed and has a very fine appearance.

Our negroes I think are quite as healthy as they were in Carolina. Individuals coming from regions of country where chill &

fevers prevail regard the chills & fever of Florida to be of a mild type. They seem scarcely to excite more sympathy than a tooth ache. We give very little or no medicine excepting quinine.

I think the place we are now living at has the appearance of being healthy. We have succeeded in getting good water both for washing and drinking purposes. This is a great consideration in this lime region. I hope ours will last. The want of facilities to market, we find a very great inconvenience, goods being shipped for us from Charleston and Savannah to Pilatka [now Palatka] & sent from there in barges up the Oclawaha to Silver Spring about 10 miles from us. We must write for things some time before we can expect to get them. This is rather hard for us who were before near enough to Savannah to send & get fresh oysters. Ocala is an improving town, it has recently been incorporated.

On the whole I think all of us are very much pleased with Florida. Mr Taylor has had chill and fever oftener than any of us, I suppose from being more exposed to sun & rain, & not being careful of himself. We are all beginning to be as venturesome as we were in Carolina & some how I hope & believe we will find this to be a healthy place.

As you may suppose, settling in the woods we have much to do. The yard is looking somewhat cleared up, but stumps in abundance stick out in waiting for the hoe & axe; building & attention to the fields & Genl Green [an illness] have placed them beyond our notice yet, but in time I hope to root them out & have a nice garden & orchard here.

Our garden is at present a mile off. Orchard we have none, only training some trees, vines etc for future setting out. A few boxes of flowers & geraniums, and our house, which is rather better than the generality of Florida houses, a kitchen nearly finished & a double servants house with the well is all that we can boast of out here. At the plantation we have all the other necessary buildings such as they are.

The Taylors were off to a satisfactory start.

A search through all the documents for the Taylors' Osceola years turns up a good deal of scattered information about the plantation and food supply. As was the case throughout the middle Florida plantation belt, the main cash crops at Osceola were cotton and sugar cane,[18] processed at the plantation gin house and sugar house and marketed in Savannah through their old agent, Major Phineas H. Behn. Because Savannah was the center of one of the few highly developed market systems of the South,[19] maintaining this somewhat distant connection was highly advantageous for the Taylors. The marketing of corn and "bine" (apparently hops) is also mentioned. The gin-house machinery could be harnessed for sawing lumber and grinding corn. Other cereals—barley, buckwheat, corn, millet, oats, rice, rye, and wheat—were planted but are not mentioned as being marketed, so were presumably for home consumption. Fruit and nut trees and vines were cultivated near the house: banana, blackberry, cherry, cocoanut, elderberry, fig, grape, orange, peach, plum, and walnut. The large variety of vegetables is especially striking:

arrowroot	cucumbers	peanuts
beans	eggplant	peas
beets	Irish potatoes	peppers
broccoli	kohlrabi	radishes
Brussel sprouts	leeks	salsify
cabbage	lettuce	squash
carrots	mustard	sunflowers
cassava	okra	sweet potatoes
cauliflower	onions	tomatoes
celery	parsnips	turnips
		vanilla

Maria maintained a sizable herd of dairy cows and a dairy house, and other livestock included beef cattle, hogs, and the usual barnyard fowl, as well as horses, mules, and oxen as work animals. The Taylors also kept a herd of sheep on a separate property along the Withlacoochie River in Levy County. The cultivated food supply was supplemented by hunting, fishing, and gathering berries as well as by supplies ordered from Savannah such as flour, sugar, coffee, oils, salt, tea, and cheeses.

As for specific menus, a letter that Maria's daughter Lydia Taylor Crane wrote to her mother in 1870 suggests that Maria's company dinners went considerably beyond the simple and hearty. Lydia, living in Pittsburgh as a faculty wife, is describing a Thanksgiving dinner she attended:

26 November 1870. Lydia Taylor Crane to Maria Baker Taylor

> I could not help contrasting the dinner they had for such a large company and what we used to do for our smaller dinner parties in the palmy days of the South. They had oyster soup, 2 turkeys and a chicken pie, sweet & Irish potatoes, parsnips, cold slaw, jelly & cranberry jam, then mince, pumpkin & apple pies, tea & coffee. Here, tho' it was considered a grand dinner. So if you have northern folks to visit, you need not worry.

The Taylors also drank well, the Baptist faith requiring moderation but not abstinence. They made red wine, a sweet golden wine of scuppernong grapes, and blackberry wine in large quantities. If equipment is any indication, considerable wine was consumed, for in a household memo of January 1857 Maria notes buying "3 doz and 3 wine glasses." The Taylors bought champagne by the basket, and a note in the 1857–63 household record lists twenty-one champagne glasses on hand (in addition to ordinary wine glasses). This beverage was served on special occasions, such as on John and Maria's twenty-first wedding anniversary when "all drank my health & happiness in a glass of champagne." Champagne was also administered to invalids.

An 1857 memorandum lists brandy and whiskey bought by the barrel, but liquor consumption appears to have been moderate. For example, John Taylor claimed three bottles of whiskey on 8 September, and not until 14 November were four more bottles "taken down" from safekeeping. Maria records her own occasional sip, and she gave out wine, whiskey, and brandy to the family, young children included, for the traditional medicinal purposes. Maria also dispensed spirits as incentive, for example sending six bottles of whiskey to "the negroes who were raising the [cotton] gin house."

Of course, Maria's Baptist faith remained the core of her existence, but matters of church organization, so prominent in the Beaufort documents, are almost entirely absent in documents from Maria's middle years in Marion County. The Taylors sometimes attended the

Ocala Baptist Church, which in 1856 had twenty-seven white and fifty black members.[20] However, services on the Florida frontier were irregular and often interdenominational, churchgoers attending wherever there was preaching. As late as 1860, the Florida Baptist Association had three times more churches than ordained ministers,[21] with one Baptist historian describing the condition of the Florida Baptist Convention from 1825–80 in these terms: "Its territory was so extended, its churches so weak and scattered, mediums of communication so exceedingly poor and methods of travel so difficult, that any form of concrete organization was well nigh impossible."[22]

Thus on the Florida frontier, it was largely up to the Taylor family circle to inculcate the basic tenets of Baptist faith: separation of church and state, a religious experience and conversion as conditions of church membership, baptism only of professed believers, worship of God according to the conscience of the individual, individual responsibility to God, governance of the church by the congregation, and the absolute independence of the local church. They also had to arrange as well as they could for the carrying out of the four ordinances of the Baptist faith: baptism, the Lord's Supper (required quarterly), funeral services, and ordination.[23] No wonder, then, that in Maria's diaries religious observances at home—family services, Bible lessons, individual devotional reading—are as frequently mentioned as church attendance.

ONE

Maria and Slavery

The relatively mild Spanish codes and attitudes to slavery and free blacks had prevailed in Florida before it became a U.S. territory in 1821. The Spanish influence persisted in parts of the state as long as a substantial number of holdovers from Spanish colony times survived. However, the migration of planters from Georgia and South Carolina into unsettled Florida lands, beginning as far back as the 1820s and booming by the 1840s, led to the replacement of the Spanish three-caste system of white, free black, slave (with many slave privileges) to the harsh two-caste white, slave system of the American South with its anti-free-black stance.[1] The Taylors arrived in Marion County as mature people with a twenty-year history of managing slaves in South Carolina, and they were surrounded by neighbors from South Carolina. Thus their attitudes and management style were unlikely to have been much influenced by whatever echoes of earlier Florida practices might still have been discernible.

Of course, slavery was the Taylors' economic base and in their Southern Baptist view a biblically justified social arrangement. Maria's own attitudes and practices can be seen in several kinds of documents. In a short essay she wrote in 1854, her second year in Florida, Maria sets forth some general views. Her daily interaction with large numbers of black people appears in the earliest of the extant diaries, from 1857. The kinds of interaction and the management style revealed here were no doubt the same that Maria had been practicing at Myrtle Hill and Osceola for some years, and are typical of those seen in her later diaries. A letter from 1860 develops her views on slavery in terms of the political situation, and a violent master-slave incident close to home related in the 1860 diary of her son-in-law Thomas Creyon Bauskett throws light on her views.

1854: "Some crude thoughts on Slavery"

The escalating national debate on slavery no doubt prompted Maria's short 1854 essay. Basing herself on scripture and contemporary "evidence" from missionaries, she echoes the views of Richard Furman and W. R. Bailey, familiar to her since youth.[2] Such views, of course, had wide currency by the time Maria wrote this piece. Certainly, she saw herself and her husband as among the "good masters."

> Have the declaimers against the Southern Institution of Slavery (once a Northern Institution until found unprofitable) ever studied thoughtfully & carefully the Negro, his character, not only as manifested at the South, but elsewhere? Are they not willing to acknowledge the really marked differences in the character of the Caucasian & the Negro?
>
> Tell me not of their degradation arising from their condition & treatment. I read of Northern missionaries encountering the same difficulties we have had to deplore. One of them writes back from Africa, "We regret to call for more stationary, but the children pilfer everything they can put their hands on, & we cannot keep slates, books, or anything else for them, & unfortunately we have no assistance from their parents, as they only chastise them for being detected & not for stealing.
>
> As for heading an article, "An Apology For Slavery"(!) I think an outrage on truth & humanity only surpassed by that of An Apology For Christianity (!!!)[3] I go out upon the broad ground that slavery was ordained by God, regulated by Him through Moses, St Paul, & others, for the benefit of society & the well ordering thereof & had that effect on Master & Servant; that the relation has been abused as every other has, as of parent & child, husband & wife, none would deny. It has been a great blessing to the African, who by coming from a land of barbarism, is being Christianized, & more or less, civilized. I have heard many of them bless God for having been brought to the South.

> "Me sing all day, me sleep all night;
> Me hab no care, me hart is light."

This is literally true with the generality of slaves, particularly those who have good masters. Were those persons who failed to read carefully & obey the vi of Timothy, doing God, or their fellow man service, when they prevailed on servants to rebel? Would not faithfulness & obedience serve more in accordance with the law, which regulated slavery on Mount Sinia [*sic*], or the gospel whose precepts & words were in concert with the law? Surely the Christian master tries to remember those, who were "in bonds, as being bound with them." Doing unto his servants as he, in like circumstances, would be done by.

Moral evil? What is moral evil? Sin? Slavery is no "moral evil." It may be connected as every good thing may with evil as eating, marrying, or anything you could name.

Maria's strong statement of slavery as a blessing to Africans may in part have been a rejoinder to Thomas Fuller, her Beaufort rival for church funds, who in an 1851 speech in Washington, D.C., had branded as fanaticism the advocating of "the perpetuation of slavery as a blessing."[4] But whatever impelled Maria to set down her "crude thoughts," they formed the theoretical base that governed her interactions with the Taylors' slaves.

1857: Maria and the Osceola Slaves

According to the 1855 tax rolls for Marion County, the Taylors held sixty-two slaves, and the slave schedule of the 1860 U.S. Census lists sixty-four. Maria's records for the first four years at Osceola, 1853–57, mention by name fifty-five slaves, including twenty-eight men and twenty-seven women. The routine interactions with these people seen in the 1857 diary center around housework, provision of clothing, tending the sick, discipline problems, and religious activities. Another area of interaction, cash dealings, is represented only in Maria's household accounts and will not appear in the following diary excerpts. However, it should be noted that Maria frequently bought eggs and chickens from the servants (12½ cents per dozen or fowl), and she paid one cigar-making servant a penny per cigar, for a total of $15.36. Such cash dealings were a common enough plantation practice within the considerable flexibility of the slavery system, and many plantation owners gave their slaves time to work for themselves and acknowledged that they owned and could sell what they raised.[5]

In 1857 Maria's house staff was performing housework for up to seventeen white people. The family consisted of the Taylor parents, now ages forty-three and forty-seven, ten unmarried children ranging in age from one to twenty-two, and newlywed daughter Mary and her husband, who spent as much time at Osceola as at their own adjoining place. Also resident in the house for some months were Miss Heermans, the governess; Maria Baker, a cousin visiting from Beaufort; and Mary Brien, an Irish seamstress.

In effect, Maria ran a fabric supply house and a garment factory, the latter with just one employee, to clothe all of the slaves. She ordered the cloth from Savannah and it came by boat to Silver Springs, a few miles away. Maria measured and cut large quantities of cloth to give out to the slaves, a job in itself. She also sewed for them, as plantation mistresses frequently did, reserving for herself the use of the sewing machine. At the same time, she was making most of the clothes for her entire family as well as bed and bath linens, mattresses, furniture covers, and curtains.

Maria was also in charge of health care for all the house servants and field hands, doing most of the doctoring and nursing herself, another role commonly played by plantation mistresses.[6] In the 1857 diary, Maria usually does not name the illnesses; other diaries reveal that the most common health problems were malarial chills and fever, dysentery, worms, and severe colds, ailments also frequently suffered by family members. In disciplinary interactions, Maria uses terms like "discipline," "chastise," and "punish" but she reveals very little of the actual measures she took.

In interactions concerning religion, Maria held the general evangelical position that religious instruction for slaves was an absolute obligation.[7] Osceola had its own chapel on the premises, primarily for the slaves' use, and Maria engaged Old John and John Williams, black preachers from other plantations, to serve as pastors to them. The Osceola blacks also came to the house for family services and attended the same church in Ocala as did the family.

The following excerpts from the 1857 diary occasionally include material that suggests the broader context of daily life in which Maria's interactions with the servants occurred. Entries marked "end" are from a separate diary section that contains several summarizing entries. First names are those of Taylor children or of slaves, mostly Maria's household servants.[8] Late in January, Maria has just returned from a trip to South Carolina:

> 24 Jan., Sat. Engaged in domestic duties, feeling unwell & much fatigued. Minty & Affy sick, had a good deal of the house work to attend to.

> 25 Jan., Sun. I remained at home [from church] gave the children their lessons, & read a sermon from Spurgeon[9] to those who remained at home. Old John & several other negroes came in to hear. Affy up & cooking.

> 26 Jan., Mon. [complete] Engaged in household duties, determined to keep house as much as possible myself & attend closely to all matters. I washed the breakfast things & set Eliza to put all her place to rights. She requires much discipline. Spent the most of the day in looking over things & altering the room arrangements. Took Sukey in & set her to sewing. She finished mattrass & mended a little.

> 31 Jan., Sat. Engaged all the morning in washing up glass & crockery, having the pantrys thoroughly cleaned & everything in them removed and washed up.

> 1 Feb., Sun. John Williams came to talk of his defalcation in not preaching, gave him a lecture on evil speaking.[10]

> 2 Feb., Mon. Had a hog salted & meat hung in smoke. Had Robin fixing up for preparing arrow root. Sent him to dig. I made a sheet to strain it in.

> 5 Feb., Thurs. Gave out moss to wash.[11] Put arrow root out to dry. Took starch out of the water, it was beautifully white. Robin gone

at the kitchen. I fixed up my presses [closets], & looked over the childrens clothes. Basted work for Sukey.

8 Feb., Sun. Old John came to hear the little negroes their lessons & I gave him Jones' catechism.[12]

10 Feb., Tues. Robin cutting up & salting 3 hogs. Rachel attended to the sausages. Put arrow root away in jars & boxes, made 25 lbs of it. Had moss beat, a mattrass emptied & the cotton opened out, filled up two mattrasses with moss & one with wool, filled 3 bolsters. Gave blankets to wash, pillow cases & 1 pr homespun sheets, had pillows filled with feathers & sewed.

16 Feb., Mon. Sent Sukey in the field. Phillis attending to the little negroes. Made[13] her patch & fill up two mattrasses. Lydia better, she helped me with patching & finishing off some of Sukey's unfinished work.

22 Feb., Sun. Mr Taylor read one of Spurgeon's sermons. The most of the negroes came in.

28 Feb., Sat. Baked pound cake with Rachel, 4 lbs of plain for a pyramid.[14] Also with Eliza 4 lbs of fruit cake for the negroes to form the base of the pyramid. Succeeded well with them all. The negroes put fill under the back part of the house. Robin whitewashed the upper part of the parlour. Phillis sick. Affy & Minty complaining.[15]

1 Mar., Sun. The two parson Johns preached at the school house.

3 Mar., Tues. The sewing machine came last night & was opened this morning & commenced work.

6 Mar., Fri. Had hams sewed up to white wash. Set Old Mary to sweep flower garden after a hard rain last night. Robin cleaned the walls & top ceiling of dining room. White washed over fire place. I cut carpet & had it hemmed.

30 Mar., Mon. Susan & Minta with chill. Robin & Tom cleaning out the well. Affy & Rachel washing. Phillis cooking dinner. I sewed up 2 skirts on sewing machine & a body [upper garment].

3 Apr., Fri. Phillis & Minty sick. Rachel complaining. I put Affy to wash clothes, made Eliza cook & attended to her doing so. Attended to having feet & tripe boiled & made souce.

14 Apr., Tues. Col Bauskett, Mr B & John[16] came over early to hunt with Mr Taylor. I attended to household duties. Sent medicine to Phillis who is sick & to Soldier. Sewed ruffles on dress for Mary & finished the sleeves, had it finished for her. Sewed the linings & collars on three coats for Mr Taylor. Nora sick, Eliza cooked dinner & waited in the house. I had the headache after dinner & slept some, read the papers. Received letter from Eliza Jane Baker. A cow gored another to death in the pen.

16 Apr., Thurs. Heard that Phillis was worse & went down to see & stopped Old Mary to attend to her, found Soldier also sick. Phillis in a critical way, gave her Dovers Powder[17] through the day.

21 Apr., Tues. Chloe came in sick. I examined into her case, gave medicine. Minty sick. I made a pie for dinner & attended to cooking it & vegetables, trying to make a cook of Eliza. She is rather a hard case. I retired early to rest last night with headache & had it all day today. Yesterdays difficulties adjusted as well as they could be. Old Mary, Sary, Soldier, Chloe, Abby & Tom sick, went down to the negro house to attend to them. Phillis still sick. Attended to the cooking with Eliza as cook.

24 Apr., Fri. Cut off some negro cloth. Cut out 6 prs of pants & stitched them up & a frock skirt for one of the servants. Very much amused at a scene between Eliza & Nancy. Sary came in complaining. Attended to her & gave out negro clothes. Minty seeming better & on her good behavior.

27 Apr., Mon. Attended to domestic duties, gave Rachel & Affy washing. Cut out three prs of blue pants for Henry's boys & a shirt for Charles, also 3 prs of white pants for Jimmy, Scipio & Sam & sewed up the most of them, finished one pair. Jim sick gave him medicine. Rachel very complaining. Old Nancy complaining, gave her medicine. Put Minty to making cegars.[18]

1 May, Fri. Gave Rachel & Affy washing. Eliza cooked & scoured. I counted out Minty's cegars. She finished 513 yesterday. Had yeast made, parched coffee. Made yeast biscuit & light bread. Made Affy & Nancy clean up fowl yard & burn it.

4 May, Mon. Affy sick, Soldier hobbled out. Eliza cooking. After Mary left I cut 7 dresses for four of the negroes. Mr Taylor ordered Phillis off from the house for idleness & gossip.

10 May, Sun. Gave Minta permission to go to Ocala. Peter went with her, he is professing conversion & I trust sincerely.

11 May, Mon. Engaged in domestic duties. Cut out pants for Prince & Peter & made them. Affy washing, Rachel very complaining. Chastised Richard & William on account of their neglect of Sabbath lessons yesterday. Put away 1050 cegars in 3 boxes.

13 May, Wed. Sent Affy in the field. Phillis came back. Eliza a new cook & Nora a new house servant keep me pretty well employed & unusually worried. Medicines & shoes came from Savannah.

14 May, Thurs. Ordered Rachel to commence taking catholicon.[19] Minty complaining. She finished 400 cegars for this week making 1536 in all. Sam & Abram have absented themselves. Phillis went home sick. Affy in the field.

15 May, Fri. I am induced to believe that Phillis has been deceiving me with respect to herself, went down to the negro house to see her & confirmed in the opinion.

16 May, Sat. Henry & Robin brought Sam in.[20]

18 May, Mon. I find Eliza very difficult to manage. She seems to have set herself in opposition & determined not to come into measure. Sent for Dr Vogt[21] to see Phillis. At night she was delivered of a dead born child.[22]

24 May, Sun. Bess, Jack, Peter, Mary, Dauphne & Chany came to talk to me about their joining the church.

1 June, Mon. Minta sick, Eliza attended to her business. I made after school[23] 3 prs of pants, a slip & frock skirt for Rachel's children.

6 June, Sat. Had the pantry cleaned. Bess thrown from her mule & leg snagged. Sent for Dr Vogt to see her. Had bottles cleaned & bottled of the 5 gallons brandy. Hemmed dress for Rachel & stitched up the body.

8 June, Mon. Gave out washing to Rachel & Affy. Cut off negro cloth for 7 or eight of the negroes, cut out two shirts for Charles, commenced teaching at 9 & got through with all the lessons & cyphered[24] with all. Had the headache all day, worse towards night. Attended to Bess' foot. Cut out six night dresses for the children. Had the beans picked.

11 June, Thurs. Went down to see Bess' wound, having it dressed with flaxseed poultices & powdered opium. Had a conversation with some servants respecting discontent.

20 June, Sat. Had a beef killed this morning, attended to having it salted & put away.

21 June, Sun. Old John came to teach the little negroes & reported a full attendance & all of them clean. Scipio came in with a sore leg.

22 June, Mon. Sewed up & hemmed 2 skirts for Old Mary, made a frock body for Nora & Letty. Attended to Eliza & her kitchen also the vegetables. Gave Rachel washing. Sent Affy in the field, put Minta to picking the beds & scalding them [for bedbugs].

9 July, Thurs. Eliza acting some better. Minta has been complaining all the week.

12 July, Sun. I went in the evening to listen to the negroes at their prayer meeting. They sang with zeal.

13 July, Mon. Called to see Rachel at the wash house, taken suddenly sick there. Gave Rachel Dover's powders.

13 July, end. One of our servants [Phyllis] has acted very badly & we strongly suspect her of starving herself to keep from work. She was so much reduced & weak last week that we had to stimulate her.

19 July, Sun. All of the negroes left the yard this morning to attend the burial of Philip a servant of Dr Keitt's. Phillis still in her house doing nothing.

25 July, Sat. Eliza acting in a very improper manner & requiring rigorous treatment.

26 July, Sun. A runaway was brought here of Dr Vogt's, he was put in the corn [house] & locked up for safe keep until his master returned. He escaped.

29 July, Wed. Attended to some sick negroes & chastised Eliza for her misdemeanors.

5 Aug., Wed. One of the little negroes got hurt in the running gear while they were grinding corn. Sent for Dr Vogt.

10 Aug., Mon. Attended to domestic duties. Rachel too unwell to wash last week, Affy washed for her to iron & she still looks badly. I hemmed a pr of pantalets for Susan & sewed up ten shirt sleeves. Taught the children. Susan & Richard sick, gave the latter castor oil. Read in the Art Journal. Minty sick and making an awful fuss. Mr Taylor reports caterpillers not so bad as the 2nd of August last year. Mr Taylor seems to be more hopeful of his cotton crop.

12 Aug., Wed. Minty still sick, Rachel taking blue pill, made her put on red flannel jackets.

13 Aug., Thurs. Attended to having arrangements made for scalding all the chambers. Robin commenced early & with Eliza to assist finished early in the day. Walked to the negro house in the evening & found out that the negroes have been stealing bacon.

24 Aug., end. Caroline devotes herself mostly to the housekeeping & to the little ones Jane & Anne who are much attached to her. She performs her duties conscientiously & cheerfully notwithstanding the annoyance of a new cook & a perverse one & a new house servant who seems more promising. Bess has done nothing of consequence since [she snagged her leg on 6 June]. Phillis the negro who has been starving herself went out last Monday for the first time

this year & picked a little cotton. Prince has been behaving very badly & is now under discipline. Three fletches [of bacon] were found in his box. Chloe had a child on yesterday the 23 of August. I have some hopes that the house servants are understanding better our management. Some of them have been quite impudent to the children lately.

30 Aug., Sun. After attending to necessary matters read in "Mission to the Jews." Mary & Mr Bauskett came over. Mr B requested Mr Taylor to go with him to search for stolen goods. Mr Taylor declined & John went. He [Bauskett] returned home bloody & wounded having been struck down by a negro with a heavy stick. Mr Taylor sent for Mssr Bowen, Johnson, Doctors Vogt & Brown[25] to watch.

31 Aug., Mon. Mr Taylor & Mr Bauskett went to Ocala to attend to the battery case. Mr B consented to compromise until Mr Williams the owner of the negro returns & if he will consent to his banishment there will be no suit. Affy, Robin, Minta sick also Jack, Nancy & several others.

12 Sept., Sat. Attended to some household matters, assorting clothes, getting up the mending, yeast made & the house cleaned up. Sent for tobacco by John to have cegars made for Brother Richard. Soldier has the vegetable garden nicely fixed off & mostly planted. I cut out a pr of pants for Peter. Dr Brown & Jones called & dined.

20 Sept., Sun. I read some to Old John.

24 Sept., Thurs. I ascertained the loss of some sugar & hams. Had to discipline several of the negroes.

9 Oct., end. Rachel's children have been all of them sickly this summer. Mr T thinks it is owing to their living in an old house and will build a new one shortly. Mary has got out of concert with Silvia & has exchanged her for Margaret with her father. Her cook has behaved badly & been exchanged likewise.

25 Oct., Sun. Mr Taylor, Caroline, Lydia, Susan, Miss Lucy Jones, Willie & Richard & Mr Bauskett went to attend the Association.[26] The wagon was rigged up for the negroes.

6 Nov., Fri. Henry confessed very improper conduct.

14 Nov., Sat. Our neighbor Mr Williams has returned with a wife said to be a pious woman. He has not behaved very handsomely respecting his negro who committed the outrage on Mr Bauskett.

19 Nov., Thurs. Robin washed & mended the sashes for me & made puddings for dinner.[27]

10 Dec., Thurs. Jane Adams [neighbor] called while we were at breakfast to request to cut out two coats for her mother. The bricklayer went to work at the chimney. I feel very unwell this morning. Had tar ointment made for Scipio's leg & had it dressed. Cut off cloth for house servants & little negroes. Cut out two jackets for Jane Adams & 5 suits for some of the field hands. Read a little. Mr Brown is having syrup ground for us.

16 Dec., Wed. Stitched up 2 prs of pants for Tom, 1 pr for Albert, 1 Maurice & 1 Milton, 1 pr for Jack, 1 pr for Butler & 1 pr for Charles. Stitched jacket for Charles, 1 frock skirt for Dauphne, 1 for Nora, 1 for Sarah, 1 for Rachel & a flannel coat, made two flannel shirts for Henry, cut out a jacket for Richard, a pr of pants for Jack & a flannel coat for Jane.

19 Dec., Sat. I made a pair of pants for Soldier, Abram, sewed up dress for Eliza, Rachel, Abby, Bess. Cut out & made a pr of pants for Ned. Minty came with complaints that they [other slaves] had stolen her flannel & some of her clothes. I made Robin arrange for arrow root, clean out smokehouse & kill two hogs, draw off syrup.

24 Dec., Thurs. Rachel came in, I put wick in the candle moulds & she made some candles, Affy ironed. Robin took all day to cut up & salt the hogs (6 more killed). I finished the aprons cut out yesterday. Sukey & Rachel commenced fixing the covering for sausages.

30 Dec., Wed. Made a synopsis of the work which the hands executed during Mr Taylor's absence.[28] Attended to household duties
& to the sick, Jupiter, Mingo & Glasco.

All in all, the diary shows that managing the servants was a difficult
and unending job, and that Maria often worked alongside her
servants and performed services for them. While Maria obviously
becomes exasperated with individual servants, she never complains
about the job in general. In this Maria differs from those many
plantation mistresses whose diaries contain bitter complaints about
having to manage slaves.[29] The closest Maria comes to a blanket con-
demnation is a statement such as "my soul has been much vexed with
the depravity of some of the servants" (7 December 1858). Probably
she accepted the role as being God-given and as her part of an
exchange that freed her from the heaviest physical drudgery. Maria
would not have liked "the washtub" and "the cookpot" any better
than had the former-abolitionist Robert ladies from her Beaufort
days.

1860: Maria and Slavery, Rhetoric versus Reality

In a long letter from December 1860, Maria develops her views on
slavery in a much more complex and topical way than is found in her
short piece of 1854. Her political, social, and religious views fuse on
the issue at a critical juncture in public affairs. Abraham Lincoln had
just been elected president in November and in another eleven days
(20 December) South Carolina would lead the way in the South's
secession from the Union.

9 December 1860. Maria Baker Taylor to James Clement Furman

Who could be otherwise than interested in the present state of
our unhappy country? particularly in the southern portion of it, to
be rendered more unhappy, if she falters in her course of withdrawal from those [the North] who consent not to wholesome
words, but despising the doctrine of our Lord Jesus Christ, dote
about questions that engender strife [slavery] and teach those
things [abolitionism] which are contrary to Godliness? Does not
the Apostle command us to withdraw ourselves from such? We

will not believe it to be an interpolation of our protestant version, & we rejoice that the South falters not.

She [the South] now knows that "Delays are dangerous" & having obeyed when commanded to "Stand still," she refuses not "to go forward" & God grant she may come forth a glorious nation, established in righteousness, working righteousness, fearing God and holding forth the Word of Life & Truth; not besotted by luxurious living, but answering, as a nation the high ends for which we are created.

Has not the Union subserved its purposes, & been instrumental in making us a great and mighty people, not only the admiration of the world, but absolutely necessary to their prosperity & happiness; and now too cumbersome to move harmoniously, cannot we afford to become detached without injury to ourselves or other nations? Would it not be a sublime & interesting spectacle, if this disolution could take place without disturbing order & harmony by war and bloodshed? The scriptures enjoin upon us to do good to our enemies & leave vengence [*sic*] to Him who judgeth righteously, & I trust the South will be mindful in her temptations of these injunctions & not seek by retaliations to avenge her wrongs.

If we set at nought His counsel, how can we expect the aid of the All Powerful One, with whom it "is a small thing to help whether with many or with few"; who can cause "one to chase a thousand & two to put ten thousand to flight." He is all our Salvation & all our trust & how careful we should be not to provoke Him to anger by our inventions! How earnestly we should beseech Him not only to direct our hearts but our minds aright.

We have been taking for the last two years "The New York Chronicle" a religious paper of high character, but anti-Slavery in its proclivities, it has pained & amused me too to watch the impulses of the Editor on this question. He has written some prize articles on Missions & you no doubt are acquainted with his writings? Pharcellus Church his name. He regards himself as being very conservative. Dangerous conservatism! Some time ago he expressed the opinion that the South was blustering & it was only "froth & foam." I felt some disposition to chuckle over the paper of the 29 Nov. Pharcellus has decidedly changed his mind, comments lengthily upon secession & its spirit, & thinks the danger so alarming that it is time "to call on every Christian man to humble himself before God" etc. and in his humility he recalls the words "froth & foam" & expresses himself very properly as being opposed to those epithets.

He never for one moment believes he might possibly be wrong, & that the Institution [slavery] has not come to nought because it was according to God's appointment. But he thinks "a wordy war" has injured the cause and that "the South is stronger today in its convictions than it was thirty years ago" and asserts that this does not prove them [the South] right, but it only proves how utterly our [the North's] thirty years reasoning has been lost upon them!!!! He insists that secession cannot "arrest the tendency of the conviction that freedom is the right of all the races & the true economy of nations," and that there is "no power in the Universe that can arrest it!!!!["] He goes on to inquire "Can a Southern Confederacy shut out the North wind? Can it silence Poets, Orators, Editors, platform Speakers"?

In the same paper is another morceau "An appeal of the Maryland Baptist Union Association" signed by Richard Fuller[30] & four others, which I presume you have seen? Before Dr Fuller can expect his voice to be regarded by Southern Baptists on the slavery question, he must go back & retract his temporizing arguments . . . in which he admits that slavery is a "moral evil" & place it where it should be, among the institutions of God to be sanctified by justice & mercy.

I turn the paper & under the caption "A singular letter" I read one dated Columbia SC nov 14th from the pen of Professor Reynolds, an old acquaintance, with introductory remarks of the Charleston Mercury, on which our Editor thus comments; "The whole thing is such a tissue of misconceptions and falsities as we have rarely seen." Is the beam in my eye, or am I right in feeling sure that Rev Pharcellus looks at slavery through cracked or smoked glasses? I think he is astonished to find all our clergy not in the same category as Dr Fuller, respecting the "moral evil" of slavery, for he [Pharcellus] sometime ago congratulated himself, that the whole southern religious press was silent upon the subject, & while politicians raved, he supposed the ministers sound [that is, opposed to slavery].

Maria is quite right about "our clergy" not holding slavery to be evil, for by 1860 the majority of southern evangelicals supported secession; through a sophisticated argument grounded in basic evangelical tenets, they had come to see in secession the working of God's will. Maria's girlhood friend James Henley Thornwell was a leading spokesman for this view,[31] and another spokesman was Maria's correspondent. Just two weeks before Maria wrote to him, James Clement Furman had given a major address as a secessionist candidate for the South Carolina convention called to respond to Lincoln's election. James was elected and gave the opening prayer at the convention that made South Carolina the first state to secede.[32]

A second document from late 1860 records a grisly event that occurred just a few days after Maria wrote to James. In a note at the end of his 1860 diary, Maria's son-in-law Thomas Bauskett tells of the murder of his cousin-in-law Dr. William J. Keitt, a frequent visitor at Osceola who had been a groomsman at Thomas and Mary's wedding in 1857.

> Dr Keitt was murdered by his negroes Lewis & Allen on Sat 18th [Dec.] between 9 & 10 pm with a razzor. A held him down & L held his beard with one hand & cut his throat from ear to ear, splitting his ears & cutting into the neck bone. Twas supposed that the woman Melvina from whose confession we derived the particulars was also present. Her life was spared in consideration of her confession. A & L were hung [on 23 Dec.]. M whipped & banished the state with ol John & Hazelius. Israel banished.
>
> Keitt was ill in bed from effects of poison by his negroes. He cried for help & begged forgiveness. Allen said we did forgive him & then beat him choked him & killed him. He had several bruises about the face. His nose was broken & his hand badly cut. His clothes money gloves razzors & stockings were stolen.

Just what Keitt "begged forgiveness" for is not stated, but considering the participation of six slaves, their killing him anyway after forgiving him, and the ferocity of the slaughter, his personal offenses must have been great. In addition, one Florida newspaper hinted at a pro-Unionist political motive for the murder, Keitt's brother Lawrence being a leading South Carolina politician. Committed to states' rights, slavery, and secession, Lawrence Keitt represented Beaufort District in the Congress 1853–60 and had participated in the famous 1856 caning of Senator Charles Sumner on the Senate floor.[33]

Maria's own 1860 diary is missing, and at the beginning of her 1861 diary, only a couple of weeks after the murder, she does not mention the incident. At the least, the murder must have stirred uncomfortable memories of the 1857 attack on her son-in-law Thomas Bauskett by a neighbor's slave. Or she may have been silenced by the stark contrast between the brutal murder and the picture of the happy slave and Christian master she had painted six years earlier in her "crude thoughts on slavery."

TWO

Education of the Children, 1853–63

Maria's primary concern during the Osceola years was the education of her many children. "Education" here is used in the broad sense of all the academic, religious, moral, and practical instruction that Maria consciously and systematically imparted to her children, either through her own efforts or through other carefully chosen educators. In pursuing this project in a newly settled territory and later in a period of severe social disruption, Maria often had to improvise, but her purpose remained fixed. While it was common enough for plantation mistresses to instruct their young children on the primary level, as Maria did, detailed accounts of how they went about it are rare.[1] However, the immense effort inherent in home instruction for a large brood suggests that the perseverance and system Maria brought to her family school were unusual.

1853–58

The measures Maria took to educate her children in the first five years of the family's residence in Florida, 1853–58, are revealed in letters of Maria's from 1853, 1855, and 1858; in her 1857 and 1858 diaries and an attached memorandum book; and in the 1858 diary of her daughter Mary Bauskett.

While still in South Carolina, the Taylors were already looking for a place "where we can enjoy advantages for the education of our children which we cannot obtain about here," but their move to Marion County in central Florida in 1853 did not improve the educational opportunities. Demographics alone were against them, for they left a long-settled district with a population of about 6,000 whites for a pioneer area with a population of about 2,000 whites. Barely established at Osceola, the Taylors began their educational attempts with Maria appealing to her academic uncle.

26 August 1853. Maria Baker Taylor to James Clement Furman[2]

> Could you not recommend me to a teacher for our children capable of giving instruction in French & Music in addition to the English branches? We have been offering three hundred dollars and board for such a one but may be tempted to increase the offer for a <u>southern</u> teacher well qualified.

Two years later the educational situation had scarcely improved, as Maria's aunt reported secondhand from Charleston.

22 June 1855. Ann Eliza Furman to James Clement Furman

> Since I last wrote to you John and Maria Taylor have been here. They both look remarkably well, and were in their usual good spirits. They seem still to be in an undecided state respecting their future place of residence. They are very much pleased with their present residence. They think that in healthfulness it is far superior to the situation which they left. They have good society and a delightful climate; these are the advantages which would induce them to remain, but on the other hand they are without regular preaching, and without the facilities of educating their children, and the idea of sending them from home for that purpose is very trying to them.

But soon some headway was made. "All of the children" includes Mary, 18; Lydia, 15; John, 13; Susan, 11; William, 10; Richard, 7; Fenwick, 6; and Dora, 5.

8 October 1855. Maria Baker Taylor to James Clement Furman

> We have employed in our family Miss Heermans, quite a pious & intelligent young lady as governess. She has all of the children

except Caroline & the baby under her tuition. John I feel anxious to have under male tuition, & Lydia we wish to send off to school. Mary will finish soon. There is a school in Ocala, but the boys are under such bad influences in the village that we do not send them there. They went awhile to Mr Bowen when he taught, but so many rowdy unprincipled boys attend the school of larger size than ours, that we feared they might be led astray by them & thought it best to retain them at home.

Lydia is very fond of books, very anxious to improve, & has both application & intellect accompanied with much strong common sense & scrupulous integrity of character with rather more discretion than is common for her years. She is very desirous of the opportunity to be educated thoroughly & "feels much ashamed in her ignorance" she says. All of her pocket money goes for books & all of her spare time is spent in reading. We have not fully determined yet where to send her.[3]

Maria's 1857 diary traces the further progress of the children's education. Miss Heermans, the governess, was still with the Taylors and remained through 23 May. A lesson plan in the 1857 memorandum book, dated January, indicates that Maria took an active part in planning Miss Heermans's instruction for each child, and the 1857 diary records Maria's own religious instruction on Sundays. For example:

> 25 Jan., Sun. Mr Taylor, Mary, Miss Heermans & Maria[4] went to Long Swamp Church. I remained at home, gave the children their lessons, & read a sermon from Spurgeon to those who remained at home. Old John & several other negroes came in to hear.

Three days after Miss Heermans departed for good, Maria picked up the daily teaching and then mentions it every weekday through the end of September. Maria was now teaching six of her children: Lydia, 17; John, 15; Susan, 13; William, 12; Richard, 9; and Dora, 7. Fenwick, age 8, had been sent to spend the rest of the year with Baker relatives in Beaufort, South Carolina. Another page from the 1857 memorandum book gives a lesson plan from the time Maria took over.

School Regulations

Read the Scriptures
Plain spelling
Philosophy
Dora—Geography
Richard's & William's reading lesson with definitions
Lydia's grammar
John's grammar
Susan's grammar
Richard cypher
Susan read or John 1st
Lydia read, cypher & write
John cypher & write
William & Susan write sentences & cypher
On Friday compositions & Multiplication & other tables

In the following excerpts from the 1857 diary showing Maria in action as educator, other material is occasionally included to suggest the context of daily life in which she maintained her school schedule and Sunday religious instruction for six children. First names mentioned other than the children above include the house servants Minta, Eliza, Rachel, Affy, and Nora; Jane and Anne are Maria's youngest children, ages three and one.

27 May, Wed. Cut out clothes for the little negroes after breakfast, & some cloth for the grown ones. Commenced teaching a little after nine & finished at one. After dinner attended to the writing & cyphering. Slept a little. Cut out 2 prs dyed pants for John & made one pr. Mr Bauskett came to tea. I tore off & gave out negro clothes.

1 June, Mon. Attended to domestic matters. Commenced teaching at nine. A good deal interrupted, by Mr Maine's coming in & spending the day, which is a very wet one. A man from Orangeburg called up for water, gave him some potatoes. Minta sick, Eliza attended to her business. I made after school 3 prs of pants, a slip & frock skirt for Rachel's children.

19 June, Fri. Sent Affy to pick blackberries for jelly, gave Minta washing. Cut out two dyed jackets for Richard. Taught from 9 till 2, & attended to compositions & sums after dinner. Also took a nap. Cut out four jackets for Willie & one for John. Read the papers. Assorted clean clothes. Anne very unwell with a cold.

27 June, Sat. I have taught school all the week & made since last Saturday 10 oclock on the machine having the basting done for me[5] 26 garments in 6 days as one of the days I could not sew at all being engaged with sickness. Taught school 5 hours during 4 of these working days & read & took a nap every day. The children do not seem to be as much interested in their studies as I would like to see them.

13 July, Mon. I have been teaching the children without allowing anything to deter me. They have improved some and seem more interested in their studies. I have received from Beaufort good accounts of Fenwick's health, improvement & conduct & pray God he may be kept from any improper influences. I was very unwell for a week & have not accomplished so much sewing work, but giving more time in the evening to the children's sums & compositions. Received a letter from Miss Heermans written from St Louis written in a cheerful strain & declining positively to return as teacher.

14 July, Tues. [Received a letter] from the Principals of the Mountain Military School[6] accepting John as a pupil for January next. I taught the children nearly all day, had them saying the tables in the evening.

Later in July, the teaching schedule was affected by a minor intrusion of the Third Seminole War (1855–58), a conflict in which 800 U.S. Army regulars and 1,300 Florida volunteers pitted themselves against 120 Seminole warriors. In July 1857 Governor Broome ordered ten Florida militia companies into service, asking the federal government to muster them into U.S. service.[7] Colonel Samuel St. George Rogers, Ocala lawyer, state legislator, and now newly appointed commander of all Florida militia in federal service, was moving the troops to Tampa, and eventually to Ft. Myers and Fort Denaud, 200 miles to the southwest, where all subsequent action of the war took place.[8] The retrospective entry of 24 August at the end of the diary and two regular July entries show Maria's attitude to the war and the interruption.

> 24 Aug., end. Col Rogers regiment has been passing here on their way to Tampa for the last month. We formed the acquaintance of the US officers who came to muster the volunteers into the US service. Ten or twelve companies have passed to fight only a handful of Indians who are brave resolute & determined to die on the soil rather than yield.[9]

> 28 July, Tues. The volunteers a number of them called up for water, the children diverted by them.

> 29 July, Wed. Attended to some sick negroes & chastised Eliza for her misdemeanors. Had to correct the children for their lessons & want of neatness this morning. I taught them and am glad to see the United States officers pass, hoping the regiment will not attract the children from their lessons again directly. A large company of soldiers came up here & insisted on having corn. Lieut Lee & Dr Brown[10] spent the evening here.

> 5 Aug., Wed. Attended to domestic duties. Taught the children from 9 o,clock till four. Read a little.

> 23 Aug., Sun. All of the children read to me in the Bible & I explained. They answered questions from all the verses. I read to them several small tracts & gave them Bible lessons to get.

> 28 Aug., Fri. The back numbers of Godey[11] came with Brown's grammar which I sent to Miss Heermans for. Nora still quite sick, made Affy cook & wash a few clothes. I taught the children. Read to them from Hebrews in explanation of the chapters of Exodus.

> 2 Sept., Wed. I taught the children until late, read only a little. Jane with fever, held her much through the day.

> 3 Sept., Thurs. I read some in Brown's grammar.

> 4 Sept., Fri. I cypher with John in the evenings in vulgar fractions.

The entries for 30 September through 8 November (1857) do not mention teaching the children, a sure sign that teaching had been suspended, and when Maria resumed on 9 November she taught for only a couple of weeks because she had to get Lydia and John ready to go away to school in South Carolina. When their father returned from taking them to school, he brought Fenwick, age eight, home from his extended stay with Baker relatives in Beaufort, so the pool of young scholars at home was replenished. With the oldest children, Maria was beginning to see the fruits of the education she had provided.

When the family still lived in South Carolina, Mary had attended Limestone Springs Female High School for two years and had since been taught at home. A test of the Baptist education Maria gave all her children came with Mary's marriage at age nineteen to Thomas Creyon Bauskett, a Catholic from South Carolina who had a farm adjacent to Osceola. Thomas was the son of John Bauskett, a wealthy South Carolina planter, prominent lawyer, and state legislator. After selling his principal plantation in Edgefield County (where Thomas was born), the elder Bauskett had moved to Columbia. Although John's father had been a Baptist, the family was now Catholic, probably through the influence of John's wife, Sophie Elizabeth Creyon, who was from an Irish family.[12]

After the wedding in March 1857, Maria began reading in Cummings's *Lectures on Romanism,* the tenor of the collection implied in the pejorative term for the Catholic faith. Maria was probably looking for both information and arguments to combat this pernicious (to her) new influence in Mary's life. Maria's attitude toward Catholicism at this time comes through in her remark about some Catholic books her resident Irish seamstress had brought into the house: "Alas that so much error should be heaped like rubbish on so much of truth."

After the birth of their first baby in January 1858, the young Bausketts planned to visit Thomas's family in Columbia, South Carolina. Maria must have been reassured by Mary's profession of Baptist faith and her baptism on 28 March, but, as Mary wrote in her diary that very day, her husband "did not want me to join the Baptist church and although I love him as well as he could possibly wish, my love to my Heavenly Father which is greater constrains me to do my duty." Still, Maria feared the trip to Columbia and preventively read to Mary from the *Lectures* as plans for the trip proceeded.

> 10 Apr., Sat. Advised Mary not to leave, but as Mr B wished she waived other consideration & I assisted her in getting ready. Made a talma for her traveling dress. They left here before 11 o'clock. Mr Bauskett & the baby both unwell. I sewed up a pr of pants for Jimmy [Bauskett servant]. Violent headache. Went to bed before supper.

> 13 Apr., end. I thank God that my daughter has had strength and grace imparted to take up her cross and follow Christ in baptism. She remained here scarce a brief fortnight afterward, and then left for Columbia to be exposed to the flatteries of the world, and the seductions of Papacy. Shall we not trust the Lord in darkness as well as in light? or shall we walk by faith when sight is dim? I will believe that what God has begun he will perfect by his own Almighty power, wisdom & grace & that my child will be preserved steadfast unmoveable in the faith once delivered to the saints.

Maria told the story of Mary's spiritually perilous trip to Columbia to her confidante in Charleston.

15 June 1858. Maria Baker Taylor to Ann Eliza Furman

> As you may suppose, the last six months, with their events, stirred within me feelings of varied kinds, in which I know you would sympathize with me. Mary with her infant; then her genuine conversion; baptism; and departure to scenes of trial for her faith & constancy; then Caroline's courtship and marriage; & Lydia & John's absence. Mother used to say, she believed I would find something to laugh at, if I were dying; if you will find the No of Harper with the wild cow defending her young from the attack of the Lion, you will see something that reminded me of myself & Mary while she is exposed to the "man of Sin," the Romish communion.

I can breathe freely now, that my child is on her way home, a true Protestant; not theoretically only, but practically; having not only withstood error, but contended for the truth, & I trust more rooted and grounded in the <u>faith</u> of the <u>scriptures</u> than before she had seen the mummeries and unsubstantialities of tradition.[13] Earthly love, with the constant kindness and affection which was shown her, and the efforts to get her into gay and fashionable balls and parties, [and] with the notions of obedience she inherited from her grandmother, made her case the more dangerous, as her only hope was in the constant and protecting care of Christ, whose blessed spirit was in danger of being grieved by any fall she might make before vanity & pride.

I received a letter from Mr Bauskett on Friday last saying they would leave Charleston today in the Everglade, so that I trust she is on her way home, made stronger by the past for any future conflicts. It will be my anxious care, so long as she remains near me, to have her go on from strength to strength. I have been much pleased with the faith and piety manifested in her letters.

At the time of writing this triumphant letter, Maria did not yet know that Mary's husband had won the next round, for as Mary wrote in her diary while in Columbia, "Mr Bauskett had our dear little child <u>christened</u> a Catholic. Oh what a sorrow what a trial to me" (13 June 1858). Late that year, Mary paid tribute to her mother and the religious education she had imparted: "How much I thank my merciful Father in Heaven for his kindness in preserving to us a kind and loving mother, who has guided me in paths of <u>virtue</u>. May he grant that not one of us may act in such a manner, as to cause her one heart-ache or sorrow, and I will always try and follow her examples, in my duty to God and to my children" (22 December 1858).

The effect of Mary's more general education is apparent in her taste in reading at this time, recorded in her 1858 and 1859 diaries: the *Iliad,* Dickens's magazine *Household Words,* Shakespeare's *Henry VI* and *Love's Labour's Lost,* George Eliot's *The Mill on the Floss,* Harriet Beecher Stowe's *Uncle Tom's Cabin,* and travel books on Africa and Siberia. In addition, every day she copied and memorized a passage from the Bible. During this time Mary was frequently sick and distressed from two pregnancies, a miscarriage, the loss of a four-month-old baby, and unpleasantness with her husband over his visits to the negro house. Perhaps her education gave Mary inner resources to pull through such difficulties.

Lydia returned from school in Charleston on 28 May (1858), just in time for her sister Caroline's wedding on 1 June.[14] Maria seemed satisfied with the results, writing that "Lydia has returned in health & improved in disposition & other respects." This one term at the Charleston school (name unknown) in 1858 at age eighteen was the only institutional education received by this child whom Maria had earlier described as "very desirous of the opportunity to be educated thoroughly." Maria nowhere explains the delay in sending Lydia to school, a plan first mentioned in 1855. However, the girl received further instruction at home. Soon after Lydia's return from school, the Taylors engaged a piano teacher for Lydia and Susan, and lessons continued to the end of the year.

Lydia was now under her mother's sharp-eyed tutelage for the next phase of her education: "I got Lydia to have the pantry arranged & the boxes filled with sugar, flour etc to begin her housekeeping systematically" (7 June 1858). Lydia led a domestic life in her parents' house until her marriage eleven years later at age twenty-nine to Edward Payson Crane.

In November 1857 John had entered the King's Mountain Military School, located not far from Limestone, the school favored for his sisters. After he had been there for five months, Maria refers to an incident she does not describe but evidently took very seriously.

> 12 Apr., Sun. I have heard with pleasure of the resistance on the part of my son to a rebellion in which he was persuaded to take a part, & although I regret deeply to hear that the abscess on his side continues to discharge, I must hope that the Lord is dealing with him for good and will not permit Satan to have dominion or power over him.

Perhaps at the back of Maria's mind was an escapade of her new son-in-law, Thomas Bauskett, who had been expelled from the South Carolina College for participating in a book-burning rebellion against the chemistry professor. John came home in July 1858 and returned to school in August, as his mother matter-of-factly records.

26 Aug., Thurs. Assorted clothes & assisted John in packing his trunk. Counted clothes for washing. Finished off the three prs of drawers for John & bade him farewell, he left for York. I made a belt for his money. Sewed up cravat for Willie, a dress for Mary & 6 aprons for her baby.

Maria refers to her oldest son again toward the end of the year.

7 Dec., Tues. John I have hopes from his letters feels the importance of consideration & a proper discharge of his duties. I pray God to change his heart in the days of his youth & to make this household one of prayer and faith.

Maria started her 1858 school year on 15 February and continued every weekday through 16 April, when she stopped for a while to prepare for Caroline's wedding to James Baird Dawkins. Teaching resumed 26 April–10 May, with the exception of one day. Things had to be pretty bad for Maria to take a day off.

28 Apr., Wed. Rachel & Minta sick. [The houseguests] left. I am with toothache nearly all day. Susan engaged with Maria [Baker] in making cake. Willie gone to Ocala with his father. I did not teach the children. Anxieties respecting the happiness of my children.[15] Held Jane the greater part of the day[16] & mended boys clothes.

After 10 May Maria had to abandon the teaching altogether to complete preparations for Caroline's 1 June wedding. She resumed teaching 7–26 June, then had to stop again due to the illnesses of many family members and servants. She optimistically started up on 1 July but was interrupted when both she and baby Anne became seriously ill. Managing only a day here and there, she gave up after lessons on 19 July. On 30 August, Maria started up again and was able to continue with some regularity through 8 November, the last entry in the year that mentions teaching. About then she had to devote herself to Mary, who was very ill both before and after losing a premature baby.

All in all, Maria's teaching in 1858 totaled only about twenty-four weeks, during which she was able to maintain steady instruction for only one eight-week and one ten-week period. However dissatisfied she must have been with this record, Maria's educational aim is implicit in the closing of her 1858 diary: "Sustain & keep them all who are the offspring of my body & may all of them be united unto thee by faith & kept from the evil of the world." She must have included her educational efforts when she summed up the year: "We have kept the faith and made some steps Zionwards."

1859–63

The education record for the period 1859–63 consists of a few comments in Mary Bauskett's 1859 and 1860 diaries, an 1859 letter of Maria's, Maria's 1861–63 diaries (the next extant after 1858), and Willie Taylor's school papers. Although the Civil War broke out in April 1861, the period 1859–63 may be treated as a unit because the children's education was only marginally affected by the war through the end of 1863. However, in the 1861–63 diaries the record itself is quite different from that in the 1857–58 diaries. Remarks like "taught the children this morning" and "heard the children's lessons" are now infrequent, and the remarks that touch on the education of the children away from home are mostly brief notations of their arrivals and departures. To make readable sense of such snippets, the presentation will sometimes resort to weaving them together in an editorial narrative rather than presenting them as discrete, dated diary excerpts of only a few words. The above differences in content and presentation should not be taken as a slackening of Maria's interest in her children's education but rather as an indication of pressing war-related concerns.

While John attended King's Mountain, Maria instructed him in the relation between faith and personal discipline.

6 May 1859. Maria Baker Taylor to John Morgandollar Taylor Jr.

My dear Son, I received your letter on Wednesday & regret to see that you are not trying to make yourself contented. A spirit of discontent can very soon spring up & destroy all our happiness, by obscuring all our blessings however thickly they may beset our path. I trust my dear boy you will not trust to your impulses but let reason rule and a sense of right, & then I am sure you will have nothing to regret. Remember that "he who ruleth his spirit is greater than he who taketh a city."

Discipline is what we all need, to make us proper men & women, and you must not kick against discipline my son, however painful it may be, discipline your mind and heart into patience and forbearance, for "it is good for a man to bear the yoke in his youth," he will learn to bear it gracefully in after life when necessity may compel him to wear it. I wish, my dear son, you were in possession of the religion of Jesus, and that you had the mind & spirit of Jesus, then I could say to you confidently "consider him who endured such contradiction of sinners against himself lest ye be wearied & faint in your minds."

I entreat you my dear Child to secure the safety of your immortal nature, the salvation of your soul. The redemption of the soul is precious, and it ceaseth [*sic*] forever. Do not let Satan or the world cheat you out of a proper and early consideration of this matter. Make the calculation now "what would a man take in exchange for his soul."

God grant my dear Son that your eyes may be opened to see the importance of securing for yourself, now in the days of your youth the friendship of the King of Kings & Lord of Lords. The Lord of Hosts is his name, all power and all Wisdom dwell with him & you may take hold of his strength and his wisdom and do valiantly. Oh hearken to his invitations and beseech him to have mercy upon you and teach and save you! I send you a little money in this, which I hope you will spend judiciously. All send much love to you. Your devoted Mother

Read this letter over at least three times and pray to God that you may not be insensible to its contents.

Mary Bauskett's 1859 diary has Johnny returning from school looking "thin and badly." In 1860 he changed from the Yorkville school to one in Columbia,[17] and Mary notes that also on his next return "Johnny looks very thin and badly." Probably because of his constant ill health from the chronically infected side, Johnny was not sent back to school in the fall of 1860. Instead, Maria took him to Charleston in November for an operation on his side, which she then backed out of at the last minute. At the next mention of Johnny, in Maria's 1861 diary, he was in the Confederate Army for the duration, marrying in 1864. His education away from home had consisted of two and one-half years at military schools in South Carolina in 1858–60, ages fifteen through eighteen.

In 1859, it was now the turn of Susan, at age fifteen, to go off to school. Limestone, the Baptist school for girls near Gaffney, South Carolina, where Caroline and Mary had been educated, was again the parents' choice in spite of the sour note that had ended their earlier association. The Curtises were still at the helm. On 30 July 1859, after several entries describing mother and sisters busily sewing for Sue, Mary Bauskett comments in her diary, "Sue left this morning for Limestone. Poor child! I know she hates leaving home, she has never been away a week in her life."

It is almost a year before Mary mentions Sue again, to report the news of Sue's baptism at Limestone in June 1860. When her father left Osceola on 7 December to bring her home, Sue had been away for eighteen months straight, a long time without her family even if the Furman relatives in nearby Greenville invited her during vacations. She returned to Limestone in April 1861 in spite of the outbreak of war and remained until December. Sue's trip home was worrisome. On 5 December, Johnny arrived unexpectedly at Osceola, apparently on leave, and reported that "Mr Curtis was to be in Charleston with Sue now." On 7 December, "John left this morning in Mr Dawkins buggy for Gainesville on his way for Susan." On 13 December, a letter came from Sue, saying she was to have been in Savannah on the 1st, and on the 17th came a letter from Dr. Curtis "saying he had left Sue at the Pavilion in Savannah in company with Miss Dozier and Hickson. He had not received Mr T's letter with check nor had Sue received mine directing her where to go." Johnny finally managed to find Sue, whether in Charleston or Savannah, and they arrived at Osceola on 19 December 1861.

Sue's schooling is not mentioned again. Perhaps sending her back to South Carolina in wartime was too risky; however, having attended

Limestone for two and one-half years, up to age seventeen, Sue had already received as much institutional schooling as had her sister Mary, and more than her sister Lydia. After that, Maria instructed Susan in household management, along with her older sister Lydia. As usual, Maria was very conscious of the principles she wished to instill, commenting on 14 January 1862, "Lydia did some mending for me, also Sue. I tried to impress upon them the duty of economy & a proper use of time, with the benefits of system."

Nineteen months younger than Susan, Willie at age fifteen through sixteen years was attending "the Academy" in Ocala in 1861. Early in 1862, the Taylors received two letters from Thomas Rambaut, their old Baptist friend from Beaufort days. Rambaut had accepted the history chair at the Georgia State Military Institute in Marietta[18] and now urged the Taylors to send Willie to school there. Assured of a strong Baptist influence, the Taylors sent Willie off to Marietta at age sixteen. Maria gave him a proper Baptist send-off:

> 9 July [1862]. Willie having everything packed left with Mr Roberds after dinner. As usual, he had many cautions & much advice. I passed rapidly over the books in the bible to tell him their character & how he should read & study them. Our heavenly Father preserve him from evil & make him one of the household of faith.

In the small packet of Willie's school papers that Maria preserved are copies in an elegant hand of lyric and patriotic poems, along with didactic pieces titled "Perseverance," "Reflection," and "Cultivation of the Mind," topics Maria would surely have approved. In his financial accounts for the term beginning July 1863, Willie lists even the minutest expenditures, no doubt reflecting his home training.[19] All in all, Willie's accounts indicate that in the third year of the Civil War, his parents were still relatively well off and not inclined to stint on education. His large expenses for uniform suit, extra pants, caps, dress shoes, and white gloves came to $278, and he bought an iron bedstead, mattress, and pillow for a total of $40. On the credit side, over one three-month period Willie received five checks totaling $900, conveyed through the Taylors' agent in Savannah. Thus he was receiving considerably more than he spent.[20]

In September 1863 the Taylors received two letters from Willie urging his father to let him leave school and enter the Confederate Army. His parents refused permission, and Maria notes that in a letter she received on 13 October "Willie says nothing about joining the army," with no explanatory comment. He could, of course, have joined the army at any time without his parents' permission. It seems odd that the Taylors were able to keep a young man almost eighteen years old out of an army desperate for men. A possible explanation is that the state of Florida was not a major theater, and the Confederate Army consisted entirely of state regiments, militias, and home guards. It is ironic that the Taylors lost Willie during wartime anyway. At the end of the fall 1863 term, he arrived home the day before Christmas, soon came down with meningitis, and died at home on 31 January 1864, two months after he turned eighteen.[21] Willie had attended the Georgia Military Institute for one and one-half years, July 1862 through December 1863, at age sixteen through eighteen years.

In 1861 at ages thirteen and twelve, "the boys," as Maria referred to Richard and Fenwick, attended school in Ocala through 28 June and resumed on 16 September. Late in 1861 Maria engaged a Miss Baker as governess for "the children," as she termed her three youngest, Dore, 11; Jane, 7; and Anne, almost 6. Miss Baker, about twenty years old and no relation, was somehow connected to Mrs. Reardon, a friend in Ocala. In January 1862 Maria decided to take Fenwick and Richard out of the Ocala school and have Miss Baker instruct them at home along with the little girls.

Miss Baker commenced teaching on 3 January 1862 and had one nine-day holiday in March and another early in June. On 11 June Maria re-engaged her to teach for two more months. "Miss Baker's Acct" reads:

July 4th Mr Taylor pd her	$103
August 5th Pd Miss Baker in full	$140

The first figure reflects deductions for some fabric Maria supplied Miss Baker for dresses. The August payment was apparently not for just the one month since the July payment but a settlement in full to that date. The Taylors, then, were probably paying Miss Baker about $280 for seven months' service, plus room and board. The worst of the Confederate inflation had not yet occurred, so this figure was perhaps modestly more than the $300 per year the Taylors had been offering in 1853.

Maria was not satisfied with Miss Baker. For one thing, the young woman left every weekend to visit Mrs. Reardon in Ocala and sometimes failed to return with the carriage sent for her on Sunday, showing up only on Monday after dinner or on Tuesday. Also, Maria had to "correct Dore for Miss B" and to call Miss Baker's attention to work of Dore's that was not well done. On one occasion, Maria "felt considerably irritated with Miss B & expressed it." The Taylors did not continue to employ Miss Baker, and no other governess appears on the scene.

In September 1863 Richie and Fen, now ages fifteen and fourteen, went off to school in Gainesville, where they lived with their oldest sister, Caroline Dawkins, and her husband, James, a childless couple. James played a significant role in the education of the younger Taylor children for a number of years. Born in Union County, South Carolina, in 1819, he was a graduate of both the literature and law departments of the South Carolina College. After practicing in Union, South Carolina, he moved to Florida in 1853 and soon had a flourishing practice that extended over seven counties. He served several terms as state's solicitor and was now circuit judge for the Suwannee Circuit of Florida, having been appointed while a member of the Confederate Congress.[22]

Gainesville at the time was a village of several hundred inhabitants[23] boasting only one school, the Gainesville Academy, which Richie and Fen attended.[24] The boys came home for Christmas, and although Carrie wrote asking her mother to send them back, Maria, uneasy over reports (mostly false rumors) of skirmishes with Union forces in the area, decided in January 1864 to keep them at home and again teach them herself along with the three youngest children.

THREE

Osceola and the Civil War, 1861–63

The Civil War broke out on 12 April 1861 with the Confederate firing on Fort Sumter in Charleston harbor, South Carolina. Florida had already seceded from the Union on 10 January. Considerably the least populous of the ten Confederate states,[1] Florida was not considered by either side to have much military importance, and not until 1864 was a relatively large battle fought in the state. For the years 1861–63, Maria Baker Taylor's only complete diary is from 1861; the 1862 diary then runs from 1 January to 4 August; the 1863 diary begins a year later on 10 August and runs through 31 December. This record indicates that, during the first two and one-half years of the war, daily life at Osceola continued much as before. Nevertheless, worries about a son in the army, bad news from the battlefronts, rumors of invasion, and shortages of goods were never far from mind. Maria writes about war-related events in her typical diary-writing style; that is, she remains brief and factual, only occasionally allowing herself emotive or evaluative language. Presumably she expressed herself much more fully in some of the many letters she mentions writing during this period but that have not survived.

The Taylor family's overall contribution to military manpower was quite limited. James Baird Dawkins, at age forty-one the older Taylor son-in-law (Carrie's husband), was a delegate to the Florida Secessionist Convention and then went on to represent Florida in the Confederate Congress in Richmond until 1863. Johnny, the only Taylor son to see regular service in the Confederate Army, first enlisted in the South Carolina home guard in November 1861 from the Arsenal in Columbia, South Carolina, at age nineteen; he then enlisted in the Tenth Florida Infantry, Company D, in February 1862 at Fernandina, Florida, shortly thereafter attaining the rank of 3rd Lieutenant. He fought under General Joseph Finegan in Florida, Georgia, South Carolina, and Virginia through the end of the war.[2]

Willie, the second Taylor son, was fifteen when war broke out and was still in military school when he died early in 1864 shortly after turning eighteen. Maria's husband, John, and next-door son-in-law Thomas Bauskett (Mary's husband) both fell under a Florida law requiring the presence of the owner or a white overseer on a plantation with slaves. Thomas, thirty-one when the war began in 1861, appears not to have had an overseer for his small place (sixteen slaves) and served only intermittently.[3] John Taylor, then fifty-one, did not serve at all; one overseer left for the war early on, and another, mentioned only when he was first engaged, presumably did not last long.

Maria aided local poor women whose husbands were away fighting and participated in the Ladies Military Aid Society. Such societies were by far the most important source of supply for soldiers in the field until 1863, when, after unsuccessful attempts at taxation to outfit its troops, the state of Florida finally came up with a central plan.[4] John Taylor is seen responding a few times to Confederate requests for labor and equipment, for which he was paid. He appears to have sold most of his sugar products to the Confederate Army, a disposition that may be considered part of the war effort. However, it also became increasingly remunerative to the Taylors, for Marion County gradually became a major source of sugar for the army. Sugar prices soared in 1863 as commissary officers scoured the area, and Florida growers frequently and successfully protested the low impressment prices initially offered.[5]

Maria does not report problems of any significance with the servants in her 1861–63 diaries, and she continued the pre-war pattern of providing them with clothing, medical attention, and religious instruction. In this regard, the Taylors' experience was typical of middle Florida, where for the most part the servants continued their accustomed lives, not threatening the security of the plantation owners; Union lines were too far away for hope of escape, especially for those with a family.[6] Lincoln's Emancipation Proclamation of 1 January 1863, freeing all the slaves in the Confederacy, fell in the yearlong gap in Maria's diaries (August 1862–August 1863), so its reception at Osceola is unrecorded.

The diary excerpts presented here detail the ways in which the war impinged on the Taylors' daily lives in 1861–63. While the excerpts thus feature this new concern, Maria's longstanding and ongoing concerns are also occasionally represented to suggest the extent of the impact of the war.

1861

At the opening of 1861, Maria had just turned forty-seven. Her daughter Carrie Dawkins, living in Gainesville, was a frequent visitor, and her next-door daughter Mary Bauskett and her family dropped in at Osceola almost every day. The Osceola household itself included nine unmarried children ranging in age from twenty to five years.[7]

[Opening prayer] Florida met in convention at Talahassee to determine her course. Be thou with this state Oh thou Arbiter of Nations & may we make Thee our trust & not be put to confusion. Direct our course. Establish us in righteousness, & let not man oppress us.

Grace be with all those who love the Lord Jesus Christ in sincerity. May charity fill our souls to the exclusion of bigotry & selfishness. And may all those who love the Lord Jesus Christ in sincerity find a place in our hearts, whatsoever name they may bear, nation they may represent, manners or dress they may wear.

13 Jan., Sun. I rode over just to see how Mary[8] was before the barouche left for church. Sister Lydia, Caroline, Lydia, Louise, Fanny, Mr Taylor & Mr Wallace[9] went to hear the Episcopal clergyman who preached in the Baptist church. I remained at home & after dinner went down to read to the negroes. I heard the children their lessons. Caroline went to stay with Mary. She sent for me in the night about the baby & I went over to see it early this morning & washed & dressed it. Sister Lydia, Fanny & myself went to Ocala & made some purchases. Consulted Dr Wilson about

Robin [servant] & got a prescription from him. When we returned home found Mr Lengle here, he dined here. I attended to household matters. Heard that Florida had seceded [on 10 Jan.]. Sue with Mary.

15 Jan., Tues. Mr Taylor went to Ocala this morning. I put buttons on the vests for him, made a pie, sewed loops on four towels & marked them. After dinner I scraped limes to make preserves for Fanny & had them put in salt & water. No mail. We heard the St Johns[10] was blockaded. Carrie stayed with Mary.

16 Jan., Wed. Mr Taylor went to Ocala, a letter from Mr Dawkins confirms the secession of Florida, Mississippi & the taking of the Florida forts.

On the advice of the Taylors' friend David Levy Yulee, then in the United States Senate, leaders of the Florida Secessionist Convention, to which Dawkins was a delegate, had moved quickly to take over Florida forts and arsenals. As of 7 January, the secessionists held Fort Marion in St. Augustine, the arsenal in Chattahoochee, and several fortifications in Pensacola Bay. Negotiations were underway regarding Fort Pickens, the main fort in the bay.[11] After these developments, Maria makes no mention of war-related events for several weeks.

13 Apr., Sat. Attended to household affairs and went to the Free Stone Springs Academy to form a Ladies Military Aid society, which we did. I called at Mary's & at Mrs Burnham's taking mutton to the latter. Returned home & commenced sewing on Sue's chemises.

14 Apr., Sun. Lydia & Mr Taylor went to the Methodist church. Mr Rivers married there. I read to the negroes in the evening & heard the children's lessons. Received an extra from Mr Dawkins telling us Fort Sumter had been attacked & after 30 hours firing Anderson had surrendered the fort. 6 vessels of war off the bars at Charleston, firing commenced Friday 12th on Ft Sumter [the first hostilities of the Civil War].

17 Apr., Wed. Prepared Preamble of constitution for publication of the Military Aid Association.

18 Apr., Thurs. Mary, Lydia & myself went to Ocala & met the ladies, who took into consideration & subscribed for the getting up of a flag for the company. They decided on one after the model of the confederate flag with the arms of the state in blue field.

19 Apr., Fri. I brought home five suits of clothes [fabric for the suits] for members of Dr Lewis' company yesterday, sent 2 of them to Mrs Collins, one to Mrs Todd, & one to Mrs Waldo & Mrs Smith to make.

21 Apr., Sun. Letter from Sister Lydia. Mary, Lydia, Mr Taylor, Willie & myself went to Ocala to hear Mr Johnson preach his sermon to fathers. Mr Bauskett also went. Mr Johnson came with us to dinner & preached at the [Osceola] chapel in the evening to a full house, all from here went out. Sallie Waldo & Mr Broome [neighbors] called up here. The papers today contained exciting intelligence. War has been declared & begun. Virginia seceded & Maryland resisting. Letter from John, anxious to go to Ft Pickens.

2 May, Thurs. I had the children Dore, Anne, Jane & Lena[12] dressed & took them with me to Ocala to see the soldiers muster. While there I saw Miss Critchfield deliver the flag to the Marion Rifle Guards. Genl Taylor [no relation] was passing through on government business. Came & made himself known to me sending messages to Mr Taylor.

4 May, Sat. Lydia myself & Sallie [Waldo] went with Mrs Owens family to attend a barbecue at Hawthorn Prairie & see Martha Owens deliver the flag to the "Marion Dragoons." She made a good speech, answered by John Martin. Mr Dupee & Capt Owens also made speeches. We spent a pleasant day among fine company, all of whom asked me to spend the night.

14 May, Tues. Received letters & papers, read them, one from Caroline. Mr Bauskett returned home & Mary left here with her children. The papers are warlike. Many troops are to Virginia apparently. Maryland knocked under & Western Virginia for the Old Union.[13] I cut out a coat for Mr Taylor today & sewed some on it. Arkansas out & with us.

20 May, Mon. Finished embroidering the letters on the flag [for another local company]. Mr McConnel & Sallie W rode up with a dispatch. Key West under Old Abe's martial law.[14]

31 May, Fri. Attended to household affairs. Dr Todd called & brought twenty knapsacks to be made up for the Hammock Guards. Contradicted reports of battles.

3 June, Mon. Looked over accounts, over sheets, fixed up presses [cabinets]. Made out bills. Cut off a white dress for myself. Cut out 20 knapsacks for Dr Lewis company & basted 12 of them. Read a little. Wrote to Mrs Reardon [Ocala friend], Caroline, & Johnny.

7 June, Fri. We heard very sorrowful accounts of the Hammock Guards on their encampment at the Prairie. Alas for the sin & folly of intemperance.

11 June, Tues. String beans. Sewed on shirt bosoms. Received papers. No letters from Caroline or anyone. Queen's proclamation, neutrality towards the beligerents to be maintained by England.[15] Blockade to be regarded if effective & privateering not piracy but no protection to be afforded to British subjects who engage in it. Sally Waldo took tea here. The little children had a party.

29 June, Sat. Washed Richard & Fenwick & cut their hair, washed Dore & Willie looked after their clothing. Put up dinner for the pic nic, dressed & accompanied Lyd, Mary, Willie & Dore to the Methodist church in Ocala. Mr Taylor, John, Mr Bauskett & Richard preceded us with the young ladies who spent the night here. Lydia presented the flag to the Hammock Guards, Willie making her speech for her. Mr Hopkins received & J Roberds made a speech. We had a pleasant pic nic at the church.

25 July, Thurs. Had some figs put in syrup & some peaches pealed & sugar put over them to be put up in cans. Anne very unwell still, Jane & Dore better. Negroes still coming in with catarrhal fever. Abram, Nancy & Mary sick & Georgy. I went over to see Mary & her baby sick. Lydia then went. Calhoun Todd called in the morning with news of battle fought on Sunday.[16] Dr Vogt called. Mr McConnel & Pasely took tea & gave us fuller accounts of battle.

29 July, Mon. Mr Taylor arrived from Savannah, well except a cold & fatigue. He left Carrie well. Could not get his steam engine for mill as there was no sheet iron to be had to make a boiler.

1 Aug., Thurs. Mr Taylor wrote to Col Dawkins respecting his election [to the Confederate Congress] & to the President [Jefferson Davis] respecting the exposed condition of Fernandina.[17]

5 Aug., Mon. Willie is much better but looking very badly. Mr Taylor went to Ocala, he is much bothered about his sugar works. No iron to be had in the Southern country for making boilers for an engine. I was engaged in sewing bosoms in shirts, in pickles, preserves & reading papers. Interesting incidents of the great Battle of Manassas.

27 Aug., Tues. No papers but the Talahassee Journal. Gov Perry calling for blankets for the troops in Virginia. I sent a piece to Mr Reynolds [newspaper editor] calling a meeting of the MAS.

10 Sept., Tues. Mrs Todd and her son called directly after breakfast. I wrote a piece respecting the cotton & blankets for the soldiers for [Ocala] Home Companion. Went to Ocala to attend to the blankets. 61 were packed up & sent off & 56 prs of socks.

13 Sept., Fri. Attended to household matters & to the sick. Knit more than a half stocking. The Perry Guards came by here on their way to Tampa. We had some cooking done for them & furnished them with many little matters, for which they seemed grateful.

17 Sept., Tues. Read the papers some. Gave Dinah washing & ordered her to come in every Tuesday to wash. Knit on sock all day & finished another pr for soldiers in Virginia. Had pillow cases made to send on there. Wound some coloured crewel with some homespun wool to knit scarfs for them, put on one & knit a little. Rachel made soap.

24 Sept., Tues. I went to Ocala today to attend the packing of articles for the Virginia Regiment. Several ladies at Mrs Reardons, we concluded to wait until next Monday & pack with the shirts which

we have to make this week. Mr Harrison the judge of Probate not very well to attend the packing today.

2 Oct., Wed. After breakfast Mrs Todd & her daughter came and I assisted her in making her accts as Treasurer of the Society. I wrote a note to Mrs Reardon in the morning by Fenwick & one in the evening on the Societys business. Sent her 15 lbs of wool[18] for army purposes & Mrs Harris 5 lbs.

10 Oct., Thurs. Sent to the office & received no mail. Mr Brown's Methodist paper came which I read. On Tuesday night Jupiter was sent to hunt for my turkeys, reported to be in Gov Broome's[19] field & his negroes after them. He came back minus 7 & we sent him again, he returned with one more broken in the back & saw signs where two had been picked. Several of the others came home with wings injured & feathers gone. We hope the Gov's negroes will behave better when he comes among them. I mended clothes.

13 Oct., Sun. No preaching anywhere today. Mary, Mr Bauskett & the children dined here. Mr Taylor read a lecture & had other exercises. I read in the Bible & in the "Whole duty of man." Mr Taylor seemed interested in the Duties of husbands & wives contained in it. I read to the negroes in the evening.

17 Oct., Thurs. Spent the morning in household duties & in darning socks. Cut out 3 tablecloths & a shirt for Sam. Reiser came here to buy wool to make clothes for the soldiers. After dinner I basted lace in dress & set off with Lydia to call & see Gov & Mrs Broome, met them coming to see us, fortunately had some cake & brandy peaches at hand to offer them. They spent some time here.

18 Oct., Fri. Received a letter from Dr Lewis offering bag of cotton to the Society. The letter had been advertised.[20]

21 Oct., Mon. Mr Wallace & Mr Watkins [neighbors] came here to make coolers for Mr Taylor to use in his sugar works. Mr Taylor called on Gov Broome. Mr Smith brought up 6 prs of drawers his wife had cut for soldiers. Mary cut & sent home [to Maria] six prs. I sent one piece of cloth to Mrs Todd.

28 Oct., Mon. Mr Taylor went to the [Silver] Springs for barrels and engaged fifty [for his sugar products]. Sent Charlie the brick-layer up to Hopkins to look at his sugar works. Mr Wallace & Watkins returned to their work today. I made Rachel boil the soap over. Negro shirts came from the Springs. Mr Taylor seems much pleased with his sugar mill which he saw today.[21] I mended Willie's coat.

1 Nov., Fri. The weather has become cooler, a long and very warm fall we have had. No call for fires yet except for several days a lit-tle in the morning. We gave the negroes winter clothes on Wed-nesday. I cut out five suits for them today.

13 Nov., Wed. I hemmed both of my frock skirts. Cut out pants for Scipio, a suit for Mingo. Cloth for Rachel, Minty & for all Rachel's children, gave her two shifts for herself & for Nora. Minty 2, Letty 1 & a woolen coat. Mrs Collins sent to ask for wool & thread.

14 Nov., Thurs. Sally Waldo rode up with the dreadful intelli-gence that Beaufort[22] was in the hands of the Yankees.

17 Nov., Sun. I received a letter from Johnny postmarked Charles-ton. He is on his way to Beaufort to defend his native state.[23] I pray the Almighty father to preserve him from all evil. I went down after dinner to read to the negroes.

18 Nov., Mon. Attended to the milk after breakfast & then spent most of the day in writing to Caroline, Susan,[24] Eliza Wallace & Sister Lydia.

23 Nov., Sat. I counted my turkeys on Thursday & had 45 in all. Dr Wilson called to see Robin & took tea here. Willie missed the chill [malarial]. Attended to domestic duties & to the sick. I sewed on flannels for soldiers. Sally Waldo called & spent some time. Mr Luffman finished the well & I paid him seventy dollars at Mr Tay-lor's request. Sally was very entertaining this evening.

5 Dec., Thurs. Lydia & myself were most happily surprised by the sudden entrance of Johnny, when we thought him at the wars.

10 Dec., Tues. Sent 1 piece of twilled cloth & one pr of tweeds to be sent to Silver Springs & Iola to be made up for the soldiers by Mrs Reardon yesterday. The box for Fletcher's company was to be packed. Mr Taylor commenced with the cane grinding today & gave the first 11 galls to the negroes.

13 Dec., Fri. I borrowed Mrs Collins [spinning] wheel & had yarn twisted today by Rachel. After attending to putting up butter I hanked it & had it washed. Gave fat tubs & kegs out to wash. Miss Baker [governess] & the children rode to the sugar works.

30 Dec., Mon. Mr Taylor brought in some nice looking sugar [from his mill].

31 Dec., Tues. The year closes upon us. It is done with its joys & sorrows. I desire to offer praise for the manifold mercies we have received & for God's preserving care over us & our household & our state. While war has devasted our land we have dwelt securely & none of our numbers are missing. We have heard of the death of dear friends [none war-related], but we mourn not without hope. Our Father we deeply thank Thee & in my present trouble respecting our son[25] I pray thee to increase my faith that I may unwaveringly trust in Thee, hope in thy mercy & finally rejoice in thy salvation.

1862

[Opening prayer] We cannot remedy the evils that surround us. We cannot make straight that which is crooked, but thou, Oh Almighty Father canst, & we beseech Thee to undertake for us & ours, & let not one of us be cut off in our transgressions.

We would desire thy special blessing upon our dear son, who is far distant from us. Our Father, draw nigh unto him & be a very present help in this his time of need & deliver him out of all his troubles. I humbly beseech to be merciful to his & our unrighteousness, & lead him in a plain path & guide him & let him not fall into sin or stumble in the way. Hold him up & give him courage & grace & wisdom to walk uprightly.

Our father we commend to thee our beloved state & country. We pray thee to protect & defend us from evil. Be a wall round about us. Deliver us from the oppression of man, from the will of our enemies & if consistent with thy Holy will, grant unto our beloved country a speedy peace.

7 Jan., Tues. Turkey. Mrs Reardon, Dr & Mrs Brown dined here & took tea. We all rode down to the sugar works in the evening. I had meat over hauled & found 25 hams & shoulders spoiled, only 17 thought good. Sent some of it to the negroes & had root tea, molasses & ashes put upon [those] most likely to keep. I finished the scarf Lyd knit.

8 Jan., Wed. Mr Taylor is discouraged about his sugar. He had the most of it cut the last of Nov. The weather has been excessively dry. The first cane ground was the standing cane which he made into syrup 75 barrels, then the remainder into sugar 8 hogsheads.[26] The cane cut in Nov they ground commencing last Sat failing to make sugar, it still fails after sundry experiments by Mr Brown [the sugar-maker], Mr Whitmire & others & Mr T has concluded to grind it all into syrup. His mill has broken several times & been repaired in wood by Mr Hussar & in iron in Ocala by workmen, at home by Gov Broome's blacksmith. Dr Waldo[27] & others in the neighbourhood have experienced the same difficulties with the cane which was cut down to avoid its being spoilt by the frost.

10 Jan., Fri. I received 2 letters from Caroline, one of them containing a letter from Johnny dated from Fernandina where he had gone immediately from Charleston to join the troops as soon as he received his discharge from the Citadel.[28] Before dinner Johnny himself arrived from Fernandina having left Caroline's last evening in company with Mr & Mrs Lipscomb. He is suffering in looks from anxiety & fatigue. I trust the Almighty Father will direct his way. I attended to household matters & knit & marked socks. Mrs Mac, Lyd, John & Susan rode to the sugar works, they practiced a joke on the negroes of passing Mrs off for John's wife. Mr Jeffords dined here & fixed the iron head to sugar mill.

12 Jan., Sun. Mary & Mr B came over to dinner. Mr Taylor read one of the Lectures of Pilgrim's Progress[29] to the family, all of whom were present except Caroline & Mr Dawkins. After dinner I put John's things in a carpet bag giving him candles, soap, arrow root, paragoric, a sheet etc. He took eight lbs of cotton with him & Willie drove him to Ocala to be in time for the stage. They attended night service in the Methodist church.

15 Jan., Wed. Rode down to the sugar house, found they had broken a mill borrowed from Mr Rammage. Mr Brown reports 158 barrels of syrup made.

16 Jan., Thurs. Caroline arrived from Gainesville. Mr Dawkins, she said, accompanied Johnny to Fernandina on Tuesday to endeavour to forward his promotion. An expected fight there from Lincoln's war vessels.

18 Jan., Sat. Mr Taylor finished boiling his cane juice today, he has made 9 hogsheads sugar & 182 barrels of syrup & molasses from about 45 acres of cane. Mr Brown the sugar maker left here today, having been here 37 days. Cedar Key has been taken.[30]

27 Jan., Mon. Caroline & myself with Jane & Anne set off in my carriage for Gainesville. Col Dawkins, Dr Butler & Johnny in Col D's buggy. We made a safe journey but did not reach Caroline's until dark.

29 Jan., Wed. I marked a pr of socks for John this morning & trimmed a red flannel shirt with black for him. Carrie took narrow braid trimming off of his military coat. We packed up his things. Caroline gave him a mattrass, pillow & two pillow slips also a comfort. He & Dr Butler left Gainesville in the cars [railroad], we rode with them to the depot.

30 Jan., Thurs. I sewed on Caroline's drawers, finished them & a chemise for her. Gave Rhoda [Caroline's servant] Caroline's scarf to wash. She overlooked Rhoda's wardrobe & commenced fitting her up to take with her to Richmond. Every thing so scarce she could make no purchases for her.[31]

2 Feb., Sun. [Maria back at Osceola]. Mr Taylor was too unwell to attend church today, coughed incessantly last night. Lydia, Mary, Willie, Richard, Miss Baker & myself went to church in Ocala. Mr Johnson preached on the final perseverance of the Saints, answering objections. Subject not yet concluded. Lydia received a letter from Johnny. He expects to go to Talahassee on Wednesday for cannon. I read the papers some.

3 Feb., Mon. I did not feel well this morning. Mr Taylor seems better. I went to Ocala to the Society. Mrs Reardon, Mrs Broome, Mrs D Broome, Mrs Rogers & Mrs Brown were the only persons who attended. Mrs Paget came in to see if we could get her some work to do. We promised to recommend her to the Society for the relief of the soldiers families. I called at Mrs Reardon's & was invited to dinner, accepted. Called to see Mrs Reynolds & Mrs Pyles in the afternoon. The latter paid me $15.00 & $5.00 for the help of poor families.

7 Feb., Fri. [Mr Brown] informed that $17.00 had been gotten for Mrs Paget & the promise of provisions. Rumours of a victory at Bowling Green [Kentucky].[32]

12 Feb., Wed. Attended to various household matters, counting over hams & other meat, having store room fixed. Butter made. Cut out 2 chemises for Dore, hemmed my travelling dress skirt. Rode out to the sugar house with Mr Taylor. The negroes are still planting cane, & leaving a quantity of good seed behind among a good deal that is spoilt.

13 Feb., Thurs. I went to Ocala today with syrup, sugar, meat & rice for the poor. Called at Mrs Broome's & left some lettuce for her. Called at Mrs Pyles & took Mrs McConnel, we went to see Mrs Lyles & Mrs Hickman [the poor], gave them each some of the articles, paid Mrs H $2.50 for work. After dinner Mrs McConnel & myself went to Mrs Paget's, Mr Mac driving us. We found her very destitute & grateful.

15 Feb., Sat. Attended to house duties. Willie killed another turkey. Had curd, pudding & custard made, boiled one of Willie's

wild turkeys & roasted. Read the Ocala paper with the news brought by Mr Dupont, that Roanoake, Forts Henry & Donelson & Florence of Alabama were taken by the Federals.[33] Mary & Mr Bauskett dined here.

23 Feb., Sun. Mr Taylor received a short letter from Johnny saying he was just leaving Georgia to bring on cannon & ammunition. I went to the chapel after dinner & read to the negroes.

24 Feb., Mon. I left home this morning for Homosasa with Dore, Jane & Anne expecting to visit Mrs Yulee. We got lost & went to the head of Crystal River, very few houses on the road, expected to have to sleep out all night, but fortunately just before sunset we came in sight of a house occupied by Mr & Mrs Wynn who had been run off from Cedar Keys by the Yankees. We were kindly & hospitably entertained by them for the night.

Since the Yulees were important figures to Maria and appear in a number of her diaries and letters, it is useful to introduce the family briefly at this point, where they begin to be frequently mentioned. David Levy Yulee (1810–1886), descended from Jewish families of Portugal, England, and the Danish West Indies, was an early Florida railroad entrepreneur whose father had owned huge tracts in Florida.[34] David Yulee was elected in 1845 as both the first United States Senator from Florida and the first Jew ever to serve in the Senate; elected for a second term, he resigned his position in 1861 to go with the Confederacy. His wife, Anne, came from a family of divided loyalties. Her father, Charles Anderson Wickliffe (1788–1869), a former governor of Kentucky and postmaster general under President Tyler, was elected to the United States Congress as a Unionist in 1861 and served his full term, but her brother enlisted in the Confederate Army.

The Taylors had known the Yulees ever since they moved to Florida, and perhaps even earlier when John was in Florida purchasing land. The families often exchanged visits on their plantations and in Gainesville at the home of the Taylors' daughter and son-in-law, Carrie and James Dawkins.[35] The Yulees' son Wickliffe was the same age as Richie and Fen Taylor, and the Yulee family included three younger daughters, Anne, Margaret, and Florida. Their plantation was located at Homosassa, about forty miles southwest of Osceola, on the Gulf of Mexico coast.

26 Feb., Wed. The Island [site of the plantation] is covered with orange, lemon & lime trees & other tropical fruits. The lime & lemon trees are ladened with fruit. The oranges have been mostly gathered. Mr Yulee commenced in 1853 to plant out this Island & has raised most of the trees from the seed. 1 single orange tree (sour) is left planted by the Indian chieftain Tigertail.

27 Feb., Thurs. Mr Yulee left this morning for Fernandina,[36] he was to go yesterday but deferred his visit through compliment to me. The family were quite distressed at the news brought them by me of the surrender of Ft Donnelson to the Yankees. Mrs Yulee has a brother in the Kentucky Confederate Regiment. Her father is a member of the Northern Congress. We rowed to an island which Mr Yulee proposes to me to try & persuade Mr Taylor to purchase & set out.

2 Mar., Sun. We have had some very serious reverses & Fernandina is to be evacuated.

4 Mar., Tues. [Maria back at Osceola] Mr Johnson left, taking with him two pigs & a can of butter we put up for him. Willie went to Ocala & volunteered to join Mr McConnel's company under the impression boys of 16 were called out. Upon ascertaining that none under 18 were called for we forbade his joining. Mr Taylor left tonight in the stage for Fernandina.

5 Mar., Wed. Quite cold last night, a frost. Gave Sarry washing, counterpanes etc. Cut off cloth for Rachel. 2 shirts for Milton, 2 aprons for Rosa, 2 for Letty, 1 frock for Letty, 1 chemise for Rosa & 1 suit of clothes for Milton. Cut off 8 yds cloth for Judy, 4 for Rachel. Cut out a strainer for arrow root & felled & hemmed it, made two prs of pillow cases. Had arrow root dug today. Robin prepared for it & then white washed dining room. I counted over the meat yesterday & had it properly adjusted for smoking.

6 Mar., Thurs. Received a dispatch saying Fernandina was taken on Sunday by the Yankees. I feel fears for Johnny as I heard Col Holland was taken prisoner & six of his men. I hope in God & trust in his mercy.

7 Mar., Fri. Mr Taylor returned home before day this morning. Gave me fuller accts of the taking of Fernandina. Johnny safe & saved all his things. I heard good accounts of him. No prospect of getting anything from Jacksonville, the people there in a panic & moving off their things. Mr Taylor thinks he has lost $1,600 worth of syrup.[37]

8 Mar., Sat. Mr Taylor attended a meeting in Ocala today. Reports that Florida was abandoned as a military necessity. A committee was sent to Tallahassee consisting of Mr Owens, Gov Broome & Genl Commander to inquire into the truth of it & protest against.[38] 2 companies were formed from this county today, making seven for the war from Marion. I attended to arrow root today. Robin finished beating it.

9 Mar., Sun. Received a letter from Johnny this morning. He is suffering from cold & in camp 12 miles from Fernandina. No preaching today. After dinner I went to the chapel & read to the negroes & taught the children. The accounts from the war are discouraging, our troops are suffering reverses but I trust now, rely only on God.

11 Mar., Tues. Mr Taylor went to Ocala today, yesterday he sent his wagon to Smyrna[39] to assist in removing 2 cargoes of ammunition & Enfield rifles which had been brought there. Some danger is apprehended that servant & team may be taken by the Yankees. They will probably be absent for three weeks. I attended to drying arrow root. Robin white washing parlor. Richard & Fenwick white washing the paling [fence].

14 Mar., Fri. Old Nancy announced the fact that Johnny had come. He is looking well, traveled all night from Gainesville on Carrie's pony. He was one of the detachment sent to burn the mills and founderies near Jacksonville, an incendiary burnt the Judson

house & a store.[40] John has lost nearly all his clothes, taken by our own men during his absence from camp to assist in removing stores from Fernandina. Mrs Yulee reached here about 9 o'clock with her four children.

17 Mar., Mon. We were busy all day in sewing for Johnny. Mr Bauskett left this morning with the wagon for Volusia[41] to assist in bringing the Confederate supplies. He put in one mule. John left this evening, gave him 2 blankets, a pr of sheets, 1 pillow. Mr Taylor sent Albert [servant] with him in buggy.

26 Mar., Wed. Put up a lunch for Mrs Yulee, who left here with her family for Homosasa about 11 o'clock. Some news from the Yankees at Smyrna, our men killed some of them, perhaps 45.[42]

30 Mar., Sun. A letter from John written at Talahassee. He does not yet know at what post office we may write him. Ordered to the Chattahoochie.[43] I read the bible in bed & the papers.

1 Apr., Tues. Mr Taylor went to Ocala this morning to see what services he could render in defence of the state, heard the report [of Federal troops coming to Ocala for ammunition]. Genl Taylor called & hurried to Ocala to see what was to be done. I sewed on chemises & doubled more yarn. Read some in the Heart of Midlothian.[44]

3 Apr., Thurs. Mr Taylor went to Ocala this morning. He saw the [Yankee] prisoners. Carried mutton for them & suet to dress their wounds. No news of importance. Our men took a cannon which they have mounted in Ocala.

4 Apr., Fri. Mr Taylor left home for Hawkinsville[45] this morning before seven o'clock. Lyd had butter made & sent by her father to Mr Alexander & the prisoners.[46] I wrote to Caroline, to Sister Lydia & to Mrs Yulee, received letters from all three of them.

8 Apr., Tues. Mr Taylor got home from Hawkinsville unexpectedly, just as we had finished dinner. He succeeded in purchasing from Foster 4 pieces of calico & 12 pieces of unbleached homespun & 2 sacks of coffee. The articles were so high that his three weeks hauling [in Smyrna] was not sufficient to pay for them.

10 Apr., Thurs. After dinner Mrs Broome called & spent a few moments. She informed that some of Mrs Simpkins & Mrs Maize's negroes had been hung for insurrectionary movements.

14 Apr., Mon. Mr Taylor set off for Hopkinsville to buy goods but returned when he got to Ocala & ascertained the goods were to be shipped by water as the Yankees had left the St John's.[47]

12 May, Mon. Mr Taylor had Dido [dog] killed for eating sheep. He received a note from C Todd last night requesting him to meet the quartermaster who wished to buy his sugar & syrup for government. He went to see him in Ocala this morning.

13 May, Tues. Mr Taylor went to Ocala this morning to see Mr Canosa.[48] I have found the reading of the scriptures very delightful recently. Commenced the NT in February & finished to Timothy this morning. Also finished in the Old Testament to the Song of Solomon. I have prayed especially for a spirit of grace & revelation to be given me in reading the scriptures. I mended summer clothes for the boys today. Mr Yulee called & said Caroline & Col Dawkins had come [from Richmond].

18 May, Sun. After dinner persons being assembled at the chapel to hear Mr Johnson [pastor who could not come], Mr Taylor went down & read a lecture to them. The negroes took up a collection for Mr Johnson & got $3.00. Mary came over to church & said Mr B was summoned to join his company.[49]

25 May, Sun. Willie went to the Methodist church in Ocala. He brought me a letter from Johnny. He has been elected 2nd Brevet Lieut & expects to be home some after his return from Savannah. I read in the scriptures & in the commentaries. Heard the children their lesson & talked with them.

30 May, Fri. Caroline & Mr Taylor came from Gainesville. Caroline was quite sick with sore throat & high fever all day.[50]

3 June, Tues. Dr Butt came to see Caroline this morning. I felt very unwell. He pronounced the case not diptheria. She took cream of tartar. Gargled with alum & had a tonic of [illegible], quinine, brandy & ginger made.[51] Medicines & liquors very scarce.

6 June, Fri. Mary came over to dinner. Col Dawkins & Willie went to Ocala to hear the news. News confirmed of the battle at Richmond.[52] Mr Brown, Dr Todd & Mr Meyers came to get Col Dawkins to give them directions & letters to Richmond. The two former have sons in the Regt & are going to look after their welfare.

7 June, Sat. Mary sent Manuel [servant] over here to be ironed.[53] He got in her store room & made large drafts upon her supplies & tried to implicate Minty [Osceola servant] as a receiver.

9 June, Mon. We are giving Glasco [servant] elder bark tea. The inner bark boiled in a pint of water down to one half for a dose, cream of tartar sometimes mixed with it. Phillis is attending to it & is improving in his health.

11 June, Wed. Mr Jenkins from Bayport[54] & Mr Bayliss of New Orleans who had run the blockade with cargo salt, coffee, and baggage & desired cotton [in exchange], came & staid all night.

18 June, Wed. Expected Capt Pratt & Mr Latrobe, who are searching for nitre caves for the confederate government, to dine here.[55] They came after dinner too late to examine those on this place.

20 June, Fri. Richie came into my room a little after daylight to say that Johnny had come home at day break & gone to bed. The boys [Richie and Fen] were ready early & set off with Wickliffe Yulee to go to Homosasa. I put up their dinner & saw them off.

21 June, Sat. Caroline sent for me this morning, she felt chilly & faint & was very sick, violent pains to hip, back & joints & high fever. Gave her aconite & salt & peach leaf tea, the latter acting as an emetic. Later in the day she took cream of tartar & minute doses of morphine. After taking morphine she got in a profuse perspiration. Glasco died yesterday & was buried today. He has been a great sufferer but seemed prepared to go. Mr Bauskett came last night & sent some things over which Johnny brought.

25 June, Wed. Rachel commenced her regular washing again for the first time for more than a year. John went to Ocala & carried 3

shirts to Mrs Lyles to have made for him & Albert. He bought a trunk of Crowson & paid for it. His pay as Lieut affording him a sufficient salary, his father has put him on his own resources, paying for his uniform & giving him some money.

27 June, Fri. Mr Cameron, overseer to Mrs Haile [near Gainesville] came to purchase sugar & syrup for his employees. Mr T sold him 700 gals at 70 cts. He dined here & told me he had come from the same part of the country I had & knew father well as a great mathematician. A letter from Mrs Yulee. The boys reached there safely. She desires me to let them stay longer.

30 June, Mon. Johnny left here this morning & took Albert with him, he went in the buggy. Caroline up this morning & looking better. Mr Taylor sent his wagon off to Bayport for salt to Mr Bayliss, who ran the blockade.

1 July, Tues. The mail boy came this morning to say that they had killed some Yankees who came up Crystal River,⁵⁶ 8 of them in a boat on Sunday last. All of them either killed or wounded & taken. A negro with them was unhurt. None of our men hurt.

5 July, Sat. Mr Burson came from Tampa & remained all night. He showed us some of the shell & ball which fell last Monday when they fired on Tampa.⁵⁷

In the remainder of the daily entries for 1862 (through 5 August), war-related events are seldom mentioned as the focus shifts to family illnesses that consumed Maria's time and energy. For example:

10 July, Thurs. Jane [age eight] had fever all night & much pain in her side and stomach, used poultices. Dr Butt called to see her, left quinine & Dovers powder for her to take. I spent the most of the day in trying to get some rest. Caroline took cal & blue pill today, is not feeling well.

13 July, Sat. Jane's fever intermitted again this morning & I gave her quinine. It returned about 10 oclock AM & was pretty high all day, very high at night. Caroline had fever last night but feels better today. I am fatigued from nursing & want of rest.

17 July, Thurs. Dore & Anne are troubled with boils also Minty. Phillis is looking better. Eliza with fever. We heard that [illegible] had taken 6000 prisoners & hemmed in Curtis. Caroline very ill with chill & fever & delirium. Sent for Dr Butt. She took cream of tartar, salt & peach leaf, warm bath & at night spirits of nettles. Mary sent for me & 3 minutes before 12 oclock had a son. I staid all night with her.

23 July, Wed. I did not feel well today. Jane is improving. Phillis sick with chill, fever, & headache.

24 July, Thurs. After attending to household affairs rode over to Mary's & dressed the baby. Found both Mary & himself doing very well. Her leg feels better. I had 24 yds of cloth shrunk for drawers & petticoats. Sewed on Mr Taylor's shirts. Mary's children still here.[58]

27 July, Sun. Mr Taylor rode to Ocala. Mrs Reardon [Ocala friend] & myself went over to see Mary. Washed & dressed the baby. Mary has been complaining of her leg & still feels weak. Anne [age six] taken with fever. Mrs Collins sent Rachel to make requests for her. Sent her a fletch of bacon. Mr Taylor was very sick all night & Anne. I slept none & sent for Robin to stay with him.

29 July, Tues. About 3 oclock Anne had a convulsion very severe. Put her in a lye bath. She lapsed all evening to a state of helplessness, not speaking & refusing to drink even water. In the morning I feared she had lost her mind from some of her symptoms. She seemed unconscious, muttering & had to be roused. Mrs Reardon slept in the room with me tonight & last night. Phillis attended to us. Mr Taylor was sick again with fever. I was completely overcome with fagitue & watching.

2 Aug., Sat. Anne seems much better, gave her no medicine today. I wrote to Caroline & Lydia & commenced a letter to Willie but felt too confused to finish it. Retired early & allowed Phillis to go home at night.

4 Aug., Mon. We were up early this morning & set Jane off on her journey to Gainesville in the carriage [to visit the Dawkinses].

Minty went with her & Robin. I cut out 2 gowns for Anne & mended & put sleeves to 2 old ones for her. Put collar on shirt for Mr T. Mended two dresses for myself. Mr Gay from Savannah dined here, his wife is in Saint Augustine which is in possession of the Federals. He stole a visit to her soon after it was taken in disguise but reports himself to have been betrayed & to have left in two hours. He thinks with three companies of cavalry he could recapture the place. Mr Taylor's crop is reported eaten up by the caterpillers.

The spaces for 6–13 August are filled with a summary of the type Maria usually wrote at year's end, and the remaining pages are blank. Thus she deliberately closed the 1862 diary in August, evidently too exhausted from nursing the sick to continue.

[Closing summary] I would desire here to record the goodness of God to me, in special mercies & deliverances out of trouble & the evils I feared from the autumn of last year up to the present time.

John who was in Fernandina as sergeant major in the 1st Fla Batalion was an object of especial mercy delivered out of trouble brought on himself[59] & preserved from the balls of the enemy during the evacuation of that place by our forces, in which he took an active part, though opposed to its evacuation. Caroline who was ill in Richmond with scarlet fever, was restored to us & being ill at our house for several months, she went to Carolina & was there frequently at the point of death & recovered. John stationed on the Chattahoochee came home ill & continued home some time in very bad health & finally recovered. Anne & Janie have both been ill dangerously so & recovered. My own health has not been good but I have been preserved through severe attacks without being compelled to take much medicine.

Florida has been threatened with invasion, but hitherto the Lord hath built a wall round about us. We have sent Willie off to a Military school, found it a difficult matter to keep him from the war. He volunteered in two companies but is not yet 17 years old.

These are only some of my Heavenly fathers dealings with me wherein judgment was tempered with mercy. A special mercy was also accorded to my daughter Mary in the gift of a son who I trust will be brought up in the nurture & admonition of the Lord. My house is not exactly as I could wish in the Lord, but I desire to take courage & trust fully in God that crooked places will yet be made straight. Mr Johnson has preached several sermons for the negroes which I hope will have a happy effect on them.

The only further mentions of the Taylors in 1862 come from Mrs. Yulee, writing to her husband in September about the visit of Lydia, Susan, and Dore Taylor to Margarita, the Yulee plantation house: "The girls are here giving us much pleasure," and two weeks later, "I am afraid the girls will leave before you come. Mrs Taylor wrote Lydia she would send for them this week. I will write her in hope of keeping them longer." Minor hostilities such as the incident on nearby Crystal River that Maria recorded on 1 July apparently were not taken very seriously. Otherwise, Maria would not have allowed the visit at all.

1863

The 1863 diary begins with the 10 August entry, a year after the closing of the 1862 diary. Because there is no opening prayer, Maria most likely began the diary earlier in the year using a notebook that is now missing. The emphasis now is on preparing, sharing, buying, and selling food.

> 11 Aug., Tues. Mr Bauskett called just from Charleston. Gave me a minute account of Ft Wagner fight.[60] Fenwick & Dore arrived from Homosassa [visiting the Yulees], brought me limes. Mr Morrison ate breakfast here & bought 4 of beef which I had salted. Mr Grigs sent a saddle of venison to sell for $14.00.

> 13 Aug., Thurs. I attended to having the walnuts beat for catsup. Put away mustard beat, put up bottle of pepper in vinegar for Cousin John Baker [in Beaufort, S.C.] to send by Mary.[61] Put up some grapes & mock olives. Bought 21 yds of cloth from Munroe Brown.

> 16 Aug., Sun. Mr Taylor myself & Dore went to Ocala to church. Mr Jones in Lake Weir & Mr Pelot preached. Received a letter from

Johnny. He expects to leave for Savannah this week, is better, will meet Mary at the road. I heard Richard & Fenwick their Bible lessons.

20 Aug., Thurs. I wrote to Willie[62] & Caroline. Packed up a basket with 50 lbs sugar & 5 jars orange and muskmelon preserves, also citron & lemons for Carrie. The sugar was packed & fixed for brother Richard [in Sumter]. I attended to household affairs & put sugar on grapes for preserves.

22 Aug., Sat. I had citron preserve made this morning. Sent 5 gals of molasses to Capt House. Received oil, tallow & beef with the tripe from him. I had part of it salted. I knit a little, read some & had house cleaned up. Cut out two aprons for Milton & a pr of pants & suit of clothes for Mingo. I had 25 sheep skins put on ashes & water a few days ago & had Robin to attend to them today. Dr Vogt sent me word he was sick yesterday & I sent him some wine yesterday & today.

25 Aug., Tues. Made several demijohns of beer.

26 Aug., Wed. I sealed up 10 bottles of wine, smoking with sulphur. Made 3 bottles of pepper catsup, put a few plums in pickle, made plum jelly & plum preserve. Mr Taylor brought me some wild cucumber very small for pickling, the first I ever saw.

29 Aug., Sat. Fenwick brought a black account of the bombardment of Ft Sumter & barbarous assault upon the city without timely warning.[63] I wrote a long letter to Johnny Friday & had a big cry about all our troubles. Our country is passing through a terrible crisis. Our children & friends in danger.

30 Aug., Sun. The fifth Sunday & no preaching any where. I read several Lectures of Cummings on the Parables. Susan read to the children. Mr Hussar came to dinner. I received a letter from Mrs Yulee. Lydia is well & desirous to return [to Osceola]. Sue went to read to the negroes. Eliza had a child last night, a son. Mr B called with letter from Mary. She got to Columbia safe.

31 Aug., Mon. Mr Taylor did not leave for Gainesville as he intended. Rain, rain. Rice getting ruined. I had grape beer drawn

off & bottled, & the grapes mashed last week put into a demijohn. Had 3 demijohns of wine drawn & sealed up one gal to send to Carrie by Mr Taylor & put vinegar on five jars of pickles. I knit some & fixed up basket to send to Carrie by Mr Taylor.

3 Sept., Thurs. I put up a bundle 2 prs of socks, 1 bottle of pickle, 1 towel, pins, thread, pine plaster & cloth to spread it on for Willie to be sent by Mr McConnel to him at Marietta. I wrote a long letter to Willie. Mr Carpenter called to see if he could get cotton in exchange for blockade goods, offered $1.50 cts for it a lb.

4 Sept., Fri. I sent socks to Mr [?'s] company & received note from him acknowledging them. A letter from Mary and Willie, he is anxious to go in the army.

5 Sept., Sat. Mr Bauskett gave me a letter yesterday to Mr Taylor requesting him to attend to his [Bauskett's] business as he was required to go into service.

8 Sept., Tues. The negroes seem better [just treated by Dr. Butt]. I gave them quinine today. My throat still quite sore. Mr Husser came here with fever on him. Gave him medicine. Anne had chill, gave her salt & mustard. Mr Taylor sent 2 wagons to Bayport with cotton & one for Mr Bauskett. I knit today and had wine made.

9 Sept., Wed. I felt very unwell this morning. Mr Taylor left early for Bayport on important business [to trade the cotton for smuggled goods].

12 Sept., Sat. Bess informed me yesterday of some misdemeaners among the negroes. Phillis been sick all the week. I understood in the evening that Mr Isby Roberds had been up here to inquire about some of his lost hogs among our negroes.

13 Sept., Sun. I felt very unwell today. Read the scriptures, talked to Mr Husser. The sick negroes some better. Jim came from Bayport with wagon & some goods.

14 Sept., Mon. I was too sick to get up this morning, took cream of tartar & quinine. I read the scriptures nearly all day. Attended to

giving medicine to the sick. Mr Taylor got home pretty late at night [from Bayport].

15 Sept., Tues. Mr Bauskett came over in the morning. Mr Taylor opened out the boxes & divided out his purchases for Mr Bauskett, who seemed much pleased. Prices for goods ranged high but they got $1.50 [per pound] for cotton. 5 doz sardines cost $100.00. Mr Husser got a pr of shoes. I put away two prs apiece for each of the boys & 2 for Mr Dawkins.

16 Sept., Wed. We sent Robin in Gov Broome's carriage to Homosassa for Lydia. I sent catsup, wine & capers to Mrs Yulee & some butter. The children sent potatoes. I put up 12 bottles of wine yesterday.

17 Sept., Thurs. I looked over some of the goods [from Bayport] this morning & got Curran & Susan to take six of the shirts badly made to sew over for John & Willie. Mrs Brown came up here & got a dress by favour at cost. Mr Taylor went to see Isby Roberds about the stolen hogs.

19 Sept., Sat. Lydia came home from Homosassa. Mrs Yulee sent Bella [servant] to accompany her as she had got her foot sprained by fall from a horse. Mrs Y sent me bananas, limes, a jar of marmalade & 2 bottles of champagne.

20 Sept., Sun. Mr Jones sent me the towels for the communion service. He & Mr Taylor had rather an angry discussion respecting the organization of the negro churches.[64] Susan & Curran [Johnny's fiancée] with Dora went to baptism. Mr Jones baptized 40 negroes.

25 Sept., Fri. I rose late, felt badly all day. Mrs Todd sent me three hanks of yarn. I wound one of them & put on a scarf for Johnny. I cut off dresses for Minty, Rachel, Nora, Letty. Gave handkerchiefs to the negroes. Eliza, Judy, Chloe & Dinah baby clothes & cut four yards of cloth for themselves.

28 Sept., Mon. Bella left this morning. Sent Mrs Yulee butter, mutton & two lambs. Dr and Mrs Brown came to dine here. Mrs Brown brought subscription paper out for the Atlanta Hospital. I

gave her [for the hospital] two new calico shirts which cost $15.00 a shirt, two bottles wine & arrowroot & vinegar

29 Sept., Tues. A letter from Johnny, he finds everything so high that $80.00 a month [evidently his soldier's pay] will not support him, has been under medical service for the week.

1 Oct., Thurs. I attended to bleaching candles or the tallow to make them & made a few. Wrote Carrie, Mary, Johnny & Willie. Mr Taylor went over the Withlacoochie[65] in quest of hogs & obtained 25 from Mr Safford formerly of Glyn Co Georgia. Anne is better. I bottled four bottles of wine & knit a little. Rachel & several other negroes quite sick.

5 Oct., Mon. Lieut Broome was spending the evening here. John Anderson[66] and Johnny Taylor came very unexpectedly from Savannah. The latter on sick furlough. I had supper prepared for them.

26 Oct., Mon. Dr Vogt called after dinner, he gave John extension of his furlough on account of intermittant fever.

27 Oct., Tues. I attended to drying beef. Curran left with John in the buggy. I put palmetto in salt for pickles. Looked over my presses & counted 49 brooches of yarn. Gave Phillis more yarn to spin. Susan very unwell with neuralgia.

30 Oct., Fri. Still having mustard & red pepper beaten. Went up to Johnny's room & read some of his letters & talked with him, put Robin to white washing my room. Received a letter from Willie, Sue one from Mary. Read the papers.

31 Oct., Sat. Mr Taylor & John left for Gainesville. Johnny seems to feel very badly on leaving. He wishes he could be by us always. I gave John 1 doz shirts of calico for himself. Gave him catsup, mustard & a bed counterpane & pillow.

2 Nov., Mon. Robin white washing dining room. Nora cleaned out the pantry thoroughly today. Phillis assisted Robin with the white washing, Minty cleaned my sashes. Rachel making candles. I knit

a little & overlooked the work generally. Letty cleaned out dining room & the pantry overhead. Anne better. I gave her quinine.

8 Nov., Sun. We read some of the Methodist sermons today. No preaching at the church. I went to the chapel & read to the little negroes. Sue taught them catechism. Gov Broome, Mrs D Groome & Curran called.

18 Nov., Wed. Had wool brought down, overhauled, assorted & weighed. Gave Rachel & Phillis 5½ lbs to clean & spin. Set Bess to cleaning 10 lbs for Mrs Lyles to spin & Phillis 3 lbs making 13 lbs for Mrs Lyles. Sent her more making 15 lbs. She sent back the 12 pillow cases & two night shirts she made. I sent bedding & articles to the sugar house for Mr Taylor.

1 Dec., Tues. The weather is very cold, a good many negroes sick with very bad colds. Nora, Phillis & Minty in the yard [house servants] & good many from the sugar sick also. Mr Venning came round this evening to get the appointment of agent of the Society to take supplies to the army.

3 Dec., Thurs. Mr T sent a barrel of sugar & syrup to the troops & barrel of oranges. I sent candles, potatoes & a few other thing to Mrs Lyles[67] by Robin with the wagon.

5 Dec., Sat. I am fifty years old today & many & varied emotions fill my mind. I trust God will give me fresh grace for my future journey in life & continue to me his unmerited favors.

8 Dec., Tues. Mr Howard called to see Mr Taylor about the impressment of sugar, determined to resist it.[68] John has a permit from Beauregard[69] to forward his. Willie writes that he has 77 cadets pledged to join him to reinforce Bragg.[70]

12 Dec., Sat. Engaged today in knitting, attending to the sick & doubling woolen yarn to send by wagon with potatoes & jug of molasses, for Mrs Lyles to twist. Dore with chill. Mr Taylor busy having his wooden mill finished, the small iron one broke yesterday. Mingo quite sick.

14 Dec., Mon. Mingo died this morning at day light. Mr Husser is here busy finishing off wooden mill for Mr Taylor, he stopped to help make coffin for Mingo.

24 Dec., Thurs. Willie arrived here at dark with Nellie & Mary Jackson.[71] He had been on to SC for them, he saw Johnny in Sav Geo & seemed much pleased with his visit to SC, saw all my friends there.

25 Dec., Fri. Another Christmas day finds us all spared. We are having sickness among the negroes & Dr Butt is attending Isaac. We hear through Willie that Pat Todd is really dead.[72] His poor mother is very ill.

26 Dec., Sat. Mary had a dining party at her house, all of the family except Mr Taylor & myself went. I was busy with lard & meat & Mr Taylor was tired out with the sugar, his large mill broke. Wick Yulee & Fen went over, Richie assisted his father.

28 Dec., Mon. Mr Yulee came & brought Yulee Dancy & Willie Forward[73] with him. He rode to the sugar house to see Mr Taylor & remained with us all night. I gave him the sugar cane champagne, which he pronounced very fine. He thought Mr Taylor's sugar fine & having planted it a long while is a good judge.

FOUR

Sickness and Death, 1864

The death of Willie Taylor at age 18 early in 1864 was a staggering personal blow that elicited by far the most emotionally unrestrained expression anywhere in Maria's diaries. In addition to exposing this new attribute, Maria's account of Willie's decline, along with the other concurrent illness among the family and servants, reveals in greater detail than heretofore her constant role of nurse and de facto doctor to the Osceola community. The strong evangelical framework Maria imposed on all of her experience also stands out in striking clarity.

Nobody in the immediate family had died since the deaths of the two young children Elizabeth and Thomas twenty years earlier in South Carolina, and eleven children had since survived in spite of the high child mortality rates of the time.[1] Although they had frequent and often severe illnesses to contend with, the Taylors must have felt relatively fortunate.

As for the immediate situation at the beginning of 1864, Willie had arrived home on 23 December 1863, on vacation from the Georgia State Military Institute in Marietta. He had first traveled to Sumter District, South Carolina, to pick up Mary and Nellie Jackson, 22- and 18-year-old daughters of Maria's sister, and escort them to Osceola, where they were to spend several months in greater safety from the war. Except for the names of these nieces and the now-familiar names of the Taylor children, all first names that appear in the following diary excerpts are those of Osceola servants.[2]

1 Jan., Fri. The Yankee blockade has become so effective that we can procure no diaries or blank books, so I am reduced to the necessity of accepting one of Willie's old books for my diary. My time is so much occupied that I can scarcely record passing events. Reminiscences of the past are pleasant, and as I have an indolent disposition to contend with, I have noted the business of each day except when I have neglected my diary too long to remember the occupations thereof.

Goodness and Mercy have followed me all the days of my life, gray hairs are sprinkling my head and a half century of my life has gone. I find very much of the carnal mind is still left in me to subdue, but I trust I desire to arise and walk before God and be perfect. Nor would I ever forget his benefits or fail to remember "the Hill from whence cometh my help." His grace has abounded to us. We have reaped a plentiful harvest, our entire family have been spared for another year, and during a time when sickness, death, trouble and War prevailed. Those who have been sick are again blessed with reasonable health, and I trust that leanesses have not entered our souls.

I would here humbly pray our Heavenly Father to continue His preserving care and keeping of us, and His blessings and favour to us, giving us heart to use his gifts to His honour and glory, and that His grace may so abound in us, that we may abound in grace unto others. I requested the children to remember this morning and during the coming year that "Christ pleased not himself" and unless we had his spirit we were none of his. They listened attentively and promised to try and think of it even in their play.

Willie, who is a member of the Military Institute is at home during vacation. He is complaining of headache and Dr Butt thinks he is threatened with meningitis. He attended Mr Alexander's sale yesterday and purchased several articles of furniture and crockery for me. One dozen plates cost $60, and half dozen goblets $61. I attended to household duties, knitting and nursing the sick. Eliza's child Jerry and Isaac are both ill. Dr Butt spent the night here.

The Taylors' confidence in Dr Butt, on whom they relied so heavily throughout the 1860s, was well placed. Zephaniah Butt (1812–83), a native of New Jersey and graduate of Jefferson Medical College in Philadelphia, practiced in several large northern cities before settling in Cedar Key, Florida, in the mid-1850s, partly under the influence of David Yulee. Upon losing his investments in 1862 with the capture of Cedar Key by Federal troops, and being indicted for practicing medicine without a Florida licence, he moved to Ocala, where he enjoyed professional success and was praised as being "at the top of his profession" and "eminently successful in his practice in this community."[3]

2 Jan., Sat. I nursed the sick and attended to domestic duties. Willie still complaining of headache, and he had so much fever he could not come out to see the young ladies.

4 Jan., Mon. Governor Broome,[4] Col Rogers, Mr J Johnson, Messrs Brown, Burns and Eichelberger, and several other men dined here. They came to appraise the sugar which the Govt desires to purchase. The boys had to sit at a second table. Dr Butt called to see the sick and dined here. He is so much engaged with practicing that both he and his horse are quite jaded. We are sending for him to attend the sick. Sugar appraised at $2.35.[5]

6 Jan., Wed. All of the boys left this morning for Homosassa—five of them—a merry crew,[6] in the wagon with Jim and Peter to accompany them. Willie took quinine[7] last night and this morning in large doses, and is much better today.

8 Jan., Fri. Georgy is worse this morning. I cupped, rubbed and administered oil and turpentine to her. Dr Butt called and recommended a blister to her spine.[8] Eliza's baby better. Mr Taylor went to Ocala to see after the sugar business. Willie, Nellie, Mary Jackson and Lydia were to dine at Rev James Owens. Dora had chills and fever. I cut off flannel for the four little negro babies and also gave Walter a woolen frock.

9 Jan., Sat. All of the sick are better. Dora and Anne are the only children with us today as the girls and Willie have not returned.

Mr Brown called, also Col Rogers. We requested the latter to purchase a piano for us at the Orange Springs.[9] I cut off homespun in
strips for shrinking for three cotton tablecloths, cut out apron for
Dora. Had ginger and orange peel beaten and potato pone made.
I have commenced attending to the milk again as there has been
quite a falling off in butter etc since it was neglected.

10 Jan., Sun. Mary sent her children over this morning, and she
and Mr B came and spent the day. Lydia, Willie and the girls came
home. Dr Butt called and thought the sick better. I read to the
children the history of Moses, and read on the Resurrection. A
man called to impress Mr Taylors teams and give him notice
thereof. Lydia went down to teach the little negroes. Willie complaining.

11 Jan., Mon. Cut off one dozen home made towels. Fixed work
for Dora. Mr Taylor received a letter from Col Dawkins containing one Johnny had sent him. Jim returned from Homosassa
bringing oysters, oranges and fish and a note from Mr and Mrs
Yulee. Isaac worse today. We sent for Dr Butt. Mr Eichelberger
came to purchase syrup for the Govt, $15 per gallon delivered at
the Railroad.[10] I got Isaac to take oil and turpentine. Marked Mr
Taylors socks. Mr Taylor sent Jack to Micanopy with two barrels
of syrup and a demijohn of syrup and some sugar for Mr Johnson.

12 Jan., Tues. Isaac much worse this evening. I went out and
stayed with him some time this evening administering medicine.
Georgy better, giving her quinine. Dr Butt called to see the sick.
Lydia, Mary and Nellie went to call on Mrs Broome and took two
canisters which Mrs Yulee sent her. Willie made a nice new bridle
for his father. Mary, Mr Bauskett, and the children also Dr Butts
dined here. Chloe came in with her child sick. Eliza's child worse,
its head drawn back considerably, it is very quiet and patient.
Willie had the fever, he was cupped, bathed his feet, and had hot
lemonade. I gave him quinine when the fever was off.

13 Jan., Wed. Willie free from fever, gave him cream of tartar and
quinine. Isaac had fever last night. I treated his case as I did Willies.

Gave them both camphor this morning. Sam has erysipelas. Isaac worse. He died about ½ after one. Chloe and Eliza both brought their children in sick. Eliza's child is in a singular way. I attended to getting a winding sheet for the dead. Cut out a floor cloth. Mended a shirt, cut out three cotton osnaburg tablecloths, making six cotton tablecloths I have cut out. Had buttons put in Willie's pants. Cut orange chips for preserves and put them in soak. Mr Husser came here this morning. Birch also came to make shoes for the family and servants. Dr Butt called and said he would not come again unless sent for. Willie felt better at night.

14 Jan., Thurs. Isaac buried today. Mr Husser left but returned to dinner and spent the night. Georgy worse. Mr Taylor gave her stramoniam[11] at night. I had my wardrobe drawer fixed, also my dairy and a piece put under the pantry floor to steady it. Made orange preserves, attended to the sick. Phillis, Sary, Old Rachel, & Morgan all with fever. The two little children still sick & brought into my room to attend to. I sent to the office a letter to Carrie & Johnny. Mr Taylor cupped Willie on his spine at night as he complained of pain. I gave Jane oil and turpentine early in the morning. She had fever last night. Bathed her feet in lye water. Gave Chloe my clothes to wash. Eliza fringed towels, Chloe sewed up floor cloth for me yesterday. I sewed and commenced binding a pair of shoes for Dora for Birch to sole. Nellie and Mary Jackson dined with Mary. Mr Bauskett called. I knit a little last night and put up preserves.

15 Jan., Fri. Georgy pronounced to be dying this morning. Gave her spirits, then oil and turpentine and afterwards wine.[12] Cupped her and put mustard plaster on her spine. The two little children seem better. I gave them sweet oil, wine and syrup. Jane better I allowed her to dress. Willie also better.

16 Jan., Sat. I attended to Georgy giving her medicine, she seems a little better. Chloe's child dismissed from the house. Eliza's child still quite sick. I had it sponged with cold water. I have 23 hogs hung in the smokehouse this morning. It is all safe and sound. I had Eliza wash the bedding the sick had used.

17 Jan., Sun. Willie and Nichols Roberts went to church in time. Georgy is worse. Susan offered to remain at home and nurse her. We received two letters from Johnny today respecting offers made for his father's sugar. He has written to Commissary Gen [?] for a permit to carry it on to Georgia. Sue read to the children and Lydia went down to the church to teach the little negroes.

18 Jan., Mon. Georgy died today about one o'clock. Dinah, Minty, and Phillis sick today. Judy and Eliza brought in their children sick. Gave Judy's child a little salts, gave it oil and turpentine yesterday. Gave Dinah's salts and peach leaf with oil and turpentine.

19 Jan., Tues. Georgy buried today. Willie has had fever for two nights and has taken quinine in the morning. I had all my towels gotten up. Knit some on Willie's socks. Had Indy sewing. Eliza did little else than mind her child. Robin salting hogs—six of them—making 29 killed, 23 in the smoke. Dinah sick and Rachel complaining. Minty better. The boys came at night [from Homosassa] and brought oysters and a few oranges.

20 Jan., Wed. Having lard attended to and dyeing cloth. Cut off 15 towels making 2 doz and four I now have of cotton osnaburgs. Richard had his oranges stolen by Milton and we had him chastised for it. Willie had two chills today and fever. Rachel and Robin sick. Attended to sausage seasoning, making liver pudding and head cheese. I gave Willie at night 10 grs of calomel and Mr Taylor scarified his neck and took some blood.[13]

21 Jan., Thurs. Willie had high fever all day and seems much weakened by the operation of the calomel. I sponged his face, gave him rhubarb and magnesia. He took a little gruel and bird soup. I attended to having yarn dyed. Eliza's child seems a little better. Rachel and Scipio sick.

22 Jan., Fri. Cut out linings for Jane's and Anne's shoes, and got Mr Taylor to make a pair of needles to knit my shawls. Attended to Willie and dry cupped him on side & neck & put poultices on his stomach. I slept with Willie last night and gave him 10 grs of quinine first intermission [of fever]. Gave him arrow root with wine

in it during the night.[14] Gave Willie another dose of quinine at ½ after 8 this morning. He took some gruel & arrow root with wine, asked for wine to drink alone. Mr Taylor sent for Dr Butt to see Scipio. The rest of the servants better. Mr Taylor scarified Willie on the back of his neck and took a glassful of blood. I rubbed his back with turpentine and his head with oil. Mr T sent for Dr Lessine[15] to see Willie, but he wrote that he could not come. Mr Puleston came & staid here all night. I slept with Willie again tonight. Mr Puleston thought the frequency of Willie's pulse was from the effect of the 30 grs of quinine he has taken since last night.

23 Jan., Sat. Mr Taylor came into my room to see Willie & thinking him worse sent off during the night for Dr Hunter.[16] I thought Willie better myself & nearly free from fever, gave him quinine. Had another low bedstead removed to his room for him to lie on during the day. Gave him oil & turpentine this morning. Dr Butt called this morning, thinks Willie doing very well. I gave him another dose of quinine at night. Mr Puleston left here early this morning for Col Summers expecting to return at night, which he failed to do, he is agent for the hospitals in Florida & to carry on supplies to our troops & is now getting sugar, syrup & other necessities for them. Dr Hunter lives forty miles from here, was not at home & did not come. Gave Willie quinine at night, rubbed his chest with oil & camphor, & his head, & dry cupped him at night. He did not sleep very well but was nearly free from fever. I put on my shawl at night. Had Eliza's child all day in my room feeding it on arrow root & wine. Jane was very sick today. I bathed her in hot lye, gave her teas, cupped her with scarifer on spine, took her in Willie's room to sleep.

24 Jan., Sun. Gave Willie quinine this morning making about 50 grs since first remission of fever. He begged to be allowed to dress & lie on the bed, he is astonishingly reduced. Took some nourishment, beer & wine today, chicken soup. I gave Willie no quinine at night. Jane had chill & very hot fever. Slept with her in Willie's room. Had a letter from my sister Mary requesting me to go and see my brother [in South Carolina], that he has not the strength to

come to Florida. I wish it were possible but with the present state of unhealthiness in my family I could not possibly think of it.

25 Jan., Mon. Jane & Willie both better this morning. Willie dressed & left his room. About 2 o'clock he had a chilly sensation followed by a slight fever. I put mustard on his spine & wrapped him up. He ate a little chicken & Irish potato for dinner & took beer & wine during the day. I put some dry cups on his chest & stomach. Knit some and attended to house cleaning. Chloe came in sick with fever and sore throat. Gave her peach leaf tea and salts as an emetic, followed in a few hours with oil and turpentine. Mr Taylor is having his rice thrashed. Gave Jane quinine this morning, Willie none.

26 Jan., Tues. Willie feeling better this morning but very weak. I gave him quinine early in the morning & last night after the fever left him. He came to the table & ate some birds & a soft boiled egg. Carrie and Col Dawkins with Anne Maxcy[17] [coming from Gainesville] passed by Gov Broome's to pick up Lyd, Sue, Nellie and Mary Jackson. They all came on together to supper. Dear Willie was lying on the lounge in my room and though rejoiced at their coming, was too sick to go out & meet them. Carrie had been much distressed by Mr Goss' discription of the illness of Willie & Jane & was delighted to find them so much better. Willie went out of the north west room into the one next. I had a nice low bedstead put in there for him. Milton attended to him. Jane was sick today with chills & high fever.

27 Jan., Wed. Willie seems better today. He walked out to the little church, but says he had to sit down several times on the way, he wanted to kill some birds for himself. Jane was quite sick again with chill & fever. I was very unwell myself. Tamar very ill. I rode down to the negro house to see her. Mr Taylor got up last night & cupped her freely, we gave her oil & turpentine followed by cal. She is spitting blood, blood, pneumonia with meningitis symptoms. We sent for Dr Butt. Before he came I had a blister put on her chest. Mr Bauskett, who called with Mary, spread it for me. Willie complained of weakness & some headache & retired early.

I had his feet bathed & his head rubbed. Johnny came from Savannah [on leave]. Willie was delighted to see him & insisted upon Johnny's sleeping with him, which I fear disturbed him as he needs great quiet.

28 Jan., Thurs. Willie complained very little. Seemed pleased to have Johnny with him & amused himself through the day in many ways. Came to the pantry for pickles & seems to like some beer Mr Bauskett sends him. He seems to be very weak & I am getting him to take iron & quinine in small doses. Carrie rode down with me [to the servant house] to see Tamar. I gave her buttermilk. I felt very unwell today & could not give much attention to the sick. Jane is very unwell.

29 Jan., Fri. Mr Taylor desired that as Johnny, Willie & Carrie had come, I should send for Mr Bauskett & Mary, that all our dear children should dine with us together as they had not done for a long while. I attended to getting up some good things for them although not feeling very well. Mr Dawkins was the only one absent of our varied but united households, & dear Johnny ventured a prophecy that it would be the last time that we would all ever dine together again. I rode to see Tamar & found her better. Anne Maxcy, Ellen & Mary Jackson, with Anne's children were here.[18] Anne seemed very lively & was teasing Willie & Johnny. Curran Broome also dined here & spent the night. Willie complains of nervousness but declined to bathe his feet. I had no quinine to give him. Before the evening closed the party sang songs & hymns. Dear Willie asked for "Home Again" & "There is a fountain filled with blood drawn from Emmanuel's veins." God grant the dear boy may have washed in that fountain, which was opened for sin & uncleanliness. Johnny slept with him again tonight.

30 Jan., Sat. Willie & Jane were both up this morning & interested in passing events.[19] His father called him to see Mr J Brown & another gentleman who rode up to the steps. I thought he looked better today than he had done for some time. He shot a few birds in the evening & rode 2 miles to the sugar house with Carrie, Curran & Johnny in the carriage. When the party returned they found

Mrs Rogers, Miss West & Miss Todd here. Mrs Rogers remained to tea. Willie ate a hearty supper but had a slight chill & fever which he did not tell me of until after supper. He seemed wearied & complained of great weakness & told me he thought he should be very ill, he wanted to take valerian[20] as he had not slept well for several nights. I persuaded him to try & sleep without it. Bathed his head in oil & camphor, dry cupped his spine & rubbed his feet, which he expressed a fear would make me sick. He did not retire till late but seemed to sleep sweetly, & promised me, if he should get restless to send for me to give him an anodyne; he seems very sensitive to noise & nervous. I got Johnny to sleep elsewhere not to disturb him, then sat up for some time to see if he would want me.

31 Jan., Sun. God be merciful to me! How can I write that my dear boy, my noble, gentle Willie is dead? Oh my Father, how mysterious is this dispensation; how lacerating this stroke to his idolizing parents & so sudden. When we hoped he was recovering & had our fears so quieted by his patient endurance & manly suffering of pains we knew not of. Precious, precious boy, I cannot bear the thought that you should have lived, suffered & died in vain. I must believe that you had a high mission to accomplish by dying, while youth & manly beauty, gentleness & controlled power so strongly marked you as one born to influence.

Oh my father that thou hast stricken me & rebuked me & chastened me sorely. I bow before thy awful mandate, destroying my hopes & striking down with a sudden blow the dear object of cherished affections. But I cling to thee, I cannot let Thee go until I find the great blessing of this, Thy great affliction. Oh grant, I do beseech Thee that by the power of God it may be made the salvation of this entire household, & the awakening of this community to a sense of sin & danger. Bright, beautiful, intellectual, docile William. With all the virtues which adorned thy character & life, thou wert only a sinner saved by grace through the blood of the everlasting covenant.

The first call I had this morning was from Johnny, before I had risen, that Willie was very sick. I ran to him, too late to help him, he was dying & exclaimed on seeing me "My Mother." Shall thus agonizing an exclamation ever be forgotten? Oh my boy! my loving obedient child! Would I not have died to save you? His father had gone to his room an hour before & finding him free from fever, induced him to take some quinine. He ate a sour orange after it; his father has the horrible fear that it was not quinine he took.[21] We were therefore at great loss what to do for him, & before a physician could be got he was gone from us to bless us no more with his dear presence.

Stunned with the awful blow I could not believe that my commanding, protecting son was indeed dead. His dear father is inconsolable, stricken to the very heart. Oh! Our Heavenly Father! Pour out thy Spirit and teach us all thy Holy Will and resignation thereto.

4 Feb., Thurs. [After the funeral] We all did little else than speak of Willie, of his many virtues & noble traits. All believe that nothing short of the grace of God, could have enabled him, under so many trying circumstances, to resist temptations that so many young men enter into. He has never taken spirits,[22] never played cards, & never taken an oath, was always as modest as a lady, & I have never, even as a child had to correct him for the slightest unchaste expression. He has always loved his Bible & read it, particularly the New Testament; as a child he spoke touchingly of a saviour's death & love, & of God's goodness. His soul could not be gathered with sinners, nor his life with bloody men.

FIVE

Confusions of War, 1864

In the remaining six months of the 1864 diary (February through July) Maria's grieving for Willie merges with her accounts of unprecedented turmoil in the Osceola community: fears of invasion, family members engaged in the fighting, impressment of goods and labor for the Confederate cause, and frustrating efforts to continue the children's education. In February, the military situation in Florida, long confined to coastal areas, suddenly moved inland. Just a week after Willie's death, Maria was sending Johnny off to meet the enemy.

9 Feb., Tues. I fixed up Johnny's clothes. Gave him two towels and four pairs new socks, 3 colored handkerchiefs and two white ones. He refused to take dear Willie's clothes. It rained before Johnny returned and I sat up for him till after twelve and had him come to my room by the fire. We heard the Yankees had landed at Jacksonville—5000 strong.[1]

10 Feb., Wed. Johnny and Mr Dawkins ate an early breakfast and left for Gainesville, Johnny on his way to Savannah to join his command.[2] I got a trunk for him for $80 and a carpet bag in which I had fixed some catsup, sardines, etc.

11 Feb., Thurs. We had intelligence today that the Yankees had captured Baldwin, torn up some of the rail road and were marching on Lake City—their numbers variously estimated. Mr Broome's family are in quite a panic, and packing to move off. Mr Taylor went to Ocala to consult respecting the public safety.

12 Feb., Fri. Mrs Rogers [neighbor] sent here early this morning in the rain to try and get a wagon to move off in. Jupiter and Jack [servants] came for permission to go with their wives, who are at Gov Broomes. Mr Taylor gave them permission to go. Sukey came to request that her husband might remain here, which was also assented to. Mrs Broome sent to beg us to come and see her. Sue, Dora and I rode over to see her. I was anxious to persuade them not to go, but she seems determined to do so. They desire me to take care of some of their things which they cannot carry with them.

13 Feb., Sat. Mr Taylor went to Ocala to see after the public welfare. We hear various reports. Mr Bauskett went with him. A company was raised, and the command tendered Mr Taylor. He was too unwell, and left too many sick at home to accept it.[3]

14 Feb., Sun. Mr Bauskett and Mr Brown called by here to tell us goodbye on their way to Gainesville to join the regiments now fighting for Florida. Mary seems willing that Mr Bauskett should do his duty & meet the present emergency for troops. I am glad to see all my children so patriotic in their feelings. Mr Brown wrote a very touching note to Mr Taylor to take care of his wife and children & act as his agent. Jack brought us the news in the night that the Yankees were at Gainesville.[4] Gov Broome sent us word. Sue and Carrie were much excited by the news but took it with considerable fortitude and heroism. I received a note from Johnny on his way to Lake City.

15 Feb., Mon. Richard drove Curran [Broome] home soon this morning and her uncle left the estate with his family and part of his negroes. Dr Waldo's family also left. I sent Mary early the news of the enemy and she promptly made preparation for them. We heard by note from Dr Brown that the Yankees were four miles from Flemington at 9 o'clock this morning, subsequently we heard that they had not left Gainesville. Mr Taylor had some corn and other things hidden from them. I got Fenwick to bury my wine. Put all spirits out of their way, and had my silver and other valuables buried. Mr Taylor put away his important papers. Some

members of Major Brevard's battalion came up here, and he himself called on his way to meet the enemy.

16 Feb., Tues. We sent Richard this morning to see Col Semmes respecting our sugar seized for the Government.[5] Fenwick went to Ocala for the news—nothing satisfactory. Many unreliable rumours. Chambers had a fight with the Yankees last night and lost two men. We hear nothing of Mr Dawkins, Mr Bauskett, or Johnny. We were informed that Dr Todd[6] had moved with his family in the scrub. Eliza wants to place herself under his protection with her husband. I had four wagon covers and nine bags made in case of necessity to remove from here. Maurice brought me a jar of peach preserves from old Clary, he says his mistress [daughter Mary next door] is determined to stay at present. Lydia fixed up the physic box and labeled the medicines. Jim Adams rode up here with a note for us to read from Joe Waldo advising his father to remain here. He has already gone however. I received a note from Mrs Reardon [Ocala friend]. She does not seem to think the Yankees will come down here. I collected what books I would be unwilling to leave behind, most religious works and one or two of dear Willie's. I wear his hair and watch in my bosom that they might not be disturbed by the invading foe should they suddenly come upon us. I wrote to Mrs Yulee and a note to Mrs Reardon. Mrs Yulee's letter was sent back as no mails were going now, the mail boy having gone to fight.

17 Feb., Wed. Mr Smith, our courier from Lake City arrived last night—the Yankees have been driven from Lake City and left Gainesville. They are fortifying on the Little St Mary's. Richard has gone to Ocala to have horses shod and hear the news. Fenwick moulding bullets. Mr Taylor making preparations for going or staying. My arrowroot has been planted and some corn. I knit a little.

18 Feb., Thurs. The weather is cold, wet and blustering. Johnny will fare badly in camps as he carried no blankets from home with him, and presume no one brought him any from camps. At night Mr Dawkins servant Tom came with the carriage horses and a

letter from Mr Dawkins to Carrie. Tom says only 42 Yankees were in Gainesville, and it is thought they wanted to get the rolling stock of the railroad. Mr Dawkins advises us not to remove, but supposes the Yankees are trying to take possession of E Florida.

21 Feb., Sun. We heard today that Mrs Rogers baby had died on the way near Blue Spring in their retreat from Florida. Mr Taylor determined to leave tomorrow for Gainesville and Lake City to see after Johnny.

22 Feb., Mon. Mr Dawkins came before dinner. The Yankees disturbed no private property in Gainesville, only some commissary stores they gave out, and carried off some negroes, two of Mr Dawkins among them. Mr Bauskett came home at night and sent us word he had seen Mrs Broome at Newnansville, and that Mrs Rogers baby was not dead.

24 Feb., Wed. I spent the day writing letters to Mary Jackson, Eliza Jane and Sister Lydia [sister and sisters-in-law in South Carolina]. Mary and Mr Bauskett with Anne Maxcy called and gave me some particulars of the battle on Saturday. Johnny safe, many of the battalion lost.[7]

25 Feb., Thurs. I spent most of the day in looking over old letters. I found one from Willie where he told me he had two room mates who prayed night and morning, whose example he followed and read his Bible. I feel thankful for this testimony that he feared God and sought to please Him. That he called on Him who never said "seek you me" in vain.

28 Feb., Sun. Richard and Fenwick went to Long Swamp to hear Mr Jones [pastor]. I was very unwell, read one of James sermons to the family and the scriptures and we had other exercises. After dinner I went down to read to the negroes. They exhibited a great deal of feeling, and Robin, Letty, Clary and Eli went up to be prayed for.

29 Feb., Mon. I had the boys cyphering and writing, and made them read to me. They are busy with turkey pens.

1 Mar., Tues. I spent the morning in reading the Scriptures and the Lectures on Pilgrim's Progress and some pieces on death. Read some to Nellie[8] and Lyd, heard the boys read and attended to their cyphering. Mary and Anne Maxey came over in the evening and Mr Bauskett. Tommy came with them. I read a piece on "Regarding the repentance of others" to all of them. I sent Fenwick to Ocala. Reports the Yankees near Camp Finegan—our troops within a few miles of them.

2 Mar., Wed. The boys attended to their lessons and cyphering this morning. We had rain last night, and raining today. The children hemming towels. I read some in Pilgrim's Progress. Remodelling a shirt for Mr Taylor. Gave Lyd and Sue 2 pocket handkerchiefs of coarse linen. I knit some on my stocking, gave Rachel and Phillis some wool to spin. Fenwick, Dora and Richard read aloud in "The Parent's Assistant." The boys caught 30 partridges.

3 Mar., Thurs. I spent most of the day in reading over my diarys since 1852. Carrie and Mr Taylor came in the evening from Gainesville. I heard the boys their reading and geography, they attended to their cyphering and writing. I am pleased to see that Fenwick's mind has so serious a turn. Carrie brought Rhoda [servant] with her. Mr Taylor seems much disappointed that he did not see Johnny. He went to Lake City passed by the battlefields and took on things for Johnny, but failed to see him. The wounded at LC seem to have excited much of his compassion.

8 Mar., Tues. We had a letter and message from Mr Yulee, just with request that the boys be sent to Homosassa to go to school with Wickliffe.[9] Also an invitation for Lyd, Sue, and me.

10 Mar., Thurs. Fenwick went to Ocala for the mail. A letter from Johnny to me and one to Lyd, both interesting and satisfactory. A letter of sympathy from Eliza Wallace containing a beautiful piece of poetry "The voice of the Departed." Also one from Maria Baker [cousin in Beaufort], very sympathizing. Gen Capers [?] wrote Mr Taylor a touching letter about dear Willie. I read them all and rejoice that notwithstanding the war there is still so much in the

world of the good and beautiful left us, and kind sympathy for those in affliction.

12 Mar., Sat. Mr Taylor received message about his sugar from the Govt agent last night and has been busy preparing for him all day by coopering and heading the barrels and hogsheads. Mr Dawkins arrived from Gainesville, bringing me some letters and some papers. He saw Johnny a few days ago and sent him a box of eatables. He was looking very well Mr D says and turned very thoughtful. He sent his father a gun he took from a Yankee prisoner.

13 Mar., Sun. I feel today that God is love. I must trust him to bring me & all my children in safety to his promised rest, not one of them wanting in the day when his jewels are gathered, but all of them bound together in the bundle of eternal life, notwithstanding the folly, sinfulness & neglect of their earthly parents, who now mourn in dust & ashes all their unfaithfulness & their omissions of duty, & humbly pray to be freely forgiven, graciously received & comforted for Christ's sake, the saviour of sinners, the life & light of the world.

14 Mar., Mon. Mr Dawkins went to Ocala and brought back the news that five regiments of Yankees were at Pilatka [Palatka] and that Finegan's brigade had been sent there to frustrate their plans.[10] Hopkins Battalion is with that brigade and I presume that Johnny is among them. May our Heavenly Father protect him from evil. Mr Taylor still preparing his sugar to be weighed. Sent Jim [servant] to Silver Spring with his tithing. He came back with the intelligence that a Battalion or Regt of Confederate soldiers were there to protect the stores from the Yankees who were expected to come down the St Johns. Jim protested against carrying his wagon lest it should be impressed.

15 Mar., Tues. Mr Eichelberger [sugar agent] dined here after weighing the sugar and paying for it. Seventy seven thousand and some hundreds. Mr Dawkins went to the sugar house to lend his aid.

19 Mar., Sat. Read the Apocryphal New Testament. Many things very fanciful in it and some excellent precepts. The historical parts I should not think are at all reliable.

20 Mar., Sun. Mr Taylor, Lydia, Sue, Nellie, Mary, Richard and Fenwick went to Ocala to church but were disappointed as Mr Jones was not there, nor any one to represent him. Minty and Judy had permission to join the church, but they went to a funeral at Gov Broome's when they heard Mr Jones was not come. I read to the children and catechized them. I went down to the chapel and read to the negroes. I felt very low spirited today.[11] I pray to God to give me right apprehensions of myself and of his dealings with me and mine, & to deliver me from all false views and unnecessary fears.

22 Mar., Tues. I spent most of the day reading and knitting. Mr Edward Haile came here in the evening to get negroes to work on the batteries.[12]

25 Mar., Fri. Caroline sent me a piece of calico containing two dresses and a piece of alpacca. The three dresses were $600.[13] Present prices seem fabulous ones. Dora remained in Gainesville with Carrie. She promised to teach her and we requested her to employ Mr Ochus to teach her music.[14]

26 Mar., Sat. I set Rachel to making up clothes for Abram, and getting him ready to go to work on the fortifications, also measured off cloth for Prince and Cudjoe who will go likewise. I had Phillis looking up the crockery and spoons and cleaning them. Nora is a very intractable cook. I was engaged in a variety of little duties. Felt very sad all day and shed many tears in remembrance of my dear Willie.

27 Mar., Sun. I went to recall the day & found it was my wedding day. Thirty years have I been married, & during eighteen years of that time, I was in possession of a bright beautiful being, who filled my heart with gladness, & of whom I was perhaps too proud, my dear Willie, whom God has recently taken from me to expand in a brighter & happier world.

29 Mar., Tues. I had some things put up for Carrie in the valise and sent her by the wagon. The negroes left for Gainesville. Several of the neighbors sent their negroes at the same time. Fenwick took up some bottles of wine and other things which I had buried in the panic about the Yankees. We had a beef killed and sent Carrie and Mary some. I read two delightful hymns headed "The Lord our banner" and "Weakness" both from the Church Militant. I put Rachel to spinning stocking yarn for me. Had a pad made for Mr Taylor's saddle. Mary sent over several little delicacies for us as she frequently does. God has blessed us with affectionate children. Oh, that none of them may come short of his glory.

30 Mar., Wed. Received a letter from Caroline, saying they were all well but very lonely, that she had heard from Johnny. He was well and near the enemy's lines.[15] The R.R. washed out by the storm will not be ready for travel before Thursday or Friday. We had occasion to correct Nora for her perverseness and disobedience. I knit some on stockings with the homespun yarn. Letty was sick. An officer appointed to impress liquors called up here to get some information, he seems to have personally impressed too much.

31 Mar., Mon. Dr Todd called to see Letty. In conversing of his own [dead] son[16] & of dear Willie he advised us to dismiss him from our minds, that he thought it had affected my health grieving so much. I would not think of heeding such advice even if I could. Tis pleasant as well as sad to think of my dear son, & to long for the time when I shall meet him again, although with patience I shall wait all the days of my appointed time until my change come [to immortal life].

1 Apr., Fri. I was mending for the boys and fixing them up to go to Homosassa tomorrow. They packed their trunks in my room. The government is hauling off the sugar purchased from Mr Taylor. A letter from Caroline. Mr Dawkins left for Savannah. Dora was learning with good heart and purpose. Mr Taylor's negroes sent to work on the fortifications,[17] Prince was already complaining. Carrie had heard from Johnny. He was reported well but not looking it.

2 Apr., Sat. The boys set off early for Homosassa to begin school on Monday. Jim went with them in a two horse wagon to bring home some oysters. The wagon broke four miles from home and the boys returned. We received a mail. The papers are somewhat encouraging to our cause. Johnny writes seriously and is very desirous that the war should end, and he get out of the way of seeing so much wickedness.

3 Apr., Sun. Mr Taylor and the boys, Anne Maxcy, Mary and Ellen and I went to Ocala to church. Mr Jones preached from the text "Without holiness no man shall see the Lord." Minty, Judy, Eliza, Chloe, Sukey, Tamar and Peter were received for baptism by the Ocala church. After dinner, all the children including the boys, Mary Bauskett, Lyd, Sue, Anne Maxcy, Mary and Nellie went to the chapel with me. I read to the negroes from the 2nd chapter of John explaining it. A good many negroes out. They seemed to sing with much life.

4 Apr., Mon. The boys left early again this morning for Homosassa. I put Minty to attend to the milk, sent Old Mary to plant beans. Phillis commenced a piece of cloth on 31st March. Rachel commenced a piece today. I took the yarn off today for knitting and sewing thread. Betsey sick. I cut off cloth for canvassing hams, 34 of them, attended to other household matters.

7 Apr., Thurs. Jim got home last night and brought me a letter from Fenwick and basket of lemons from Mrs Yulee. Mr Venning came yesterday evening and remained all night, he brought me the Governor's letter and some certificates having acted as agent for our [Military Aid] Society to carry on supplies to the Army of Tennessee. I advised him to write to the Governor for amount of his expenses.

8 Apr., Fri. This day has been appointed by the Confederate Congress and confirmed by the President to be set apart for fasting, and prayer for the blessing of Almighty God upon our efforts to maintain our liberties and independence. That he would vouchsafe to us His aid in this our extremity and cause us to bless and praise his name.

12 Apr., Tues. Peter came from Gainesville with the cart and brought Carrie's trunk with the articles Mr Dawkins had purchased in Savannah for us and another gentleman had procured in Augusta, mourning goods. The articles were extremely high. Mr Yulee's overseer came from Homosassa to purchase corn. He brought me a letter from Richard, who professed to take much pleasure in the two chapters he has to read daily in the Scriptures.

16 Apr., Sat. Cudjoe ran away from the fortifications and came home this morning.[18] We are having some beautiful flowers from the garden. Received a letter from Dora, her first to me and very well written. She wrote "tomorrow is my birthday, I will spend it in reading my Bible and try from then to be better."

17 Apr., Sun. All of the family except Mr Taylor and myself went to Scott Spring to see the negroes baptized. Mr Jones baptized fifteen. Minty, Jim, Peter, Judy, Sukey, Tamar, Chloe, Eli [all from Osceola], Mary Bauskett's Chany, Dr Vogt's Abe. I read in Romans. Picked up in the library this morning some documents of Swedenburg[19] and read some. After dinner I went down to the church and read to the negroes, and talked to them.

18 Apr., Mon. We received a mail, a letter from Johnny. Mr Taylor had one from Major Behn [Savannah cotton agent], Capt Anderson, and Mr l'Engle.

John W. Anderson to John M. Taylor, Savannah, 11 April 1864.

I rec. your kind message relative to the Tierce of sugar & gladly would take it if I knew how to get a permit for its transportation. I believe Genl Finegan alone could grant it. I have no access of approach to him. My son Robert is in command of all the Cavalry in your state, but I do not know when to address him, if I can ascertain I will write & see whether he can do anything for me.

Prices & scarcity keep us almost in a state of starvation & those who were easiest before the war & have kept from all filthy speculations & gave themselves & their all to our country are the greatest sufferers. I trust that a good God hears our cries & groanings & as Capt of the Host will take charge of us & lead us to success &

victory & drive our cruel & abandoned enemy from our shores & give us peace & prosperity.

22 Apr., Fri. Betsy & Eliza are better today. Dr Butt called in the evening to see them. I read some more in the Epistles of Ignatius [apocryphal]. I had Anne and Jane sewing on their pantalets. I sewed on their chemises and fixed their work for them. I burnt several literary articles which I thought calculated to corrupt, one of them a translation from the Hebrew sent me by the translator.

24 Apr., Sun. Morgan ill this morning. Dr Todd saw him, giving veratrine[20] to him and Betsy. He had Eliza blistered over the left lung, also put upon veratrine. I read in the Scriptures also in the "Plan and Philosophy of Salvation." Mr Taylor read the last lecture on the "Pilgrim's Progress." After dinner I read some and found Morgan so much worse that we sent again for Dr Todd. He thought it useless to give him anything as he could not possibly live. I had him stimulated, remaining with him the most of the evening.

26 Apr., Tues. Morgan was buried this morning. Mr Smith brought Abram up, found him in the act of running away [from the fortifications]

27 Apr., Wed. Mr Taylor is having considerable trouble with three servants whom he sent to work on the batteries. Prince and Cudjoe have both run off, and Abram has to be put in confinement. After dark Major Lay, Mr Haile, 2 Miss Paynes and Miss Cameron of Virginia called up and spent the night. Major Lay is on Beauregard's staff and came on official business. I was to have gone to Gainesville yesterday, but Mary is too sick for me to leave home. A letter from Richard [in Homosassa]. He has run an orange thorn in his knee.

29 Apr., Fri. With some misgivings I left home for Gainesville this morning after hearing Mary was better. Had a very good journey and stopped with Mr Johnson [Baptist pastor] in Micanopy. I had conversation with him in the evening. This is the first time I have seen him since dear Willie's death—he wrote us a very sympathizing letter when he heard of the event. I took some tea and clarified

sugar to Mrs Johnson, and a little butter. Gave her little boy $10.00. He is an interesting child.

2 May, Mon. After we had all retired Johnny came, having walked seventeen miles to reach the cars [railroad]. He seemed much fatigued and very hungry. Carrie had supper got for him. He gave me an account of Col Hopkins trial and his being called on as a witness.[21] Johnny has only 24 hours furlough and has to leave tomorrow.

3 May, Tues. I talked all the morning with Johnny. Mr Yulee called and he and Mr Dawkins wrote to Gen Anderson for Johnny, Mr D wrote to Gen Finegan.[22] Mr Dawkins and I accompanied Johnny to the cars as far as Baldwin. I had much conversation with Johnny on the cars.

4 May, Wed. Wrote to Mr Taylor and determined on sending Robin home tomorrow with carriage and horses, and remaining until Monday. I put up a "Mercury" [Charleston paper] for Mr Taylor in which is an obituary of our dear Willie, written by some friend in Carolina, which is truthfully and beautifully expressed. Johnny discovered it in the paper when he was here on Tuesday and pointed it out to me. Carrie brought me a pamphlet—a review of Swedenburgenism by Dr Pond answered by Mr Cabell, a layman, with an introductory letter by Mr Craile.[23]

7 May, Sat. Mr Dawkins took Jane, Anne and Dora to fish and staid all day. Prince made his appearance this morning from camps, represents himself as being dismissed, says Cudjoe got there on Thursday.[24] I wrote to Mr Taylor and sent some papers to him by Prince. I wrote to Johnny. Cut out two bodies and two pairs of drawers for Dora, and made one body. Wrote some in my diary. We hear of fighting in Virginia and victories on our side in the Mississippi Dept. Carrie finished my dress today, all but sewing on the skirt.

9 May, Mon. Miss Dozier called in the evening, she informs us that one of Mr Ben Dupont's brothers was to be shot or hung for being a traitor. We heard some particulars of the battle in Virginia. General Longstreet severely wounded and other prominent officers

killed and wounded. We have repulsed the enemy. Mr Phelps [Baptist pastor] took tea here and Mr Yulee came after. We conversed of demonology. Carrie got the Commentary to assist us. We also spoke of the existence and manner of the Divine Presence. I am truly of the opinion that the deep things belong unto the Lord our God, save those that are revealed to us and our children. The finite cannot comprehend the infinite. "Keep back thy servant from presumptuous sins." I rode to the stores and purchased some black pins, a tooth brush and some castor oil. One quart of oil cost $30.00 and four rows of pins $1.00.

10 May, Tues. Mr Yulee came over to breakfast and brought me some letters and papers from Mrs Yulee. I left Judge Dawkins at 6 o'clock and arrived home at 6. I found all well at home except Phillis and Eliza, who are still on the sick list, but up. I felt very tired and had a bad headache which kept me awake a long while.

11 May, Wed. Felt feverish and unwell but went over to see Mary and found her better [from bronchitis]. Mary lent me the Al Koran which she had borrowed from Sally Waldo. When I returned home I found six or seven soldiers at our house of Capt Fickling's [?] company, he among them, on their way to Brooksville [forty-five miles west]. They took tea here.

12 May, Thurs. I went over to see Mary. When I returned I found Mr Yulee there, having travelled all night from Gainesville in a panic about his family, having heard the Yankees had burnt Brooksville and were committing other atrocities. [added later:] All false reports gotten up by alarmists. They had taken Tampa [on 6 May] and made some of its most prominent citizens prisoners. Major Snell, a confederate also taken. He was engaged to haul a mill for Mr Taylor from that region, who will now in all probability be defeated in getting it in time for the sugar crop. Mr Taylor and Mr Yulee went to Gov Broome's and to Ocala. We had exciting news from Virginia. Gen Jenkins, a very brave officer from S.C. was among the killed. Johnny was at a military institute under him before the war began. Longstreet severely wounded.

14 May, Sat. Put Nora and Letty to cleaning up the house. Anne coughed last night. I knit on my stocking, cut out one dozen towels, six tablecloths, two pairs of sheets. Finished reading all I desired to read of the Koran.

The "Mr Crane" frequently mentioned in the following entries is Edward Payson Crane, the tutor whose instruction the Yulees had invited Richie and Fen to share with their son. They had originally engaged him sometime in 1863. Crane, age thirty-two, was a Presbyterian minister from the state of New York and a graduate of New York University and Union Theological Seminary in New York City. He had been in Florida since 1857.[25] David Yulee wrote to his wife about Crane: "Besides being very well educated, he is very intelligent & I believe as you say a good man, deserving respect" (29 May 1864). His association with the Taylor family became permanent when he married Lydia Taylor in 1869.

17 May, Tues. Mr Yulee's wagon came with Mr Crane, our boys, and Wickliffe Yulee. Wick came with the fever on him, he looks very badly. We had blackberries for the first time today. I enjoy reading the Scriptures very much. Such works as Swedenburg's & the Koran are calculated to endear the Holy Scriptures to the rational man and true Christian. I cut out the negroes clothes, Richie assisting.

19 May, Thurs. Minty sick. Phillis and Rachel complaining. I gave Wickliffe [castor] oil and turpentine, he is still in bed. I arranged the rooms with Letty and moved the beds to their proper places. Had a bedstead put up in dining room, and Wickliffe put in there. Gave him laudanum at night.

20 May, Fri. Sent for Dr Butt. He came and gave Wick quinine and calomel. His fever rose. I sent for Dr Vogt, fearing he might have convulsions. He administered morphine to him in minute doses which had a happy effect. I spent the day in nursing the sick and household duties. Mr Blunt, a government agent, spent the night here last night. Mary, Mr Bauskett and the children dined here. The rain prevented Mary from going home and she spent the night here with the children. Mr Snell, who was released by

the Yankees, came here today and dined, he gave us an account of his capture at Tampa, and of his release. He described much disturbance in that region.

21 May, Sat. Received a letter from Mrs Yulee saying she would be here tonight. Mrs Yulee's carriage came at night with English servant and three children [Nannie, Maggie, and Flory Yulee]. Mrs Yulee camped out on the road with Mr Yulee.

22 May, Sun. Mr and Mrs Yulee arrived here in time for dinner. A mail was brought. A letter from Carrie to me, 1 from Nellie Jackson, 2 from Johnny to Sue and his father, 2 from Curran to Lyd and Sue, 1 from Miss Cameron to Lyd and some business letters. Johnny left for Virginia on Tuesday.[26] Negroes held meeting at negro house so I did not go to chapel. Mr Crane had small congregation in Ocala.

24 May, Tues. The negroes still sick.[27] Mr Yulee, Mr Crane and myself were again discussing the nature of devils cast out of persons by our Saviour. Mrs Yulee and Lyd chimed in. I received a letter from Carrie by Dr Vogt's boy. Johnston fallen back at or near Atlanta. Johnny's address, Petersburg, Va, Finegan's Brigade.

27 May, Fri. The sick are improving except Dinah who is still quite sick. Dr Butt did not call, it rained hard. I heard that Mary was better and up. I knit some, went to the negro house to stay with Dinah awhile.

28 May, Sat. Cudjoe came home [from the fortifications].

30 May, Mon. I read some letters to Mrs Yulee today of dear Willie's and some about him. Dr Butt called to see Dinah, thought her still quite sick. Mrs Yulee received a letter from Homosassa saying the Yankees had burned the island home, and destroyed or took off the things from there. The negroes, except Tom had all proved loyal and escaped from them. The messenger said they [Yankees] were in a boat pursuing the Yulees.

2 June, Thurs. I went to see Dinah, found her better. We had a mail yesterday, a letter from Johnny, Carrie and Dora [in Gainesville] and one from Mr Behn [agent in Savannah]. Johnny writes

from Columbus [Georgia], called a half hour in Macon. Was detailed to bring on troops from West Florida. Mr Behn sends his accounts, and writes that he had sent Albert [Johnny's servant] on to Macon with Johnny's trunk.

5 June, Sun. Mrs Yulee, Mary Jackson, Susan, Maggie and Nannie Yulee, Fen and Richard went to church in Ocala and heard Mr Jones preach. Dora read to Anne, Jane, and Flory [Yulee] and taught them hymns and Bible lessons. I read the Scriptures. We heard the Yankees had been driven from Camp Milton, and our diminished troops are holding Baldwin. It rains too much for me to go to the chapel, as I had St Anthony's fire [skin inflammation]. Received letters from Johnny written from N Carolina.

6 June, Mon. Mr Yulee went to Ocala this morning and returned with three men to go to Homosassa with him to see to the Yankee doings on the Island.[28] They left here before dinner. Mrs Yulee cut off five pairs of shirts and one odd one, and four towels and put all the girls and children to sewing on them. I assisted in cutting them out and knit on a pair of stockings for Dora. Mr Taylor is troubled with stricture of the chest and shortness of breath, which seems to distress him at night even while asleep. He also has severe pain in his arm and leg which I think is from sleeping in a draught.

9 June, Thurs. The men who went with Mr Yulee to Homosassa returned today and called here. They report the dwelling house burned up and almost everything destroyed on the Island. The plantation has been left unmolested. Mrs Yulee takes her losses with Christian fortitude but mourns the library. A letter from Johnny written at Charlotte, N.C. on the 30th. He had called in Columbia to see Col Bauskett's family.

14 June, Tues. Mr Taylor complains very much of the grass in his cane and the wet weather coming on. Sue is busy making a dress. She seems very unwell. She told me of a very remarkable dream she had, of dear Willie reading to her from a green book.

18 June, Sat. Mary and Anne both took tea here last evening. They send the children over frequently.[29] Nannie Yulee is looking much better. I knit and attended to household affairs. The post boy rode

up and gave us some news from below. Some runaways were taken with a boat of Mr Yulees and some things from the place. Marve Edwards headed the expedition, and Madge, a blockade runner, had bought their things from the conspirators who had stolen them. Mrs Yulee had a letter from Mr Crane.[30] He is anxious what are to be the future arrangements, and his own part in the play.

19 June, Sat. Abram returned early this morning from the batteries, discharged from further duties. He brought a letter from Mrs Bauskett to Mr B, and one from Carrie to me, containing a letter written to her at Johnny's request from Fernandez, to say that he was then well & too busy at the breastworks fighting [at Petersburg, Va.] to write himself. Albert was well and acting as nurse in hospital.

21 June, Tues. Mary and Mr Bauskett, Anne Maxcy and her children came here to dine today. Mr Yulee rode in to Ocala and engaged a hack to assist in taking his family to Gainesville. All of the young people have been engaged in learning to play and playing chess. I put on stocking for Jane and knit it, and one for Dora for her to knit. Mr Taylor seemed fretted that he cannot work his cane for the wetness of the land, and that his corn is much eaten by the squirrels. I opened Fenwick's boil at night, it is a very large and painful one. He seemed relieved and slept. Sue was sick. She took blue pills and oil.

22 June, Wed. Whilst I was preparing a lunch for Mrs Yulee, a buggy came up with Mrs McNeal and her two children. She wanted breakfast, and her buggy fixed and her horse rested, all of which she secured and also got a bushel of corn. She is just from Marietta where she went to see her son in the first Fla Cavalry. Her husband fell at the Battle of Olustee. Mrs Yulee and all the family left here this morning except Wick, who was quite sick with an affection of the bowels. Mrs Yulee was much affected at leaving and all the children were sorry to go.[31]

23 June, Thurs. After my every day exercises of reading the Scriptures, I attended to household duties. Put some beans, cucumbers, and young corn with onions in salt for pickles. Dr Moody drove

Mr Delorme up here, a young man just from Sumter [South Caro-
lina] come on for Nelly and Mary, sent out for by Mr Jackson for
them.[32] All the girls rode to pick berries with Mr Delorme, Wick
and Richard. Old Mary finished her soap. I went to the negro
house to see Phillis and Nancy, who are both quite sick. Mr
Delorme brought me a letter from Eliza Jane Baker [sister-in-
law]. She writes very affectionately and feelingly of dear Tom.[33]
Says that he was delighted with dear Willie, and thought him a
noble, splendid looking man, and that he was so gentle and tender
in his manner. She invites Lyd [Taylor] to go and live with her.

25 June, Sat. I wrote to Carrie, Eliza Jane Baker, and Mary Jackson [sister]. Attended to household duties, commenced letter to
Johnny. Had keg filled with sugar and put up some arrowroot for
E.J. Baker.[34] Had candy made and put up for Mary's children,
Richard's and Gule's children. I put up dresses for Rachel, Rosa,
Guly Baker and Charlotte Furman. Arrowroot for Sister Lydia,
and dear Willie's woolen gloves for Uncle Samuel [Furman], a
handkerchief for Daphne [servant] and some spices for Mary. The
girls expect to leave tomorrow to be in time for the cars on Tues-
day. Anne Maxcy came over with the children and took tea here.
Mr Yulee's wagons with negroes came up here. We gave Mom
Cicely and some of them dinner and vegetables. Mary and Mr B
came by here to take tea. We received a mail, a letter from Johnny,
Uncle Samuel [Furman], Major Behn and Curran Broome. Uncle
Samuel's is one of sympathy and expresses much admiration of
dear Willie's character. Johnny writes he has been in considerable
fighting, and has had five bullets to pass through his clothes and
blankets.

28 June, Tues. Mr Taylor complains of oppression of the chest and
drowsiness. I put Lydia and Sue to finishing off stockings which
Mary and Nellie left unfinished for the boys. Set Jane and Anne to
fixing calico shirts for Johnny. Mr Johnson and Mr Ives called,
reported Captain Dickerson had again captured 16 deserters. This
is his fifth capture.

29 June, Wed. Rode to the plantation with Mr Taylor to get vegetables and cucumbers for pickling. Mr Crane and Richard came

[from Gainesville] after we had returned. Mr Crane will remain with us we hope for the remainder of the year.

1 July, Fri. Mr Crane commenced teaching the children. Anne, Jane and Dora went to him, with Fenwick and Richard. Wickliffe Yulee will not start at present on account of his health.

4 July, Mon. I put Letty to washing up the things on Saturday as she had been sick several days, and put Milton to scouring. Gave Minty pants to hem for Johnny and jackets to fix. Anne and Lydia took a shirt to make for Johnny. The children all went to school today [Crane's tutoring]. The boys remained in late as their lessons were not perfect. Jane offered Mr Crane some calico shirts. She seems delighted to have an opportunity to study. We are getting a few melons. I did a little mending, ripped and fixed the shirts and knit. Tamar came in sick. Nora still sick, gave her calomel.

5 July, Tues. Susan cupped Nora and Tamar who are still sick. All the children attended school. Mr Crane seems always ready to explain Scripture in a modest manner. We offered him to take Willie Forward to stay with us for him to teach, which seemed to gratify him over much. He wrote immediately to Judge Forward respecting it. I bottled off some wine. Sue has had a violent headache all day and seems much depressed.[35]

6 July, Wed. The boys had good lessons yesterday, and Mr Crane got through with them earlier. I hope the boys and he may prove blessings to each other, also Dora, Anne and Jane. Dr Moody came up here at night to tell of a report that the deserters and Yankees were coming down the Withlacoochie. He went off to see into truth of it, but returned after we had retired to say there was no truth in it. Mr Taylor and the boys soon had the guns loaded up. Jane and Anne [ten and eight years] seemed much frightened. Anne wished the Yankees were all wounded to make them sorry enough to stop. Jane wanted to know if they knew God.

8 July, Fri. Mary sent me word that Lena [Bauskett, six years] was very sick. I went over after dinner with Anne Maxcy. Mrs Crutchfield was there and gave us some news of the 4th Fla regt killed.

Finegan's brigade reported as having acted a conspicuous part in repulsing the enemy in the first attempt on the Weldon Road,[36] capturing 400 prisoners and driving off the enemy. I saw some soldiers near the pond and invited them to supper, but they declined. Mr Crane commenced fixing and tuning the piano.

9 July, Sat. Set Patsey yesterday to waking up the family by ringing bell at sunrise. The family have been up earlier in consequence. Sue had a letter from Curran, she writes that she thought Johnny converted.[37] I truly hope that my dear, dear Willie though dead, will continue to speak to us all of the great importance of the preparation for that City whose builder and maker is God. Johnny's letter received was dated on the 17th. We have heard of him up to the 22nd.

10 July, Sun. Mr Crane preached at the chapel. Mr Williams and part of his family and a number of others came to hear him. In the afternoon he preached from the prayer of the leper "Lord, if thou wilt, thou canst make me clean." The house was pretty full of negroes and whites. Fen and Richard got their Bible lessons. I heard Jane and Anne their hymns. Old Mom Nelly came here to ask the news from her mistress and to attend church.

11 July, Mon. Sent for to see Tommy [Bauskett, two years] this morning by Mr Bauskett. Found him ill, he had convulsions and Dr Butt remained with them all day. I paid him three visits, dined and staid all night with him. We heard today that Petersburg was taken by the enemy, and Johnston had fallen back to Chattahoochie. Also that Beauregard with a large body of cavalry were on Arlington Heights expecting to take Washington.[38] Dr Butt called to see Nora, thought her pretty sick.

16 July, Sat. Richard and Mr Crane left for Gainesville [for a Presbyterian conference]. I set Mom Mary to boiling soap and Robin to making castor oil. I feel very unwell today. Nora, Peter, Cudjoe sick. Old Phillis made her way up here. I set Judy to spinning wool today.

19 July, Tues. Susan is teaching the children during Mr Crane's absence. I had blackberry wine and jelly made today and stewed

peaches, the first of the season. Last Sat I received a letter from Johnny, and one from Curran containing one of his. He came near being captured, was one of those who drove back the Raiders from the Petersburg and Weldon R.R.

20 July, Wed. Col Snell called up here with a telegram. Our troops in Maryland doing damage to the R.R.s and Canals, threatening Baltimore and Washington. In the evening Mr Crane and Richard returned home in Mr Dawkins carriage. They could not get off on the R.R., a part of it having been burnt by the enemy. They brought me a letter from Carrie inviting Lydia to go to Gainesville. They also brought a telegram. Our troops had had a battle and were retreating from Washington. Nora was very ill yesterday and we sent for Dr Butt, he staid here last night and left her better this morning. He pronounced that she is threatened with abortion.

23 July, Sat. We feel deeply anxious respecting the armies. Mr Betts called here to beg supplies for the hospital at Madison, Ga. We sent in to him today a barrel of molasses, 30 lbs sugar, 2 lbs soda, 2 pillow slips, 1 bottle of wine, 1 of catsup.

26 July, Tues. I finished reading the papers today, and read some in Harpers. Had plum preserves and jelly made, and put the mash with syrup to ferment. I felt very very sad today, and gave vent to a long fit of crying, when thinking of my dear precious Willie, and how much more I might have done to make him happy and good while he tarried with us here. Dear, noble boy, may your virtues only live in the future. I wrote to Lydia and attended to the sick.

28 July, Thurs. Dr Moody called up just as we were going to breakfast, to notify us that the volunteer troops are called to meet the enemy on the way to Lake City.[39] I gave Sue calomel this morning and several doses to the negroes. Got Robin to making hand barrows for drying peaches on. I cut up peaches today until dinner and engaged fully in household matters. Mr Taylor went to Ocala to see what was to be done by the company which he sent his name in to—he thought the orders exceedingly impractical and advised others.

29 July, Fri. Spent the morning with several of the servants assisting in cutting peaches. Susan was exceedingly ill today with congestive chill. Her chest very much affected and she was threatened with convulsions. We used prompt remedies, sent for Dr Vogt who came immediately and administered calomel and morphine. I slept with Sue at night. She seems to have very little desire to live since our dear Willie's death.

30 July, Sat. Dr Todd called on his way to join the troops at Ocala with three days rations. Gov Broome wrote to Mr Taylor to say the company was ordered to leave tomorrow morning at 4 o'clock. I had haversacks made for Richard and Mr Crane, wallets, etc, and had rations for some days cooked for them, all after night as the messenger did not come until sunset. I gave Mr Crane dear Willie's jacket.

31 July, Sun. This morning is exactly six months since my darling boy fell asleep so calmly but so suddenly to me. Lord! Give me all gracious feelings concerning this terrible event. His [God's] providence ripens fast, unfolding every hour. I can already record many events which would have been very, very trying to him [Willie].

Not a fortnight after his death, our State was invaded and many fled in terror to seek homes elsewhere, while all felt there was no security from the foe. The battle of Olustee was fought in which his brother John took a part, and since then the foe has been in Marietta, and despoiled that beautiful town, burning to the ground the Institute buildings in which he was acquiring military and scientific training, for further usefulness to his country, which he longed to serve.

God had higher work for my dear boy I must feel assured, and took him from all these trials to act in another sphere, more adapted to his pure nature. Now we are again invaded and this morning my dear Richard has left us to go and assist in repelling the enemy which again threatens us at many points in the state. God only knows what is before us. A dark hour seems to have come, and in God only is our trust as there are scarcely any troops left in the State to defend us. Richard is only 16, his teacher accompanies him, both of them prepared to fight. I do trust I have not seen his face for the last time. He is a brave good boy and will do his duty.

I will now close this book as a diary, and not encroach any further upon its pages, which I value for the items here recorded by my beloved Willie, and the writings he has left in it. He tried to get a diary and blank books on his way from Marietta, and failing to do so requested me to use this book "and tear out the scribblings," which I rejoice that I did not permit him to do. He gave me another book containing his French exercises, which he said I could use if he did not return to Marietta. His wishes I regard as sacred, and will delight to use the book, as I have done this one, feeling that he still contributes to my wants, as it gave him pleasure to do in life. Oh! How precious is the knowledge that the <u>love</u> of Jesus is <u>stronger</u> than a <u>mother's</u> love. How delightful the thought, that amongst his chosen one—"sought out"—and safely housed,[40] is my own beloved, gentle, beautiful Willie.

Richie Taylor and Edward Crane were mustered into Captain E. D. Howse's company of the Home Guard. They took part in the only military action anywhere near Osceola at this time, a skirmish in Gainesville on 17 August in which 175 Confederates routed a slightly larger Federal contingent.[41] This is the only Civil War service recorded for Richie.[42] Fen Taylor at age fifteen was also a participant,[43] so evidently he left Osceola for Gainesville shortly after Richie did. Both boys would have fallen under the 1864 Florida law declaring all white males ages fifteen to fifty-five not already in the army to be members of the state militia and subject to call. No further military service for the boys is recorded; they evidently returned home for the remaining nine months of the war. As for Johnny, after the close of Maria's 1864 diary he was hospitalized in Richmond on 30 August, married Curran Broome on 15 September, and was furloughed home on 26 September. He returned to his post in Virginia late in February 1865 and was present at the Confederate surrender at Appomattox on 9 April 1865, which ended the Civil War.[44]

SIX

Education of the Children, 1864–73

After the war ended in April 1865, the education of the youngest Taylor children remained a pressing concern for Maria and John. Jane having died in December 1864 at age ten, there now remained the teenagers Richard, Fenwick, and Dore, along with Anne, who was six years younger than Dore. In addition, Johnny, now a married man, was back on the scene, his religious education, in his mother's opinion, still not completed. The diaries for 1865, 1866, 1868, 1869, and 1872 are missing, but letters of 1866, the 1867 diary, family letters from that year, the diaries for 1870, 1871, and 1873, and letters from 1872 and 1873 bring to a close Maria's account of the education of these children. For the most part, the children as teenagers were attending school away from home, and some of the education-related material consists of brief and scattered notations of their arrivals and departures. To build a coherent picture from this type of information, much of the presentation will consist of editorial narrative that weaves these bits together, supplemented by information from other sources about the schools Maria mentions. More-continuous diary and letter passages are presented in the usual form.

It is certain that Fen attended the East Florida Seminary after being tutored by Edward Crane;[1] because he and Richard were treated as a pair, it is likely that Richard also attended this school. The East Florida Seminary was one of two schools established by the state school law of 1851 for the training of teachers. Located in Ocala until it moved to Gainesville after the Civil War, the seminary had to close in the early years of the war because it lost teachers and students but then reopened in the fall of 1864.[2] Thus the boys probably attended the seminary in Ocala for a little more than a year, from the fall of 1864 after returning from the Gainesville skirmish they fought in to the end of 1865. The state law had mandated an ambitious curriculum, but the school itself was a modest undertaking on the high-school level.

The Taylors must have wanted something better, and on 7 February 1866, only ten months after the war ended in April 1865, Maria was writing to Ann Furman that "Richard & Fenwick left here ten days ago with their father for Virginia on their way to Genl Lee's School. Mr Taylor did not expect to go any farther than Savannah." On 13 February she wrote Ann, "Mr Taylor arrived last night, having sent the boys off to Lexington in company of Mr Orf a merchant of Savannah." Apparently, then, the boys at ages eighteen and seventeen were to attend Washington College (later Washington and Lee University) in Lexington, where Robert E. Lee, the great Confederate commander, was now president. However, a letter from Richard to his mother only two months later places the boys at the Maryland Military Institute in Baltimore.[3]

23 April 1866. Richard Furman Baker Taylor to Maria Baker Taylor

My Dear Mother, I received yours of the 3rd on last Thursday, containing advice on how I ought to behave. I have been trying to follow all of the advice you gave me before I left home & I will continue in doing so. I have made considerable advancement in my studies since I came here. We have left the class that we went into, when we came we were a little behind it.

We had quite an excitement here on last fryday evening. We were just about to commence drilling, when one of the boys on line was ordered to button up his coat, by one of the officers. The boy steped out of the line & struck the officer five or six blows. The officer drew his sword and cut him very badly over the eye, and cut his arm to the bone. The boy was sent home the next day, nothing was done to the officer as he was perfectly right in doing what he did.

Did you get a copy of the rules of this school? I sent you one. If you did, don't think that I will be late every morning, at revilee, we get up now at 5 oclock I have not been late once since I have been here. In fact I have not but three dimerits that I know of. They read out the reports every fryday evening & they have not read out but one for me. That was for lying on the bed. Since I got those three, I keep clear of the bed. Fenny is well and sends much love to all, give my love to all, kiss Annie for me and believe me dear Mother to be as ever your affectionate son R.B. Taylor

In her 1867 diary, Maria notes on 9 February that "Richard's and Fenwick's reports came," and on 18 March that they "had just arrived from Maryland, the school broken up." Thus the boys attended the institute for only the one year, February 1866 through February 1867.[4]

The rest of the 1867 diary shows Richard, now nineteen, working on the plantation but still in some ways under his mother's tutelage, for she tersely notes on 11 August, "Reprimanded the Richards [son and visiting nephew] for incorrectness of speech." Some effort was made to improve Richard's position, for on 12 November Maria records that "Mr Taylor wrote to Mr Johns Hopkins of Baltimore respecting a place for Richard." However, there is no record of an outcome to this appeal to the influential financier and railroad entrepreneur,[5] and the 1870 diary finds Richard still laboring on the plantation, as he continued to do for some years.

Fenwick's case was different. His mother had earlier noted his "serious mind," and in June 1867 at age eighteen he continued his education in the form of reading law with his brother-in-law James Dawkins while living with James and Carrie in Gainesville. On 22 March 1870, Maria remarks briefly, "Fenwick was admitted to the practice of law today. He was 21 the 10th of this month." Fen then entered into partnership with James, his practice thrived, and two years later he was able marry Amelia Evans Haile of Kanahapa plantation near Gainesville.

In 1864 Dore (earlier "Dora") at age fourteen had been sent to Gainesville to live with and be taught by her sister Carrie Dawkins, but by early 1866 she was attending the Gainesville Academy (soon to become the East Florida Seminary), then the only private school in Gainesville for whites.[6] The school must have been a relaxed affair, for Dore was back home 15–27 March, again 4–15 May, and school let out the middle of June. Dore did not return in the fall of 1867. Thus after three years in Gainesville, her formal education ended in June 1867 at age seventeen. Dore had also studied piano, as had all the daughters, and Maria considered her the most talented. Of Dore's repertoire, Maria mentions only that she played Haydn.

Dore returned home in July and soon her domestic education was continuing under the demanding supervision of her mother, who commented on 22 December, "I had occasion to reprimand Dore for unwillingness to comply with my requirements." After several years of domestic life on the plantation, Dore had a socially and intellectually enriching experience that may be counted as an extension of her education. At age twenty-one through twenty-two, she spent the year October 1872 through October 1873 in Pittsburgh, Pennsylvania, with her sister Lydia and brother-in-law Edward P. Crane, the Presbyterian minister who had tutored the Taylor children in the 1860s. Edward and Lydia had married in July 1869, and Edward was now a professor at Western University (later the University of Pittsburgh). With the Cranes, Dore enjoyed the advantage of a milieu that was considerably more sophisticated than any she had yet encountered, and she attended lectures, concerts, and academic social gatherings. The atmosphere of the household itself was intensely Baptist, Edward's denomination notwithstanding, and Dore was baptized in one of the Pittsburgh Baptist churches amid "exercises, sermons & hymns."

In a letter to Maria from Pittsburgh, Dore gives a lively exhibition of the Baptist education that her mother and older sisters had imparted.

11 June 1873. Dore Taylor to Maria Baker Taylor

Yesterday a young lady who is a baptist came to see me. She boards with her aunt, who has a large family; and as they are all presbyterians, poor Sallie has a hard time of it to keep up her baptist principles. After sitting awhile she said "Dorie I wish you could have been at the presbyterian church on Sunday. I heard a sermon that was pretty hard on the baptists, and it rather convinced me." I said very well Sallie lets hear some of those convincing arguments that the young brother used. [Sallie presents his arguments.] I said well if sprinkling is for circumcision what is for baptism, both was done to Christ. Lets read the fifth chapter of Galatians. I think Paul tells us we are released from that bondage and if we do not accept freedom from all of those laws laid upon the jews, we cannot accept it from any. We read the chapter together and she seemed quite satisfied on that point and said she did not know there was anything in the New T. Well, said Sallie, "Dorie you are cute [acute]. I am a strong baptist and I'll remember all that & not let my head get turned again."

I have a class of boys in the Sabbath School, young gentlemen, I presume they consider themselves, from the frequent twist their fingers give toward the direction of their mouths. I was not atall pleased with the way they prepared their lessons, so I told them a few Sundays ago that really their lessons did not do justice to their moustaches. I wish you could have seen the mingled look of amusement and provocation which they all put on. However they prepared their lessons better afterwards.

Dore returned home by way of New York City, where her brothers John and Richard had entered commercial life, and she remained at Osceola in a domestic capacity until her marriage in April 1874 to William Christian Wallace.[7]

Just as Maria witnessed the triumph of the Baptist education of her daughter Mary after Mary was married, so her efforts with her son John came to fruition when he was a married man. In 1870 Johnny, now twenty-eight, was living next door to Osceola with his wife, Curran, and their small child, having bought the Bausketts' place in 1867. In spite of a lifetime of religious instruction, Johnny had not yet confessed his faith. But now in 1870 Maria's hopes were raised and she applied herself anew, and with ups and downs, to his religious education.

13 May, Wed. Johnny came home to supper. I had a long talk with him about baptism & church membership as he expressed the desire to be united to the church. I told him I thought according to

the Commission that teaching should go before baptism. "Go teach all nations baptizing them."

24 May, Tues. I finished letter [on religion] to Curran. Johnny came here & I read it to him & talked to him about the church & his committing himself to it.

25 May, Wed. Johnny called, Mr Taylor & I conversed with him on the subject of communion & Baptist Church Government.

27 May, Fri. Johnny called over this morning. He spoke to me about joining the Baptist Church, thinks them too illiberal for him to join them. Perhaps if I had had less of false liberality I would have seen him more decided in the <u>faith</u> of the <u>Bible</u>. <u>Good</u> should not be called <u>evil</u> nor <u>evil good</u>, nor should error ever be justified for the sake of being liberal. True <u>charity</u> embraces <u>truth</u>.[8]

Maria probably said something to this effect directly to Johnny and got him back on track.

30 May, Mon. Mr Bishop[9] returned early in the evening. Johnny took tea here & we all had a conversation on the subject of baptism & church membership. Mr Bishop proposed to baptize John on the 4th Sunday in June & he promised to think of it.

11 June, Sat. Johnny informed me yesterday that he had made up his mind to be baptized when Mr Bishop came here on the 4th. He had written to Mr Crane of his intention & received advice from him not to join the Presbyterian church as he did not believe in infant sprinkling. I feel greatly rejoiced that he has determined to put on Christ & try & come out from the world & serve the Lord.

12 June, Sun. Johnny notified me of his desire that I should write to Mr Bishop to come prepared to baptize him. We all sat up pretty late at night, Johnny, Richard, Fen seemed to enjoy each others company, & Mr Taylor seemed happy with them. I read a part of a sermon to John & Mr Taylor & prayed our Father to make me more effective in His work.

26 June, Sun. We rose early this morning & made all necessary preparation for attending church. We called at Scott Spring, all

the family except Richard, who felt sick, & witnessed the baptism
of our son John, Mr Bishop officiating. Sue Waldo, Alby[10] were
the only white persons except the family present. Some negroes,
Samuel, Mannie, Druscilla & a few others. After the ordinance we
went on to church & Mr Bishop preached & the Lord's Supper was
administered. In giving the right hand of fellowship he made a
very touching address to Johnny. Mr Bishop went home with us
and preached in the evening. Who is he that overcometh the world
be he who believeth that Jesus is the Son of God.

Johnny left four days later to join his wife and baby in New York
City. The young Taylors were in debt to Curran's uncle, former
Florida governor James E. Broome, and part of the repayment was
for Curran and her sister Julia to run a boarding house he owned in
New York City. Curran and the baby had already left, and Johnny
was in effect joining them to seek his fortune, anchored by his wife's
job. Maria took comfort in his new status as a baptized Christian.

> 30 June, Fri. It filled me with sadness to see John leave us for a new
> home, but I pray God to uphold & keep him from all evil, to direct
> all his way & bless & prosper. We have nothing to give him but a
> blessing. We rejoice he has a wise, powerful & loving Father to
> supply his need & make his way prosperous.

Anne, the youngest child by six years, was educated at home
through age fourteen. Maria writes little of her teaching of this lone
pupil, but her perspective is clear: "I spoke with Anne of the blessings
of letters, printing & other discoveries & inventions, & all from God
who gave man the skill & wisdom to invent & execute for the good of
others."

Late in August 1870, Anne at age fourteen went to Gainesville to
live with Carrie and James Dawkins and attend school, the fourth of
the younger Taylor children given this advantage by the childless
couple. Anne entered the school of Miss A. M. M. Clarke, which
advertized itself as an institution "for young ladies and children
where all the acquirements of a polite and finished education may be
obtained." The school, which had opened in 1866 or 1867, was one of
the first three private schools in Gainesville. Maria paid tuition of $25

per one-half quarter. Anne completed the 1870–71 school year in June, with Richard, Fenwick, and Dore attending her final examination, such occasions being public events at the time. On 26 June Maria noted simply that Anne "took the 1st prize at the examination."

In September 1871 Anne returned to Gainesville with the Dawkinses, who had spent much of the summer at Osceola. Carrie had been sick during that time, and Maria was uneasy about the whole group. As it developed, the situation all fall was not conducive to Anne's studies.

> 22 Sept., Fri. I regretted to see Carrie, Mr Dawkins, Anne & Sophie[11] leave this morning. Carrie seems better but I fear not strong enough to travel. Anne is complaining & I fear she will be sick.

> 8 Nov., Wed. [In Ocala Richie] heard that the yellow fever was back in Gainesville & Mr Taylor is minded to send for Anne & Sophie. Richie said he would go.

> 9 Nov., Thurs. Wrote to Carrie urging her to come stay with us until the danger from Yellow fever is over. Richard left here for Anne & Sophie after dinner, expecting to get a buggy in Ocala & go part of the way to Gainesville tonight. I sent letter to Carrie by him & Mr Taylor one to Mr Dawkins urging him to come with Carrie.

> 13 Nov., Mon. Richie came at night with Sophie. Carrie was too ill for Anne to leave her.

> 17 Nov., Fri. I feel very uneasy about my children, Carrie, Mary, Fen & Anne. How much I wish I could be with them all & help them.

Fen, also living in Gainesville with the Dawkinses, was equally in danger of contracting the fever. As for Maria's concern over Mary,[12] this daughter had borne twins earlier in the year; one had already died, and the other was now very ill and was expected to die. But Maria was kept from "them all" by her husband's serious illness and by other illness at Osceola. With these family crises on her mind and having to nurse Carrie, Anne must have found it difficult to concentrate on her studies.

A little later in 1871, Maria made a comment that implies some of the values she wanted to instill in Anne and that were perhaps already evident in the young girl: "I read in Anne's book 'Home Sunshine.' The sentiments expressed throughout I entirely accord with, it is the spirit of true piety manifested in action, & Mr. and Mrs. Gordon were represented as possessing strong minds & good sound sense" (3 December).

Anne did not return to Osceola for Christmas, remaining in Gainesville to take care of Carrie, who was again ill. However, in December 1871 Maria met at Osceola a new member of the Dawkins household, the man Anne was to marry, Julius Addison Carlisle. Julius's background was similar to Anne's: a large plantation, devout (if Methodist) parents, and many siblings. In 1863 at age seventeen, Julius had enlisted in the Confederate Army while a first-year cadet at the Citadel, where he had quickly distinguished himself by placing last of the whole student body in conduct. He had just arrived in Gainesville upon jumping bail and fleeing his home in the Goshen Hill section of Union County, South Carolina, also James Dawkins's original home. Julius was among 200 Ku Klux Klan members arrested when the writ of habeas corpus was suspended in Union County on 10 November, after months of unrest following two Klan raids on the Union jail in January 1871 that resulted in the lynchings of ten black militiamen accused of killing a white man.[13]

On 20 December Maria writes of Julius's first appearance at Osceola: "Fenwick came from Gainesville after we had dined & we got dinner for them. He brought Mr Carlisle with him from Union SC. After dinner they went to the sugar house & did not return until after we had retired." For the next two days she pointedly mentions that Richie, Fen, and "Mr Carlisle" came home too late for dinner, and the 23 and 24 December entries have been removed from the diary.

In a letter to Ann Furman, Maria indicates that in January 1872 Anne was still at school in Gainesville. However, John Taylor died on 13 March,[14] and Anne arrived home too late to see her father alive. Even if she returned to Gainesville to finish the 1871–72 school year,

Anne cannot have profited much from her schooling, beset as she was by the yellow fever epidemic, Carrie's illnesses, her father's death, and the distraction provided by Julius.

On 1 September 1872 Anne left home "to be in time for her school." At some point Anne changed schools, from Miss Clarke's to what Maria calls "the Gainesville School" or the "High School." This was probably the East Florida Seminary rather than the public school, for at this time the Gainesville public schools used pro-Union textbooks and were controlled by boards that included black members,[15] conditions that Maria would have found unacceptable. Anne graduated the following spring.

12 June 1873. Maria Baker Taylor to Ann Eliza Furman

> Anne brought her diploma from Gainesville & did not get the measles before the examination as I feared she would. She graduated at the Gainesville School in June. She was Queen of May, by unanimous vote. Millie [Fen's wife] wrote me that she looked so queenlike & performed so splendidly & gracefully that she felt like applauding her & that Fen said he felt proud of his young sister. It is the second time she has been elected Queen, and her mother thinks her a very sweet girl.

In Maria's Baptist view, Anne had graduated just in time. Here Maria is speaking of her trip home from a visit to her daughter Mary in St Augustine.

21 August 1873. Maria Baker Taylor to Ann Eliza Furman

> We had a pretty Nun on board, not so revoltingly dressed as those in Augustine, for hot weather; she was from the West, & laughed, & talked merrily with the Capt. We also had Mr and Mrs Meany on board, a ritualistic clergyman, educated at Oxford, England. I heard him preach the Sunday before, in the Episcopal Church, in St Augustine. To be honest, he should have preached in a Catholic pulpit. He is pastor of the church here, in Gainesville, & elected to be the Principal of the High School here next session. I am glad Anne has graduated.

Anne was at school in Gainesville for a total of three years, finishing at age seventeen. Unlike Dore, she had no further enriching experiences to extend her education. At age eighteen and one year out of high school, Anne married Julius Addison Carlisle in August 1874.

SEVEN

The Taylors and the Freedmen

A letter from 1866, the first post-war document from Maria's hand, suggests something of the Taylors' attitudes and situation just ten months after the Civil War ended.

7–8 February 1866. Maria Baker Taylor to James Clement Furman

We have heard with sadness of the condition of our native state & of how she has been spoiled by the ruthless hand of the Invader & we are truly glad that so many of whom we were so anxious have fared so well while others have met with insult & poverty. Mr Taylor heard that Mr Benjamin Bostick was reduced to absolute want, was living in his wash house & suffering for the absolute necessaries of life.[1] The whole of the Robertville & Pipe Creek country has been desolated. God has been truly good to us, & except from the emancipation act we have met with no property losses to speak of except some $60,000 or $70,000 in confederate money. We continue our old occupation [farming]. Mr Taylor has organized a strong force & is much more hopeful of free labor than he was a short time ago.

Respecting the state of our church here, [it] is at present without a pastor & principally given up to the freedmen for preaching purposes. I was in hopes Mr Taylor would have been able to make some estimate of what the church could offer a pastor, but he seems to think the income from free negro labor is so uncertain that he cannot tell what to promise & he is almost the only member, who gives anything at all. He will see some of the members in a few days & try & ascertain what can be done.

The 1867 diary,[2] the next post-war document, will serve to illustrate race relations at Osceola under Reconstruction (1865–77) just as the 1857 diary served that purpose for antebellum times. The abolition of slavery had not diminished the number of black people Maria was now dealing with: she names fifty-eight freedmen in her 1867 diary alone, whereas her combined records for 1857 through 1864 mention fifty-one slaves.[3] Obviously, the Taylors' economic base remained the labor of the many black people at Osceola, but of course the new dispensation brought about an unsettled and worrisome situation for all, on both the household and plantation levels.

In 1867 the Osceola household consisted of John and Maria, now fifty-seven and fifty-three, and six of their children: two unmarried adult daughters, Lydia, twenty-seven, and Susan, twenty-three; two sons, Richard, twenty, and Fenwick, eighteen; and two younger daughters, Dore, seventeen, and Anne, eleven. John, twenty-five, and his young family lived on the adjoining farm, which he had bought from the Bausketts.[4] Also on the scene was Major Remley, the Freedmen's Bureau agent, who was very friendly with the Taylors. They frequently turned to him because the regulation of black labor and the administration of justice in cases involving negroes were among his duties.[5] Apart from family members and Remley, all other persons referred to in the following excerpts from the 1867 diary are freedmen (some mentioned with last names) unless otherwise indicated.

1867

[From the opening prayer] My most ardent desires for the year are, that God would vouchsafe to this family an abundant supply of spiritual blessings in converting grace, and communion with Him, who is the author of our salvation, that we be guided into all truth and in the faithful and wise discharge of all our duties, that we may provide things honestly in the light of all men, and abound in grace to others. . . . We would like to discharge all the relative duties of life faithfully, with a proper appreciation of them, neither giving an undue value to them, nor under rating them. We would enjoy truly and wisely, as the gifts and blessings of God, our personal relations, and the comforts which surround us, submitting ourselves and them to His disposal.

5 Feb., Tues. Johnny came home and brought two negroes [from South Carolina].

6 Feb., Wed. Birch returned with 9 negros and more to come.

7 Feb., Thurs. Mr Taylor discharged Tom Johnson today for refusing to split rails.

8 Feb., Fri. The wagon went to the Springs for Richard's trunk, and for some of the other laborers. Mr Taylor sent Prince with John Dawkins to bring some negroes from Indian River.

9 Feb., Sat. Finished a coat I have been making for several days for Gilbert Patience, also finished his pants. Andrew, who was hired the first of the month, seems to show no disposition to attend to his business. I had to do it for him today.

11 Feb., Mon. I hired Grant today to attend to my garden and other matters. I am having the cabins fixed up.

13 Feb., Wed. I attended to the garden and had some soap looked after. Had some pickle boiled [by Grant] and put on beef that was boiled yesterday. Some negros came from Charleston for Johnny. Prince Williams came and his set. Nora sick, attended to her and gave her opium.

14 Feb., Thurs. I discharged Andrew today. He is habitually so very idle. Had the garden ploughed and Irish potatos dug, and planted over. Finished off the soap. Johnny got Lee Wallace [nephew] to go to Gainesville with a telegram to stop forty negroes he hears are coming on to him for work.

16 Feb., Sat. Andrew came in with his foot sprained. He was impudent and Johnny discharged him before the day closed. I was busy with the garden planting Irish potatoes. Grant butchered a pig for me on trial and told me of his engagement with Affy.

18 Feb., Mon. Robin fixed the gin for ginning short cotton. Had rice beaten and various matters attended to. The wagon came from Smyrna with fifteen grown negroes, besides children. John Dawkins and the two others that left did not return.

20 Feb., Wed. Mr Taylor seems very uneasy about the provision question. Corn very scarce, he fears we will not be able to feed all the hands he has. Gave Affy and Grant a talk about their intended marriage, and my conditions of receiving her in the yard again. I gave Grant some clothes to be married in.

23 Feb., Sat. I ascertained 25 pounds of coffee stolen.

27 Feb., Wed. I offered to give Louisa washing. She seems fearful that she will not be able to do it and went to her uncles. I am more than willing she declined as my obligations end. I had sweet potatoes planted yesterday. I walked to the negro house and church to see sick negroes, engaged Josephine Cannon to do my washing for me.

2 Mar., Sat. The goods [from Savannah] were opened and the negroes came up to get some clothes.

4 Mar., Mon. Grant commenced smoking the meat, he worked a while in the garden. I had the table mended and the room fixed with lock. Rachel came yesterday and looks badly, she is here today, and says she has gone into her new house near Ocala. Spent the afternoon waiting on the free darkies[6]—their wants are innumerable.

7 Mar., Thurs. Engaged in attending to sick negroes. The servants about the yard annoy me very much with stealing articles of clothing, silver, crockery and food, I presume to supply those who have set up for themselves.

9 Mar., Sat. Dinah came here today and talked about Samuel's accusations & his preaching. Old Mary came by here sick and had her cupped.

13 Mar., Wed. Old Mary left here after receiving her donations. She looks quite used up & but for her pride would desire to return to us. Heard bad accounts of Patience and Joe Morgan. Talked to Old Affy and Grant about removal if they failed to comply with contract.

17 Mar., Mon. Affy came in to say she would come in tomorrow if she was well enough. Sukey came after dinner to hire to me. She works very well by the day for 37-½ cts.

23 Mar., Sat. Patience is worried with charges of purloining the keys for Joe Morgan by the negroes.

25 Mar., Mon. Affy came in today to say she was ready to work. Mr Taylor fixed a trap for the rogues [thieves] in the store room. The boys, Richard B and Lee [visiting nephews] helped Birch shingle to get him to make a ploughstock for them.

28 Mar., Thurs. Thomas finished my closet and put up the stove, Birch assisting him. I was busy most of the day in directing them about these matters. Gave Sarah washing. Had light bread made and assisted with cakes and some other eatables for the picnic. Several of the little children sick among the blacks. The boys went to hunt with Birch.

1 Apr., Mon. Birch brought me a fine wild turkey which I had roasted in the stove. Grant seems very idle and negligent of his business. Josephine came up and declined washing any longer for me. Some of the negroes who desired her place had told her some falsehoods, about my being dis-satisfied. I accepted her quit.

Noteworthy in the April part of the diary is the absence of any mention of the occupation of Florida by Union troops that began on 1 April in anticipation of the declaration of martial law on 8 April. The Reconstruction Act of 2 March 1867, passed after every southern state except Tennessee refused to ratify the Fourteenth Amendment, divided the South into five military districts with supreme authority invested in the army commander. This situation evidently had no immediate effect on life at Osceola.

2 Apr., Tues. Got Chany to come and wash for me.

3 Apr., Wed. Busied all the morning in attending to the clothes. Chany took out another bundle & I did some ironing and attended to the stove. Dinah came to ask for salt. Mr Taylor dismissed Grant today and he and Affy left. The latter is a good riddance, being a very mischievous, self willed person.

8 Apr., Mon. The two Richards [son and nephew] are engaged on the farm, Robin and Sam working with them. I engaged Else and Bess to wash and gave them out the washing in the evening for tomorrow. Thomas fixed two locks and fixed the stove.

11 Apr., Thurs. Patience still trying me with perverseness and carelessness. Lock left open and spoilt.

12 Apr., Fri. I intended to dismiss Patience today, but she anticipated me and did not come to cook breakfast. Louisa undertook to attend to cooking and washing up things and did very well. Patience failed to get up my things. I was engaged some in the garden and in household affairs. I gave Patience notice to leave here. She has lost 3 silver spoons and innumerable things of various kinds for me.

16 Apr., Tues. I attended to household matters. Else sick and Bess. Got Abby to wash for me and engaged Amelia to do my washing for a month.

18 Apr., Thurs. Mr Taylor left early this morning to go in the stage for Gainesville. Richard accompanied him to Ocala and went on to Silver Springs to see if the provisions had come for the horses and laborers. We have been buying corn at high prices since the first of February, also oats and hay.

20 Apr., Sat. The negroes all went to Ocala to attend a mass meeting. Mr Owens, Mr Gary, Mr Goss [Ocala lawyers] and some negroes addressed the meeting.

21 Apr., Sun. Louisa sick this morning and Harriet Horde came in and cooked for me. Was very pleasant and cooked very well.

Alex Britton sick. Dinah and Sukey came here and the former talked a long while.

22 Apr., Mon. Louisa still sick and I determined to prepare breakfast myself, which I did washing hominy for the first time in my life. I was rather glad that Mr Taylor was not at home to criticize. Phillis came up and remained to cook the other meals. I went down to the quarters to see Louisa and Alex Britton. Both of them pretty sick.

23 Apr., Tues. Phillis came up again to cook today. Louisa sick. As Phillis is a good cook I got some lessons from her and assisted her. The stove is a very good and convenient one, and I will feel more satisfaction and ease in attending the culinary department.

24 Apr., Wed. Louisa came in this morning but looks weak. Phillis came up to cook. Went down twice to see Alex Britton and Kitty, both sick, the former very ill.

26 Apr., Fri. Phillis still cooking. Louisa complaining and doing but little. Amelia brought home the clothes alright and I hope she will do well as a washerwoman. Sam has been sick since Wednesday.

27 Apr., Sat. Minty brought me my sheets and tablecloth etc that Patience stole, and were taken from her trunk in Ocala.

28 Apr., Sun. Sam still sick, gave him medicine. Alex Britton very ill. Dr Vogt[7] attending him. Mr Taylor had fever this evening. Sue and Lyd went to Currans after reading to the little negroes.

29 Apr., Mon. I walked down to the cabins to see Alex who is very ill. Gave Josephine a little washing to do for me. Spoke to Alex of Jesus as the friend of sinners and our Advocate. Louisa still complaining. Fenwick went to Ocala and heard something of the things I lost. He attended to Alex.

30 Apr., Tues. Alex said to be better—he was pronounced dying last night. Set Louisa to cleaning up the house. Alex died about dinnertime. Prince Williams came to get plank for coffin. Brick

brought me 8 doz eggs from a man who is raising them by steam at Gib Browns. Old Lucy came to beg a shirt to bury her son in.

1 May, Wed. Phillis came in to cook today. Alex burial took place and there was quite an effort for display on the occasion, and nearly all the plantation left their work to attend.

2 May, Thurs. Phillis sick. Nora cooked for me today. Attended to household affairs and commenced sewing on pants for Richard Baker [visiting nephew]. Nora put in a plea to have a pair basted for her.

3 May, Fri. I attended to having the house cleaned up. Stopped Robin [from field] to scour. I basted and fixed a pair of pants for Birch for Nora. Phillis cooking for me today. Louisa scalding rooms, sunning beds. Priscilla came up for breakfast, and I put her cleaning knives etc.

5 May, Sun. Priscilla came to help with dinner, she was extremely ill with pneumonia when she came here in Feb, but is recovering now and comes up to get something nice from the table.

15 May, Wed. Rosanna brought her baby up here with spasms. Gave her powders of calomel, Dovers and quinine for it, & some red flannel.

20 May, Mon. Phillis came in the morning and cooked breakfast for me and the other meals. Mr Taylor learned that they had taken a quantity of sugar from his sugar house. Sent for Major Remley to come and see after some of the Freedmen whose crop is likely to spoil for want of work.

23 May, Thurs. I cooked breakfast altogether this morning by myself. Fenwick got me water and wood. Lydia attended to the household affairs. I also cooked dinner and supper, and got on pretty smoothly, considering it was my first attempt.[8]

24 May, Fri. I have not hired anyone to cook. Nora occupies the only house I have for cook or house servant, and she is not in a situation to be turned out of it [pregnant]. With some system the

household affairs can be conducted by us. I accomplished the cooking myself today, & sewed some, mending clothes.

25 May, Sat. I attended to the culinary dept all day and prepared some things for Sabbath. Mended clothes and put up the clothes washed by Amelia. Easter sick and she undertook it all. Scipio sick. I was sick myself and retired early. Almost all our sugar and syrup reported stolen. Mr Taylor had it brought up today [for safe-keeping].

26 May, Sun. Phillis cooked today. I felt very unwell but got up. Robin went to see Patience. I sent her some arrowroot.

2 June, Sun. Alex Whorden has several children ill. His daughter came up to cook for me but I sent her back after breakfast to help nurse them. Bess cooked for me, volunteering her services.

6 June, Thurs. Mr Taylor and Major Remley rode over the several crops. Peter's and Alex Whorden's reported in bad condition. Major Remley dined here. Phillis complaining, Sarah More assisted her in preparing dinner and I attended to the vegetables. Ajean came in to wait. Robin attended to breakfast and Lyddy. I made catsup after dinner and prepared supper.

7 June, Fri. Sarah came in and Robin to get breakfast. Phillis sick. Major Remley left here this morning. Mr Taylor continues to hear accounts of the stolen sugar and molasses. Peter Morgan involved. He gave the first information to Mr Taylor of the parties involved in it.

8 June, Sat. Scipio came up to see me. He looks badly. I gave him quinine, spirits and some mutton.

14 June, Fri. Birch came to say Nora was sick. I went to see her several times.

15 June, Sat. Hired Dinah to assist Sarah [Dinah's daughter] who is complaining. Sarah Buzzard and herself ironing at the stove. Nora was delivered last night of a dead child. I went to see her several times through the day. I had headache all day and felt very tired at night.

24 June, Mon. [Maria was very sick for a week] I feel better of fever, but am suffering otherwise very much. Bess has waited on me very faithfully ever since I have been sick, and slept in my room every night. The negroes seem disposed to be very attentive except Minty. We sent for Dinah who is quite sick, to come and stay with her daughter [Sarah More]. She seems glad to come. Mr Taylor went to see them today.

4 July, Thurs. Johnny stopped at Ocala to dinner and heard a Radical speech from Mr Goss [lawyer] to the negroes. Samuel Small and Major Remley also spoke. Dr Butt[9] called to see some sick negroes. I read the Scriptures, attended to sick negroes, went to see Nancy and Whorden.

8 July, Mon. Lieut Armstrong and Major Remley came here and dined today. Went to see Nancy who is quite sick. Henry & Whorden sick. Major Remley reprimanded Wallace Dawkins[10] for his resistance to authority. I went to see all the sick negroes. Jupiter got hurt from a mule.

9 July, Tues. Sarah More the cook sick today. Dinah, her mother cooked breakfast. Sarah had a daughter during the day. Alex Whorden and Nancy very sick. Gave them medicine.

10 July, Wed. Sarah Buzzard came in to cook for us this morning. Waiting nearly all day on sick negroes. Prince Williams was very perverse today about having plowing done. Sarah B was taken sick after dinner and left her washing to Chany.

14 July, Sun. Minty came in after absenting herself for a long while and shewed a disposition to oblige and be useful.

19 July, Fri. Henry reported very sick. Carolina came up here in the night, was very ill & disturbed us asking for a Dr. We sent him to the quarters. Tom here sick.

20 July, Sat. Sewed and attended to physicking the sick. Old Nancy came up and told me of a good many travels [travails] she had had, think she fancies I wont live very long.

21 July, Sun. All the family went to church except myself. I went to the negro quarters to see the sick, conversed with Henry on religious subjects. Frank Williams very ill. Sent for Dr Butt to see him, he came in the night.

22 July, Mon. Mr Taylor went early to the quarters to see the sick. Whorden objects to have hands hired to work his crop. He has been sick for three weeks & various members of his family have been sick for long periods all through the year. Cook and washerwoman both unfit for duty. Sent for Bess to wash, Dinah contented to remain a day longer. The most of the Freedmen are gathering fodder.

24 July, Wed. Bess brought in her washing, very well done. Dinah left. I paid her for her services in flour, sugar, meal, meat, soap, etc. She has been here over a month, more than half the time nursed, physicked and rationed, all of which I gave her for ten days cooking.

25 July, Thurs. Old Whorden and his son in law, Sam Boyd made a violent resistance to authority when Mr Taylor sent John Craig to work in their crop.[11] He sent John C up to Ocala to the Authorities, and Major wrote him an impressive order to desist or be arrested. Mr Collins came here to ride over Whorden's crop and remained to dinner.

26 July, Fri. Mr Taylor gave Henry a severe reproof for interfering with John Craig and ploughing. Learned that Patience trespassed on the premises today.

27 July, Sat. Tom came to get salt, meal, tobacco etc etc and brought 2 little chickens to obtain them. Poor fellow! he finds it hard to live on his own resources in the woods. Experience is often a necessary teacher. I was writing to Mary when Rachel and Maria came to have their accts settled up. I gave Rachel sugar and cloth.

29 July, Mon. Isaac Elmore failed to come for his rations on Saturday, the regular period for receiving them, and came to demand them this morning, and being refused, he went to Ocala to make

a report but gained nothing by his visit. Peter went to report Wallace Dawkins, one of the Freedmen, for offense against him and his wife. Mr Taylor sent Margaret off from here.

30 July, Tues. [complete] Richard Baker [nephew] shewed me a letter he received from Mr Richardson making offers to Mr Taylor to act as his agent in planting here next year, and bringing out negroes to do so with. John Dawkins came up to say that Peter [Morgan] had cut his brother [Wallace Dawkins] very badly with a knife in the field. Mr Taylor sent a vehicle for him and went down immediately to the field with Dr Vogt, who found three very bad wounds. Maj Remley and Mr Priest, the sheriff, who were coming for Wallace, took Peter to jail.

1 Aug., Thurs. Richard Baker went to Ocala and heard that Peter had made an effort to break the jail & had been chained. I was very much annoyed by Martha Morgan, annoying me by her presence and her persistence to see me.

2 Aug., Fri. Chany came to beg for some medicine for Old Minty. I sent her meal and flour yesterday. She [Minty] is an object of charity. Several of the negroes came up to gossip about Peter and his wife and Wallace Dawkins condition. Tom Johnson came to settle for his share in crops and seemed well satisfied.

3 Aug., Sat. Old June and Joe Mitchel came for settlements. Old June in a fine humour. Joe begged for medicine for Sukey who is sick when he is hired. A good many came up on this place for favors. They go to Ocala to register today their names.

7 Aug., Wed. Sarah Buzzards little girl Caroline died very suddenly today while we were at dinner, before her mother could get down to see her. Lyd made a shroud for it.

8 Aug., Thurs. I was sick all day with fever. Sarah's child was buried today. Seabrook broke the buggy and tore the harness to pieces without asking permission for him to take it. Sarah More cooked for me today. Bess staid in the room all night with me.

9 Aug., Fri. Sarah Buzzard came up and finished washing the clothes. She looks much distressed at the loss of her child.

10 Aug., Sat. Mr Taylor went to Ocala to attend church meeting. Mr Goss [Ocala lawyer] and Smart Wilkinson's cases were somewhat canvassed there, the former for open communion, and the latter disrespect to the pastor. Smart came to see me today, and disclaimed any such intention, said he would make ample apology. I gave Smart $5 and 7 yards of osnaburg for attending as sexton to the church.

12 Aug., Mon. Mr Taylor having Prince's corn broken in and measured. He is disposed to be dis-satisfied in his temper and pretty self willed. Peter has been bailed out of jail by Mr Goss. Mr Taylor told his [Peter's] wife not to stay here, she is not under contract and is a mischievous person. Bess called for her washing. Sam Floyd very sick and a good many other negroes.

21 Aug., Wed. Dinah and Peter More got some grapes for me to make wine. I employed Scilla in wine making and paid her as soon as the work was finished.

22 Aug., Thurs. Old Nancy came up with many requests and long travels [travails]. Bess, Thomas, Gilbert and Joe Morgan sick. Josephine Cannon had a daughter.

23 Aug., Fri. Sarah Buzzard pressing grapes for me, Anne assisting her.[12] The constable came here for Isaac Elmore, one of the Freedmen, for disobedience, violation of contract, theft and idleness. The two Richards went up to testify of the theft very reluctantly. Robin, Peter More, & S all engaged in Tom's services to dig grave, make coffin and go with ox cart for corpse [Sarah's child]. Mr T's wagon borrowed.

25 Aug., Sun. Minty came in and asked me to read for her. I read a sermon and several chapters for her & read several chapters myself from the Methodist Pulpit South.

27 Aug., Tues. Mr Priest came for Wallace Dawkins and the witnesses in his and Peter's case.

1 Sept., Sun. The negroes are having quite a revival. All the girls [daughters and niece] went down to Sunday School in the evening, but declined having it as they [the negroes] had a meeting there and they [the girls] remained to it. It seemed to excite Anne very much and I had to rebut some of the false impressions she received.

4 Sept., Wed. Mr Taylor, Johnny and Richard T again went to Ocala. The trial of Peter Morgan and Wallace Dawkins did not come off yesterday.

6 Sept., Fri. Henry B quite distressed about his lands to find Joe M has the No 5 [lot]. Henry had it arranged first, but does not like to have a fuss and is for giving it up. Tom B sent for a conveyance for Silvia's child's corpse. It died last night.

8 Sept., Sun. Bun Dawkins begged Mr Taylor to hire him next year.

10 Sept., Tues. Mr Halliday left here this morning to enter lands for the freedmen. A letter from Bertha Richard recommending Mr Harvin to take charge of this place with fifty white laborers. Mr Taylor is anxious to give up the charge of so many freedmen.

11 Sept., Wed. I attended to Cawline's work in the garden. Bun Dawkins accidentally shot a little child of Peter Counts. It died in a short while.

12 Sept., Thurs. We rose early this morning and left home before 7 o'clock to attend the funeral, The corpse did not arrive until about 1 o'clock. Mr Perry officiated. A jury of inquest met here to sit on the child of Peter Counts.

16 Sept., Mon. The negroes are bringing in very little cotton. Peter Morgan picked 55 lbs. I heard Eliza's child was dead.

17 Sept., Tues. Phillis came to ask for sugar and physic for Eliza's child Henry who was not dead as reported. Carolina planted cauliflower and cresses and split rails. Old Nancy came up. Quite a revival among the negroes.

22 Sept., Sun. Peter Counts came up to fuss at Richard about his son, whom R had slightly thrashed.

25 Sept., Wed. Carolina did nothing and left. Old Adeline came with her child. She had given it too much laudanum.

26 Sept., Thurs. Old Adeline's child no better. I had it given camphor, coffee, sweet oil, used cold water and mustard plasters. Sent for the Dr to see it. Old Nancy came up to ask for a way to go to church. Patsey, Nora and a number to be baptized of the colored people.

29 Sept., Sun. The negroes came to borrow mules to attend a great baptizing among their own color. Some of the freedmen killed a cow last night.

30 Sept., Mon. Mr Taylor and Johnny went to Ocala on business. Robin (col) subpoenaed to sit as juryman. Quite an era in the South. Mr Taylors employees idling dreadfully.

2 Oct., Wed. Minty came to ask for mule and vehicle to go to Ocala for some bedding she had there. Dinah sent to get medicine. Mr Taylor ordered Tom Jenkins to leave here. Mrs Horde (col) came up to make a fuss about her child, Callie, and some shells she had taken.

6 Oct., Sun. Patience and Lyddy quite sick. Robin came to ask Mr Taylor to send for the doctor for them. Dr Vogt called.

7 Oct., Mon. Mr Taylor and Fenwick also Johnny went to Ocala to attend court. The judge did not attend. Some little excitement about the negro jury. Court postponed. Dinah came to ask for sugar and pepper for Old Mary. Mr Taylor has to be very positive with Prince.[13]

8 Oct., Tues. Sukey Jupiter came to beg for castor oil for her child. Henry came to ask me for the pony. He came today to ask for a mule to go in search of Charles, who has left him since Sunday.

9 Oct., Wed. Sukey Jupiter sent to beg for laudanum, Mose for tobacco, neither of them working here. Scipio came up to see

about his accts. Exhibited great stupidity but a determination to be honest.

11 Oct., Fri. I sewed some, wrote a letter for a freedman. Had wine drawn off. Robin assisted me. Drew off 6 gallons of red scuppernong, made 1½ gallon of winter grapes first quality, and 6 qts of white scuppernong.

12 Oct., Sat. Johnny's freedmen obstreperous about putting cotton in gin house. Carolina came for a settlement.

14 Oct., Mon. Dinah came to beg for medicine and cards to spin with. Alex Whorden brought in some pumpkins with his corn today. Carolina came in to beg Mr Taylor to see about his land for him.

16 Oct., Wed. Samuel came here with papers showing that the polls were open for registration.

21 Oct., Mon. Mr Taylor and Johnny went to Ocala to attend a meeting (public) for promoting immigration to this state to cultivate the lands.[14] Cut out some work for Minty. Richard Taylor went to hunt with Mr Scales for Mr Bauskett's cattle. They were not successful. Found one for Mr Taylor. The negroes seem to be killing off the stock everywhere.

23 Oct., Wed. Amelia and Minty came to take up clothes. I read the papers, which are jubilant North and South over the Democratic victories. Mary (col) disposed to be stubborn.

25 Oct., Fri. Mr Taylor seems to think it will be necessary to discharge the most of his hands, as they have made little or nothing and seem determined to do nothing. Peter is behaving very badly.

27 Oct., Sun. Lydia went down to the negro quarters to teach the little negroes Sunday School.

29 Oct., Tues. Minty seems to be obliging and useful the last month.

2 Nov., Sat. Mr Taylor, Johnny and Mr Collins went to Ocala together to attend the immigration meeting. They resolved on

sending for white laborers for the country as the negroes have come short of our expectations. Old Nancy came up and seems troubled at her prospects for another year.

8 Nov., Fri. Mr Taylor made an effort to get a loan from the firm of Strong and Roper through Mr Fowles on mortgage of plantation, as our crop has entirely failed after large expenses for the freedmen.

10 Nov., Sun. Lydia went down to read to the negroes. Sarah More sick, Sarah Buzzard cooked. Old Adeline and Nancy came up to see me.

11 Nov., Mon. Robin came to ask for use of vehicle to go with Patience and her child to the Silver Spring, to take the boat for Carolina.

12 Nov., Tues. Sarah Buzzard came to cook today, Sarah More sick. Peter's and Prince's home got burned up this morning, with their rice, fodder, corn etc etc also some clothes, rifles and money. Richie thinks "what came from the water, goes to the water."

14 Nov., Thurs. The negroes nearly all went to the election.[15] Mr Taylor gave Minty a talk about the conduct of the negroes.

16 Nov., Sat. Robin and Henry came in to attend to business and Mr Taylor read them both some questions propounded in one of the Tallahassee papers to the black voters & a speech. Tom came to ask Mr Taylor to lend him some mules, which favor was granted.

20 Nov., Wed. The negroes tried to resist sending their cotton to be ginned in Ocala, but finally yielded. One of the Freedwomen brought her child to see me, she had given it my name. Mr Taylor disappointed about the ginning of his cotton.

22 Nov., Fri. Mr Taylor went to Ocala to see Major Remley to have Prince Williams accounts settled and him removed from here. Black Betsey came over to see us. Says she has left Morton.

Amelia came here to boil the soap over. I was busy most of the day in attending to it.

25 Nov., Mon. Major Remley came here and spent the night. Peter More came to ask if I wanted Sarah to cook for me and I told him "No." Sarah also came to inquire for herself. Mr Taylor was busy arranging accts for settlement with Prince Williams.

26 Nov., Tues. Peter Counts refused to come to Major Remley when sent for. Major Remley returned to Ocala. Prince Williams left here today. Ted commenced work.

27 Nov., Wed. Mr Taylor and Johnny went to Ocala to attend a public immigration meeting. A soldier came out here twice in search of Peter Counts for disrespect of the Authorities. [Letter] from Genl Wayne respecting immigration [Irish labor to replace black]. Henry brought up his potatoes and banked them.

28 Nov., Thurs. Mr Taylor sent Richard this morning to demand the potatoes kept back by some of the negroes. Cannon sent those he had. Joe Morgan, W and Bun Dawkins, Sam Boyd and Peter Counts refused. Mr Taylor went to Ocala to attend to it. Wallace came to apologize and brought note from Major Remley. They all brought up their potatoes.

29 Nov., Fri. John Dawkins came up to talk with Mr Taylor about staying with him next year. Mr Taylor desires to send off Peter Counts and Sam Boyd. I gave Adeline Whorden yarn to size and to wind for weaving. Phillis came to help with arrowroot.

5 Dec., Thurs. A host of hungry negroes came here. Sarah Buzzard sick. Phillis up to strip arrowroot and attended to some other matters. Finished with the arrowroot.

7 Dec., Sat. Wallace Dawkins came up early this morning for Mr Taylor and himself to make an agreement for the next year. Mr T refused to stay longer on his bond and gave him notice to leave.

15 Dec., Sun. Mr Taylor sent to the sugar house for Mat Haynesworth [visiting cousin] and Richard Taylor who staid there last night. They fear negro trouble and fire.

16 Dec., Mon. Mr Taylor very busy making up his accts with Freedmen. They are very largely in his debt and I presume will

never pay. They owe over $4000. This amount would make him pretty easy if paid. The whole country is in a deplorable condition from loss of crops.

17 Dec., Tues. Robin and Henry Buzzard salting hogs. The sugar mill does not work well. The iron rod broke and Mr Taylor sent Peter Morgan to Ocala to have it mended; he returned without it.

18 Dec., Wed. Sugar mill not fixed yet. Mr Taylor sent Peter off early this morning with a note to the blacksmith to fix it. I made out the accts of our house servants today & of the washer women.

19 Dec., Thurs. Sarah Buzzard tied up lard for me yesterday, and I had it put away today. Sarah More coming about again. I told her what her acct was. Mr Taylor had boys stay at sugar house at night [to protect it from thieves]. Affy and Sukey Jupiter came here. Affy seemed disposed to try and please.

24 Dec., Tues. Richard had sugar, syrup and all the things brought up and put in store room [for safekeeping]. Robin fixed a place for it yesterday and this morning. Spent nearly all day looking over accts.

27 Dec., Fri. Sarah More came for money or an order, her husband is largely in debt. Dinah at work here. John Dawkins and old Whorden came up and want to stay here next year. Johnny says he has no hands yet.

28 Dec., Sat. Henry Buzzard came to speak to Mr Taylor about staying here another year. Sarah More left here today. Richard went to Ocala to see after the stolen cotton. Mr Taylor spoke to Old Nancy of Joe Young, Joe Morgan & Gilbert Morgan & their ill conduct. Rosanna brought in the clothes very well washed and ironed.

29 Dec., Sun. Lydia went to the church [Osceola chapel] in the evening, and found it in a bad fix, not yet cleaned out & a hole burned in it. No negroes around the building.

30 Dec., Mon. Mr Taylor went into Ocala and took Joe Young, Gilbert Morgan and Joe Morgan to the store of Mr [?] to see if they

were the cotton carriers [thieves]. He said they were not. Sarah sick and we had a very late dinner. Old Charlotte cooked. I mended clothes, attended to having the ground prepared for Irish potatoes.

31 Dec., Tues. Old Whorden still fixing the potato ground. Mr Taylor rode over land yesterday with Robin for him to choose where to settle & with Scipio this morning. I settled accts with Minty and bought two turkeys from her. Sarah Buzzard about again.

[From the closing prayer] I close up another Diary under circumstances of great mercy and goodness. Many fears with which the beginning of this year found me troubled and perplexed have not been realized. Death has not entered the family circle, and though we have had much sickness and perplexity, the mercy of God has been over us & we have had our wants supplied & been brought safely through our trials. Our minds have been much filled with the cares of the world and with anxieties for the morrow, & we feel ashamed that we have not been able to render a childlike trust to our Heavenly Father.

[From the opening prayer of the 1868 diary, found at the back of the 1867 diary] Give us proper servants, and deliver us from the evil, the unfaithful, the destructive, and the slothful.

Five months later, Maria summed up the state of the plantation in 1867.

29 May 1868. Maria Baker Taylor to Ann Eliza Furman

In common with other southern planters, Mr Taylor failed last year in his crop, incurred large expenses for nearly, if not quite, a hundred freedmen, the most of whom he discharged in debt to him to from twenty seven to three thousand dollars, with no prospect of ever collecting any of it from them. Money has been scarce, interest high, ruinous to a planter, particularly with pd labor of such a character & such exhorbitant wages as we give in Fla. So that this year for the first time I may say we have really felt the times to be hard, & yet, through it all, we have been bountifully fed, & our anxieties are greater than our wants. God is good, we may fully trust Him.

Johnny is living near us & planting the place formerly owned by Mr Bauskett, but he is not satisfied to endure the watchfulness necessary to planting [with] freedmen with success, & wants employment for himself in which he may dispense with Sambo's radical notions. I see Uncle Charles [Furman] has been induced to meet the Democratic Convention [in South Carolina]. I was so glad to see so respectable a body named & so much unanimity manifested in its action. I trust it may be the dawn of a brighter day for the South, though I fear the radicals will not be displaced until their malice has been satiated by farther sufferings of our poor people, white & black.

Maria would have a long wait for this displacement in Florida. A week after she wrote, the new legislature was seated. Out of seventy-six legislators, a radical majority of fifty-three, including nineteen freedmen, had been elected.

EIGHT

Financial and Emotional Crises

In 1869 the emphasis in Maria's concern with plantation affairs again shifted, this time from labor problems to the mounting financial crisis with the plantation as a family business operation. These material difficulties merged with the emotional crisis Maria suffered over John Taylor's declining health in 1871 and his death in 1872. Legal documents from 1869 and 1871, the 1870 and 1871 diaries, and letters from 1870 and 1872 reveal the intertwining of these profoundly unsettling concerns.

The plantation difficulties were, of course, symptomatic of postwar conditions in the whole area. Cotton production in Florida dropped from about 65,000 bales in 1860 to about 40,000 bales in 1870, and the total value of farms from about $16,500,000 to about $10,000,000 in the same period.[1] While 1869 documents from Maria's hand are lacking, two legal documents indicate that by then the Taylors could no longer keep the place running on their own.

The first document, dated 23 February 1869, records John Taylor's sale of a one-half interest in 1,388 acres to Samuel A. McDowell for $21,000, plus a one-half interest in "all tenements, appurtenances, rents, issues, and profits."[2] This acreage was almost the entire plantation except for the eighty-acre homestead. How the Taylors became acquainted with Dr. McDowell, a dentist from Carlisle, Pennsylvania, is unknown. Maria had acceded to the sale, giving up her dower right in the one-half interest.[3] McDowell paid John Taylor $5,000 cash and signed two notes, one for $5,000 due on 1 April 1870 at 6

percent interest from 1 January 1870, the other for $10,500 due on 1
January 1873 under the same conditions. McDowell's collateral was
of course his one-half interest in the plantation; also, John was to have
all of McDowell's interest in the crops until McDowell paid his debt
in full. On paper, McDowell and John Taylor were now equal part-
ners in the plantation.

The second document, dated 27 October 1869, records John's sale
of the eighty-acre homestead parcel to Maria for $200, "for her and
her children's benefit as she may see fit to confer it upon either or any
of them." This move assured Maria of a roof over her head. Maria
immediately took over the management of this property and its produce, and such references as "my field," "my house in the field," "my
rice" occur frequently over the next two years, for example on 19
October 1871: "Mr Taylor had my short cotton weighed 1975 lbs &
commenced ginning it."

Early in 1870 the McDowells were living with the Taylors at Osceola, and efforts to resolve the financial difficulties with the plantation
continued.

> 11 Jan., Tues. I wrote a long letter to Lydia. Mr Taylor wrote to her
> & Mr Crane[4] about a loan of $25,000 or the sale of his place to a
> company & I wrote on the same subject.

> 14 Jan., Fri. Mr Taylor & Dr McDowell had a conversation about
> the place today, & he [McDowell] signified his determination to
> stand up to his purchase. Mr Taylor consented to remit the inter-
> est on the $10,500 for one year.

> 31 Jan., Mon. Dr McDowell wants to get out of the purchase. Mr
> Taylor feels it would damage him materially if he [McDowell]
> fails to comply with his obligations. Johnny made a new proposi-
> tion to Dr McDowell to take his purchase off his hands & sell him
> his place. Mrs McDowell seems disposed to make up for the Dr's
> want of affability. He seems entirely out of sorts & not disposed to
> oblige at all in any way the family.

> 1 Feb., Tues. Mr Taylor spoke to Dr McDowell for his final deci-
> sion & he [McDowell] is determined to give up & have nothing
> more to do with the place as he cannot afford to run it without

involving his friends & risking their property. Mr Taylor went to Ocala to have an injunction taken out against Dr McDowell.

In February, McDowell sold out the corn and fodder he had on hand "on his own private account," although all proceeds were supposed to go to the Taylors until his mortgage was paid off. At this point the McDowells left Osceola. John Taylor had in the meantime borrowed money on his remaining half of the plantation from Mrs. Stringfellow, a Marion County resident, and Major Phineas H. Behn of Savannah, his factor (business agent) since the Taylors' Beaufort days. It was common for planter and factor to have this kind of long relationship and for the factor to become identified with the well-being of the planter's estate.[5] In this case, Behn was intensely identified, for he had been extending John credit against his crops for some time and was now in effect part owner of Osceola.

As expected, McDowell defaulted on his April payment, and the Taylors were now trying to sell the McDowell half as well as their own, either separately or as a package. In May they had a nibble for the McDowell interest from a Mr. Dozier, a connection of Major Behn's, and John hastened to respond to the request for information about the plantation. The letter is in Maria's hand, so it is probably a copy she made for the Taylors' own records. After accurately explaining the legal situation with McDowell described above, John gives considerable detail about the plantation.

7 May 1870. John Morgandollar Taylor to L. Dozier

It is too late now for any other party to put in now to work the crop of this year or to share the profits & expenses. The crop is well under way, on a small scale, on my own hooks.

Out of courtesy to your questions, I would say, that I have about 85 acres of corn, very promising, about 70 acres of cotton, a fair stand & about 30 acres of cane a medium fair stand,[6] but small as usual at this season, a small patch of potatoes to furnish vines for the main crop to be planted in the summer. Should a purchaser take Mr McDowells half interest, say to him, there is a fine engine all up & ready to run, smoke stack too short by 10 feet, for a proper draught. Engine said to be 30 horse power with 40 feet of shafting & pulleys to drive any machinery which may be wanted on a plantation, such as cotton gins, grist mill, thrasher etc. all which should be procured & put up at an early day, as they would pay well it is believed.

We have on hand, but not yet put up, a large sugar mill complete in all its parts, also two batteries, 5 kettles each, supposed to be able to manufacture 8 to 10 hogsds of sugar per day. A saw mill, if attached, would saw lumber for plantation purposes, & profitably for neighboring wants. There is not a saw running in 10 miles, that I know of, & a great demand for lumber.

He should also be informed that I would expect him to comply in full with McDowells engagement to pay $5000 at once minus the excess he paid in mill & engine, purchased by Taylor & McDowell in June last, & to assume also the payment of his note $10,500 due June 1873 or earlier as his share of the crops may enable him to do, as per mortgage, also in Sept to put in 6 or 8 mules, as may be agreed upon, & provisions for them also, to pay half expenses of planting the cane crop in Oct & Nov. I hope there will be cane enough to plant 100 acres in Nov & replant the [?] when it may be necessary. But, I will expect to have paid the half expenses of planting & working so much of the crop of cane now growing as I may give up to plant jointly for the year 1871. I think it would pay well to a purchaser to finish the mill at once on joint expense, put up the shafting, procure a saw etc, & saw, grind, & gin cotton on tole this fall. The sugar mill will not be needed before the 1871 is mature.

I believe a successor to McDowell, who would carry out the original programme, would certainly make a large per centage upon his outlay, for it is a conceded fact, by all, who are acquainted with my plantation, that it is among the best in the country & has so far as I know a better start in seed cane, than any other place in the country. Any one desiring to purchase is invited to come & see for himself.

A few days after writing this letter, John checked his acreage figures and Maria remarked on the result in general terms ("planters").

11 May, Wed. Mr Taylor was quite worried yesterday to find that there was less cotton planted than he thought, he measured the land partly, which should have been done in Dec or Jan had not adverse circumstances prevented. Planters should be particular to know exactly, what they plant & have it laid off in acres to pay laborers accurately for their work. System & punctuality is very necessary in farming & planting.

A few months later, Major Behn became pressing about John's indebtedness on his brokerage account; no progress was made on the sale of the McDowell interest through Behn's connection; other prospective buyers came and went; and the Taylors were advertising through friends, relatives, and newspapers for a lender or purchaser for the plantation. Johnny Taylor, active on his parents' behalf in New York City, put the situation bluntly in the following letter. The close relationship between planter and factor is again apparent when Johnny expresses faith in the helpfulness and honesty of "Old Behn" in spite of the Taylors being his heavy debtors.

22 November 1870. John M. Taylor Jr. to John M. Taylor Sr.

My Dear Father, Yr last letter was rec'd this evening. You misjudge me if you think I can get tired of your letters, to the contrary I am always glad to hear from you. Though sorry to see you so low spirited. I keep on trying to help you find a purchaser but I tell you they are scarce. To my three last advertizements I have only rec'd 3 replies, out of the millions of people tis rather discouraging.

I rec'd a letter from Mr E.G. Eastman who is now in Jacksonville Fla. I gave him the particulars & asked him to go down & see your place. He may go & he may not. I rec'd the certificates & have shown them until actually they are nearly worn out. Today I rec'd the enclosed letter from Mr Turnbull, he writes that he still has intention of going to Fla. I hope he will & I hope he will buy yr place, but the mortgage [Behn/Stringfellow] & judgment [McDowell] you will find are very serious obstacles in the way.

I will from time to time put in advertizements & solicit replies, but I have, to be frank lost all confidence in selling or finding a lender. I have dispaired of my own place [next door to Osceola].

The judgment, tho I have it from Harney that he is willing to let it run another year, operates against me. They ask me why have you not paid this small amount? a question which required the statement that "I never had the money."

I wrote Fen the other day a plan which if followed will reduce your condition as to debts just to your own time. Tis to sell Mc out. You or Rich buy him in, then Judge Dawkins forclose mortgage for Mrs S[tringfellow], & Rich buy in every thing. The money which you hold of Mrs I will buy it all & it can be obtained, or reborrowed from her. The two opperations does not weaken her security in the least, & will obtain a suspension of duns for you. Old Behn will be glad to ask legal interest, & in the course of time Richie can pay him & any dollars that you owe. He is not the man to take undue advantage of his appearant ownership in yr whole estate.

This may appear to you as unjust, but understand me that I do not propose for you to hold from yr creditors their just dues but by this means you obtain time to pay every dollar. You can then sue McDowell & if he has anything in Pa you can get it. Yr creditors will be glad to take his notes for yr debt.

I have thought of this matter & this is the most feasible plan that I can think of. Every thing too must be done quickly & if possible let it all be done by the time Mrs S debt is due. You confess her debt & sanction the foreclosure is the plan.

In haste my dear Father Yr affec Son JMT

In 1871 the Taylors pretty much followed Johnny's convoluted plan, having found no better solution. Maria's diary for that year explains the situation.

2 Jan., Mon. Fenwick went to Ocala to attend to some business with Judge Goss, but failed to see him, he had papers attended with reference to selling this land of Dr McDowell's to get judg-ment for an execution. I spent some part of the morning hunting up some items for Mr Taylor of expenses for the mill. Mr Taylor's business affairs are in a very critical situation. I trust a merciful Father will make the crooked places straight and enable us to maintain our integrity and provide for our household.

3 Jan., Tues. Mr Taylor received two letters from Major B who seems to be very hard pressed for money & declared himself unable to run the place any longer.[7]

6 Mar., Mon. Richard & Mr Dawkins went to Ocala this morning. Today the sale of one half of Dr McDowell's in this place is to be sold at Mr Taylor's suit, by the sheriff. Richard bought in the land & mill, which were sold today for $315.

What Richard bought was 887 of the 1,388 acres in which McDowell had originally contracted to buy a one-half interest, McDowell having long been in default on his mortgage payment and no purchaser having been found. Also included were the steam engine, boilers and fixtures, and sugar mill. Soon after, on 3 April, Richard bought McDowell's interest in the rest of the plantation for $35 (see diary entry). Five months later, on 9 September, Richard conveyed to Maria 1,311 acres with "love and affection for and toward my mother," for the sum of one dollar.[8] Thus as of September 1871 Maria owned the entire plantation. This conveyance, although undertaken primarily to shield the property from John's debts, had some plausibility, for Maria knew as much about running the place as John did. However, that the Taylors were able to bring off the transfer of property at all owed much to Florida's innovative and early Married Women's Property Act of 1845, which had been designed specifically to protect a wife's property from her husband's debts.[9]

The last six months of the 1871 diary tell a dismal tale. In spite of all the maneuvering, the financial situation at Osceola continued its downward slide, and unprecedented friction arose between John and Maria, each struggling with illness and daily demands. Other stresses took their toll. In Gainesville, Carrie was given up for dead several times during a prolonged illness, and Fen caught the epidemic yellow fever; three of Mary's children were staying at Osceola while Mary, now living in St. Augustine with her new husband, bore and lost twin daughters; Richie was having to sleep in the sugar house to prevent theft. The following diary excerpts focus on plantation affairs and John's physical and psychological decline. Maria's reactions, among which her own spells of illness should probably be counted, may also be inferred from her read-between-the-lines style of reporting unpleasantness. At first, John and Maria appear as a companionable couple.

16 July, Sun. Both Mr Taylor & I were much gratified with receiving the papers Mrs Gary[10] sent us, particularly with Uncle James address on "Ministerial Education" delivered at the Southern Baptist Theological Seminary.

17 July, Mon. The girls are laughing at Mr Taylor and me for talking so much of old times.

19 July, Wed. Mr Taylor's foot painful again. Mr Taylor complains of his foot & of general debility, he looks thin.

27 July, Wed. I cleaned out the press after breakfast & in doing so a bundle of our old love letters fell out of a small basket, which I took up & in waiting for the cook after finishing the household affairs I began to look over them. While I was giving out dinner Mrs Rogers & Mrs Reardon rode up to spend the day & after receiving them I had dinner prepared for them & enjoyed their company very much. After they left Mr Taylor & myself read a number of the old letters together & had some laughs & merry making. I wanted to burn them, but he said, No!

31 July, Mon. Wrote a letter to Messers Butler, Chadwick, Gary & Co, agents of the Immigration Society & sent them $5 for a ticket. I sent them the $5 considering it will not be lost in aiding immigration to S.C. to assist in lifting her from her present degradation, if it is the will of our Heavenly Father to get something to aid His cause & pay Mr Taylor's debts, some of them due to widows & orphans in need.[11]

5 Aug., Sat. Mr Taylor complaining very much of his liver & debility.

6 Aug., Sun. We had rather an unpleasant morning, Sarah's mutterings culminated in Mr. Taylor's threatening to pay her husband up,[12] & drive them off the place.

7 Aug., Mon. Cut out a pr of pants for Mr Taylor & sewed on two prs on the machine, Mr Taylor assisting me. Mr Taylor felt sick

yesterday & took Gregory's pills last night & they benefitted him very much. He is taking qui today. Mr Taylor has no patience with Sarah Buzhart & her vulgar impudence.

8 Aug., Tues. Richie went to Ocala & took letter from Mr Taylor to Major Behn asking for money to pay Henry Buzhart to discharge him on account of his wife's impudence & intermeddling with everything, & somewhat for his own unfaithfulness & carelessness. Mr Taylor pd Sarah Buzhart & gave her a plain talk.

13 Aug., Sun. We had not a pleasant time at dinner. Mr Taylor seems to be excited towards the Buzharts, & some things said were unpleasantly & not correctly interpreted, he said. I had a talk with Richie which neither of us found pleasant respecting the conversation at table. He went off in the evening to the camp ground & stayed a while.

14 Aug., Mon. I had very little or no sleep last night, tried to humble myself before God for my sins, neglect of duties, love of ease, pride & unbelief.

15 Aug., Tues. I finished my letter to Mr Crane & enclosed a statement of what is to be done to get the fixtures to the engine, mill etc completed, made out by Mr Taylor for Major Nicodemus. Mr Taylor received a letter from Major Behn authorizing him to draw on him for money to pay Henry Buzhart.

17 Aug., Thurs. A terrible storm arose last night & continued blowing & raining all day today. House thoroughly wet & trees blown down in all directions.

18 Aug., Fri. The storm of wind & rain still raging without intermission. Richard went down to see after the fences. The gin house still standing, a number of acres of corn & cotton entirely under water, trees blown down over the other parts of the field & branches wrenched off. The palings around the garden, grape yard, flower garden & orange yard for the most part blown down, peach trees uprooted, horses & cows stalking the fields, & what was three days ago a fine prospect for harvest much injured.

20 Aug., Sun. I read the scriptures & a little in the religious papers. Talked with Mr Taylor a good deal & felt we had spent a very unprofitable day.

21 Aug., Mon. Mr Taylor called Henry Buzhardt & settled his accounts with him & told him he could have till Saturday to make arrangements to go off.

22 Aug., Tues. I gave Sarah Buzhart a dress.

23 Aug., Wed. Mr Taylor called to see Mr Caleb Wallace & called at Old Henry's, who had quite a tirade against Sarah & Henry Buzhart, pity some of the things he said had not been known before they were dismissed.

25 Aug., Fri. Quite a wind & storm arose last night during the night much rain fell which continued all day blown from the east, I had work to keep the rooms in the east end of the house dry. Only sewed a little, drying up water all day. Mr Taylor seems depressed & not in a very good humor. Richie tried to have a beef killed several times but failed, it stormed so. Mr Taylor congratulating himself that his house stands the storms so well. God is our helper in the storm & in building, or we labour in vain.

26 Aug., Sat. It cleared off in the night & we had sunshine this morning. Oh that he who stilleth the storm would calm all the disordered elements of this household & give us all peace with Him & with each other.

8 Sept., Fri. I tried to sleep but could not succeed & felt used up. Mr Taylor came & talked to me while I was lying on Richie's bed in dining room on an + exciting subject.[13]

11 Sept., Mon. Mr T seems unusually provoked with what he hears of our late cook Martha Carlisle & her slanders. I did not feel like discussing agitating subjects.

26 Sept., Tues. I did not feel well this morning. I did not sleep very well last night. I spent the day in trying to humble myself before God. Fasted & prayed for the preservation & conversion of myself & family from the love & practice of all evil. "The slightest sorrow

for sin is sufficient if it produces amendment, and the greatest sorrow is insufficient if it does not." Colton.

29 Sept., Fri. Mr Taylor received a letter from Mr Long informing him that Mr McConnel had put note into his hands for collection & the administrator of Wilsons Estate, amounting in all to $224.[14]

30 Sept., Sat. Mr Taylor wrote to some gentlemen in Savannah requesting money.

5 Oct., Thurs. Mr Taylor had a letter from Major Behn, urgent for money. God grant us the ability to satisfy him. Mr Taylor with the blues all day.

10 Oct., Tues. I rose very early & walked toward carriage house to meet Mr Taylor but found him coming from the garden looking very unwell. I did not feel well all day. I have considerable heaviness of the heart lately. My liver too out of order & my head is aching & heavy. Sometimes I feel as though the rest of the grave would be welcome.

22 Oct., Sun. Mr Taylor was taken with a fever about 12 o'clock & with severe vomiting, which lasted some time, was delirious all evening. He took pills at night & I prepared qui pills to be ready.

24 Oct., Tues. Mr Taylor seems quite weak & sick this morning, at breakfast but would go down to the gin to fix it up, he has fever. No crop & no prospect of relief from his financial difficulties seems to press upon his spirits & make him sick.[15]

1 Nov., Wed. Richie & Fen went off before breakfast to Ocala, Fen had to be there by 9 o'clock for court. Mr Taylor was not pleased to have them leave before breakfast. Before Mr Taylor left for Ocala he told me something which I will not write. My thoughts of God today have been very precious. My only hope is in Him. I had a long talk with Mr Taylor tonight about some matters which disturb that can change & he promises to try.

3 Nov., Fri. Got Mr Taylor to try on his [basted] pants. He is uncommonly gloomy. Johnny tries to cheer him, but he seems to try to persuade himself that nobody cares for him in the face of

palpable facts. Mr Taylor wrote to Dublin Ireland & sent letters by Fen & Rich.[16]

7 Nov., Tues. Mr Taylor called at Joe Waldo's mill to see about collecting some money due by the freedmen. Mr Taylor quite sick & wanted me by him all evening. He took pills at night. Read pretty late in the Book of Job Revised Translation.[17]

10 Nov., Fri. Finley came & pd Mr Taylor $37.00 of his debt.

13 Nov., Mon. Chill again this morning & fever all day. Bad headache at night. I slept in the parlour I had such a headache. Sue got up during the night and made tea for her father and me which I found very palatable with some toast. Mr Taylor quite sick again, he took Dover's powders & morphine. Johnny went to Ocala to attend to Mr Taylor's tax affairs.

19 Nov., Sun. Before dinner Mr Taylor was taken with dumb chill[18] & fever which lasted all evening & part of the night accompanied by vomitting. Mr Taylor took 10 gr of cal with ipecac & a little magnesia.[19] He took blue pill & calomel last night & talked to Johnny, Dore & about religion. Yesterday he professed to have clear views of Christ which were precious to him.[20]

20 Nov., Mon. Mr Taylor got up & took qui. He was up very much through the night & I gave him tea twice. I felt unwell with loss of rest. About eleven Mr Taylor was taken with another dumb chill followed by vomitting & fever. I rubbed his spine with kerosine. The fever lasted until after night, when he took qui.

21 Nov., Tues. Rose early & made tea for Mr Taylor. He did not have fever during the day, his eyes looked hollow & he seemed much debilitated but walked out several times to look after the potatoes. At night he had fever & I gave him Hydrage & Dovers powder later, & during the night one of the blue pills Dr Moody sent.[21] I got up during the night & made some sage tea for him; he was up a number of times through the night.

23 Nov., Thurs. Mr Taylor free from fever but seem very much fretted & worried about business. He is having the rest of my potatoes

dug. Cutting & banking cane in the field. I had a chill followed by fever. Tried to do a little sewing work but could not effect much. Mr Taylor went to the field.

24 Nov., Fri. I got up this morning & tried to attend to business but felt very unwell all day, at night had a high fever all night & did not go to sleep until 2 o'clock. Tried to sew a little through the day.

29 Nov., Wed. I had fever all night but was not awake so much. Took oil this morning & a little turpentine. Nauseated all day. Fever continued till night when I took qui. I felt too sick all day to wash & dress. All day under the influence of medicine. Mr Taylor went to Ocala & attended to his business satisfactorily. He heard Dr Vogt had sued him for less than fifty dollars for visiting the freedmen.[22]

2 Dec., Sat. I slept only 1½ hours last night & got up feeling bad, dressed & ate a little more breakfast than I expected. I made out a list of cows & calves & named the youngest of them. Heard some new things about myself at dinner. I have been led through a very mysterious way by Him "whose ways are just, & whose counsels wise" & I do trust He will pardon all my manifold sins & take me to Himself at last, in purity & peace.

4 Dec., Mon. I suffered very much last night & Mr Taylor got up & waited on me. I found laudanum relieved me & I slept some & woke with an awful dream of seeing eight murdered bodies. I attended to a few household duties. Mr Edwin Williams called up & informed Mr Taylor that the tax collector Mr Ferguson had been murdered & robbed & left in the road above Micanopy with his throat cut from ear to ear. I had some meat overhauled today by Sam, he had orders to cut & bank some cassava for me. I took cream of tartar & feel better in the evening.

11 Dec., Mon. I had fever yesterday & felt very unwell at night, got up sick this morning. Mr Taylor is very unwell. I fear he may have chronic diarhea. Mr Taylor went to the sugar house twice today. I assisted Grace with her dinner, had tripe boiled & feet cleaned. Rhina picking my cotton, Curran making dress for Lena [Bauskett].

"Be not wise in your own conceits." "Recompense to no man evil for evil." "Do good unto all men especially unto them who are of the household of faith."[23]

12 Dec., Tues. Mr Taylor went to see Mr Dilaberry to get him to hunt with Signior Nicoletti [visiting Venetian]. I cut out 5 prs of pillow cases for my bed & fixed up my presses. Walked down to the cow pen & went to look for a good place for a grave yard on this place as I do not like the place near Mr Collins.

13 Dec., Wed. "As much as lieth in you live peaceable with all men." Seek peace & preserve it.

16 Dec., Sat. Mr Taylor went to Ocala & remained until late, going & coming by the sugar house. He rode Bob & got a fall from him. He saw Mrs Reardon who seemed to be much troubled about various things & professed to be anxious to see me for comfort. I finished making the ten pillow slips & commenced marking them.

17 Dec., Sun. The buggy is broken & no one went from here to Ocala to church today. I read the scriptures & some in Keeble's "Christian Year."[24] I was very unwell myself today & much nauseated.

25 Dec., Mon. I felt much nauseated this morning again & was sick all day, kept hoping to be able to write but was disappointed. Mr Taylor sat & talked with me a good deal today. He seems much troubled on every side but more hopeful & patient than usual. The children appear to be enjoying themselves with the contents of their stockings. My head rings with qui.

26 Dec., Tues. I got up & dressed feeling better had to lie down some during the morning. Dr Moody called to see Mr Taylor about paying his account, says he is broke & needs all the funds he can get.

30 Dec., Sat. Letter from Major Behn to Mr Taylor, not pleasant in its insinuations.

31 Dec., Sun. I would at this the close of another year record with thankfulness the goodness & mercy of God, who has abundantly

supplied our wants & we have neither lacked for food or clothing
& I have been able to pay up all my laborers & all my obligations.
God grant that some of our trials may never come again & the old
ones never be renewed, but that God's restraining grace may be
around us, & discriminating wisdom be given us to direct our steps
aright. The disastrous storms & rains occurring in August & the
following months, ruining the crops, have left us in a situation of
prostration in our temporal affairs, we feel that only God can help
& deliver us & enable us again in integrity & uprightness to discharge all our obligations to our fellow men & I pray Him
earnestly so to do.

Over a year later, Maria summed up this trying period:

7 March 1873. I spent most of the day in getting up my towels,
straining & looking over wine, & reading over my diary of 1871,
the last year of my married life. It was full of cares, trials & affliction. The Lord pardon all the sins of it & remember them no more
against any of us forever.

John Taylor died on 13 March 1872 at the age of sixty-two. The
1872 diary is missing, but in a letter she wrote to a cousin about a
month later Maria tells of John's death and expresses her appreciation
of his character.

18 April 1872. Maria Baker Taylor to Dora Furman Hutson[25]

I presume my letter to Sister Lydia has given you information
of Mr Taylor's death. I say <u>death</u>, but I cannot feel that he is <u>dead</u>!
I only acknowledge to myself that he has entered upon <u>life</u>. A new
beautiful & glorious life. I can only listen to the voice of <u>faith</u> in this
bereavement. I dare not let <u>nature</u> speak!

I feel every day the wisdom of God, in his command; "six days
shall thou labour etc." What a panacea for grief is employment!
And my hands are full, in the increased duties & responsibilities,
which devolve upon me, in the exigences, which follow the loss we
have sustained, by his death, whom we all so dearly loved, & who
has, by our loss, himself gained the bliss of Paradise.

Mr Taylor was no self righteous Pharasee, deserving the woes denounced by our Saviour, against all such; but an humble Christian, ever ready to exclaim; "God be merciful to me a sinner."

His death seemed very sudden to us, for he was very busy about the farm on Tuesday 12th, was cheerful, sat up till 9 oclock, attended to family worship as usual, & seemed interested in the papers & letters handed us after night, & slept sweetly, until 10 oclock, when he woke with a start, telling me he was dying! & I believe he was; for in about an hour, perhaps not that long, he fell asleep, never to wake, until he woke in eternity.

Yet he had been sick a long while & had lost more than 60 lbs of flesh. He had felt for some time that his end was approaching & often spoke of his expectation of not living long. [He] Said frequently he would not live through April, if till then, & was making preparation for the change [from mortal to immortal life] growing in grace & in a knowledge of Jesus Christ.

He had been telling me of a visit he paid on Monday, the day before his last, in which he had indulged in some pleasantry, & feared he had descended to levity, which he spoke of as one of his easily besetting sins. Three nights before his death he told me a dream, from which I had unintentionally wakened him, saying, "Oh what a delightful dream you have woke me from! I was with a number of our deceased friends, among them Aunt Kitsey Maner [his mother's sister], & she said to me, 'Oh John you don't know what a delightsome land Heaven is! Your mother is here & other loved ones that you long to see, & John you will see them soon, for you will soon be here.'"

I remarked to him that I presumed he thought it a dream of warning? "Well," he answered, "I would not be sorry if it was. I would not like to leave you & the children, & would willingly stay, if I could be of any service, but in my present health, & incapacity for business, I feel that I am & will be more a burden to my family than anything else." Considerable conversation ensued between us & he spoke of dying with no apprehension, said he could not always trust, as he wished to, but felt Jesus was his friend, & he would gladly die & be with Him & be freed from the strife of life & sin & be at rest.

He died peacefully & calmly, without a groan or struggle, on the 13th of March, the month we were married, thirty eight years ago.

Of the children, only Susan and Dore were at home when their father died. John and Richard were in New York City; Carrie, Fenwick, and Anne were in Gainesville; Mary was in St. Augustine; and Lydia in Pittsburgh. They all came as soon as they could. Maria speaks of them to her correspondent.

My children are great comforts to me. They have much of their fathers affectionateness & energy & are not sparing of it where I am concerned. I am gratified to find our friends & relatives appreciated Mr Taylor so much. I think that even his infirmities were the extreme of some noble & generous virtue & am glad I am not alone.

Almost heroically, John Taylor had forced himself to continue with his daily responsibilities literally to his dying day and in full expectation of death. Perhaps "the infirmities" Maria had in mind were the irritability and depression he felt when in his last years he was unable to provide well for his family or to fully meet his responsibilities to others. The last significant mention of John in Maria's writings appears thirteen years after his death, when upon moving the family graveyard, Maria chose an epitaph for his new tombstone: "We mourn the more because there are so few who in life's struggles bravely act their part."

NINE

A Time of Transition

After her husband's death on 13 March 1872, Maria's final three years at Osceola formed an interim when she had major decisions to make about the plantation, her future as a widow whose parental responsibilities were coming to an end, and her attitudes as a member of a changed social order. Letters from 1872–75 and the 1873–75 diaries[1] trace these closely related concerns as Maria's middle years drew to a close.

Early in 1872, Osceola was still home base for Maria and her four unmarried children: Susan, thirty; Richie, twenty-five; Dore, twenty-two; and Anne, sixteen. Richie would soon have a connection with a New York firm that would take him away from Osceola for several months each year, Dore would soon be spending a year in Pittsburgh, and Anne was often away in Gainesville. Of the married children, the two who lived in Gainesville, about forty miles north, were often at Osceola with their spouses: Carrie, thirty-seven years, and her husband, James Dawkins, fifty-three; and Fen, twenty-three, who had married in February, and his wife, Millie, twenty-one. James and Fen were in law practice together, and James was also a Florida Circuit judge.

Maria and her children were not the only people concerned about the fate of Osceola. Major Phineas Behn of Savannah, who still held a large mortgage on the plantation as well as other debts of John's, was all business in a letter to James Dawkins as soon as he heard of John Taylor's death.

20 March 1872. Major Phineas H. Behn to James Baird Dawkins

Yours of 15th at hand I regret very much to learn of the death of Captn Taylor. I heard of it the day previous & wrote you to Gainesville. I understand from you Mr Fenwick Taylor will remain on the plantation & assist his mother.[2]

You say again the seed cane has been injured and only about six acres more has been planted. 40 acres in sugar. Are the 40 acres in cane all that is planted. Last year there were 65 acres cane, 6 more added makes 71. Capt Taylor was anxious to plant 30 acres of cotton with fine seed & ten bushels of fripp seed, which he gave me an order for when I saw him last & which I had purchased in Charleston & forwarded. The Fripp seed are coarse. Labor is very much demoralized and every opportunity used for neglect of duties & to steal. If you have not been misinformed & only 40 acres of cane are planted, it will not require so much to carry on the work as Captn Taylors calculation was to plant from 80 to 100 acres, 30 acres cotton.[3]

I do not think the risk of carrying on the place should be borne by me altogether. Will you take equal obligations with me for Mrs Stringfellow.[4] The profit of any to be equally divided between her and myself & the amounts credited on our claims. Losses if any to be divided equally also. Am very glad the Capt left a will, Mrs Taylor is executrix. I have no doubt with Mr Fenwick Taylor's assistance to his mother the laborer will not idle. Nor could they steal, which unfortunately is a terrible propensity with them.

Assessments of the value of Maria's plantation in 1872 varied. In March, Johnny was trying to sell it in New York City for $60,000. In a letter to Maria of 4 June 1872, Behn places the value at $77,400, Maria having a clear equity of $34,000 after deducting mortgages and other debts. Later in the year, family discussions of what to do about mother and Osceola had evidently begun.

28 October 1872. Maria Baker Taylor to Ann Eliza Furman

My children have been at me to sell out here & go somewhere else where they would have easier access to me; & the girls &

Richard, who insists on staying with me, as a protector & assistant, would be more in society.

The night your letter came I had one from Gov Broome[5] informing me he had had an offer of an exchange of property, for this plantation, if I would include my Homestead, worth nearly $70,000, with only a slight incumbrance, on said property; he sent me memorandum, of equities etc, & Richard & John both wrote[6] to beg me to accede as it was a splendid trade, including a large farm in Jersey with 2 story house, in fine order, stables, barns, having gardens, 1000 grape vines, 1000 peach trees, 100 fruit trees & 4 acres in small fruits, strawberries, raspberries etc, within 2 hours ride of New York, by rail.

On Monday, after the letters came, as sick as I was I telegraphed that I thought (on paper) "it was a good trade; take it up & include homestead, & Mr Dawkins would state terms." But when he arrived in New York & looked into it, he did not think it would suit my wishes. So he came back without trading & assigned me my Dower, in addition to my homestead; & I hope they will all be satisfied for me to remain the rest of my days here, & come sometimes to see me.

However, things were not so easily settled. A few months later, Maria confided thoughts about the situation at Osceola, the challenge of new times in the South, and her own personal development.

15 February 1873. Maria Baker Taylor to Ann Eliza Furman

Well, I have read over all your "rigmarole," as you are pleased to term it, about not making me that hoped for visit, & I have concluded that "my final hope is despair" respecting your coming this winter. Times & events are so shifting & changing that I scarcely feel certain that next winter will find me in my present home, even if I live, which has now been my home for twenty years & seems to be almost a part of myself. The fruits & flowers I had planted, & even the large forest trees of live oak were set out under my eye.

I would like very much tho', if you would tear yourself away & not have so many "Lions" turning you out of the path; like the good Old Pilgrim of Bunyan, our <u>Baptist</u> friend, you would find them chained if you would only pluck up courage enough to advance. Feebleness of purpose won't do in these days of Yankee goaheadativeness. We will be pushed entirely out of ranks, if we don't pluck up & put vacillating aside & <u>dare</u> & <u>do</u>. I feel more & more the inconvenience of old habits of thought, feeling & action & want to get rid of every thing that is not good; I want to hold fast to that <u>which is</u> good. The "axe has indeed been laid at the root of the tree," in this country, & we poor southerners have felt the heavy blows, but, if they contribute to ripen the purposes of God, shall we receive good at His hand & not evil? God forbid! The war with all its ravages was only God's sword, which we needed, to cut off our sins & make us a wiser & better people, or the sooner fill out the measure of our iniquities.

I enjoy nice books & good books yet, & <u>will</u> take time to read them. I agree in the sentiment that when we consider the <u>wisdom</u> of a man's life, we must not leave out what he has <u>left undone</u> when we state what he <u>has done</u>. We can only stand a certain amount of pressure & it is better to avoid the wear & tear of doing what somebody else can do better, or as well as we can, & with more ease & comfort, & do what <u>we can</u> intelligently & skillfully, in its place. If we could all know what our <u>talent</u> was & improve <u>that</u>, we would be more successful in doing good. I have never yet felt as though I knew what mine was & feel the importance of knowing it more than ever <u>now</u>, that I have no children to bring up.

In March and April 1873, Maria was hopeful that Osceola could be sold through Alonzo G. Grant, an immigration and land agent from Dublin, Ireland, who inspected the place, made sketches, took photos, held meetings on immigration, and then left.[7] Nothing came of a later exploratory visit by a Mr. Ashley of the West Indies, who was looking for a sugar plantation. By April 1874, Maria had even less reason than ever to maintain her own establishment.

8 Apr., Wed. Carrie brought down Dore's trousseau, some very nice & pretty things. We are greatly indebted to Carrie for her judicious selection & the timely aid she has given as we are to all the children for their generosity & affection. I trust God will bless & preserve them all from want. Mrs Gary [Ocala friend] came &

helped me make a plain cake & sponge cake, also orange pies. She brought three cakes she had made for me at home. Millie [Fen's wife] made jelly.

9 Apr., Thurs. We were all busy all day making preparation for the wedding. Mrs Gary remained here last night & long enough to trim the fruit cake she baked. I made custard & blancmange early in the morning. Millie made trifle. I made ambrosia of cocoanut & orange. Mr Dawkins, Mr Carlisle & Fen came after dinner [from Gainesville]. They brought me oranges & light bread, We had a rainy evening. The groom did not arrive until ½ after 8 o,clock. It was so rainy a number of those invited did not come. The supper was more than sufficient for twice the number of guests.

The groom was William Christian Wallace, a Gainesville druggist eighteen years Dore's senior. John Taylor's aunt, sister, and now daughter married into the same Wallace family, which had origins in both South Carolina and Kentucky. William's brother Caleb owned a plantation next to Osceola.

Selling the place became more pressing for other reasons besides Dore's moving on.

16 June 1874. Maria Baker Taylor to Ann Eliza Furman

John is making an effort to sell this plantation,[8] which is eating its head off with taxes, none of it being planted this year. I only plant on my own place & Richie's,[9] & only a small crop for myself; Richie pays expenses & has the bulk of the crop. He will soon go on to New York, being an agent for the mercantile establishment of Aaron Chaflin & Co, & it being necessary for him to be there, during the fall business season.

Richie, his mother's mainstay on the plantation, left on July 26. On the recommendation of her son-in-law Edward Crane in Pittsburgh, Maria engaged a Mr. Jackman of Pittsburgh to put the plantation machinery in order and to serve as general assistant. James Dawkins undertook to supervise the arrangement with Jackman. Jackman arrived on June 18, followed by teenage sons George and Harry in July, and Mrs. Jackman and two younger children on August 1. The

Jackmans were lodged in the main house until other quarters could be readied. Thus they were there during the preparations and gathering of the family for Anne and Julius Carlisle's wedding.

> 13 Aug., Thurs. We all got up early & Nan[10] was married at ½ after 7 o'clock & all of them left as soon as we could get over with breakfast, which everyone seemed to enjoy. I put up lunch for the party. Mr Tomkies[11] arrived in time to marry the couple. I put up dinner for Mr Jackman & Mrs Jackman went down with the children & spent the day [at the mill]. We heard the hogs were in the corn & Fen went over & had them put out of the corn. I put away crockery, spoons, knives etc & had scalding done.

This second 1874 wedding removed yet another reason for Maria to maintain a family home. As the 1874 diary continues, Maria's difficulties with the Jackmans are added to the many other things she has to take care of, while Fen and James come down to help when they can. Immediately after the wedding, Maria turns her attention to the Jackmans' quarters, an abandoned church that had to be moved.

> 14 Aug., Fri. I felt very unwell yesterday & today, wrote a long letter to Richard yesterday & wrote to Johnny & Lydia today & to Nan, and only attended to a few household matters. Mr Jackman had John [servant] & the wagon to haul wood, & Robin began to take down the church. Noland came to see after the cows.

> 17 Aug., Mon. Plant Irish potatoes. I tried to get the oxen rigged up to carry the church down. Tom Johnson brought up front wheels & fixed spoke & attached the wheels together. John helped him gear up the oxen, but he & Harry Jackman let them get away & broke up the whole hauling. John cleaned out the [out]houses. Drayton & George helped him. I sewed some. Commenced hauling corn, hauled 4 loads.

> 18 Aug., Tues. Cabbage seed. Hauling corn with 1 wagon. I had to get a driver for the ox wagon & kept the oxen up here. Drayton's misdemeaners with the mule put us to much trouble. Harry lost stirrup from Richie's saddle. Fen went to engage Cephas Gordon to haul the church & succeeded.

20 Aug., Thurs. Fen worried to find Daisy ridden hard by Harry Jackman without permission. Helped Drayton get breakfast & dinner & got most of supper myself.

21 Aug., Fri. Sarah More began work. Sent Drayton to Ocala, he did not return until after dinner. I received a letter from Lydia, some papers. I attended to household duties & read the [Godey's] Lady's Book. Mrs Jackman sick. Ceasar Gordon hauling the church down to be put up at the engine.[12]

24 Aug., Mon. Mrs Jackman quite sick this morning & Mr Jackman remained to wait on her & sent for a physician. Fen went to Ocala & had the mill taken there to mend & the buggy taken in there to be mended. He saw Mr Agnew about my coffee, flour, meat, & package of shoes, none of them forthcoming yet. I waited on Mrs Jackman some.

25 Aug., Tues. Plant beets, turnips, carrots. Mrs Jackman still quite sick & Harry [Jackman] also. Henry finished shingling the little corn house. Millie making pants Fen bought for Harry Jackman. Still hauling corn. Mr Jackman went to Ocala for the mill but returned without it, brought the mail.

26 Aug., Wed. Fen took Henry Buzhardt & planted turnips, beets, carrots, Hubbard squash, cabbages in the cowpen for me. Mrs Jackman called for much attention. Mr Jackman ground corn.

27 Aug., Thurs. Mrs Jackman thinks herself ill & I was frequently up & down stairs to attend her.

28 Aug., Fri. Attended to household matters. Mrs Jackman still sick & requiring much attention. I tried to write some. I was busy all morning, salted up beef. I sat down to write some but Mr More came & I had to entertain him. I felt very tired at night with nursing etc.

30 Aug., Sun. My day was pretty well spent in nursing Mrs Jackman. Dr Butt came to see her & gave her medicine. George Jackman with fever. Fen gave him cal. Harry sick all day with a boil. I gave Mrs Jackman 15 grs of quinine. She came down in the parlour.

31 Aug., Mon. Grandison gave notice his mules were out & one of Mr More's horses out. They were gotten up & Mr More left about 12 o'clock. Mr Jackman found the boiler burst & could not grind. He & Fen went to Ocala to see after having it mended. George took oil today. Gave Mrs Jackman pills left by Dr Butt who called to see her yesterday, 3 or 4 doses of turpentine. She came down stairs & lay in my room & in the parlor, fell down three or four times. I found it necessary to be positive with her [speak sternly].

1 Sept., Tues. Mrs Jackman appears worse this morning. Clear symptoms of typhoid. I gave her oil & small doses of turpentine. Dr Butt came & gave her blue pill & quinine & continued turpentine. I gave her anodyne at night. She was much more patient today & tractable.

2 Sept., Wed. Dr Butt called to see Mrs Jackman this morning. I gave her 10 grs of quinine. Two white men came with a part of the saw frame.[13] One wagon broke down & left its contents 13 miles from here. They tarried here all night. Fen went with wagon & got the blacksmith's tools & he will be out here today.

3 Sept., Thurs. I gave Mrs Jackman the quinine & medicine left by Dr Butt. She is decidedly better. Fen was very busy today attending to George & Harry sick.

4 Sept., Fri. I feel very unwell. Waited on Mrs Jackman & gave her nourishment. I attended to the farm business weighing cotton etc. Wrote to Mrs Nicholes, finished Curran's letter, wrote PC to Mr Dawkins. Read a little & gave Mrs J her medicines. The white men came back & brought the machinery they left behind. I gave them dinner, fed their horses & gave them food for themselves & horses by the way.

6 Sept., Sun. Mrs Jackman still sick. Dr Butt called to see her. I did very little else than wait on her, read the scriptures & the religious papers some. Dr Butt called & pronounced Mrs J convalescing. Mr Dawkins came in the evening & Thornton Stringfellow with him. I concluded my letter to Lydia. Sue got supper for Mr Dawkins. Carrie sent me bread pickles & jelly by him & he brought me sugar, meat & lard.

7 Sept., Mon. Jane [servant] left this morning. Mr Dawkins went to see after the mule business. John Craig began to haul Dr Wallace's corn from Howse field with one wagon.[14] Mrs Jackman sent George for Dr Butt & he came & pronounced the visit unnecessary. Thornton Stringfellow had a chill & fever in the evening. I had his feet bathed & gave him hot tea.

10 Sept., Thurs. Sent Henry to the Springs for flour, meat & potatoes, he only brought 2 barrels of flour. Mr Dawkins also went with Thornton Stringfellow there to get white lead. I finished letter to Richie, wrote PC to Fen & put up some papers for Lily Furman & sent George to the office with them. He brought me a letter from Lydia & one from Richie with which I was much pleased. Mrs Jackman decidedly convalescent.

11 Sept., Fri. I attended to household affairs. Mr Dawkins & Thornton still here. I read some in the morning in New York Herald & the Witness. Made up accts etc. After dinner I rode to see Robin & went to the engine with Mr Dawkins. They have just finished patching the boiler & Mr Jackman is putting the attachment up.

12 Sept., Sat. Mr Dawkins had the house moved to the engine.

14 Sept., Mon. Mrs Jackman up & out again. Mr Dawkins went to Ocala & to the mill & did not return to dinner. I attended to household matters. Wrote to Mary Ansley,[15] Lydia, Dore & PC to Aunt Ann. Gave rations to Dr Wallaces hands & to the cotton pickers. I weighed cotton. Read a little.

15 Sept., Tues. Mr Dawkins gave me accts to look over & memorandum of agreement with Mr Jackman. I made up my own accts, looked over his.

16 Sept., Wed. Strawberry plants. Mr Dawkins got the large wagon today & finished hauling the house down for Mr Jackman. I had some difficulty in getting John to go on with the corn. He was very provoking about the horse & left Mr D afoot. Eli broke gin. I wrote to Carrie & Fannie before I retired. Weighed cotton & gave out rations.

18 Sept., Fri. Mr Dawkins went to Ocala this morning. Sent telegram to Carrie to come on here. She telegraphed that she could not leave Mr Carlisle, who was ill with fever. I am very sorry & uneasy to hear of his illness. George came up with the telegrams. Mr D wrote me he had a lunch with him [in Ocala] & would not come to dinner. Mr Dawkins came home greatly worried that the mill is not ready for running & because Carrie could not come.

21 Sept., Mon. Henry came to beat out my rye, but found the rats had destroyed it all. I mended Loulie's dress & had a good deal of business to attend to. I wrote to Millie, Carrie & Anne to send by Mr Dawkins when he goes. Weighed cotton & gave rations to hands.

22 Sept., Tues. Mr Dawkins showed me memorandum of agreement between him & Mr Jackman & gave me some directions about his business. I was busy with accts & writing. Wrote note to Mr Dawkins at mill after he left & sent Drayton to go with him to Ocala. He [Drayton] brought me letters from Carrie, Richie & Curran & note from Mr Dawkins. Henry Buzhardt worked my patch & ploughed a little.

23 Sept., Wed. Settled with John Clement. Drayton cooked. I dismissed Sarah today & pd her up in full. Settled with Henry Buzhardt & Carolina Mikle. Finished letter to Richie. Wrote to Mr Dawkins, Carrie, & Curran. Weighed cotton. Assorted Irish potatoes & had some planted & the patch hoed by Henry Buzhardt. The horses all came home of their own accord & I salted them. I weighed cotton & gave rations.

25 Sept., Fri. Florie [Jackman] quite sick & Mrs Jackman uneasy about him, called upon me frequently to advise for her. I attended to farm matters weighing cotton & had Claiborne cutting hay. Drayton cooked & I assisted him. Found no time to write or sew. Noland came to see me about his cows, meal etc. I settled up with Carson & had my Irish potatoes washed & overhauled. Prince sent word he could not go to Gainesville tomorrow with Mr Dawkins wagon.

26 Sept., Sat. Neither Sue nor myself are feeling well. Florie still sick, Old Mooney came back but had the chill & had to leave again. The mill ran but the patrons were discouraged & many did not come.[16] I had to give Mrs Jackman a plain talk.

28 Sept., Mon. Mrs Jackman with fever. Sent breakfast down to them [at the mill] by George and ascertained he had been threshing down my oranges. I went to look after Mrs Jackman some. Sunned some of my bedding & the Irish potatoes. Minty sent me some pea seed.

30 Sept., Tues. Mrs Jackman too sick to move today. I sent gin down & her trunks & a mattress. Prince sent me over a letter from Carrie he brought from Gainesville, they will be here this evening. Mrs Jackman concluded to remain. Carrie & Mr Dawkins came, & she was not near so much worried by the travel as usual.[17] George came up & went to bed sick.

1 Oct., Thurs. Dig your potatoes & plant oats or rye. Put rye in corner next to Dr Vogt's. Mrs Jackman removed this morning. I felt very unwell. Mr Dawkins went to the mill & saw Mr Jackman who also came up here for his wife & took her down to her house.

The Jackman family and other labor-related difficulties not mentioned in the diary evidently produced the exasperated state of mind Maria expresses in a virulent attack on two eminent champions of the black race: Harriet Beecher Stowe, the renowned author of *Uncle Tom's Cabin* (1852) and author of an 1870 exposé of the personal life of the English Romantic poet Lord Byron;[18] and Stowe's brother Henry Ward Beecher, nationally known Congregational preacher and former prominent abolitionist, now in the limelight as defendant in an adultery lawsuit. The coincidence of "Topsy" being the name of both a mischievous young female slave in Stowe's masterwork and an annoying young male servant of Maria's provides the transition into the attack.

30 September 1874.[19] *Maria Baker Taylor to Ann Eliza Furman*

Your letters always revive & quicken my feelings, & I like to write before they are defaced by the daily cares which often harrass me, in my contacts with Darkies[20] whom I cannot control & whose parents will not manage them. If I could only tell you my complicated troubles of this morning (just 9 o'clock) you would laugh & marvel, at the patience I exercise, as the children do,[21] but I think my boy Topsy has put the "last hair on the camel's back" this morning & must go somewhere else to get his butter & bread. As Sister Lydia would say, I wish Mrs Stowe & her "delightful Brother" Beecher, had him tacked to them for life. In fact some of his accomplishments, in the way of ogling, would just do for that Adonis & his artful "Betsey."[22]

What has our fair, beautiful & once much favored country come to? Wickedness stalks through the land, & sin unblushing holds up her nakedness exposed to view. I blush for the nation when I think of Beecher's defence, Moulton's exposes of his hypocritical baseness, or as the Savannah news calls it, "Beecher's nastiness," & of American papers having regular runners to catch up & report to an impatient & curious people, all the slime. But I have digressed & upon a theme I would not dwell; words could not express my indignation & scorn. Oh, that the South may long be kept from Northern isms!

It is a pity Mrs Stowe went way over the water to hunt up Lord Byron's crimes. A little patience would have enabled her to find a tale, so in unison with her depraved tastes, nearer home. Excuse the above, the name of "Topsy" reminded me of these excresences on the body politic, "Beecher & Stowe"!!! Throw a vail [*sic*] over these ebullitions & let us pass on to some thing more pleasant.

Since Carrie came we have had some variety in our household experience. Mrs Jackman & family moved out the day after she came & what with bed ripping, blankets, sheets & quilt washing & house cleaning, I have been kept "pritty" busy & my head is a little cooled off from the quinine ringing sound it had in it while the brood were here; deliver me ever from Northern trash; presumptive, assumptive! "Nothing but a shoveling will do for them." Southern crackers are not so bad.

The diary shows Maria's concerns about the plantation continuing.

2 Oct., Fri. Ned busy cleaning up the house. A telegram came for Mr Dawkins to say that two Cubans would come by the boat to look at the place, & be here in the morning. Rhina sent me Louise's[23] clothes unwashed, & I had trouble to get them done as the negroes have gone to a camp meeting for the most part. I felt bothered by the press of business. I am glad Mrs J got off.

3 Oct., Sat. Mr Dawkins went early to Ocala & remained there & at the mill till late in the evening, when he brought out 2 Cubans, Mr Huertes, & Mr Williams who took tea with us & spent the night. Mr Govine [Cuban] & Sue played & Carrie played for them on piano. Mr Govine Sr could not speak English but his son spoke very well. They were very agreeable. The engine boiler burst today, no one here.

5 Oct., Mon. We rose early & Mr Dawkins & myself went to the Springs with Louise & remained there all day waiting for the boat to take her, at last had to leave her & arrived home late, found Carrie & Sue anxious about us. I left Louise with Nora & Saml Small. Mr Williams & Roy promising to take care of her for me until the boat arrived. I saw one of the Glory of France roses today at the Springs.

6 Oct., Tues. Plant your cane as soon as you cut it. Sue Floyd cooked. Mr Jackman came up to see Mr Dawkins who is rather indifferent about spending money to be thrown away so carelessly.[24]

Toward the end of 1874, Maria stated yet another reason to wind up her affairs at Osceola: "Today is Curran's & my birthday. I am 61 years old & in the course of nature cannot expect to live much longer" (5 December 1874). Maria never expresses any desire to keep any of her children with her down on the farm, but rather exhibits her own "goaheadativeness" in a recommendation for a young cousin in South Carolina.

20 January 1875. Maria Baker Taylor to Ann Eliza Furman

Could not Bollivar [Furman] do better in business in New York if he could secure a place than he does at planting? Perhaps

Johnny could assist him in getting a place, he has aided several young men in securing good situations. Richie finds his business in New York much more paying than planting,

Nevertheless, Osceola remained a lively locus of family life during Maria's last year there. For example, in just the two months of March and April 1875, Lydia and her baby Maria came from Pittsburgh for a stay of two months, picking up Carrie and Anne in Gainesville on the way. Maria noted on 8 March with obvious gratification that with the exception of Mary all of her daughters were with her—Carrie, Lydia, Sue, Dore, and Anne. Also in the house at the time were Johnny's wife and children, Dore's husband and new baby, and, off and on, Carrie's husband. After Johnny's family and Carrie left, Mary's children Sophie and Willie Bauskett and stepdaughter Kate Ansley arrived from St. Augustine for a visit.

Perhaps even such a family-centered person as Maria was glad to leave on 28 April for a trip that took her away from Osceola for more than six months as she visited Mary in St. Augustine; relatives in Charleston; Lydia in Pittsburgh; Johnny and Richie in New York City; and Carrie, Anne, and Fen in Gainesville. While on the trip, Maria showed her desire for North-South reconciliation in two letters to the editor she sent to the *East Florida Banner* (Ocala):

> The Baptist convention [in Charleston] was in progress when we arrived, and an able body of divines was present from all the Southern States, and some from the North came, with kindly greetings, and I trust returned to their houses, with the conviction that we have as much practical faith as they in our Lord's positive announcement respecting the necessity of forgiveness, if we desire to be forgiven.
>
> I attended the commencement of the Western University and that of the Pennsylvania Female College, under Presbyterian patronage, and thought their exercises and essays highly creditable, having nothing to shock my southern patriotism, or wound its sensativeness. On the contrary, I felt reassured that in these institutions nothing was taught to cherish animosity to the South. We find the Pittsburgers a very courteous, friendly and hospitable people.[25]

A little later, during her first visit to New York, Maria found much that was reassuring in this northern city also. Her sons were busy but attentive, and she encountered in-laws and other southern friends living there, including her old friend from Beaufort days: on 22 August, "Johnny went with me today over to Brooklyn to hear Mr Rambaut preach. He greeted us very cordially."[26]

Between the time Maria returned home on 5 November 1875 and the end of the year, the "open house" at Osceola resumed with various combinations of Sue, Dore and husband and baby, Fen, Richie, Johnny and his family, Mary's son Tommy Bauskett, Carrie and James Dawkins, and Anne and her baby Millie. Maria termed these visits after her return "a pleasant reunion."

In spite of this ample fulfillment in family life, Maria seems to have felt that she had missed something. On 5 December 1875, she wrote a curiously sweeping statement: "I am 62 years old today, & I look back with regret on the many profitless years of my life." Typical of her laconic diary-writing style, she does not expatiate. However, "profitless" is a term she uses only to express dissatisfaction over time not used to good purpose; thus she is not here referring to the economic failure of the plantation, nor would she regard her years of childrearing as misspent. She seems rather to be articulating a sense of unfulfilled potential in herself, reminiscent of her earlier remark about needing to discover her own talent.

Nevertheless, thoughts of her family dominated as Maria looked to the future. On 17 December she recorded, "Johnny has bought Mrs Dozier's place in Gainesville & wants me to break up & go live with him." She accepted the invitation. In expectation of her new life in Gainesville, on New Year's Day 1876 Maria prayed for herself and her children.

> Make me in all the future more faithful & wise in the performance of my duties to Thee, to my children & in all the relations of life. Lord help us to be true to each other & may no root of bitterness springing up trouble us. Father I pray Thee to make me a blessing, particularly to my children.

Conclusion

At the end of her middle years, Maria was free of what were perhaps the two most demanding life tasks that had absorbed her entire adulthood: educating her children and supervising a large number of black people. Hence overviews of her accomplishment with the children and of her attitudes on race in her final years on the plantation will conclude the account of this phase of life.

In June 1873 Maria at age fifty-nine had accomplished a major life project that had engaged her for almost forty years. She and her husband had seen six daughters—Caroline, Mary, Lydia, Susan, Dore, and Anne—and four sons—John, William, Richard, and Fenwick—through primary education at home and institutional schooling away from home at ages ranging from fourteen to nineteen. The education of her children was unquestionably Maria's highest priority in terms of time, effort, thought, and material resources, and she pursued it tirelessly under the difficult circumstances of removal to a new territory, war, and social upheaval. Maria must have frequently found the results discouraging.

The Taylor parents were equally concerned about educating the girls and the boys, an attitude that is not surprising given that in the Baptist scheme of things the ultimate purpose of education was the salvation of the immortal soul, and the souls of men and women were of equal value. In the temporal realm, these beliefs would have been supplemented by the attacks on the notion of female intellectual inferiority launched by southern intellectuals and religious leaders from 1830 to 1860.[1] The variations in the educations of the individual children are assignable to external circumstances, most importantly the Civil War and hard times after the war, and the ages at which the children were affected by those circumstances.

In choosing schools, the Taylors looked for a Baptist influence, and while the children were away Maria continued to impart religious and moral instruction through letters. When the four youngest Taylors lived with Carrie and James Dawkins to attend school in Gainesville, Maria was assured that they were receiving a strong Baptist influence through Carrie, of whom Maria wrote to Ann Furman: "All [of the family] think her a model woman. She is a true Christian woman, who has been properly exercised by her trials, which have been varied. She is one of the charitable types of Christians, very unselfish & self denying" (16 June 1874). With her five consecutive years at Limestone, Carrie had received the longest and most consistent institutional education of all the children, and with her husband's full concurrence she generously furthered the education of her youngest siblings.

As for social education, the children grew up among the best society the sparsely settled countryside and the villages of Ocala and Gainesville had to offer, for the Taylors' holdings placed them in the planter aristocracy of Florida, and James Dawkins was a prominent man in the region. Persons who moved in wider and more sophisticated circles found the children to be desirable company, evident when David Levy Yulee proposed educating Richie and Fen with his son Wickliffe and when Mrs. Yulee invited the younger girls for house visits and reluctantly saw them depart. The result of Maria's social education of Carrie is suggested in Mrs. Yulee's comment, "We had such a delightful time with Mrs Dawkins [age twenty-seven]. She is so lovely."[2]

On a deeper level, Maria understood courtesy to be a manifestation of Christianity, as she explains in one of her "Grandmother's Letters," didactic pieces for children she was writing in the 1870s. In this one, addressed to "My dear Grandchildren," Maria summarizes what she must have taught her children of the meaning of etiquette.

> [The Bible is] the very best Book of Etiquette, or more properly of politeness, from which etiquette springs. It enjoins us to be

courteous to all men, without exception, good, bad, or indifferent, without respect to persons. I do not understand how a disciple of Jesus can be impolite. He lifted not up his voice in the street but was gentle to all. Courtesy, politeness, and good manners should characterize the Christian & should be practiced in youth to become perfect. It springs from the heart & is doing unto others as we would have them do unto us. Not set phrases, nor forms unsuitable to the circumstances that surround us, but the quick sense to set them aside when they would be distasteful or irksome.

Maria considered the Bible to be also central for intellectual education. Again, the "Grandmother's Letter":

Who would not seek to be intellectual? The Bible above all books quickens the intellect, enlarges the heart & mind. "The entrance of Thy word giveth light. It giveth understanding to the simple." Then if the simple would understand knowledge, let us seek it in the Scriptures. Let us drink deeply at this fountain of true wisdom, the wisdom that cometh down from above.

In their system of education, the Taylors showed little ambition for their children in an economic or professional sense. Their sending their sons to military schools suggests that they shared in some degree the antebellum view that the purpose of the southern system of education was to teach its white citizens to effectively control slave labor.[3] However, in Maria's letter to Johnny and Richie's to her when the boys were in military schools, the emphasis was on their learning to control themselves, not others. In other words, for Maria the training in self-discipline and obedience to authority in such schools was primarily a matter of building Christian character (with God as the ultimate authority). Maria explicitly stated in her diary her belief regarding this issue: "I every day acknowledge more & more the necessity of teaching children self control & exercising it daily ourselves. To crucify the flesh with its affections & lust is very painful, but is nevertheless very necessary" (28 March 1875).

Throughout her life Maria evinced much less interest in her children's temporal fortunes than in their immortal souls, as her daughter Lydia summed up a few months after Maria died: "Our dear

Mother put heaven in front of all earthly desires for herself and us, and thus we must hope and strive to reach it."[4] To attain the grand goal of education, the key was obedience to God's will as learned through the Bible: "Search the Scriptures, Old & New," Maria adjured all children. "They will make you wise unto Salvation."

Long and strong echoes of Maria's many teachings can be seen in traits a contemporary colleague saw in her son Fen during his thirty-five years on the Florida Supreme Court (1891–1925). Justice Jefferson B. Browne credited Fen with being equally firm in standing against demands for faster criminal convictions directed largely against blacks and demands for infringing the property rights of corporations, saying of Fen, "Where hate and fanaticism have run riot, and the public careers of men threatened unless they would bow to its behests, he has stood unmoved and unshaken." Fen must have had his mother in mind when he himself said that greater attention should be paid to "the inculcation in them [the country's youth] with the rigid principles of old-fashioned honesty and integrity . . . and a proper respect for age, law and order, and the rooting out from their minds the idea that the acquisition of money is the only thing worth a life's striving." Attributing to Fen wonderful strength of character, fearlessness, and massive intellect, Browne yet found his most admirable qualities to be his gentleness and tolerance.[5]

In her diary for her last year at Osceola, Maria names thirty-five black neighbors and servants, although she was at Osceola for only six months that year, but in the combined documents for the next twenty years, spent in Gainesville, very few black people are mentioned. Thus one major concern of Maria's forty-two years as a plantation mistress, her interaction with large numbers of slaves and then freedmen, ended abruptly at the conclusion of her midlife years in Marion County. A sampling of diary passages gives some idea of the view of black people Maria had arrived at as this intense involvement drew to a close.

Already in 1867 some evidence of accommodation to changed times appears in Maria's neutral comment when Robin, for years her mainstay as both slave and freedman, was called to jury duty: "Quite an era in the South." By 1871, in referring to another longtime servant, Maria chose a respectful term that she would perhaps not have used in slavery times: "Abby came with a message that Old Minty was dead. She must be very old, perhaps 90 or more. I gave Abby some clothes to bury her in, & regretted that I did not see the old lady in her illness" (12 April). On the other hand, when the family found Smart Wilkinson, the black sexton of their church, and his friend Murphy seated on the front porch one Sunday, Richard "invited them out of their seats," the Taylors "not being yet prepared for social equality" (9 July 1871). Still, the turn of phrase here is mild rather than indignant. The tone was different in another incident. When the freedmen John Clement and Amos Graham "came to beg me to let them off about Dr Wallace's horses which they have been riding," Maria "felt disgusted" and sarcastically referred to them as "our voters" (20 October 1873).

Maria remained forthright in her dealings with servants about wages. For example, when Henry and Grace got married, "Sue fixed up the table for Grace, & I was pretty busy in getting up things for her"; but two days later when "Henry came to know what Grace's wages were, I checked his presumption by informing him & telling him, if he wanted it higher he must go elsewhere to get it; she is mostly kept for her good temper, being very inefficient" (12 May 1873). However, Maria also often evenhandedly records blame and praise, for example, "Phyllis cooked breakfast & dinner. Oscar was very crooked & idle this morning, took five hours to milk 9 cows & bring 3 buckets of water 20 steps. Nancy helped & Phyllis did some cleaning up. Affy sent Scip Reed to borrow the oxen & cart to take her cotton to town. I sent several commissions by him, which he executed very well" (10 October 1873). If an exacting employer, Maria was concerned to deal fairly, writing on 4 January 1875, "We would express our sincere thanks that we have been enabled to discharge our obligations to all our servants the past year."

On a more personal level, ordinary helpfulness prevailed between Maria and her black neighbors, Maria and her daughter Sue lending a hand in a variety of ways: when Grace got married, "Busy in dressing Grace's cake and fixing off some other matters for her. Sue busy all day with Grace's 'fixins'" (9 May 1873). "Patience came to say Phyllis was quite ill. Sue went to see her & carried some tea, sugar etc for her" (13 June 1873). "Phyllis came to get me to read a letter from

Sukey for her" (29 November 1873); and "I sewed on some sewing work to help [Josephine] Cannon" (4 May 1874).

Visits from Charry, Affy, and Minty kept Maria informed of Ocala news and doings in the black community: "Minty came here & had a long talk on various subjects; brought some eggs with her. There has been a great hubbub in the St Joseph's church & Prince deposed from his office" (29 November 1873); but Maria felt she had to justify listening to malicious gossip from a black person: "Old Affy told me a long tale of Ocala slander in which A.W. [a scapegrace friend of Richie's] was mixed up. I listened to her contrary to my usual practice as I felt by so doing I could clear or justify an innocent party" (8 May 1874).

Attitudes apparent in actions of Maria's son Fen during the 1870s evince moderate attitudes toward race that may be ascribed to the family as a whole. In one instance, Fen was one of three lawyers requested by the court to examine Florida's black U.S. congressman Josiah T. Walls for admission to the bar, and Fen enthusiastically recommended him.[6] In another instance, Fen protested the poor treatment a lawyer for a black defendant received at the hands of an Ocala judge.

Finally, during the years on the plantation, Maria and the servants who were her mainstays formed friendships that continued after her move to town. In an undated sketch of Maria, her granddaughter Ellen Sutton Wallace wrote of the former servants, "The most beloved were Robin and Minty, who married each other, and Maum Affy. In later years Robin and Minty owned a very nice little home and place in Ocala and were good citizens. After Robin died, Minty came often to Gainesville to see Grandmother, staying a few days or a week. She would always bring a basket of fried chicken and cake." And looking back in 1880 on former servants, Maria herself commented nostalgically to Ann Furman, "There are so many of the old negroes that I would like to see a sketch of before the 'Old Times' passes from memory."[7]

These vignettes and backward glances suggest a relatively mild form of racism given the time and place. It is unlikely Maria ever forgot the southern evangelical view that, in spite of their ordained inferior social status, blacks were "intellectual, moral, immortal" human beings who like whites "were created in the image of God,"[8] a view that was certainly more humane than the contemporaneous anthropological attempts in the North to prove that negroes were a subhuman species whose brains had different proportions from those of whites.[9] In her 15 February 1873 letter to Ann Furman, Maria had spoken of the need to reassess her "old habits of thought, feeling & action," and it is tempting to assume that her views of race were among these. However, in the letter she gives no clue whether these views were among the sins that God intended to "cut off" through the ravages of war in order to "make us a wiser & better people" or among the good things from the past she wanted "to hold fast to." If Maria did not reconsider the validity of her racial views in the new social order, she would have needed to expend great psychological energy to avoid so huge a component of her "old habits."

But however she managed her "thought and feeling" on the race issue, Maria was largely quit of the "action," as she was of other consuming responsibilities at the end of her midlife phase in Marion County. She would no longer have to deal with freedmen, manage the plantation, educate her children, or run a large household. Of the responsibilities she would assume next, some would be new projects, others continuations of old projects in new configurations. Some would be freely chosen, others implicit in the situation she chose to enter.

Four

OLD AGE IN GAINESVILLE, FLORIDA, 1876–95

Introduction

When Maria at the age of fifty-nine had expressed a yearning for self-discovery, by the standards of the day she would have been regarded as "old." However, the construal of the category "old age" is a product of the personal imagination, the physical state of the body, and the surrounding social world.[1] Throughout the final stage of her life, Maria sustained a positive self-image that empowered her to undertake new projects and new versions of earlier projects. Images of growth and accomplishment reveal what old age meant to Maria. For example, at age seventy-seven she states that the desire of her old age is "to bring forth fruit," however small, and at age eighty she sees herself as finally "settling" into spiritual knowledge after years of gradual learning. These attitudes were supported by the other factors that determine self-image in old age. Until her final year, Maria's health compared favorably with that of other family members. As for her social environment, the family circle constantly stimulated her with its needs and expectations, and her religious community accorded her a bit of recognition for her writing. At the same time, death was never far from Maria's consciousness; as she wrote in her diary at the age of sixty-two, "Passing away is written in characters not to be mistaken, on everything" (4 April 1875).

When Maria moved to Gainesville early in 1876, it was a bustling, rapidly growing county seat with a population of about 2,000, the majority of whom, like the Taylors, had South Carolina connections. Maria had known the community well for a number of years, and in one sense she was living as she always had—that is, in the midst of her large family. Perhaps the biggest change was that she never again maintained an independent household. Maria never expressed regret over leaving her independent household at Osceola, and her only regret about not having her own place in Gainesville was that she did not feel she could invite out-of-town relatives for long visits.

Five of Maria's seven married children and their spouses were living in Gainesville at the time: Carrie and James Dawkins, John and Curran Taylor, Fenwick and Millie Taylor, Dore and William Wallace, and Anne and Julius Carlisle. Daughter Sue made her home with the Dawkinses until she married in 1884, and afterward lived near Gainesville. Son Richard and his wife Kate lived a few miles south of Gainesville at their country place on Lake Wauburg and came into town frequently. Carrie and Richie remained childless, but among them the other children produced fifteen grandchildren during Maria's Gainesville years to add to the nine surviving grandchildren born earlier. The Gainesville family circle was further extended by the many relatives of James, Curran, and Millie who lived in town or a few miles out, a secondary family network often supplemented by visiting South Carolina relatives who typically stayed for several months. As for Maria's other two children and their families, Mary (formerly Bauskett) and her second husband, William Ansley, were on the Florida east coast, just a few hours away by train; only Lydia and Edward Crane were relatively inaccessible, living in Pittsburgh and then in Germany.

At various times, Maria had her headquarters with Carrie, John, Fen, and Anne, whose houses were in easy walking distance of each other. However, she often left her "base" to stay with one of the other families when needed, sometimes for weeks. She apparently felt equally welcome at all of her children's houses, and most days she saw most of her family members. No doubt the prosperity enjoyed by the family as a whole helped to ward off potential generational conflicts, for Maria's children in and near Gainesville were well positioned. James Dawkins and Fen Taylor had a flourishing statewide law practice; William Wallace ran his own drugstore; Julius Carlisle was variously Clerk of Circuit Court and businessman; and John Taylor traversed the state as a salesman for a New York City firm.

Richard Taylor was an orange grower as well as a traveling salesman for another New York firm.

An 1883 account of Gainesville lists the Dawkins and Carlisle houses as among the "fine residences" of the town and describes the Carlisle residence as being surrounded by a four-acre orange grove.[2] Maria recorded her pleasure in these surroundings: "The orange trees in the yard are loaded with blooms, the atmosphere is filled with their perfume" (11 March 1885). Richie's place she described as "near a beautiful lake, in a hammock of beautiful trees, of great variety. Orange trees growing & soil for a beautiful garden of flowers & vegetables & the best facilities for raising poultry. The house is pleasant" (12 June 1882). James, John, Fen, and Julius also owned farmland in the county, and Julius had phosphate mines. In addition to the attractive places and economic security with her children in Gainesville, Maria had her own resources. She gradually gave to her children or sold off parcels of the Osceola and other Taylor property, but for some years she realized a bit of income from tenants. Much of the money from the land sales went to pay off mortgages, and in 1890, eighteen years after her husband's death, Maria was selling forty acres of "my lands in the phosphate regions" in Levy County to pay his estate taxes. Still, she died possessed of property in Alachua and Pasco counties.

Relatively privileged as she was, Maria still had many trying circumstances to cope with. Poor conditions of public health and sanitation constantly affected the family; various fevers—typhoid, dengue, yellow, scarlet—were endemic or epidemic, and measles, whooping cough, and diphtheria were feared diseases. Some family members also suffered from worrisome chronic ailments. Carrie was reduced to invalidism by a condition in which pieces of her backbone splintered off and emerged through setons that had to be constantly tended to. Sue was afflicted with severe facial neuralgia, and Johnny periodically broke out in a painful and debilitating rash. Maria was the preferred nurse for those afflicted with these and milder illnesses, as well as for births and deaths.

Other kinds of difficulties arose, and Maria suffered along with her children. The alcoholism of son-in-law Julius Carlisle was a constant source of unpleasantness for the whole family, and for years William Wallace failed to set Dore up with her own house. Sue's husband John Beard made a precarious living teaching school in small Florida settlements, provoking contention in his school boards and being fired at least twice. After teaching at Western University in Pittsburgh for fifteen years, Lydia's husband Edward Crane suffered an emotional and physical collapse upon being dismissed; in 1888 David Yulee used his influence to obtain a consulship in Germany for Crane, but Maria apparently never saw Lydia and her family again. Maria's last years were also saddened by the deaths of close family members.

Church life was of course more regular in town than it had been in Marion County, and over the years Maria attended Sunday services about half the time, usually noting the reason when she did not go. She also served for years as treasurer of the Ladies Benevolent Association and did her share of the work for LBA fund-raisers. However, she was not a bustling churchwoman. Her religiosity was more significantly demonstrated through private reading and writing, through many kinds of service to the family, and through one episode of commitment to a missionary cause.

ONE

Reading and Writing

Maria's reading was a lifelong habit that both formed and expressed the quality of her mind. She regarded herself as a person of intellect, as did others in her small provincial circle. For example, Judge William A. Hocker of the Florida Supreme Court stated that Maria had "the finest intellect [I have] ever known in a woman,"[1] and her Gainesville pastor C. V. Waugh, who later became a college professor, described her as "broadly cultured in the arts and sciences."[2]

The following discussion of Maria's reading provides an overview of everything she is known to have read and therefore of the intellectual resources she commanded in her old age. Most of this record is found in her diaries, the earliest extant dating from 1857 when Maria was already forty-three, and a bit of physical evidence survives in the form of a few books known to have been owned by the Taylors. As for her writing apart from her diaries and letters, Maria composed poems and short prose pieces throughout her life. Some of these have already been presented, and more will follow as components of other topics. The discussion here will be confined to Maria's writing of pieces for Baptist newspapers, an endeavor distinctive to her old age in which she deliberately set herself forth as a public author.

Reading

Maria read to explore issues that interested her, to increase her fund of knowledge for her teaching, and for pleasure in lighter moments.

One item in particular, *Cyclopaedia of English Literature* (Boston 1847), suggests a conscious effort at self-education and providing culture in the home. The inscriptions indicate that the Taylors acquired the two-volume anthology in 1848, when Maria was thirty-four. The long subtitle describes it as "A selection of the choicest productions of English authors from the earliest to the present time connected by a critical and biographical history, elegantly illustrated." The two volumes, totaling about 1,400 closely printed pages divided into seven historical periods, consist of snippets from a great number of authors ranging from "the Anglo-Saxon writers" to early Tennyson and Dickens. Represented are poets, novelists, dramatists, essayists, "metaphysicians," "historical, critical, and theological writers," travel writers, biographers, political economists, and "writers on science." From this resource, Maria would have received some idea of the scope of English literature and the important names of the tradition. Considering her omnivorous reading habits and the lack of libraries where she lived, Maria must have become very familiar with the contents of the *Cyclopaedia,* and her pedagogical eye would have been caught by the editor's statement that one of the purposes of the anthology was "to introduce the young to the Pantheon of English authors."

Of the reading Maria records in her diaries, religious works consistently predominate. She read the Bible every day, her favorite Old Testament books being Genesis, Psalms, Isaiah, and Daniel. She also read and re-read John Bunyan's great Baptist work, *Pilgrim's Progress,* and commentaries on it. Of the many authors of sermons Maria mentions over the years, three appear most frequently: John Wesley (1703–91), founder of Methodism; Thomas de Witt Talmage (1832–1902), a nationally renowned American Presbyterian preacher and editor; and Charles Haddon Spurgeon (1834–92), the best-known British Baptist preacher of the century (dubbed "the modern Whitefield"), who for years commanded huge congregations in London. Maria also read George Whitefield (1714–70) himself, a cofounder of Methodism; the British Baptist Andrew Fuller (1757–1815); and the famous American Congregationalist preacher Henry Ward Beecher (1813–87), even after she was scandalized by his adultery. These divines were persons of intellect and leading figures in their field.

Biblical exegesis was also favored reading, as were histories of the scriptures, the reformation, the Waldenses (an early Protestant sect), the Baptists, the Muslims, and the Mormons (authors all unidentified), as well as the more general *Ecclesiastical History* by the German theologian Johann Lorenz von Mosheim (1694–1755), a work praised by the great English historian Edward Gibbon as "full, rational, correct, and moderate." Maria also read original works by Martin Luther (1483–1546); Emanuel Swedenborg (1688–1772), the Swedish mystic (whom she termed "a very remarkable and singular man"); and Johann Friedrich Oberlin (1740–1826), the Alsatian religious activist. Biographies of religious figures in her reading ranged from works on early Christian martyrs and Mahomet (by Washington Irving) to lives of various American and English churchmen and female church workers (one "a saintly Methodist lady"). Maria also read innumerable religious tracts published by the American Tract Society.

Every Sunday Maria found time for "the religious newspapers," among them regional Baptist papers published in Richmond and Atlanta and occasionally even a Catholic periodical. Besides news from churches and denominational colleges, sermon digests, and debates on theological issues, these papers published international and national news and feature articles. Maria was thus well informed about the current state of religion in the country. A national magazine with a popular religious bent that Maria often read was *Frank Leslie's Sunday Magazine.* Lavishly illustrated with large, handsome engravings, the magazine offered a potpourri of short articles on history, geography, ethnography, social customs, and natural history as well as sentimental verse, anecdotes, serialized novels, short sermons, and Biblical exegesis. A regular reader of this publication would have a large if haphazard collection of information at her command.

Maria also read a number of secular periodicals. She faithfully perused the local papers and leading Florida dailies, and of the New York City papers she occasionally saw the *Times,* the *Sun,* and the *Herald* (sent by her sons from their business trips); from time to time she subscribed to South Carolina papers, for example, the *Rural Carolinian* and the *Charleston Courier.*

Brief descriptions of the best-known of the national magazines Maria read indicate that she "kept up" in a variety of areas. *Godey's Lady's Book,* best known now for reproductions of its fashion plates, contained moralistic fiction and poetry by popular writers, but also pieces by such luminaries as Longfellow, Hawthorne, Poe, and Emerson. *Harper's Monthly Magazine,* advertizing itself as containing "only material that could be read aloud in any family circle,"[3] was another staple of Maria's reading. Although Maria never particularizes the contents, during the time she was reading it, the magazine published novels of Dickens, Thackeray, George Eliot, Howells, and Henry James. *Scribner's Monthly,* another genteel magazine Maria saw occasionally, may have interested her for the Civil War memoirs and debates it featured.

The *North American Review,* generally considered the most important intellectual magazine in the country, provided a different perspective. Edited variously by James Russell Lowell, Charles Eliot Norton, and Henry Adams, the magazine stated as one of its missions to "acquaint its readers with the best from abroad." It also discussed presidential elections, labor problems, divorce, evolution, and agnosticism, and its review essays covered books on travel, law, history, and biography. The *Review* was the most elevated of Maria's periodical reading; it must have challenged her thinking about many issues of the day.

As for her acquaintance with the canonical English authors, Maria makes specific mention of substantial reading in Shakespeare, Spenser, Milton, Pope, Edward Young, Defoe, Coleridge, Walter Scott, Byron, Tennyson, the Rossettis, and Dickens. Of the second or third rank, she mentions the Scottish poet Thomas Campbell and the novelists Edward Bulwer Lytton, Benjamin Disraeli (the sometime prime minister), and Charles Reade. Of the now-classic American authors who were her contemporaries, Maria mentions separately only Longfellow, Bryant, Stowe, and Twain. To these British and American lists should be added the authors Maria must have known from the periodicals discussed above. Of continental literature she mentions reading only George Sand's *Consuela* and "a Russian novel."

Maria read a good deal in general history and biography, for example, a volume on "the world's great empires," English history by David Hume and Thomas Babington Macaulay,[4] a book on "the early period of English history," a history from the accession of Queen Victoria to the Congress of Berlin, a biography of Henry VIII, and, interestingly, a biography of the English abolitionist William Wilberforce (1759–1833). On the American side, Maria enjoyed accounts of the Civil War, including biographies of Robert E. Lee. Books on Admiral Perry's Japan expedition, Stanley's explorations in Africa, and G. E. McCall's letters on the American frontier supplied a touch of adventure,[5] and she delved a bit into science with *Cosmos* by Alexander von Humboldt (1769–1859) and "a physical geography of the sea."

Especially in her later years, Maria indulged herself in novels by "the popular authors," with which "Fenwick generally keeps us well supplied," for times when she felt "too unstrung for anything but light literature"—but never on Sunday. The level of this reading is apparent from such titles as *Married at Last, Mamselle's Secret, Not Wisely but Too Well, Ward or Wife, What He Cost Her,* and *A Woman's Secret and How She Kept It.* Maria's comments vary: "a worthless piece," "not much of a book," "abounding in sentimentalism [apparently a pejorative]," "good morals exemplified." One comment indicates more fully what Maria liked to see in a popular novel: "He is a fine writer, morals pure, Religion not puritanical . . . [he] has fine discriptive powers. Keeps up his characters with wonderful consistency. None of them are without their blemishes." Such works and the names of their authors have vanished without trace.

Maria read other popular material a cut above these ephemera. Among women authors in this category are two Americans, A. K. Green and Mrs E. D. E. N. Southworth, and two English writers, Frances Havergal and Marie Corelli, whose attractiveness to Maria may be surmised. Anna Katharine Green (1848–1935), creator of the first female detectives in literature and author of the famous early mystery novel, *The Leavenworth Case* (1878) and thirty-eight other mysteries, "portrayed women as characters of primary importance who refused to be victimized,"[6] a feature that may account for Maria's reading a number of her novels. Emma Dorothy Eliza Nevitte Southworth (1819–99) was an immensely popular writer of serialized rags-to-riches novels, one of which sold two million copies. Her success has been ascribed to "the simple black and white morality of her tales, her fine melodramatic touch, and her innate story-telling ability." Maria read several of Southworth's novels, perhaps finding the first attribute especially attractive.

Frances Ridley Havergal (1836–79), a favorite of Maria's in her last years, wrote poems in the style of hymn texts. One commentator has praised Havergal's work for reflecting "a remarkable depth of spiritual insight gained both from introspection & from the Scriptures which she studied incessantly." Maria described Havergal as "very spiritual," and no doubt found her of particular interest as a fellow practitioner, for at the time Maria was trying her own hand at writing poetry in hymn style. Maria had mixed feelings about Marie Corelli (1855–1924). She described Corelli's *A Romance of Two Worlds* (1886) as "a Swedenborgian novel—some things very heretical, but a growth in grace, & daily communion with God to this end suggested by its contents." Maria's curiosity about alternative religious experience probably sparked her interest in Corelli, an interest that waned with subsequent Corelli novels she described as "horrid books, full of evil & heresy & so graphically & passionately written."

Maria also read a number of novels by two popular male writers, Edward Payson Roe (1838–88), an American Presbyterian minister turned romantic novelist, and Georg Moritz Ebers (1837–98), a German Egyptologist at the University of Leipzig who wrote a number of historical novels set in ancient Egypt. Maria enjoyed Roe for his "constructiveness & ready wit." Ebers she read more seriously, considering him "quite a writer," and felt that she was learning history as well as being entertained, as she did with John Esten Cooke's Civil War romances. Finally, like everyone else, Maria read Lew Wallace's best-selling novel *Ben Hur* (1880) and Edward Bellamy's *Looking Backward* (1888).

Writing: Baptist Newspaper Pieces

In 1873 at age fifty-nine, Maria began a new project, namely, writing poems and short essays for Baptist newspapers. She may have been encouraged to seek publication at this time by the appearance in print after the Civil War of a remarkable number of women novelists, journalists, and essayists,[7] but the determining factor was probably that with her parental responsibilities nearing an end, she had time for this more demanding kind of writing. Her last mention of a published piece appears in a December 1885 diary entry, when she had just turned seventy-two. Thus Maria sustained this project for at least twelve years, 1873–85 (the 1886 and 1887 diaries are missing). Maria unquestionably took her public writing seriously. With rising ambition after breaking into print with several items during 1873–75, she wrote new poems and short prose pieces, solicited criticism from her college-professor son-in-law, and revised earlier efforts. Of course, she had her disappointments, for a number of the pieces she sent off were not accepted. Of those she records as having been published, nineteen proved to be recoverable from Baptist archives.

Maria brought a large measure of self-awareness to this new undertaking, which she expressed to her favorite correspondent in general terms on the subject of public writing. In an 1875 letter to Ann Furman, Maria at age sixty-two reveals her sense of the Baptist writing market and her ambition. That is, the reasons Maria lists for Ann to publish the memoir no doubt express Maria's own purposes.

28 January 1875. Maria Baker Taylor to Ann Eliza Furman

> I hope you did not lose, in the house burning, & war accidents the material which Aunt Susan had prepared for a memoir of my grandfather [Richard Furman]? I want to ask you, with your leisure and ability, to go on & finish it without delay. "Time & tide wait for no man" is an ancient aphorism, but a very true one. Baptist history, statistics, & reminiscences are in great demand, being all the vogue at present, &, as going in on the tide is just the thing, avail yourself of it, & push this memoir through, for the benefit of the denomination spiritually; in justice to his (Grandpa's) memory & the gratification of his family & descendents, & to your own benefit pecuniarily. Could you not begin it in some prominent Baptist paper, by contract, & see the result?
>
> I hope my proposition does not shock your sensibilities & bring upon me Byron's malediction of Scott, in British Bards & Scotch

Reviewers. If it does just remember that he made himself obnoxious to the same charge afterwards & was perhaps more entitled to be called the "groveling" Byron. If I could wield your chaste & accurate pen, & had the materials (judging from your letter in Religious Herald) you are so willing to furnish to others, I would not hesitate a moment. I hoped to have seen the proposed work long ago, but I believe one member of the family have waited on another, until the time is passing away & only Dr Brantley's short sketch likely to be in existence.

What would you think of my turning authoress & sending some of my rough writings before the public in the shape of "Grandmothers papers"? Containing familiar letters, short sketches of persons, & places, & things & occasionally a sentimental tale, all true but a little? Write me soon & frankly & let your heart & mind be single.

Maria commented directly on her goals in her public writing when she submitted a piece to her uncle James Clement Furman for the *Baptist Courier,* the paper he had recently founded in Greenville, South Carolina. She tactfully bows to James's superior judgment but also presents her credentials as a writer; that is, she is not asking for consideration as a relative.

23 January 1878. Maria Baker Taylor to James Clement Furman

I take the liberty to enclose you a piece I have written on a subject [unknown] which has recently attracted much attention here & in Europe. If you deem it worthy of publication in the Courier, your Baptist paper, will you be kind enough to give it the necessary corrections & send it on for me, as I desire to be incog. . . . I like strength, perspicuity & simplicity of style; you will smile & think I will hardly attain to them. I do not aspire to beauty of style, though I do admire it, but I would like to write something to do good, something to correct the errors of the day & lead the heart & mind to virtue, God & happiness. One of the editors of the Florida Baptist requested me to write for that paper last year & again this, which I did last year under several assumed names. One of them was "Sarah Maria," a part of my maiden signature.

Besides wanting "to do good," Maria certainly hoped for some recognition for her published pieces and reproached Ann Furman when this favored correspondent did not respond to her work: "Did you receive an Index with a piece of mine headed 'A Fragment,' which I sent you last fall? You never acknowledged it. I sent you another piece 'A voice from the Better land'" (11 March 1885).

Maria's pieces appeared in three Baptist newspapers. One poem appeared in *The Religious Herald,* a widely circulated Baptist weekly published in Richmond, Virginia. The rest of her religious writing appeared in two related Baptist weekly newspapers, *The Florida Baptist* and *The Christian Index.* Maria first began writing for the Florida paper in 1877 at the invitation of one of the editors, W. N. Chaudoin,[8] whom she had met through her pastor in Gainesville. A few years later the *Baptist* was incorporated into the *Index,* and some of Maria's pieces then appeared in this "Florida Baptist" section, others in the *Index* proper. Published in Atlanta, the *Index* was itself already an amalgam of Georgia, Alabama, and Tennessee papers. Appearing in a substantial four-column, sixteen-page format, it was probably the leading southern Baptist paper at the time. Thus Maria had the satisfaction of seeing herself in print in journals that were well respected in her community of faith.

Brief excerpts from Maria's published poems and prose pieces reveal the topics that interested her and the styles that define her capacities as a writer in her old age.

Maria must have been deeply gratified when the *Herald* featured her forty-three-line blank verse poem on the front page of its 4 June 1874 issue. The editor states that he "cheerfully accepted it" as the final word on a debate that contributors had engaged in over several months. Maria's poem (untitled) is essentially an elaboration of the epigraph she chose, Isaiah 55:9: "For as the heavens are higher than the earth, so are my [God's] ways higher than your ways, and my thoughts than your thoughts." Thus, rather than addressing the topic under debate, whether Christ suffered in his divine aspect as a result of his sufferings in his human aspect, Maria asserts that human reason cannot comprehend the mysteries of the divine, a point that would, of course, lay to rest any theological debate. With its clichés of theological contrast—finite/infinite, earth/heaven, human/divine, reason/faith, change/constancy—the poem is devoid of original basic thought. However, the first lines show that Maria had some grasp of writing in a lofty style and setting up an opening.

> Oh, can this earth, though beautiful it be,
> And bearing impress of a hand divine,
> Can it afford a single picture true,
> Of that far lovelier land, that distant
> Home, whose loveliness is not born of earth?

In subject matter, Maria continued to content herself with expounding the central tenets of her simple faith, apparent in "Truth, Light and Love," a fifty-one-line blank verse meditation on Christ's "amazing love" published in the *Index* of 1 November 1883. The last lines of this performance indicate that Maria also had a sense of effective closure.

> Dear Lord, Thy quick'ning Spirit give with power!
> Oh, help us yield to Thee and own Thy sway!
> Take thou possession of our inmost souls.
> Oh, cleanse and make them harmonious with Thine
> In holiness, in love, in every grace!

Maria turns her attention from Jesus to Satan in a much shorter blank verse poem, "The Evil Power," from the 13 December 1883 *Index*. Maria effectively brings out Satan's ceaseless activity by the simple device of rearranging the words of Job 1:75 to place the prepositions in a single series with emphatic repetition of "and," a device she then repeats with the verbs.

> Bewailing want of Omnipresent power,
> But going to and fro, and up and down,
> He enters into man, and works and tempts
> Weak men, through him, to go astray.

In a very long poem (110 lines), curiously titled "A Fragment," Maria works up that popular Victorian theme, the death of a female child. A few features of Maria's version are distinctive. For one, her emphasis is different from some of the best-known Victorian treatments of the theme, for example, the suffering child as sacrificial victim in Dickens's Little Nell or the saintly exemplar Stowe makes of her Little Eva. By contrast, Maria's emphasis is not on the child but on the mother and her success in bringing the child to die willingly (since it is God's will that she die) and thus save her soul. Early in the poem, Maria sets the reader up for the expected plea for the child's earthly life with the repetition of "save," then takes the turn to spiritual salvation; in addition, the repetition both hammers home the point and conveys the mother's desperate anguish.

> [the mother] / Then besought: "O, Master, save my child!
> Save, save! Oh, save my child! Not, not her life, —
> I ask not this—but save, oh, save her soul!

In a calmer mood the mother later calls on Christ

> To wisely guide [me], and now give grace to speak
> To that dear child, the words of peace and love,
> Of faith and hope in Him, mighty to save,
> That she, His beauty seeing, would admire,
> Nor hesitate to go to Him for life.

Thus the mother is portrayed as teacher of the ultimate paradoxical lesson: death, which Maria describes as "the slave / So oft employed as porter to unlock / The gates of Paradise to the redeemed," leads the believer to everlasting life. In this deathbed scene (which does not directly parallel an autobiographical situation), Maria has restructured a convention in order to celebrate the role that absorbed so much of her own life, that of teacher to her children and grandchildren with the grand aim of saving their souls.

The best that can be said for these poems is that they are thought through, have a dignified if simple seriousness, and demonstrate a decent technical competence. Perhaps with some readers Maria achieved her goal, to "lead the heart & mind to virtue, God & happiness."

Maria's first prose piece in the *Index* was an obituary for Thomas Willingham, a South Carolina friend, in the 7 August 1873 issue. The most notable feature is her command of a stately Johnsonian syntax that lends a ritualistic quality suitable to the genre.

His social and religious temperament was ardent, earnest and demonstrative—he did nothing halfway, but thoroughly, hence he exerted great influence, social, moral and religious, as far as he was known. To the cause of God and the poor, to the helpless widow and the orphan, he was sympathetic and liberal. It was in the relation of husband and father he is worthy to be held up as a model;—loving, confiding and respectful as a husband; tender, affectionate and indulgent, but prudent and firm in discipline as a father.

Maria's other prose pieces are explicitly didactic. In the 1870s Maria was working on her "Grandmother's Papers," varied writings for children in epistolary form that she hoped to publish as a series. However, only one ever appeared in print, in the 20 May 1880 *Index* as "A Letter from Grandmother." Written in a quiet teacherly style that does not condescend to young readers, the letter contains Maria's only extant comment on the religion-versus-science issue of the time. After adjuring children to "love, venerate and believe the Holy Scriptures," Maria further instructs:

> Even if learned and scientific men should tell you something contrary to the Bible, don't believe them, however plausible they may be. Never try to make the Bible come to their statements; for believe me, all real science will yet come square to the Bible and when the great scroll of the earth is unrolled, the rocks, fossils and other created matter will have written upon them the same truths as the books of the Holy Scriptures.

In three other pieces Maria becomes the teacher/preacher to adults as she employs several strategies typical of the pulpit: excoriation, exegesis, and parable. While these pieces are in the nature of mini-sermons, they display more structural variety than the typical evangelical sermon pattern, consisting of enunciation of fundamental truth, followed by application and call to repentance and faith. In her piece appearing in the 5 February 1878 *Florida Baptist,* titled "Fagots from an Old Stick," Maria begins with a few plain truths, then builds to a rhythmic harangue.

No character appears to have been more offensive to the Saviour than the Pharisees. He felt a contempt for them; how could he feel otherwise? He knew their littleness, the unrighteousness of their fancied righteousness, the helplessness of their boasted strength, the blindness of their presumption, the intenseness of their hypocrisy. Notice their accusations;—"your disciples eat with unwashen hands." Ye blind traditionalists! Ye idolaters of creeds! Eat with unwashen hands! What have you done with widows' houses? Are your father and mother provided for?

Maria adopts the sermon strategy of Biblical exegesis in "Patience under Injury," in the 17 December 1885 *Index*. In this mini-sermon she demonstrates the conciseness she claimed as one of her stylistic goals. Her text is II Samuel 16:11, "Let him alone, and let him curse; for the Lord hath bidden him"; the context is that King David stops his followers from killing a man of the house of Saul who was cursing him as he [David] fled Jerusalem at the time of Absalom's rebellion. Maria does not need to explain this context to her Baptist readers, and she launches out immediately after the quotation.

These words [the text] are a manifestation of the perfect confidence which David had in God, and his deep submission to the divine will; and they evince the patience and forbearance he could exercise under injuries.

After briefly elucidating David's character, Maria turns to the application.

How unworthy and small appear numberless resentments indulged in, when we contemplate David's conduct under the trial of this cursing. Oh, that we had the same practical, abiding faith in the care and wisdom of God, in his justice and forbearance. David felt that he was wisely and justly punished, and that the Almighty would terminate it in good season, therefore, he could charge his indignant followers to "let him curse."

In "Economy" in the 28 May 1885 *Index,* Maria made use of another mode of sermon instruction, the parable. This time, instead of exemplifying a principle and then inviting her readers to apply it to themselves, she presents the principle and then illustrates it. Her text, "Gather up the fragments that nothing be lost," serves as a reminder that the learning of proverbs and maxims had been a prominent feature of Maria's early education.

> Proverbs are terse expressions of truths, mostly of practical character, important for us to know, remember, and energise. To those who despise economy, regarding it as meanness, allied to stinginess, when exercised in small matters, we would call attention to the words of our Saviour at the beginning of this [piece], of divine force, and quite as clear and simple as the common proverb, "waste not, want not." It assures us of the dignity and honorableness of economy, from the highest standpoint.

Maria then places her parable in times modern enough to lend an air of reality but sufficiently distant to suggest the "olden days" suitable to the genre.

> The exemplification of this [the honorableness of economy] will be found in an anecdote related by an agent travelling in the South forty years ago, to collect funds for missionary purposes. He was advised to visit, during his tour, a merchant of standing and capital, who was represented to him as being a liberal giver to all benevolent objects.

The story takes its ritual course as the agent, seeing the merchant tell a clerk to pick up a scrap of paper, "naturally (?) concluded there was too much closeness here for generosity to abound to him." But, of course, the merchant is able to give him a large donation, precisely because he saved every scrap.

Perhaps one of Maria's impulses in these writings was to try her hand, in miniature, at the varieties of preacherly discourse. If she had been a man, she would probably have become a Baptist preacher. As a laywoman, Maria must have been gratified to participate in the public discourse of her religious community, if only with such mites as these.

TWO

Serving the Family

In such a large extended family as Maria's, someone was always in need of care, comfort, or counsel. Much as family members cooperated in helping each other, Maria was both the center of the family support system and its chief operative. Given her practical Christianity, Maria would not have found a merely honorific matriarchate to be attractive.

A variety of documents illustrates the many-faceted nature of Maria's service to her family during her old age. First, letters from 1876 and 1877 show her leading the family in bringing solace to one member. Second, the 1882 diary as a whole illustrates how incessant the demands on Maria were. Next, diaries and letters that reveal two distressing situations occurring in 1880 and 1884 suggest Maria's Christian stoicism. And finally, in the 1889 and 1890 diaries and a poem from 1890, Maria copes with the sickness and death of her youngest daughter, Anne, and then commits herself to the care of Anne's youngest daughter.

Late in 1875, Dore, Maria's second-youngest child, went with her husband, William Wallace, and their baby Kate to live in Alafia on the Florida west coast near Tampa. Dore did not want to go, and Maria was uneasy about the move to such a primitive and hard-to-reach place. Maria and her unmarried daughter Sue had gone to St. Augustine to be with daughter Mary for the birth of Mary's ninth child when the call came from Dore. Maria tells the story of her "sad journey to dear Dore."

30 October 1876. Maria Baker Taylor to Ann Eliza Furman

The night after Mary's baby was nine days old (Hope Lea Ansley, a pretty little blonde baby) I received a letter from Dore written on a bed of illness, a few words at a time & wishing so much, without asking, that some of her family was with her. Sue & myself were both with Mary, so I determined at once to pack up & get to Dore as soon as possible, no easy undertaking, & leave Sue to take care of Mary & the baby. So on Wednesday morning I left Augustine by way of Jacksonville for Gainesville.

Fenwick & Mr Dawkins would not consent for me to take the route by hack of four days travel over a rough road with poor vehicles, so Fen went to Cedar Key[1] to procure me a passage by water & as no steamer could be relied on to come there, & none were on hand, he procured for my accommodations a schooner, intending to accompany me. I remained with Millie [Fen's pregnant wife] on Sat when he left for Cedar Key. On Monday he telegraphed me to come on the train, & I went immediately on board the schooner to leave that night.

Fen had his baggage on board but I insisted on his returning to Millie, as I did not leave her well & felt uneasy for him to be away from her. He had pd for the schooner only for his use & mine but obeyed me as I was pretty preemptory, so I went alone with two white men and one colored, & we had a safe & pretty quick passage two nights & a day & a half on the way.

They landed me at Dr Wallace's wharf not 100 yds from the house. Dore & the Dr came to meet me & from the boat I asked for little Kate. When Dore answered "She is dead, Mother," I was truly shocked & could not control my feelings, particularly when I saw how wretchedly Dore looked.[2] When I went to the house I had the satisfaction of seeing her remains before they were committed to the grave & of following them there. She had died of congestive fever after 5 days illness, during which her mother nursed her constantly, notwithstanding the debility under which she was suffering from previous illness. Poor child, she said she felt as if a load was lifted off her by my coming.

I remained with them a month & did all I could to comfort & help them. There are few mail facilities there, & I did not write many letters. Fen said he would go to see Dore & try to bring her back with him.³ She did not like to leave Dr Wallace alone, but felt anxious to be with us all; Johnny has written to Dr Wallace to bring her <u>here</u>. It was a great trial for me to return without her, as I hoped when I went to Tampa to bring her back.

3 January 1877. Maria Baker Taylor to Ann Eliza Furman

I make my headquarters at John's, but I am now at Millie's [Fen's] as she is not well & I promised Fenwick, when he left for Tampa yesterday [on a law case], to remain with her until his return the latter part of next week. He goes early enough to be in time, if possible, to see Dore. Sue accompanied him to go on to Dr Wallace's to spend some time with her sister. John left here Monday week ago on a traveling tour & expected to take Alafia in his route, so that Dore, with one visit of a month from me, two from John, three from Fenwick, & a long one from Sue, will not feel that she is so very far away from us.

Not long after the traumatic Alafia experience, the Wallaces moved to Gainesville at Dore's insistence, but Maria remained worried for years that William would again take Dore away to some godforsaken place.

Maria's incessant care of the afflicted seen in the 1882 diary was not unusual. For example, in April and May 1881 Maria helped her Gainesville families through about twenty cases of measles and scarlet fever, after which, as she told Ann Furman, "I was ill myself with threatened pleurisy, & had seven visits from a physician" (26 May 1881).

In 1882 Maria was first concerned with her oldest child, Caroline, and her husband, James Dawkins. As Maria summarizes in the diary, "At the beginning of this year my daughter Caroline [forty-seven] who has been suffering with spinal affection for 3 years is much better, but still confined to the house. Judge Dawkins [sixty-two] appears to be a confirmed invalid & has but little use of his right hand [from a stroke in 1881]." Maria, herself now age sixty-eight, went every day to help.

> 14 Jan., Sat. I slept not well last night, felt feverish, nervous & restless. Went about 10 to Judge D's, found Carrie suffering terribly with neuralgia. We bathed her with salt & water, & chloroform & camphor relieved her. Judge D was a little better. I rubbed him with camphor & staid with them all day.

On 18 January news came from Fernandina of the death from heart trouble of Maria's grandson Thomas Bauskett, who at age nineteen was "a promising youth, preparing for the medical college." Maria went to her daughter Mary and stayed for a week, giving solace. After several days, Maria could note that "Mary felt better & got up but is very weak. She seems wonderfully sustained [spiritually]." However, in her diary Maria does not express grief over losing Tommy even though she had been very close to him; she saw him almost every day when the Bausketts lived next door to Osceola, and when Mary remarried after Thomas Bauskett's death and left the area, Tommy had remained at Osceola under Maria's care from age eight to thirteen. Instead of writing about the dead, Maria rendered practical assistance to the living: when she returned to Gainesville, she took along Mary's youngest child, six-year-old Hope, for a long visit. Maria then resumed her routine care of her Gainesville families.

> 12 Feb., Sun. I put my room to rights & went over to Judge D's, he seems better. Carrie not well. I rubbed him & then went over to Millie's. +Found her sick in Kate's room, she had been sick several nights. Fen was not well. I went over to Nan's to see her children, whom she left to go to the Methodist church with Mr C's sisters.[4] I returned to Fen's to dinner, only Fen & myself & Tom Haile [Millie's brother] were at it. Millie not well, I staid all night with her. Fen drove me to Curran's to get my gown.

On 16 March, Maria moved in with Fen and Millie to help Millie in the last stages of pregnancy. After Carl was born, Maria stayed for another month before returning to John's house, which was "headquarters" at the time. After all of the extensive care Maria had given others thus far in the year, her children reciprocated by insisting that she attend the Southern Baptist Convention in Greenville, South Carolina, and making up a purse for her.[5] There she had the joy of seeing eminent clergymen, old friends, and many relatives, including Ann and James Furman. When she left on 18 May after ten days in Greenville, Maria wrote, "Parting with my relatives whom I never expect to see again was very painful to me."

June and July brought long visits to Richie at Lake Wauburg and Mary in St. Augustine, where Maria proffered her usual assistance in household routine and minor illnesses. A more demanding situation arose in August, when Millie Taylor took the children to North Carolina, leaving Fen alone in the house but under the family eye.

> 20 Aug., Sun. I met Nan on her way to church. She informed me Fen had fever & I went with her & I stopped there. Fen sick all day, in the evening his fever increased & the pain in his side & he sent for Dr McKinstry.[6] He [Dr.] said he had congestion of the liver & needed prompt remedies. He put on a blister.[7] I staid all night & did not undress but dressed his blister through the night.

> 25 Aug., Fri. I felt very tired & got up late. Attended to Fen's blister through the night & early this AM I gave him cinchona[8] at 7. I waited on him all through the day, his blister painful & pains in side & abdomen. Nan called & sent my dinner & Fen's to us as she has done all the while. Mr Carlisle called as he does every day. Fen's blister painful & needed dressing through the night.

Later in the year, Maria's engagement in a variety of services for members is seen as she spends a typical Sunday interacting with her family.

> 26 Nov., Sun. I dressed to go to church but Millie expressed a desire to go & I staid with the baby & she & Nan went to the Presbyterian church & heard Mr McCook preach. John came over with Gilbert [his son] & sat awhile with me & went over to see Mr Dawkins & Carrie. John seems a good deal worried. After Millie returned from church I rode home with John to dinner. Nettie [John's daughter] had chill, fever & headache. I waited on her,

bathed her feet & gave her aconite.⁹ I returned to Millie's late & called to see Mr D & Carrie. Read to Ena [Fen's daughter] & Carrie from the paper. Millie slept in my room.

After spending some months in North Carolina in an attempt to improve their health, the Dawkinses arrived home in November: "Judge D returned feeble & unable to attend to his courts & he came & took dengue [fever] after their return home" (diary year-end summary). Carrie too continued ailing, and Maria took care of both of them much as she had at the beginning of the year. Maria then received a summons from a different quarter.

15 Dec., Fri. I put my room to rights & after breakfast went over to see how Judge D & Carrie were. I had not been very long before I received a telegram from Richie asking me to come to him as he was sick. I returned to Millie's & got ready. Fen came to go with me, & I called again at Carrie's & went off on FSR [Florida Southern Railroad]. George¹⁰ met me at the depot & on our way out a heavy rain drenched us. I found Richie quite sick, I think with dengue & Kate not well. Richie was glad to see me & asked me to sleep by him all night

Although Kate was well enough to go "to Micanopy to have a mattrass made" and family members came to visit Richie, Maria at sixty-nine was chief nurse.

19 Dec., Tues. Richie seems better this AM. The Dr did not come out, busy with his oranges, shipping them. I helped with the house fixing & waited on Richie. I did not sleep any last night, gave him the medicine during the night.

20 Dec., Wed. Richie complains of weakness & bad feelings. Sent in for the Dr. I gave him gelamine last night & it did not agree with him, combined with nitre. Gave aconite, also rhubarb & then qui at 4 when the fever lessened. His head perspired very much last night & the rhubarb operated freely this AM. Charlie [hired man] sick with giddiness & fever, gave him aconite at night. The Dr rode out in the PM on his own horse & thought Richie better, put him on turpentine emulsion, which acted nicely. I gave Richie about 12 grs qui today.

25 Dec., Mon. Richie better, his head perspired profusely last night till 2, gave him chicken soup through the night. I slept very little & feel stupid & giddy. I got up at 6, & dressed as soon as I got water. Slept by Richie at night. Kate slept on the sofa.

28 Dec., Thurs. Richie had a very bad turn with bronchitis last night & vomited a good deal of phlegm before he was relieved. I kept on my clothes all night & watched him giving him remedies etc. He was better this morning & took qui. I caught fire & had my neckerchief burned. I cut off the burn, cut it round & hemmed it. I was in Richie's room nearly all day, he was very restless.

29 Dec., Fri. I slept well the first part of the night, but awake with him mostly after 12, & waiting on him. He was restless & wakeful. The Dr came & thought him better. Rain, rain. I gave Richie paragoric & he slept some time. Kate sick & slept all the morning. Kate with severe headache, I got her to take a Seidlitz powder. Gave Kate cal at night. The Dr came & thought Richie improved. He slept very heavily through the night. I had no rest.

At the end of the 1882 diary, Maria prayed for Richie and all of her sick children.

Father I pray Thee now for Richard that he may be saved. Spare his life for Thy service & put a new song into my mouth & his, & let none of us persist, in spending their "money for that which is not bread & then labor for that which satisfieth not." Father I pray Thee to raise up my children who are sick to serve Thee, may not one of them go down into the pit.

Maria's arduous labor to save Richie continued through January 1883, and he was months more recovering. Without doubt he owed his life to his mother's devoted care. Richie lived to be eighty-four.

Maria's reaction to acutely distressing situations was to help as best she could before and after, but to accept the crisis itself as the will of God. This attitude is apparent even in a situation in which Maria could easily have given herself over to self-reproach.

In 1880, Maria's son John and his wife went to New York City on business, leaving their two older children, Willie and Nettie, in Maria's charge in Gainesville. Her terminally ill brother Richard Baker then requested her to come to him in Mayesville, South Carolina. After receiving the parents' permission, Maria took the children with her to Mayesville, and while there Willie, age eleven, had a hunting accident. In neither her diary nor the long letter she wrote to Ann Furman does Maria indulge herself in "if only I hadn't taken the children."

5 October 1880. Maria Baker Taylor to Ann Eliza Furman

> [Willie] had lent a short shot gun against a tree & was looking up at a squirrel, & leaning against the tree himself, when he supposes the gun slipped & in falling shot him, with his face turned up. The load entered the left cheek & passed out at the corner of the left eye near the nose, tearing the socket bone of the eye so that it had to be taken out, & mangling the face dreadfully; fortunately no large blood vessels were injured, as he was half a mile from here & might have bled to death, as Chandler [Baker, also eleven] was the only person near him, & not large enough to bring him home.

Maria watched over Willie day and night until his parents arrived and noted without further comment that Willie turned away from her, preferring the hired nurse.

Maria no doubt instructed her children in acceptance of misfortune as God's will. However, a letter from a second distressing situation suggests that Maria was not the chosen confidante when they could not attain Christian resignation. Maria's daughter Susan Taylor Beard, who married at age thirty-nine, had her first child in 1884 at age forty, and Maria, then seventy, went to South Carolina to be with her. The baby soon died, and Sue confided her true feelings to her sister in a way that would probably have called forth efforts to correct her attitude from her mother.

23 June 1884. Susan Taylor Beard to Lydia Taylor Crane

> Thank you dear Sister for your recent affectionate & sympathetic letters, written to both Mother & myself. How I wish that I could cheerfully give up the dear little one, who was to add so

much to my life. But I cannot! Even now my selfish heart longs to have him back, yes even from the Better Land! My little baby that I did not even know & may not know even There, if I am permitted to reach Heaven. O Lyd if he had been spared only for a short time till we could have known and loved each other, perhaps it would not have seemed so hard.

But I must say no more & know you are shocked at what you will think my rebellious spirit. I do not mean it thus, & I do try so hard to feel that it is for the best & I pray against wrong thoughts & entreat for the christian's spirit of resignation, but this feeling when it comes only lasts temporarily and I soon find I am still unsatisfied.

Thank Brother Edward for his kind loving words and ask him to pray for me that all this may be for my eternal welfare.

At the beginning of 1889, Maria, now seventy-five, was living with Fen and Millie Taylor; next door were the Carlisles—Maria's youngest child Nan, Nan's husband, Julius, and their six children: Millie, thirteen; Carrie, eleven; Kitty, ten; Tommy, seven; Maria, five; and John, seventeen months. The opening prayer of the 1889 diary strikes an optimistic note.

1 Jan., Tues. I am a wonder to myself! I never expected to enter upon my 76th year. Hitherto the Lord hath led me, may He keep me by the Almighty power through Faith unto Salvation; may His mercies & benefits be continued through this year to us all & be received with grateful hearts.

However, Nan fell sick on 16 January and Maria became concerned.

18 Jan., Fri. I went over to see Nan, found her with severe headache and brought the children over here to say their lessons. I called again to see Nan after school.

19 Jan., Sat. Rose early. Weather cooler. Read the Scriptures. Knit some. Read several tales in Frank Leslie [popular magazine]. Called to see Nan, who is quite sick, several times and sat some with her. The Dr there once. I finished Millie's orange chips and put them in two pans. Cut out collars for Mr Carlisle's shirts and

put on one and fixed wristbands for Nan. I fixed the Treasurer's book of the L.B.A. [Ladies Benevolent Association], also fixed my own books. I had Maria and Kitty to come over to Fen's with me, washed them. I kept Maria all night. Read to them and amused them.

20 Jan., Sun. Rain, rain. No preaching in any of the churches today. I read the Scriptures and in the Tabernacle sermons. I read a good deal to Maria in Acts of the Apostles and she seemed quite interested and was good all day. I called several times to see Nan, and feel uneasy about her. She seems so weak.

21 Jan., Mon. Nan still quite sick and Mr Carlisle in bed sick, he had to send for the Dr last night. I rubbed him, waited on Nan, who cannot be up and seems quite weak. Knit on Maria's stocking, peeled oranges for preserves for Nan. Rainy murky weather. I still have Maria here to take care of and have her sleep with me.

24 Jan., Thurs. After putting the room to rights I went over to see Nan, found her sick, weak and with headache. I remained some time and waited on her, rubbed her with sweet oil.

26 Jan., Sat. I went over very early to see Nan and breakfasted with her. Went over to see Carrie, found her quite sick with fever but better. I sat with her till 12 and went over to Nan's and bathed her feet. Her head quite painful. Fever and great nausea, difficult to keep her warm. Millie Taylor called and sat with her awhile. Dore called. I called a few minutes at Dore's on my way to Carrie. Dr Wallace[11] sent me bottle of wine.

28 Jan., Mon. Clear and windy cool. I still have Maria here. Went over to see Nan found her still with great debility, nauseated and inclined to be cold. She is applying cold to her head. I breakfasted at Nan's then went over and taught the children. Mended garments for Maria. When school was over went back to see Nan. Carrie [Dawkins][12] wrote me Dr McKinstry thought her critically ill. She is so desirous of having quiet that good nursing is difficult. I staid from 12 to 9 PM with Nan, bathed her feet.

31 Jan., Thurs. Nan still very ill. A number of persons called to offer their services to sit up or nurse. I did not teach the children but remained with Nan all day. Millie Taylor taking care of the children except John who stays with his Aunt today and night. I feel extremely anxious about Anne. Sue came and sat up with her at night and I lay down with Millie [Carlisle] without undressing. Got up several times during the night to see after Nan and once fell on my face and bruised my forehead.

1 Feb., Fri. Nan still very ill. Sue remained for some time and returned home. Uneasy about Taylor [Sue's little son], who will have her near him. I had a letter from John respecting the Osceola land, which I tremulously answered. Anne seemed anxious to be alone and quiet. Often uttered ejaculatory prayer and suffers with her bowels, wanted mustard plaster. Mrs McDowel [nurse] came and sat up with her all night. Dr McKinstry also remained all night. I slept some with Millie [Carlisle].

2 Feb., Sat. The Dr left after 5. Mrs McDowel left at five. I took my place with Anne before she left. At 6 Nan went to sleep and slept until ½ after 10. I felt very glad and hoped to see her wake up refreshed and better, but alas, she was worse in every respect and was very nervous and excited. I sent off for the Dr and for Sue and they both came. I staid all day and until after supper, and as Sue and the Dr both were to stay, I went over to Millie's to change my clothes and sleep with Maria. Before 11 Fen woke me up to say that Mr Carlisle thought Nan was dying.

3 Feb., Sun. [narrative continues on diary page of this date] Millie [Taylor] had gone over, and we followed as soon as possible. My dear child was nearly breathing her last when we got there. Sue, Mr C, Millie and the Doctor were with her, and the nurse. It was not long before the heart rending announcement was made that she was no more. Mr C and I were kneeling by her bed. God knows best, loved most, and he took her away! At 3:30 her funeral was conducted at the Methodist Ch by Mr Corr, assisted by Mr Curry and Mr Pike. She was buried by her dear little Julius[13] for whom she called early Sat. AM.

4 Feb., Mon, I went over early this AM to Mr Carlisle's. Found Sue still there with Taylor. Mr Carlisle requested me to remain and take charge of the house and children. I had Allisson and Charity to help with necessary arrangements, and Leaky Redland [servants] came for some washing. Maria not very well. Carrie Dawkins offers to take care of the children in a letter to Mr C but he had written to his sister Sue. Carrie came with Millie and remained all night and found the lines Nan repeated, from Bryant's Thanatopsis.[14]

5 Feb., Tues. Maria was quite sick last night and some fever this AM. Complained of cold and feverish. I gave her soda and kept her in, attended to her diet. Carrie [Dawkins] seems very much depressed and not well but she would return home this inclement morning. I was very tired but busy all day, burnt coffee in the rooms, took curtains down and put up some things.

9 Feb., Sat. Clear—the weather cooler. I attended to household duties. Heard Millie Taylor was sick and went over to see her and found her in bed. I returned and put Carrie and Kitty to mending their clothes, assisted them to do so. They finished their work and went off in the evening to have a pic nic. I went over again to see Millie and found her with fever. Put mustard on her stomach, gave her ice and rubbed her. I went home and wrote and put up week's clothes.

On 27 February, Maria's new companion in caring for the Carlisles arrived: "Miss Sue Carlisle[15] came today. She looks well. She was very sweet and sympathetic, a fine Christian character. I am truly glad the children have secured her care of them and Mr C has affectionate help and sympathy."

Maria's restrained tone immediately after Nan's death is in marked contrast to the anguished outbursts she had allowed herself twenty-five years earlier when her son Willie died, and, unlike her recurring thoughts of Willie, Maria mentions Nan only once over the next several months. Maria finally wrote about her feelings ten months after Nan died. In the summarizing section at the end of the 1889 diary, Maria sketches the background of Anne's illness and then delivers a eulogy. In the first paragraph, Millie is Nan's oldest child, Maria and John her two youngest; Maria reverts to the more formal "Anne" as she addresses her daughter's spirit.

After a trying summer [1888], during the yellow fever epidemic from which we went in the country trying if possible to escape, we did not return to Gainesville till Dec. Millie and the children were not well and I went to them as soon as possible. Maria was very ill in Dec. and would have no one but her mother to nurse her. Then John was ill with mouth very sore, a stubborn case and Nan was pretty much exhausted as she exerted herself also to get things to rights after long absence from home and in Jan she was taken sick, being beforehand prostrated, yet none of us realized how ill she was until death came on the night of the 2nd of Feb at 12 o'clock and took her from us.

Did I write that death came? Not death. She did not die. She only entered upon life! Free from the cares, the pains and anxieties of a life on earth. She has entered upon the rest and joy of heaven. God took her: willing, active, self denying and conscientious, he called her to Himself for higher work. Blessed Anne! Beloved child! Lovely in character and person. Beauteous in conduct to me, and in all the relations of life. Ever amiable and forbearing: an example for others. Ever truthful and good. Dear Anne, thy cherished wishes are all dear to me! Thy dear children—precious memories of thyself, as dear to my heart as thee. I rejoice in being spared to comfort them, and bestow upon them some of the love they will miss of thine.

On every side are souvenirs of thy filial affections and loving attentions. How could I forget thee? Never! Never! Thy memory is sweet: Always gentle, always faithful, always true, always trusting. I can only feel that you have passed from this to eternal, blissful life. Rest and peace are thine. When my work is done I hope to join you and rejoice with you. Until then may our Heavenly Father keep me and thy dear children from evil and from doing evil.

Maria's final working through of her loss of Anne is her funerary poem dated July 1890 and printed in August 1890 in the *Christian*

Inquirer, a Baptist weekly published in New York. Apart from its significance as continuing her grief-work, the poem both articulates Maria's version of wifely duty and speaks to her daughter's marital situation. In a 19 August 1890 letter to Ann Furman, Maria writes:

> But you know a married woman has "to please her husband," & happy for her if she obtains the wisdom from above to win him, to make her pleasure his, while she feels that caprice & selfishness do not control <u>her</u>, but an honest, & earnest desire to please God, & bring her husband, with herself, in subjection to Him. Woman's influence is powerful! Who can measure the extent of her accountability?

As for Anne's situation, she had much to contend with in the alcoholism of her husband, apparently a longstanding affliction, for a brother in South Carolina had written "liked his likker" across a photo of Julius as a young man. Maria herself never explicitly mentions Julius's failing, confining herself to comments like "Anne told me something I did not like to hear" or "Anne gave me several pieces of information that pained me very much." Similarly, Maria does not specify the offense when early in 1882 she writes that Julius had to go to Jacksonville to stand trial and then pay a fine of $3,000, but his alcoholism was probably somehow involved. However, Maria expressed her indignation in general terms in an untitled poem, which she claimed she wrote to support the temperance cause. This seems unlikely as a single motive, for Maria does not mention the cause anywhere else in her writings, and her faith would not necessarily have prompted her to be active in it. Indeed, the poem begins, "With bar rooms we have no debate" and instead targets "our lords" "Who leave their homes for such resort / Whence crime & stench decocted come / From whiskey's self & whiskey's scum." The last lines of the poem probably speak directly to Anne's unhappy marriage:

> One swig! and where has manhood gone?
> Alas! alas for hopes undone!
> Weakness ensues, a frenzied brain
> Has left no firmness to restrain

The strong desire man has for drink!
Then, ere you take one—pause & think
Of those who love, who fain would try
To shield you from malicious eye
To guard you from a bar rooms fate
To fall, & fall!—to lose estate!
Just one word more before we part —
Strong drink destroys the human heart!
I know not how, but love goes out
The mind a chaos filled with doubt.

In her funerary poem, "In Memory of Mrs. Anne Carlisle," Maria implicitly praises Anne's behavior toward Julius in terms reminiscent of her counsel on husband/wife relations. The passive traits of the opening yield to traits requiring self-discipline and moral courage:

Lovely and gentle her walk was through life,
Humble and quiet, contented to serve,
Unostentatious, avoiding vain strife,
Bravely enduring with firmness and nerve. . . .
Truthful, transparent in conduct she stood,
Glossing no faults for fear of offence,
Loving the erring, herself pure and good,
Candid and faithful, without false pretence.
Wounds from her lips were the wounds of a friend,
Wisely directed and tempered by love;
Kisses deceitful, in bitterness end,
Candor and faithfulness come from above.

After Sue Carlisle arrived from South Carolina to assume charge of her brother's household, Maria moved back to Fen's home next door but took over full care of Maria Jr., Anne's youngest daughter, who in effect then became Maria's child. Maria also constantly helped with the other Carlisle children and household, and when Fen moved his family to Tallahassee in 1891, Maria at age seventy-seven went to live with the Carlisles. There she amply kept her promise to Anne's spirit to love her children as her own.

Maria's service to her family members continued to within a few weeks of her death at age eighty-two. Perhaps they saw her as the "blessing, particularly to my children" that she had prayed to be when she moved to Gainesville.

THREE

Teaching the Grandchildren

For many of her Gainesville years, Maria maintained a school for her grandchildren. This endeavor took much of her time, but beyond the almost daily "I taught the children," her references to it are scattered and brief. Nevertheless, these items—found in all of the 1879–95 diaries and in letters from 1876, 1886, and 1888–93—are numerous enough to permit a reconstruction of the extent and characteristics of Maria's teaching, which she faithfully pursued in the midst of the other family demands already seen. Due to the nature of some of the material, the presentation here will sometimes resort to weaving very brief references to the topic into an editorial narrative rather than presenting them as separate diary excerpts of only a few words.[1]

Maria's school was in session September through May, Monday through Friday, nine o'clock to one o'clock. Her clientele consisted mostly of her grandchildren, but occasionally she also accepted children of in-laws or family friends. At any given time, the children could range from age four years to twelve or thirteen, when they customarily entered the East Florida Seminary or the Gainesville Academy. The number of children she taught at a time varied from two to nine. All told, sixteen grandchildren passed through Maria's school, the children of her sons John Taylor and Fen Taylor and of her daughters Sue Beard, Dore Wallace, and Anne Carlisle. In addition, sometimes a Bauskett or Ansley child of Maria's daughter Mary would attend her school while paying an extended visit to Gainesville.

The curriculum included religion, reading, writing (composition and penmanship), grammar, arithmetic, geography, history, current events, and a smattering of Latin for the oldest children. Maria probably gave her charges at least as good an education as they would have received in one of the regular elementary schools.

Maria's cash accounts record varying figures for tuition, but her basic fee appears to have been $2 per month per child. Her attendance records (in her diary entries) and the demographics of her clientele suggest that she prorated for the age of the child, spells of absence due to illness, the number of children from one family, and out-of-the-ordinary services a parent had rendered her. For example, Maria charged Julius Carlisle $25 (rather than $30) for teaching three of his children for five months.

In comparison, Maria herself had paid $25 a half-quarter in the early 1870s for her daughter Anne to attend a Gainesville school. Assuming that a quarter was three months, that fee was about four times Maria's charge although it was for a higher level of education. However, Maria was apparently also receiving room and board from her children, for her meticulous cash accounts show outlays only for such items as stationery and stamps, personal laundry, toiletries, and gifts. The most regular of these expenses, the laundry, cost her $1 a month, half of one child's fee. In one of her better years, Maria received a total of $69.25 in tuition, so the teaching gave her a bit of spending money beyond her basic needs. Her charging anything at all perhaps indicates that she wanted her enterprise to be taken seriously, and her children probably insisted on extending a material and systematic token of their appreciation.

Maria's teaching began the year of her move from Osceola to her son John's house in Gainesville. As she wrote to Ann Furman on 30 October 1876, "I amuse myself by teaching John's children every day. They are obedient and affectionate." As she had when teaching her own children, Maria strove for the regularity of an established school, and only the most pressing events could force her to break off. For example, in January 1880 she gave off the week during which Dore had a baby and her enfeebled brother Richard Baker and his young son Chandler arrived from South Carolina for a visit. A few excerpts from the 1880 diary illustrate other constant features of Maria's teaching.

> 9 Mar., Tues. Taught the children their lessons which they were a long time at. Willie [Taylor, eleven] began his new Latin grammar yesterday.

> 24 May, Mon. Taught the children. Willie [Bauskett, thirteen] came over & I examined & taught him. Studied some myself looking over several of the Latin Grammars, one that Fen sent me.

> 1 June, Tues. I knit some & practiced some in the rule of three & fractions.

> 2 June, Wed. Put my room to rights & taught the children, ciphered & studied until dinner & knit some.

> 30 July, Fri. Taught Willie Bauskett & Nettie & had Willie read the scriptures & write a letter to his father to which I added some.

> 4 Aug., Wed. Taught all three children this morning. Taught Willie how to read the newspapers & made him understand the situation of Afganistan & Great Britain.

Lacking the 1881 diary, all that can be known of Maria's teaching that year is a brief note at the beginning of the 1882 diary: "Taught Willie [Taylor] 347 days in 1881." Because she usually took summers off, Maria probably gave this intensive instruction to be sure that Willie would be prepared to enter the Gainesville Academy. The 1882 diary shows Maria still living at John's and now teaching four children, Willie and Nettie Taylor; Willie Broome, Curran Taylor's nephew; and Willie Phillips, the son of a local doctor. Maria was particularly careful to keep track of the financial arrangements for the two boys who were not her grandchildren, with such notations as "WP time up," "Willie [Phillips] has only been here 10 days since his month began," or "WP and WB begin new month." On 8 May Maria went to the Baptist Convention in Greenville, South Carolina, and, although the normal school year was almost over when she returned on 23 May, she resumed her school for two more weeks, no doubt to round out the fiscal month. Clearly, she ran her tiny school in a businesslike manner.

Probably for the first time since she took up residence in Gaines-ville, Maria did not start up her school in the fall of 1882. On 13 Sep-tember, Willie Taylor, now thirteen, and Willie Broome entered the Gainesville Academy, Nettie was having severe eye trouble, and the next grandchild of school age, Millie Carlisle, seven years old, was in North Carolina until November. Maria, however, still had unfin-ished business teaching her own children. On 17 November she writes, "I had a talk at night with Fen [thirty-three] on his skepti-cisms. Oh, that he may turn." The family difficulties noted in the pre-vious section continued well into 1883, and Maria did not hold school that year either. While waiting for more propitious circumstances, she vented her pedagogic energies on Harriet, a young black servant in her daughter Carrie's house.

In September 1885, Maria began holding regular school for five grandchildren: three Carlisles, Millie, ten; Carrie, eight; Kitty, seven; Ena Taylor, seven; and Gilbert Taylor, six. Little Richie Wallace, five; George Taylor, four; and Carl Taylor, three; were sometimes allowed to sit in. The school day began with the scriptures and ended "with reading & explaining history to them." School ran until 24 December, when Maria gave a holiday until 4 January 1886. As she had with her own children, Maria continued to attach great importance to main-taining a regular school schedule whatever else might be going on.

22 February 1886. Maria Baker Taylor to Ann Eliza Furman

> I am only out of Anne's room a few moments, where I have been sitting to try & keep quietness so she may sleep, as she pre-sented us all yesterday with quite a splendid kinsman, Julius Carlisle. . . . I hope both Nan & baby are doing well but she has a severe cold contracted a week ago. I am fortunate (as I teach in my own room here) in the day of the baby's birth on Sunday. Nan sick on Sat & Monday a national holiday. So I will only give one day holiday besides, viz Tues. These little circumstances may appear trivial, but to me they are pleasantly providential.

There are no documents for 1887, but the opening of the 1888 diary shows Maria's school in full swing, with four Carlisles, two (Fen) Taylors, and Richie Wallace, ranging in age from thirteen to six. John Taylor and his family having moved to Brooksville, Florida, Maria, now seventy-two, had moved in with Fen and Millie and was holding school next door at the Carlisle house. Maria continued to keep an eye out for teaching material, for example, by "reading some in scientific subjects," and as always, she "read to the children at night and told them stories."

During the summer of 1888, while visiting Richie and Kate at Lake Wauburg, Maria put in extra duty with her twelve-year-old granddaughter Hope Ansley, there on a visit from St. Augustine. Noting that Hope "does not appear interested in her studies," Maria characteristically persisted nonetheless. But she had some unwelcome relief from teaching in the fall of 1888, when the women and children of Maria's families and Maria herself scattered to the countryside or nearby villages to escape a fearful yellow fever epidemic. Hence from 19 September through 8 December, Maria had to confine her teaching to reading to the children when she saw them on visits. The day after she returned to Gainesville, Maria resumed teaching two of the Carlisle children (Fen's children remained in the country), and continued through 22 December. In January 1889 Millie Carlisle, now thirteen, entered the East Florida Seminary, and Maria was left with Carrie, Kitty, and Tommy Carlisle, and Ena and Carl Taylor. In addition to the regular school hours, Maria prepared informal lessons for the evenings: "Read Romeo and Juliet and King Lear. Told Carl and Maria and Ena the story of Romeo and Juliet at night" (23 January 1889).

The 1889 teaching was, of course, interrupted by the death of Anne Carlisle on 3 February, but on 11 February Maria took up school again. After having "all the children around me in my room" on Sunday the 10th, Maria notes on 11 February, "I taught the children, interrupted by [condolence] callers," then hit her stride again on the 12th: "I taught the children and got through with their lessons notwithstanding the callers." As usual, on Sundays Maria taught all the children their Bible lessons and read to them, and she was also instructing the girls in sewing every day. Maria had an occasional triumph, as on 5 March: "Glad to see Kitty interested in reading out of school." A complete diary entry exemplifies the context of daily living in which Maria's teaching took place.

8 Apr., Mon. I rose early, breakfasted at Mr C's. Maria slept with me last night. She does not seem very well today. I went over to see John. He is quite sick fever all day. I gave him some whisky to day which he relished very much, the liquor said to be 10 years old & Dore brought it for me to take.[2] I helped Miss Sue get up the washing. Looked after Mary's [servant] washing. Taught the children, was a long time with Carrie's arithmetic. Went over to Millie's after dinner. Carrie Dawkins called, I went over again to see John. No better. The Dr sees him several times a day. Carrie [Dawkins] staid with him. Maria & Carrie [Carlisle] staid at Fen's. I told them stories at night. Evans still quite sick.[3] I hemmed 2 neck ties for Maria. Richie Taylor called & we talked about religion.

At the end of May, Maria put great effort into preparing the children for their final examination. It was the custom of the time for year-end examinations to be public, celebratory events, and although Maria's "public" was only a few family members, she made as much of the occasion as any regular school would. And of course, the children had to be nicely dressed.

30 May, Thurs. I rose early, put my room to rights. Taught the children. They reviewed their studies. I was busy with them nearly all day & sewed on Maria's & Kitty's dresses. Went over to Mr Carlisle's several times to see the children & Miss Sue. She called over here.

31 May, Fri. I put my room to rights & made preparations for reviewing & examining the children. Miss Sue Carlisle & Millie [Taylor] were present & thought they acquitted themselves well, particularly in reading & speaking. I dismissed the school for the summer. After dinner I prepared their reports. Mr Carlisle came after supper & heard the children speak.

In June, Julius Carlisle took his children for a protracted visit to his family in South Carolina, and on 17 September 1889 Maria wrote to Ann Furman: "I began teaching Ena & Carl on the first Mon in Sept, both are quite interested in their studies. Since Dore's return her son Richard comes, & is eager to learn. When dear Nan's children return I shall be kept busy." Tommy Carlisle arrived home on 6 October, and on 7 October Maria comments, "Tommy came to school today. He has forgotten a good deal and grown a good deal in person."

With the return of the rest of the Carlisle children on October 29 (1889) Maria was teaching eight grandchildren: Carrie, Kitty, Tommy, and Maria Carlisle; Ena and Carl Taylor; and Richie and Ellen Wallace. Bessie Haile, a niece of Millie Taylor's, made a ninth scholar. The children ranged in age from twelve to six; Maria was soon to turn seventy-six.

> 19 Oct., Fri. Studied the new method of teaching grammar. I do not like it in all respects as well as the old, also looked over the histories & the arithmetic.
>
> 23 Oct., Wed. I studied the maps some.
>
> 6 Nov., Wed. I spent the afternoon in studying the new method of teaching grammar.
>
> 22 Nov., Fri. I was engaged all the forenoon teaching the children & with their tables & compositions after dinner.
>
> 26 Nov., Tues. After school I fixed up the book with the children's marks. Looked over the children's compositions at night.
>
> 27 Nov., Wed. I taught the children, they got through early. I spent the most of the day after their lessons in cyphering & studying.
>
> 29 Nov., Fri. Read this AM until school [at 9 o'clock] except putting room to rights. Taught the children, all present except Ellen. After 2 before we closed. Compositions & arithmetic kept us late.

In the opening meditation of her 1890 diary, Maria, now seventy-seven, summed up blessings that included the opportunity to serve her grandchildren.

> With a grateful heart I hail this beautiful morning of a new year. Having passed my 76th birthday, I have reason for thankfulness for the health & strength I enjoy, together with all the merciful loving kindness of my Heavenly Father. That my life has been prolonged to love & care for my dear grand children, whose mother was called from them the first of last year, is abundant cause for

gratitude, nor would I fail to recount all the many mercies that crown my days & years & beseech Him for a continuance of them & for blessings upon every member of my family & their families.

Maria resumed teaching on 2 January (1890) with the same eight grandchildren, Bessie having dropped out. In addition to the formal instruction during the week, Maria was still giving Sunday Bible lessons, reading or telling stories in the evenings to all the children, and acting as mother to her six-year-old namesake Maria Carlisle, who usually spent the night with her. However, Maria's energies began to wane, for she now mentions discipline problems for the first time. One of her remedies was to write "some verses for the children to memorize." The poem reads in part:

> Loving word & loving deed,
> Gently spoken, gently done,
> Kindle in us love we need,
> Bless us with the love we've won.
> Then, dear children, let it rule
> All your thoughts, your words, your life.
> In the play room, in the school,
> Never once indulge in strife.

In spite of the exhortation of the last line, Maria reported in the 24 April entry, "I taught the children. Kitty tripped Tommy up & hurt him pretty badly. I gave him salt & put Pond's extract on his head." Maria ended her 1889–90 school year with even more of a flourish than usual.

22 May, Thurs. This morning I had the children getting ready for their examination. Miss Sue [Carlisle] came over & Millie [Taylor] & they passed very well through their recitations, reading etc & acquitted themselves very well. After dinner I took the children over to recite their poems for Carrie [Dawkins]. Mrs Davis & Miss Davis present & appeared pleased. Kate & Richie [Taylor] took tea at Millie's & after tea the children all but Carrie C recited for them & Fen & Millie Carlisle & Mrs Haile.

During the following summer vacation (1890), Maria did quite a bit of informal teaching. For example, on 7 July "the children came & said Psalms & the Lord's prayer & all of them read. Maria wrote & Kitty cyphered some. Assorted [news]papers to read to the children." And on 8 July, "the children came again & I read to them & heard Thomas read. Tommy, Kitty, Carl & Maria had some arithmetic, writing etc."

School began rather lamely in the fall of 1890, partly because Maria's oldest scholar was ready to move on.

1 Sept., Mon. Went over to Mr C's & began school with the children. They said their Psalms & I excused Carrie, Ena & Kitty by request [of Miss Sue]. Heard Tommy & Kitty their lessons. Carl not well.

2 Sept., Tues. Taught the children all of them present of Fen's & Mr Carlisle's children. Richie & Ellen [Wallace] will not come before Oct. Carrie's eyes still painful. I tried to teach her to knit, & did not have her read or study.

24 Sept., Wed. This is my last day with teaching Carrie. She goes to the [East Florida] Seminary tomorrow. Gave her a long lesson in Grammar & Geography. Dear child! I hope she will do well there.

3 Oct., Fri. I taught the children, was in till one. Read & studied the new methods of writing & arithmetic. At it all evening.

8 Oct., Wed. After dinner I looked over some histories & books for the children.

28 Oct., Tues. Taught the children. Thomas absent. I sent for him & he said Psalm & prayer & returned home.

3 Nov., Mon. All of the children present. We were interrupted somewhat by the kitchen taking fire.

18 Nov., Tues. Taught the children. Kitty was not well & came late. The boys behaved badly & I had to punish them. John [three] came & after behaving well he was disobedient. School was kept in till after dinner.

24 Nov., Mon. I taught the children. Make out their reports of deportment & progress every day.

At the end of the year (1890) came gratifying news about one of Maria's first generation of scholars: Fen was appointed to the Florida Supreme Court. Maria's only comment on this honor: "Fen is receiving a number of letters & telegrams of congratulations on his appointment, which I trust he will fill with wisdom & ability & a deep sense of his obligation to serve Thee faithfully." However, at this point the educational outcome with the grandchildren seemed less than promising.

30 Jan., Fri. I taught the children. Thomas absent. The month is over today, Ena & Kitty have had grippe & lost almost half their time. Tommy & Richie have also lost some days. I was the most of the afternoon engaged in making out their monthly reports.

6 Feb., Fri. Taught the children, they tried me considerably with their frivolity & I used a switch to one or two of them which I regret, having avoided it so far.[4]

9 Feb., Mon. Taught the children. They were very noisy & unruly today.

16 Feb., Mon. I taught the children, was sorry to punish Thomas for laughing & talking.

28 Feb., Sat. Made out reports for the parents of my grandchildren. It took me quite a time as I only had blank sheets [instead of printed forms] & had everything to do with the pen.

Writing to Ann Furman a little later, Maria gave no hint of all these difficulties: "Teaching five days until one, during the week, does not leave me much time, when I am cut off from writing by gaslight.[5] I teach eight of my grand children & their parents appear satisfied with their progress" (30 March 1891).

As the end of the school year approached, Maria noted teaching "Richie & Thomas a little book-keeping," reading "some of the history of Elijah to Tommy & Carl & Maria," and herself studying "a little in grammar & history & in the Scriptures." The 1890–91 school year ended more quietly than usual on 3 June, when Maria "went to Mr Carlisle's to tea, & the children said their speeches for him & he looked at their compositions."

At the beginning of the 1891–92 school year in September, Maria had only two scholars, Kitty and Thomas Carlisle, Maria Jr. being in South Carolina with Miss Sue. Ena Taylor, now thirteen, entered the East Florida Seminary, and Carl Taylor and the Wallace children did not begin with Maria until October. Then:

> 23 Oct., Fri. Got up at six but found it impossible to stand up & returned to bed. My head was strangely affected & I was apprehensive of paralysis. I got up soon after breakfast but had to use a stick. The children came but I could only have them write & cypher.

> 24 Oct., Sat. Dore called with Harney [her little boy] brought message from Dr Wallace, advising me to give up school teaching & go & live with them, that he would do all in his power to make me happy etc. I appreciated the invitation & felt grateful for the kindliness of feeling. I felt better today, but still stumbling around.

> 13 Nov., Fri. I taught the children. All of them were naughty today & worried me except Ellen, Maria & Taylor [the three youngest]. I went over to see Miss Sue—& I presume she thought me impertinent—about the children but I want their errors to be eradicated.

> 18 Nov., Wed. Taught the children. Richie [Wallace, eleven] did not come. He began school at the Public School.

Perhaps the family wanted to reassure Maria of their love, for they made a special effort for her seventy-eighth birthday. However, the school situation did not improve.

> 5 Dec., Sat. Carrie [Dawkins] sent me a note inviting me to spend the day with her & Carl offered to drive me. Kate [daughter-in-law] came & went over with me. I was surprised to find in the yard at the gate to meet me so many of my children & grandchildren. They had gotten up a surprise birthday dinner for me. The day was pleasant & we had a fine dinner & an enjoyable time.

8 Dec., Tues. Miss Sue without a servant & the school interrupted with Kitty, Maria & Thomas having to leave here several times [to help Miss Sue].

9 Dec., Wed. Kitty sick, Thomas with employment for his father. Ellen failed to come. Carl in demand for errands & as Maria was the only one at school I gave holiday.

18 Dec., Fri. I taught the children, only Kitty, Tommy & Carl present, did not finish lessons till 1.

21 Dec., Mon. Taught Thomas and Carl. None of the other children came. Kitty excused to help her aunt.

23 Dec., Wed. Taught the children. Gave them holiday until 4th Jan 1892.

The diaries for 1892–94 are missing, but a letter to Ann Furman of 9 January 1892 shows that Maria took up school as she had intended, however shrunken her clientele. Shortly thereafter Maria suffered such a bad spell that her daughter Lydia in Germany wrote to her sister Dore upon receiving the news: "Your letter has made me so unhappy that I burst into tears every where and in the night when I realize the fact that our dear Mother may even now be lying in her last resting place!" (16 January 1892). But Maria recovered well enough from that and another episode to be teaching later in 1892, "writing hurriedly" to Ann Furman on 17 October, "After putting my room to rights I wrote the foregoing, before breakfast, & now find it is nearly time to ring the bell for my little scholars. While at Dore's, where I spent six weeks, I got a fall down several of the stair steps, but fortunately did not have to go to bed. As the children have come I must close." Just who was left in the school is not specified.

In the next extant letter to Ann, of 3 November 1893, Maria does not mention any teaching of her own but informs Ann that Carrie and Kitty Carlisle are both attending the Seminary and that Millie Carlisle "has her diploma, but is to begin on Monday a course of Latin & Algebra, with a finished teacher in those branches. She is ambitious to be prepared as a first class teacher," an ambition that must have gratified Maria. A year and a half later, Maria had still not completely given up teaching, for in a letter of 11 April 1894 she writes to Ann that she hates to leave "my little scholars," although "Kate & Richie have been pressing me to go to Wauburg this month, when it is pleasant there & plenty of vegetables." By the opening of 1895, Maria was teaching only the two youngest Carlisles, and Julius put John, age seven, in public school on 16 January. Mercifully, Julius left young Maria, now eleven, under her grandmother's tutelage. "Taught the children," the weekday diary note of so many years, now reads "taught Maria."

When the days of the school thus came to an end, Maria had taught her grandchildren over a span of nineteen years, from age sixty-two through age eighty-one. In a letter Fen Taylor wrote to his mother shortly after moving to Tallahassee at some time in 1892, he implies one reason why Maria's children were content to have her teach their children for so long: "Ena is doing well at school, but I'm afraid Carl's school is too overcrowded with scholars for them to receive enough individual attention" (undated). From their own experience of their mother as teacher and from observing her daily efforts with her grandchildren, Maria's children knew that their children received individual attention from a teacher who was dedicated to their intellectual and moral welfare, and who maintained loving but unswerving discipline.

Clearly, Maria should have stopped before she was too old to control her pupils and before the adults signaled their disenchantment by taking the children away from their lessons to run errands and do chores. Toward the end, it seems to have been one of those family situations that no one quite knows how to bring to a graceful conclusion.

FOUR

Memorializing a Friend

From 1885 to 1891, Maria memorialized her friend Anne Wickliffe Yulee through her work for the *Mission Populaire Evangelique de France,* better known by the name of its founder as the McAll Mission. Her endeavors for this organization—recorded in letters from 1885–87 and 1891 and in the 1885 and 1891 diaries—reveal two facets of Maria not yet seen: the intensity of a friendship and her charitable work beyond the parochial level.

Obviously, Maria's adult daughters satisfied much of her need for intense relationships with women. In the ordinary neighborly sense, Maria was sociable with a number of other women, but she did not seek out extra-familial society for its own sake, especially in this final phase of life. For example, she would frequently make gallons of ice cream for a church social and then not attend, or she would decline a dinner invitation issued to the whole household. However, Maria did have a few intimate women friends outside the family, one of whom was Anne Yulee, wife of David Levy Yulee, Florida railroad entrepreneur and prominent politician.

Maria had known Anne Yulee ever since the Taylors' arrival in Florida in 1853, but the two women never lived in drop-in proximity, their relationship developing largely through infrequent cross-state visits at each other's homes and through letters Maria mentions but that have not survived.

Shared interest in religion was at the heart of Maria's few intense friendships, such as in her friendships with Ann Furman and Maud

Gary, a close Ocala friend who like Maria wrote pieces for Baptist newspapers. The same basis is apparent in Maria's obituary tribute to Anne Yulee, published in the *Florida Mirror* (Fernandina) of 18 July 1885. After speaking of Anne Yulee's "fidelity and constancy as a friend" and her "conspicuous traits of energy, perseverance, courage and promptness," Maria describes her piety as "of no ordinary type," but rather as "a living, abiding principle." Further, Anne "loved the Lord Jesus in sincerity, and her 'goings out and her comings in were before Him.' Firm in doctrinal views, she was ready to receive experimental knowledge with the humility of a childlike nature and a Christianlike spirit." These attributes were similar to Maria's own.

David Yulee responded to Maria's obituary of his wife with a proposal.

25 August 1885. David Levy Yulee to Maria Baker Taylor

> [Thank you for] the beautiful tribute by which you gave us so much occasion of grateful obligation to you, in always reminding me of the very warm affection our dear departed entertained for you. You mention an interest she took in the McAll Mission in France & quote from a letter of hers. I am aware of the very warm concern she felt in that excellent work, & of her desire to promote it. It would seem to be appropriate that her wishes should be carried out by our aiding the association she desired to be formed in her own state. Would it be imposing too much upon your affectionate remembrance of her, if we ask you to lead in the formation of the auxiliary society she suggested, & to enter at once an annual subscription from her family of two hundred & fifty dollars? If you are willing to undertake the promotion of this evangelical charity, no doubt the ministry of the church in Florida of all the denominations would take the labor of organizing the movement under your direction.

Thus Maria at age seventy-one was to supply the hard work and the Yulee family the better part of the money for this undertaking.

Robert Whitaker McAll (1821–93), an English Congregational clergyman, founded his nondenominational Protestant mission in 1872, opening his first station in the communard quarter of Paris.

Described by one of McAll's associates as "the pioneer act of modern city missions in any country," the project was directed "not to Roman Catholics, but to free-thinkers, whether atheists or well disposed to religion," although, of course, it made some converts from Catholicism.[1] When Maria became interested in 1885, the organization had reached its zenith with a total of 130 mission stations, or *salles,* forty-two in Paris and environs, the others scattered over France, Algeria, Tunis, and Corsica. The American McAll Association, formed in 1883 with headquarters in Philadelphia, had a number of state auxiliaries, most of which sponsored a specific *salle.* Among the Mission's offerings were Sunday schools for children, Bible classes for adults, medical clinics and dispensaries, industrial schools for girls, childcare instruction for mothers, temperance meetings, fraternal meetings, home visits, distribution of religious literature, and lending libraries.

Confident that Maria would find this operation appealing and concur in his proposal, David Yulee immediately wrote to McAll, who replied with this information:

1 October 1885. Robert Whitaker McAll to David Levy Yulee

> You are aware that our numerous auxiliaries in America are worked by devoted Christian ladies, a certain number appointing themselves as a Committee, & a large number becoming collectors in the several churches to which they belong. How far a similar organization could succeed in Florida you alone can judge.
>
> Some years ago a devoted Christian lady in England, Lady H. Knox, desired to found & sustain an added station in Paris. She selected the most destitute & populous neighbourhood, called the Gare d'Ivry, inhabited by the poorest & most ignorant of the working people. The place may be regarded as a little centre of light & love in the midst of a most dark & degraded neighbourhood. The proposition made [by the board] was that this mission hall should be named "Salle Yulee," & that you should be invited to assume the responsibility of its annual cost.

McAll then detailed a budget that came to $540 per year.

The Florida Auxiliary of the American McAll Association was the largest-scale organizational work Maria had ever undertaken. In addition to the motives of memorializing her friend with a significant labor and the enlarged scope for her own abilities, Maria's adoption of this cause was probably given impetus by the great increase in foreign missionary activity among southern evangelical women in the 1880s.[2] Maria would have been well informed about this movement through her reading of the religious press. In Florida, the contribution of women to such enterprises was accepted and well recognized, women having been accorded seats on the Florida Baptist Missionary Board "upon the same terms as the brethren" in 1881.[3] By late 1885, Maria had plunged into the McAll Association work.

> 30 Nov., Mon. Fen called over & brought me letters & a package of pamphlets of the McAll Mission from Mr Yulee, two letters from France, one from Mr Newel & one from Mr McAll. I taught the children & then read them & looked over Mission documents. Fen goes to Jacksonville tomorrow. I wrote to Mrs Baker by him about McAll Mission, sent her some Records.[4]

> 1 Dec., Tues. Mr Curry [Baptist pastor] called by request & I showed him the letters & papers on the McAll Mission & requested him to deliver an address & aid me in getting up an association auxiliary to the Americans for the Evangelization of France. I had a pleasant conference with him.

> 3 Dec., Thurs. Mr Curry called after supper & we had a pleasant conference about the McAll Association, but he is not very hopeful of a great success.[5]

> 5 Dec., Sat. I went over to see Fen after breakfast, he was not up & I went in his room to see him & gave him letter to Mr Yulee to read respecting the McAll Mission. He thought there was nothing in it to involve us in responsibility to Mr McAll.[6]

> 14 Dec., Mon. Mr Pasco [Methodist minister] called to see me by request & we conversed on the subject. I lent him the pamphlets. I went in the evening to see Fen & showed him the piece I wrote on McAll Mission for the paper. I returned to Nan's, made a few changes & fixed it for Fen to have published. Retired late.

16 Dec., Wed. Mr Waugh [Baptist pastor] called for me & I went to see Mr Dunham [Presbyterian clergyman] & wife, talked of the McAll Mission. Called at Mrs Crawford's & Mr Pasco's for books but failed to get them. Called to see Mrs Manly. Mr Carlisle brought letters from Sue, Lyd, Mr Crane & Mr Yulee, the latter sent $300 for the McAll Mission.

19 Dec., Sat. Called at Mr Pasco's for pamphlet & to tell him about meeting at his church [Methodist]. Not at home, saw his son who called afterward at Carrie's with message. After dinner talked with Curran then went to Mr Waugh's & was there some time to confer with him about the McAll association. Mr Curry called & we decided to have it at the Baptist church on Tues. Wrote notes to Mr Pasco & Mr Dunham requesting them to notify [their parishioners of] McAll meeting.

22 Dec., Tues. Mr Curry called & we made up the programme for the evening. I sent to ask Mrs Jackson & Mrs Crawford to attend the meeting. The one was sick & the other absent. After dinner I went to the Baptist church & a Fla McAll Auxiliary Association was organized, Mr Curry & Mr Waugh speaking & RF Taylor [Fen] acting Secry. I returned home, felt very tired. Wrote to Mrs Chase [National McAll Secretary in Philadelphia] & sent the letter off.

23 Dec., Wed. Signed check of $300 & enclosed in letter to Mrs Chase & sent by Mr C to the office for French mission. I called to see Carrie & went to Curran's & Mrs Fosters & at Mr Waugh's saw Mrs McGill & read her [my] letter to Mrs Chase.

With the organization in place and the first big contribution in the mail, Maria, now seventy-two, wrote a week later in her 1885 year-end summary, "I was truly glad before the year closed to be somewhat instrumental in carrying out Mrs Yulee's wishes & organizing a Fla McAll Auxiliary, a very laudable enterprize."

Maria assumed the position of corresponding secretary. In a letter to Ann Furman early in 1886, Maria admitted that the auxiliary "does not 'take like wild fire,'" and added that by 1 June the Auxiliary had to raise $250 for the *salle* beyond the Yulees' $300. In addition, the new organization paid the expenses for a speaker from national, who "was very interesting, giving us an estimate of [McAll's] earnestness, zeal, wisdom & economy in the work, all of which must have been divinely bestowed" (22 February 1886). In spite of this inspiration, Maria did not succeed in raising the $250 by June.

3 June 1886. Maria Baker Taylor to David Levy Yulee

> On Tuesday last at a meeting of the Board of our Fla. Auxil-
> iary the Treasurer read a letter with acknowledgement of the
> funds sent by you & by us, from the Treasurer of the National
> Association. By unanimous resolution of the Board, the ladies
> request that you will receive our heartfelt thanks, for so graciously
> & promptly meeting our renewed calls upon your generosity, after
> the liberal contribution of your family to our Auxiliary. Rev. R.W.
> McAll has written us several very encouraging letters respecting
> the usefulness of the work done in the "Salle Yulee de Florida."

As chief fund-raiser for the auxiliary, Maria must have been relieved to learn from McAll that some of this work was paid for by other organizations: a medical dispensary funded by "Scottish patronage & without additional expense to us" and mothers' and working women's meetings funded by the Quakers.

David Yulee died in October 1886, and thereafter Maria worked with two of the Yulee daughters, Maggie Read and Nannie Noble. If the Yulees still had to come to the rescue after their initial annual con-tribution, it was not for lack of zeal on Maria's part. Her correspon-dence record shows that she wrote 158 letters for the auxiliary in 1887, and ninety-five more during the first five months of 1888, both to raise money and to establish local circles. A fragment of a rough draft of one of these letters, dated 27 January 1887, indicates the tack Maria took.

> Rev W.N. Chase kindly sent me your name, & I take the liberty
> of writing & enclosing you a preamble & Constitution to be adopted
> by Circles of the Florida Auxiliary to the McAll Association, hoping
> that I may rely on your cooperation with us? Our organization
> is entirely undenominational, composed of Christians of all the
> churches, & we try to work together in the common cause, of

giving the Bread of Life to enlightened and civilized France, with her millions of sceptics & infidels, of ignorant & degraded.

Her McAll address list suggests that Maria "worked" her acquaintanceship thoroughly. It includes members of her immediate and extended families (including some in South Carolina, Georgia, Alabama, and New York), area clergy, Gainesville friends, old friends in Marion County, and business and professional associates of her children. Her perseverance (to her, one of the Christian virtues) paid off, for with a typical individual contribution of only $1, the auxiliary was able to meet its 1890 obligation in full by 14 April.

Maria had advanced in the organization to being twice elected vice president for Florida in the national association while retaining her Florida auxiliary post of corresponding secretary. After all of her dedicated labor, Maria was mortified to learn that on a visit to Paris in 1891, Wickliffe Yulee, her friend's son, had not been able to find the Salle Yulee de Florida. It took Maria several days to frame a letter to Mrs. Bracq, the national corresponding secretary (diary 27–29 January), and the gist of her letter becomes apparent in three letters of response.[7]

Maria's tone must have spelled trouble, for Mrs. Bracq took time to marshal her forces before replying, writing to Dr. McAll and apparently also to Justine Dalencourt, a volunteer in the *salle* whose work Maria knew and respected. Mrs. Bracq then dated her reply to Maria 4 March, but waited to send it until Dr. McAll's letter from Paris had a chance to arrive in Gainesville and until she received Madame Dalencourt's letter, which was addressed to Mrs. Bracq but obviously intended for Maria. Thus a barrage of letters struck at about the same time: Maria received Dr. McAll's letter of 4 March on 19 March, and Mrs. Bracq's letter with Madame Dalencourt's enclosed on 22 March.

4 March 1891. Emma W. Bracq to Maria Baker Taylor

Americans come home every summer saying, "We made diligent search for the McAll Mission, and could find no one who knew anything about it," and this for the simple reason that even the name of the founder is seldom heard in connection with the

Mission. It is called "Mission Populaire," and <u>this</u> name is well known.

I do not know whether the name "Yulee-Florida" is found over the entrance or not, but I doubt if the hall is ever designated by that name in Paris. It is probably known as Gare d'Ivry, the name of the locality. It has been found impossible to get the French people to <u>pronounce</u> the foreign names that we have imposed upon them, and so Beach Memorial is known as "Les Terues," the New York hall as "Rivole," the Baltimore hall as "Bonne Nouvelle," Boston, as "Barbee," Phila. as "Rue Royale," and so it must be so long as the halls exist, a Frenchman cannot manage these strange names.

We have invariably designated the halls in Paris by their <u>American</u> names in all our published accounts in the "Record" and elsewhere, so that in this periodical alone the name Yulee-Florida comes before 8,000 readers. I cannot imagine a more beautiful or a more precious memorial than the many precious souls that have been born into the Kingdom in that hall—it is one of the most fruitful in the Mission. What does it matter that the converts cannot pronounce the name of the family by whose generosity they have received the Bread of Life, so long as they have learned to love the name of Jesus their Saviour & the way to heaven?

I am very sure that Mr. McAll will do all he can to make this hall a memorial. If the name "Yulee-Florida" is not over the entrance it should be—this is about all that could be done. I earnestly hope the Yulee family will continue their contributions to this hall. To close it would be to deny thousands in the course of one year the healing of the body and the healing of the sin-sick soul.

For his part, McAll is careful to mention that "the family of our late dear friend Mrs. Yulee adopted the Salle as a memorial of their venerated mother." He emphasizes the specifics and efficacy of the work.

4 March 1891. Robert Whitaker McAll to Maria Baker Taylor

Scarcely could there be found, in any part of the world, a darker or more degraded neighbourhood than that in the very centre of which this much blessed mission-hall is placed. Far removed from the centre of the vast city, though peopled by an immense throng of the poorest & most uncared—many visitors to Paris would have no idea of the existence, within the fortifications, of such a district.

M. Saynd [the young preacher] is regarded with the utmost affection by the people. The excellent Madame Justine Dalencourt founded in the Salle a very large & useful Mother's Meeting, which prospers to this day, & has also been the means of bringing many to the Saviour. Not a year has passed in which a series of marked conversions among old & young has not been recorded. The Free Dispensary, open twice a week under the care of Dr. Honore Estraband, our devoted young French medical missionary, has brought not only physical healing but spiritual light & blessing to many a poor neglected one.

I add a list of the activities of the station for each week, which will show you how completely the Hall is utilized for its beneficent purposes [detailed schedule follows].

In addition, 4 of the attendants open their houses for cottage-meetings, & in the summer, open-air services are held in sur-rounding courts. Very many visits are systematically paid by our missionaries, the Doctor, & our devoted Christian ladies. Many of the people have joined the neighboring evangelical churches, of various denominations. I add some cuttings from our new Annual Report (now in the press) which record a portion (only a part) of the triumphs of the gospel witnessed at the Salle Yulee of Florida most recently. To these are to be added similar records respecting the Free Dispensary, from the pen of our medical missionary. I will send these by next post.

By contrast to McAll's tone, Justine Dalencourt, a volunteer for both the Protestant Mission to Working-Class Women and the Salle Yulee, writes in an emotional vein.

5 March 1891. Justine Dalencourt to Emma W. Bracq (but intended for MBT)[8]

"Yulee" and "Florida" are for me more than agreeable abstrac-tions; they are almost friends with whom I sense the sweet com-munity of aspirations and interests to the glory of the Savior.

Mrs. Taylor tells me that "the faith of our Florida friends has been made stronger on reading my last letter & realizing that we are not laboring in vain in 'Salle Yulee Florida.'" Our women (to speak only of my assembly) are almost all Roman Catholic by birth; of 250 I have at the most 10 protestants; this means that they have not only much to learn but also much to unlearn, which is always difficult, humanly speaking, but the powerful Light triumphs over everything and we have some remarkably transformed lives: from dark mountains of sin they are as melted at hearing of the love of God and of Jesus Christ for the sinner.

What would you say, accidentally visiting a public hospital in Paris where all religion is officially banned, if passing behind a row of beds you were to hear a half-lowered voice declare that the most crimson sins can disappear and seem whiter than snow? Wouldn't your heart leap for joy if one told you that this is a woman, previously a raving drunkard, who without the Salle Yulee Florida, founded in the middle of that populous quarter, never would have known that there is for the alcoholic as for the less depraved sinner, a powerful Savior, who came to break the chains of the captives?

I do not wish to close my letter without transmitting the affectionate message of recognition from about 90 family mothers who were present at my meeting yesterday afternoon. I gave an explanation of the words "Yulee-Florida" which one reads under the entrance door (the inscription doesn't need to be renewed); I repeated that which I understood Mr McAll told the assistants one evening at the annual meeting; and a goodly number of them [the mothers] were much touched that such far away strangers were interested in their souls. I have wanted to good advantage, for their development, to tell what I know about the Yulee family, their desire to honor the memory of a pious mother and to perpetuate her Christian endeavor here and establish the Bible in this area.

In conclusion, if we want to honor the memory of our dearly beloved who were people of good deeds and of good intentions, let us rather give a pair of socks or of shoes for a poor child than a crown of glass beads for their tomb. It is well understood by those who will one day accompany me to my last resting place, that instead of strewing flowers around my remains, they will contribute to a collection to do some good for the poorest among them. And one poor woman who has lost her mother (whom she had brought to Christ) has said that on the day of the anniversary—in memory of the deceased—she will make a gift of a good scarf to her poor mother-in-law, because if her mother could see that action she would be far more content than with a bouquet on the grave. This is really Christian, isn't it?

Maria took the letter to her daughter Carrie to translate. Depending on how good Carrie's French was, Maria may have been spared a full understanding of Dalencourt's many condescending remarks.

In spite of the epistolary efforts of these three good people, they did not accomplish their purpose of keeping Maria's hard work and the Yulee money in the mission. Maria had already dissociated herself and she did not reconsider. Nevertheless, during the month of March 1891 she was punctilious in winding up her connection with the mission.

> 5 Mar., Thurs. I wrote postals to Curran & to Maggie Read & letters to Fen & Mrs Gary respecting "Salle Yulee." Wrote note to Mrs McDowell & sent subscription paper to her to collect for the Fla Auxiliary.

> 9 Mar., Mon. After dinner Ena drove me out to make collections for the McAll Mission. The horse on the right of buggy very restless & curtailed our ride. Called at Mrs Wilson's got her subscription. Saw Mrs Fluellen, called at Mrs Chapin's & she promised to try & collect for the Auxiliary.

> 19 Mar., Thurs. I wrote a letter to Mrs Bracq dissolving my connection with the Paris mission.

> 27 Mar., Thurs. Wrote to Mrs Wilson [auxiliary president] respecting the dissolution of the Fla Auxiliary & sent her report to read. Mrs Scott signed it for me yesterday as Vice President.

In writing to a cousin about the end of the Florida Auxiliary, Maria does not mention the difficulties outlined in the correspondence above, but gives other reason for withdrawing.

31 March 1891. Maria Baker Taylor to Dora Furman Hutson[9]

The Treasurer & President had both resigned & not been replaced, &, as Cor. Sec. of the Aux, & Vice Pres of the Association[10] I found my duties onerous, with the funds to collect, & some of the largest contributers in Italy, Washington, N.J. & Richmond, besides some in S.C. & various parts of Florida, but I have closed it all up now, & sent on the funds in time for the report of the fiscal year, & written, & sent letters this A.M. to Maggie Yulee Read & Mrs J.C. Bracq, Gen'l. Secretary to the Association, with report of the Fla Auxiliary.

So you will admit I have reason to congratulate myself, at my age, for having through,[11] for I find it trying & often impossible to see to write at night.

For whatever mix of motives, Maria, now age seventy-seven, called it quits. One of the Yulee children thought the withdrawal from the mission was precipitous, maintaining that "a year's notice should be given the officials about the Salle." However, Maria's other friends and relations probably breathed a sigh of relief—no more solicitations. Fortunately, the whole episode ended on a friendly note. On 8 May 1891 Maria "received a pleasant letter from Dr McAll. It was kind in him to write." And on 11 May Maria wrote a reply, no doubt also "a pleasant letter."

FIVE

Approaching Death

In her last few years Maria's major concerns were to come to an understanding of the meaning of her life and to continue her accustomed
activities as best she could. These concerns are reflected in summarizing reflections on her family and her faith found in letters and
poems dated 1891–95 and in her diary from 1895, the year of her
death.

One reason Maria valued her lifelong correspondence with Ann
Furman was that it linked her to her family of origin; in a retrospective mood at age seventy-seven, Maria expressed to Ann what this
formative influence had meant to her.

12 June 1891. Maria Baker Taylor to Ann Eliza Furman

  The Furman character, I contend, is a particular one, which
should not be eclipsed in its individuality by all its mixtures with
foreign elements. I don't think I say this in any spirit of pride,
which needs correction. Because it is the character which has been
formed, from generation to generation, of deep rooted Christian
principles & blended & sent in the beautiful Christian casket of
courtesy of our Saviour's own making. "Do unto others as you
would have others do unto you." Some of the family needed to be
reminded that they are not commanded to love their neighbors
<u>better</u> than themselves.

  The longer I live the more I understand the necessity of good
training by godly people, who know how to control themselves to

control others. I bless God for my dear Mother, my dear Father, & my dear good brother Richard, & for my dear Grandfather, & I cannot enumerate all whose love & precious influences were so good to me.

Mother's constant, silent refreshing, like the dew, began when I took in the first kindly act, the daily unselfishness, & self sacrifice, the freedom from revenge. Then dear Father, how he loved me, how patient & particular, how he tried to make me feel <u>above</u> doing anything wrong or dishonorable. How I knew he would give me anything in his power good for me, & to make me happy.

I have been writing of my types [exemplary archetypes] who let me into the secrets of deep & joyous things. I think your heart will respond. I think you will understand me. Oh, I want "to bring forth fruit" in old age! What if it be not large, but small? Small fruit may be very sweet & luscious. Even the cup of cold water is rewarded.

Distinctive to Maria's final years is a small set of unpublished devotional poems, all dated 1893. In contrast to the long, blank-verse discourses she published, these poems consist of rhymed stanzas in standard hymn meter that show a firm grasp of the hymn-text genre. In substance, they are Maria's final literary expression of her spiritual faith and hope. "The Higher Life," in the hymn meter 6.6.8.6 (syllables per line), is a good example of Maria writing in an aspirational mode.

The Higher Life

Mount up my soul, mount up,
    Grasp higher joys above
They are within thy reach in Christ,
    Wrapp'd in His richer love.

Illimitable pow'r
    Illimitable grace
Stand pledg'd to save rebellious man,
    Lost gifts, more than replace.

Free'd from the stain of sin,
That ugly thing of earth,
Made holy through the blood of Christ,
By the celestial birth.

Then mount my soul, mount up,
And grasp the higher prize.
It is within Thy reach in Christ—
"Come unto me" He cries.

Another of Maria's poems, headed with the scriptural motto "They who will to do His will shall know the doctrine," is in a more determined mood. The repetition of the key line in the first three stanzas is a convention of the genre, but noteworthy is the progression in grammatical person as the hymn becomes more inclusive.

I will to do His will,
The world doth me oppose,
But Christ has overcome the world
And so should we our foes.

I will to do His will,
But, Oh! this flesh is strong,
Calls loudly for indulgent sway,
Inclines me to the wrong.

I will to do His will,
But Satan ready stands
To capture mind & heart & soul
To yield to His commands.

Then watch, awake & strive,
Gird on thy armor bright,
Thy sword unsheath for use
Be ready for the fight.

Aye watch, awake, & wait,
Our Captain's gone before.
He is our King, our strength, our shield
Our guide to the blest shore.

"An Invitation" (8.7.8.7 trochaic) is in a militant, hortatory spirit. The sequence of the last lines of the stanzas is nicely worked out as the sinners advance from the "penitential" to the "Heav'nly" throng. The effect of Maria's hymn texts is better understood by imagining them being sung to hymn tunes in matching meters. For example, the next poem could be "heard" as sung to the hymn tune "Stuttgart," familiar as the musical setting of texts such as "Earth has many a noble city" and "Come, thou long expected Jesus"; or to the hymn tune "Hymn to Joy" (Beethoven), familiar as "Joyful, joyful we adore thee."

An Invitation

Come ye sinners, mighty sinners,
    Ye have serv'd the world too long,
Let not Satan be your master,
    Join the penitential throng.

Manifold are your transgressions,
    But our Lord is great & strong,
He can pardon, He can heal us,
    Join the penitential throng.

Ask Him for the true religion!
    Choose the right, reject the wrong,
He will give you strength & wisdom,
    Join the penitential throng.

Ask Him for His Holy Spirit,
    That you truly may belong
To the hosts that seek forgiveness
    In the penitential throng.

Ask Him for His blood & merit,
    And for faith & love so strong,
To appropriate His graces,
    And to join the Heav'nly throng.

Since Maria greatly admired the hymns of Frances Ridley Havergal (which are still found in standard hymnals), some influence from

Havergal might be expected. However, Havergal's feel for the genre is more overtly emotional and personal than is Maria's, qualities that in a lesser talent such as Maria's could have fallen into a meretricious sentimentality. A year after she composed these simple, sturdy statements of her faith, Maria at age eighty still had a sense that she was spiritually unfinished.

11 April 1894. Maria Baker Taylor to Ann Eliza Furman

> How many noble & lovely ones have gone before us! Like us, I presume, they all felt the evil of sin. They all needed the pruning hand, sinned, had to confess & receive pardon from Him, who "knoweth our frame that it is dust." Peter prays that "the God of all grace who hath called us unto His eternal glory, by Christ Jesus, after that ye have suffered awhile, make you perfect, 'stablish, strengthen, <u>settle</u> you." The settling seems to come last. Many of us are "ever learning" & are so slow to come to a "knowledge of the truth."

To the end of her life, Maria remained committed to the care of her adult children's souls. For example, on 15 March 1891 she notes in her diary, "Wrote to Richard [forty-four] on the authority of the Scriptures. Wrote to John [forty-nine] on faithfulness of God to reward Godliness & integrity & trust in Him." In a family-circle poem she wrote in 1893 at age seventy-nine, Maria reviewed her success in the project she had devoted herself to for almost sixty years.

Home Thoughts of my Children

Dear children Lord, Thou gav'st to me,
 A precious trust, to rear for Thee!
Thou know'st all & Thou can'st tell,
 Where I have err'd, or where done well.
If I have fail'd, dear Father, deal
 With gentleness my failures heal.

Carrie & Mary, Lydia too
 Thou did'st with piety imbue.

Perfect them Lord, that purified
    They in Thy Heav'nly courts may 'bide,
Where no distracting cares molest,
    A perfect Home, a perfect rest.

Susan & John too sought Thy love.
    Oh, that they steadfast, faithful prove!
Father! Thy Holy Spirit give
    And teach them on Thy word to live.
Oh, may they find their Saviour still
    Gracious to them, & <u>do</u> His will.

Dear Richard does not yet profess,[1]
    But in his heart doth Christ confess
As King of Kings, as Lord of all.
    Now at <u>His</u> feet oh, may he fall,
Whose blood alone can cleanse from sin,
    Whose Spirit quickens life within.

Dora & Fenwick, children dear,
    Great Saviour, wilt Thou keep them near,
Nor let them from Thy pastures stray,
    To lose the narrow Heav'n bound way?
As they Thy Holy Name profess
    May, then, Thy Holy Spirit bless.

Dear Willie, Janie, Anne, three
    I feel assur'd are now with Thee,
In Thy Celestial joyous Home,
    Where Thou in love did'st bid them "come,"
There earth's allurements tempt no more,
Nor ills e'er mar that blissful shore.

Thomas, Elizabeth, home too,
    Their hearts were knit in love, they grew
In oneness, close in death they lie,
    One grave conceals from human eye
Their beaute'us forms, & safe above
    They know each other, still they love.

These valu'd treasures, only lent,
    I feel assured that God has sent
And He hath length'n'd out my days.
    I shall a sacred altar raise
And wholly consecrated live,
    Remaining strength, to Jesus give.

In her last diary, from 1895, Maria is still recording her usual activities: teaching, sewing, reading, writing, visiting, and caring for the sick in spite of her own infirmities. For example, although she was down to one scholar, her twelve-year-old granddaughter Maria Carlisle, Maria was still tenacious in keeping to her teaching schedule.

8 Feb., Fri. Ground covered with ice. I taught Maria. Busy all the morning. Fell on the ice some after dinner & got my right side very much hurt by a fall on the ice. Miss Sue waited on me very nicely. Sue called, Carrie stayed all night.[2]

9 Feb., Sat. Dore[3] called, she has neuralgia. I am glad today & tomorrow are not school days. I remained on my bed all day, cannot move my leg or my foot without assistance & great pain. Used peppermint as a lotion & Pons extract. Porous plaster.

11 Feb., Mon. I felt better this morning, could move my foot a little, using same lotions. Letters from Mary Ansley & one from Carl [grandson]. Carrie went home & spent the day & came back at night. I taught Maria. She nurses me nicely.

26 Mar., Tues. Clear pleasant day. I feel weak & short breathed. I taught Maria. Read the papers & read history.

29 Mar., Fri. Taught Maria. My sinews still painful but walked a little across the room. Carrie came to spend the night.

On 30 March, Maria's grandson Carl Taylor died suddenly of appendicitis a few days before his thirteenth birthday. He was visiting his Haile grandparents at their plantation Kanapaha near Gainesville, Fen and his family having moved to Tallahassee in 1892.

30 Mar., Sat. Greatly grieved to hear of dear Carl's death, Fenwick's only son. I was unfit for work which I promised to do.

Wrote postals to Richard, Sue, John & Mary with sad intelligence. Carrie returned here when she heard the news. All of us truly grieved.

31 Mar., Sun. Carrie made a wreath for me for dear Carl. Maria busy trying to get flowers. A number of emblematical floral tributes were made. Dear Fen, Millie & Ena called on their way to Kanapaha. Miss Sue, Thomas, Maria & John went to the funeral, also Dore & her children. Richie & Kate were out & quite a concourse. Carrie, Kitty & I were at home.[4] Ena returned with Mrs Haile & Bessie [Haile].

1 Apr., Mon. Fen & Millie came today & Mrs Haile Sr with them. Fen came over to see me & we talked some time. I taught Maria. Read some, was glad to have several visits from Fen & Millie & Ena, Carrie here.

2 Apr., Tues. Maria did not say any lesson today we were so much interrupted by company. Ena, Mrs Haile Sr & Jr & dear Fen & Millie called. Fen came by himself & sat sometime. I gave him a piece I wrote on Carl. I felt so sorry for Mrs Haile.

3 Apr., Wed. Fen & Millie left today. They called to see & bid us goodbye, my heart bleeds for them. Taught Maria under difficulties. Ena remains till Saturday. Sent verses to the Sun.[5]

Maria's 8 February fall on the ice crippled her permanently, and her accounts of her daily activities are now frequently punctuated by remarks such as "feverish and feeble," "sick and on bed nearly all day," "felt very unwell," or "up but feeble"; and some days she was able to write nothing at all. Nevertheless, days off from the lessons were granted only when young Maria, not Maria herself, was sick or was claimed for errands by Miss Sue

Writing letters, of course, was another lifelong activity that Maria persisted in. Her last extant letter, dated six months before she died, has a valedictory quality. Ann, one year older than Maria and long a confirmed invalid, was contemplating a visit to relatives in Greenville, South Carolina; the other places mentioned are residences of some of Maria's children. To the end, Maria observes the old proprieties of address in the relationship.

27 June 1895. Maria Baker Taylor to Ann Eliza Furman

My darling Aunt,

I have been trying to begin a letter to you every day this week but have felt too feeble & unwell to overcome interruptions, in fact I think I ought to be in bed & not to take the few steps I do, which set my breath & pulses going. My dear, good, patient Aunt, you give me truly a noble example! Do I lack the pluck to take it, when you, in your helplessness can look forward to doing so much? A journey? A journey to Greenville! While I am appalled at a short trip to Wauburg Lake, [or] 12 miles to Rochelle, to see Sue. A journey to Tallahassee being as impossible as flying.

I ought not to write of myself as you so persistently show your aversion to egotism, but I feel differently & want to know all I can about you, & who to tell me but yourself? So, I set you a contrary example & have ego prominent. I admire Paul exceedingly, as a great working self sacrificing apostle, & he did not hesitate with his I's to make himself known, so you will have to excuse me.

I imagine you in a soft cushioned, rolling chair with every body ready & willing to wait on you, & you anxious to do all you can for every body else. I hope our hearts are getting purer & purer & less selfish every day, & that our Blessed Redeemer will present us blameless, with exceeding joy, before His Father's throne, not for any works of righteousness which we have done, but by the thorough work which he has wrought in us by His Almighty power.

Do write me when you can. Present me kindly to the family circle & imagine, if you can, a warm, loving embrace from the affectionate heart & flabby arms of a very wrinkled, bony, old woman, who thinks she was once, is now, & always will be your loving niece, MB Taylor

In October, Maria rallied enough energy to be concerned for her fifty-one-year-old daughter Sue Beard, who was living a few miles from Gainesville in Rochelle with her husband and young son Taylor.

16 Oct., Wed. Taught Maria. Clear, cool day. Dore & Kate called on their way to Rochelle to see Sue. I ciphered some, read & sewed

on a skirt. Curran called & took me to ride the first time I have been out for two years.[6]

17 Oct., Thurs. Dore & Kate called & gave distressing accounts of Sue's sickness.

19 Oct., Sat. I was busy all day sewing & mending clothes for Maria & myself. I feel some stronger. I feel very anxious about Sue & wish I could go & be strong enough to nurse her.

20 Oct., Sun. I read a sermon. Curran sent Gilbert [her son] for me to go & spend the day with her. He drove me carefully & I had a pleasant time & a nice dinner. Returned in time to read Dr McArthur's sermon & other devotional material. Kate & Ellen[7] went to Rochelle to see Sue.

21 Oct., Mon. Kate called, reports Sue very low.

23 Oct., Wed. Taught Maria. She had cold. Richie went to Rochelle to see Sue, found her ill, telegraphed for Dr McKinstry [family doctor], he also sent for nurse Abbie, 7 miles in the country to nurse Sue. He came back at 1 & went on traveling tour & I did not see him.

25 Oct., Fri. Taught Maria. Letter to Kate from Mrs Fay [in Rochelle] last night saying Sue was better. Richie got home tonight, glad to hear from Sue. He & I had an ecclesiastical talk. Kate, Millie, Eva & Bessie went to the Opera house. I am glad the Mikado is over.

30 Oct., Wed. Wrote to Sue. Dore went to Rochelle to see Sue who is ill. Dore called to tell me of Sue.

31 Oct., Thurs. Carrie letter from Mrs Fay, Sue worse & she & Dore determined to go to her.

3 Nov., Sun. Curran came for me & I went to church with her in time to partake of the communion & enjoyed myself. I dined with Curran. Called to see Mrs Haile Sr who is sick at Evans.' She looks bad. Mr Charles Haile there with his brother Thomas.

"Mrs Haile Sr" was Millie Taylor's mother, Serena Chesnut Haile. The Taylors had known the Hailes for decades, and the two families had lived parallel lives. About twelve years younger than the Taylors, the Hailes had arrived in Florida from South Carolina a year before the Taylors, bringing a large workforce and establishing themselves on a 6,000-acre plantation near Gainesville, where they reared fourteen children.[8] Maria's attention soon reverted to Sue.

4 Nov., Mon. Received two letters from Carrie, Sue very low & not expected to live.

5 Nov., Tues. Taught Maria, had her go & get money order & get money from the bank for me. I wrote to Dore, to Carrie & Mary. I have decided to go see Sue. Mrs Wilson will go with me.

7 Nov., Thurs. Curran came for me soon after breakfast to drive me to the station. We called at Dore's & she went with us. Mrs Wilson accompanied me to Rochelle. I found Sue very ill & perfectly willing to depart & be with Jesus.

8 Nov., Fri. Mrs Wilson returned. She seemed to feel unwell. Sue asked me to stay Friday which I did. She is calm & peaceful. I felt very weak & had to lie down the most of the day. Mam Abbie is a splendid nurse & all the neighbors are so kind.

9 Nov., Sat. I sat some with Sue. She is calm & lucid & my intercourse with her very satisfactory.[9] I bade her farewell & returned on 2 oclock train to Gainesville.

13 Nov., Wed. Taught Maria. Kate came to tell me that a telegram had come announcing dear Sue's death. She staid only a few moments. In the absence of all my sons & Dr Wallace, she & Dora to make all the arrangements necessary.

14 Nov., Thurs. I had a chill last night & severe pain in the side. Dora called. Dear Sue's funeral took place at the Baptist church, Mr Hundley officiated. She was buried by Mr Dawkins.[10] Carrie came from Rochelle sick, Sue's body was brought from there. She died conscious, relying on Jesus.

Maria's statement on November 7 that Sue was "perfectly willing to depart" was not a sentimental wish but the perception of the entire family, as a comment from Lydia Crane, writing from Germany to her sister Dore, makes clear: "You write that Sue was so glad to go, and be at rest. Was her life then <u>so</u> unhappy with her husband? or was it the poverty of which she so much suffered?" (13 March 1896).[11]

On 17 November, Maria attended church for the last time, where she "heard an excellent sermon from Mr Geiger on the parable of the fig tree [Luke 13:6–9]." That same day she saw Mrs. Haile for the last time. Two weeks later, Maria had her last birthday.

> 5 Dec., Fri. I am 82 years old today & feel thankful to God for the prolongation of my life & trust it is for good to others. May I be perfected for death when it comes. Read the paper & attended to little duties.

> 7 Dec., Sun. We heard this am that Mrs Haile died last night at eleven passing away quietly. After breakfast I called to see Millie & her mother's remains. She was funeralized & buried today. A good woman & a pleasant friend. I read, did not feel well.

> 8 Dec., Mon. Maria had severe cold but said her lessons. Millie Taylor came over to say goodbye. She went to Kanapaha to put away her mother's things. I began a letter to Lydia but my eyes failed & I put letter away, had fever & coughed very much at night.

Maria's final eight diary entries show her confined to her room with the grippe but writing to the *Christian Herald;* reading a tale of the Civil War and a devotional tract; hemming a skirt; being concerned about the health of Miss Sue and young Maria ("not well enough to say her lessons"); and receiving visits from Johnny (who brought her "a bottle of brandy & some medicine"), Johnny's wife Curran, Dore and her daughter Ellen, and Millie Taylor on her way back to Tallahassee after her mother's death. Maria's final entry:

> 16 Dec., Tues. Murky morning, not very cold. Cistern very low. Maria better. I had an appetite for breakfast. A letter from Lydia last night. She sent Command Me, a nice Christmas gift.

The pages for 17–25 December are blank, then in the space for Thursday, 26 December, appears an entry in the hand of Maria's eldest child, Caroline Taylor Dawkins: "Through with earth & all its trials, tonight at 8:30 her pure spirit was called from earth to heaven. C.T. Dawkins."

Maria was survived by seven children, Caroline Dawkins, Mary Ansley, Lydia Crane, John Taylor, Richard Taylor, Fenwick Taylor, and Dore Wallace; twenty-two grandchildren; and six great-grandchildren. She was buried in the Carlisle plot in Gainesville's Evergreen Cemetery, since relocated to make room for a highway. No trace of Maria or the Carlisles is to be found in the new location, but perhaps the epitaph on her tombstone read as her daughter Lydia thought it should: "Thy word is a lamp unto my feet and a light unto my path."

Epilogue

Taken together, Maria Baker Taylor's writings form an autobiography that possesses virtues inherent in this informal genre: specific truths that give face to reductive generalizations; insight into women's situations as women themselves perceive them; a particular subject's manner of constructing reality from herself outward; and the assertion of the importance of the individual life, however ordinary or obscure.[1] These values are given substance by contemplating a few kinds of significance that may be ascribed to our particular subject's life.

On a simple generational level, Maria was a transmitter of her culture to a greater extent than the uncertainties of American family life at that time often permitted. She was the product of parents who came to maturity in the late eighteenth century and exerted a strong formative influence on her. A stable and powerful personality herself, Maria in turn was a major figure in the lives of her own children far into their adulthood, the eldest survivor being sixty years and the youngest forty-five when Maria died. As for her grandchildren, the youngest to know her well lived until 1969.[2] Thus Maria may be viewed as the focal point of a family culture that flourished for more than a century.

In other areas of significance, there are elements both alien and familiar to present-day experience. After Maria's death, her daughter Lydia Taylor Crane singled out the two traits of her mother that she would miss most: Maria's emphasis on family unity and her devotion to the spiritual well-being of individual family members. Even translated into contemporary arrangements and the higher secular concerns, these values may or may not be attractive to the present-day reader. Furthermore, even the most empathetic reader may find it difficult to judge Maria's way of dealing with her basic experiences, so alien have these experiences become—holding and selling slaves and managing basic care for a sizable black community, bearing thirteen children and rearing most of them over a forty-year period, running a household for up to twenty people at a time without modern conveniences, providing two generations of children with formal home-schooling for more than fifty years, nursing sick family members day and night, and meeting the constant emotional demands of a close-knit extended family. Even the present-day senior citizen who longs for distant family would think more than twice about immersing herself in family cares as Maria did in her old age. But alien as her external circumstances now seem, Maria's notions of order, steadfastness, and service are familiar basics of the civilized life in any era.

The main instrument Maria had for meeting the formidable challenges of her life was her unquestioning religious faith. On one level that faith no doubt functioned as a subliminal survival mechanism. But even though the basic tenet appears simple—everything is ordained by God and the believer has only to accept His will—Maria as intelligent believer still faced an imposing challenge, because great principles must be consciously and constantly interpreted. Through self-awareness and self-examination, Maria had to figure out what it meant in practical terms to conduct herself like a Christian in the minutest details of everyday life; she often had to subdue her own powerful will to accept terrible outcomes as being God's will; and she had to generate meaning from such events to serve as guidance for the future. Thus to a considerable extent Maria's faith was a conscious construction on her part, although of course grounded in a culturally inherited framework. Much the same can be said of the set of values developed by any thinking person.

In a combination that may seem somewhat paradoxical today, Maria's unquestioning faith was housed in a mind that was both inquiring and capacious. But it was not a mind equipped with the originality to challenge basic social arrangements of race and gender, in spite of the contemporary ferment on such issues, which Maria was aware of from her extensive reading. Maria's forte lay instead in doing a loving job of keeping things going within the accepted social framework. Rather than being a social reformer on the great issues of her day, Maria was a former of the souls directly under her care; but like the social reformer, she believed fervently in a great idea—for her, salvation—and strove tirelessly toward it for herself and her family.

All in all, Maria's ability to sustain her demanding role in life for so long at such a high pitch speaks of a strong mind and determined character powered by a remarkable physical constitution. Perhaps Maria should be placed at the high end of the range of the ordinary, or perhaps she can be seen as a fitting representative and spokeswoman for the millions of obscure women who have always made order out of chaos and kept things going.

The last word on Maria goes to a thoughtful obituary by C. V. Waugh, a Baptist pastor who had served as editor of the *Florida Baptist* and was now an academic at Florida Southern College in Lake City. In his eulogy Waugh explains his relationship to Maria. His estimate of Maria's intellectual accomplishments and published writings is valuable in suggesting how these accomplishments looked to an educated person of her own religious community, the only public she cared about. Waugh's ambiguous comment on Maria's "liberality of soul and spirit" also catches the eye. Does he mean that people who did not know her well thought her more liberal than she really was, or that she was more liberal than she appeared? More likely the latter.

C. V. Waugh's Obituary of Maria Baker Taylor[3]

Sorrow fills my soul tonight for I have just heard that on the 26th of December my beloved friend, Mrs. M. B. Taylor fell asleep. It was a pleasure to have been for twelve years her pastor and for twenty years her loved and loving friend. She was almost mother to me and mine during my long residence in Gainesville. My dear association with her of long continuance, enables me to speak advisably of her worth. I was her preacher, she was mine. Many a time have I sat at her feet to hear her unfold to me the word of God. She was mighty in the Scriptures, mighty in Theology, broadly cultured in the arts and sciences and an extensive reader.

Intellectually she was a princess among women. As a writer of prose or of real poetry she had few superiors. Many of her productions on matters of religion or theology, or verse would do honor to any whom the world greets as masters. It is to be hoped that her children may take of her writings and give them to the world in some permanent form.

She wrote a great deal. Some twenty-two years ago there was a great discussion going on in the papers as to "Did Divinity Suffer?" This provoked an article from her in blank verse, masterly in manner and truly Miltonic in execution. I was residing in Virginia at the time and little dreamed of ever knowing the author. The article struck me so forcibly that I put it in my scrapbook. Her pen I often enlisted to help me with the Florida Baptist and frequently she wrote for the Index and in earlier days for the Witness.

Mrs. Taylor was one of the most Godly of women, living and acting out her religion at all times. Her home life is too sacred [to discuss publicly]; as a friend she was true as steel. Though advanced in years when she moved to Gainesville, she nevertheless became an earnest, active church worker, the Pastor's strong ally, ever willing and ready to help him execute his plans, invaluable as a counselor and auxiliary; others might falter, she never. Forward, onward, upward, never backward.

A large manner of my success in Gainesville was due to her words of cheer and her helping hand. Zion's walls were precious in her sight and sweet the assembly of God's children. As a Baptist and as a Christian, she was firm and true. Her liberality of soul and spirit was misunderstood by some who did not know her real ideas of matters. Owing to a fall she was unable to attend church and her soul was filled with longing to do so. Of this she told me last June, in her own sweet way. She said, "Soon we shall all meet in the Father's house above, then we shall go no more out." Her losses have been heavy, her grief and sorrow intense, but she has ever borne it all with sweet Christian resignation.

Eighty-two years were the measure of her life and these all filled up with good works. She was spared long to bless her children, and their children's children bless her memory. Her faith in the Lord and His Christ was simple like that of the child in its parents. It was clear-cut having no mist at all about it. Religion and religious spirit was a reality to her. Her faith admitted no doubt nor incertitude. She was ready when the Lord came and is now at rest with Him.

FINIS

Notes

Introduction

1. William Cowper (1731–1800), British poet, considered the poet of the evangelical revival of his time.

2. Their aspirations have been described as "to appear richer than one's neighbor, to set a heavier table, to drive a fancier carriage, to sail a larger boat." Theodore Rosengarten, *Tombee: Portrait of a Cotton Planter with the Journal of Thomas B. Chaplin (1822–1890)* (New York: Morrow, 1986), 25.

3. Rachel N. Klein, *Unification of a Slave State: The Rise of the Planter Class in the South Carolina Backcountry, 1760–1808* (Chapel Hill: University of North Carolina Press, 1990), 42–43.

4. James A. Rogers, *Richard Furman: Life and Legacy* (Macon, Ga.: Mercer University Press, 1985), 151.

5. See the bibliographic note at the head of bibliography for a brief summary of the major categories of the complete MBT material.

6. The years of the extant diaries: 1857, 1858, 1861, 1862, 1863, 1864, 1867, 1870, 1871, 1873, 1874, 1875, 1880, 1882, 1883, 1885, 1888, 1889, 1890, 1891, 1895. There is every reason to believe that Maria also kept diaries during the missing years.

7. For example, see Virginia Ingraham Burr, ed., *The Secret Eye: The Journal of Ellen Gertrude Clanton Thomas, 1848–1889* (Chapel Hill: University of North Carolina Press, 1990), 364; and Judy Nolte Lensink, *"A Secret to Be Buried": The Diary and Life of Emily Hawley Gillespie, 1858–1888* (Iowa City: University of Iowa Press, 1989), 19.

8. A motive here may be the traditional judging of a woman by "the skill with which she manages to keep undisturbed the smooth pattern of daily living," as Elizabeth Hampsten puts it in *Read This Only to Yourself: The Private*

Writings of Midwestern Women, 1880–1910 (Bloomington: Indiana University Press, 1982), 71. This typically Victorian standard was in place even earlier, for Martha Ballard, an American midwife diarist who died in 1812, "deliberately excluded family quarrels from her entries." See Laurel Thatcher Ulrich, *A Midwife's Tale: The Life of Martha Ballard, Based on Her Diary, 1785–1812* (New York: Vintage Books, 1991), 336.

9. The epilogue serves also as the conclusion for part 4.

10. Franz Boas (1858–1942) was the most prominent American anthropologist of his time.

11. Lensink, *"A Secret to Be Burried,"* xii; Hampsten, *Read This Only to Yourself,* 14, 26; Virginia Walcott Beauchamp, *A Private War: Letters and Diaries of Madge Preston, 1862–1867* (New Brunswick, N.J.: Rutgers University Press, 1987), xxxiii; Robert Manson Myers, ed., *The Children of Pride: A True Story of Georgia and the Civil War* (New Haven: Yale University Press, 1972), xii; Minrose C. Gwin, ed., *Cornelia Peake McDonald: A Woman's Civil War. A Diary, with Reminiscences of the War from 1862* (Madison: University of Wisconsin Press, 1992), 3; and Elizabeth Fox-Genovese, *Within the Plantation Household: Black and White Women of the Old South* (Chapel Hill: University of North Carolina Press, 1988), 38.

One

Introduction

1. The "i" in Maria is long and is pronounced as in "I."

2. Present-day Sumter. The entrance drive to Oak Grove, now blocked off, can still be seen on the south side of U.S. highway 521 just south of the intersection with SC 441 at a bend in the road.

3. Cassie Nicholes, *Historical Sketches of Sumter County* (Sumter, S.C.: Sumter County Historical Commission, 1975), 71.

Family and Formative Background

1. Harvey Toliver Cook, *The Life Work of James Clement Furman* (Greenville, S.C.: Furman University, 1926), 325–26.

2. Thomas's political affiliation is unknown.

3. Thomas means two doors on each side of the facade, not on the side of the building.

4. The implication is that Catholics are not Christians.

5. Larry Koger, *Black Slaveowners: Free Black Slave Masters in South Carolina, 1790–1860* (Jefferson, N.C.: McFarland, 1985), 136, 144.

6. A "sizeable number"; see Michael P. Johnson and James L. Roark, *Black Masters: A Free Family of Color in the Old South* (New York: Norton, 1984), 26.

7. The Furman Theological Institution was located in the High Hills near Oak Grove from 1829 to 1834. It was a very small affair, having only one teacher until 1831, when Samuel Furman, Maria's uncle, joined the faculty.

8. Maria's letter describing the meeting exists only in Harvey Toliver Cook's 1926 biography of James Clement Furman (17–18). Cook gives neither date nor addressee, but identifies the writer as JCF's niece, Mrs. Maria B. Taylor, "an eye and ear witness of James C. Furman's preaching in his twenty-second year."

9. In his autobiography, J. Marion Sims narrates several college escapades with Richard Baker. See J. Marion Sims, *The Story of My Life* (New York: Appleton, 1884), 119–25.

10. Maria's widowed sister-in-law, who lived with the Bakers.

Schooling

1. Such enterprises were common among planters of the time. Typically a small group hired a single teacher and provided housing for the school; see Rosengarten, *Tombee,* 175.

2. Founded in 1764 by the Philadelphia Baptist Association, the college became Brown University in 1804; Wood's father, Richard Furman, was instrumental in sending a number of South Carolina students to the institution (see James A. Rogers, *Richard Furman,* 124–25).

3. James Lyons Furman, "Reminiscences of an Octagenarian," 1905, Thomas deSaussure Furman Collection, 5, 16. Furman describes, respectively, the building and the curriculum. Thomas deSaussure Furman provided a typescript of J. L. Furman's memoir. Evelyn Gaillard Rhame, present owner of Oak Grove, provided information about the archaeological excavation of the Woodville site.

4. Archaic term for sequence.

5. William H. Pease and Jane H. Pease, *Private Values and Public Styles in Boston and Charleston, 1828–1843* (New York: Oxford University Press, 1985), 72.

6. Letter of 20 April 1841 to Henry's brother James Clement Furman.

7. Klein, *Unification of a Slave State,* 294.

8. Wood Furman, Samuel Furman, and Thomas Baker.

9. Identified in the next letter as a Miss Brainard.

10. A term meaning "this month," often abbreviated "inst." Thomas no doubt meant to write "ultimo" or "ult," meaning "last month," as the letter referred to obviously arrived at least one month before 5 March.

11. Identifications of persons mentioned in the letter: "your sister Lydia" is Lydia Dick Baker, Maria's widowed sister-in-law; "your brother" is Richard Baker, Maria's older brother; "your aunts" are Maria and Susannah Furman; "Caroline" is Caroline Haynsworth, Maria's second cousin; "Jno Haynsworth" is Caroline's older brother; "Elizabeth" is Elizabeth Haynsworth, also a second

cousin but not a sister of Caroline, and apparently attending a different Charleston school; "the doctor" is Dr. James Haynsworth, Elizabeth's father; "the children" are Maria's younger brother, sister, and niece.

12. Letter writing was a valued accomplishment in nineteenth-century society generally, competence being "expected of all who aspired even to what we might term lower middle-class status"; Marilyn Ferris Motz, *True Sisterhood: Michigan Women and Their Kin, 1820–1920* (Albany: State University of New York Press, 1983), 10. Hence Thomas's concern to instruct Maria in improving her letter writing and his later statement that her letters will be an indication of her educational progress.

13. British poet, playwright, and essayist.

14. Jean E. Friedman, *The Enclosed Garden: Women and Community in the Evangelical South, 1830–1900* (Chapel Hill: University of North Carolina Press, 1985), 100.

15. Anne C. Loveland, *Southern Evangelicals and the Social Order* (Baton Rouge: Louisiana State University Press, 1980), 20.

Suitors and Wedding

1. Sims, of course, is in error here. It was Thornwell who was Presbyterian.

2. Sims, *Story of My Life,* 107–8.

3. Benjamin Morgan Palmer, *The Life and Letters of James Henley Thornwell* (Richmond, Va.: Whittet and Shepperson, 1875), 52.

4. Donald G. Mathews, *Religion in the Old South* (Chicago: University of Chicago Press, 1977), 176.

5. Eugene D. Genovese, *The Slaveholders' Dilemma: Freedom and Progress in Southern Conservative Thought, 1820–1860* (Columbia: University of South Carolina Press, 1992), 28.

6. The implication of the term is unclear, as most adjectival uses of "dutch" are derogatory. Perhaps here it signifies "in-law."

7. Thomas Baker's will (dated 1 April 1839) stipulates that the value of the slaves given to his two married children be assessed and counted as part of their shares in order to equalize the shares of the unmarried heirs. Because Thomas specifically excepted counting a gift slave who had since died, it can be assumed that Maria was given at least two slaves.

Conclusion

1. The book is among the few volumes from Maria's library that have survived in the Wallace Collection.

2. Rufus William Bailey, *The Family Preacher* (New York: Taylor, 1837), 26–58 passim.

Two

Introduction

1. The economic development of upper St. Peter's Parish is traced in Lawrence S. Rowland, Alexander Moore, and George C. Rogers Jr., *The History of Beaufort County, South Carolina* (Columbia: University of South Carolina Press, 1996), 1:297–312.

2. Robert Wilson Gibbes, *Documentary History of the American Revolution* (New York: New York Times, 1971), 3:239–40.

3. By 1820, Henry Taylor was the second-largest slaveholder (205 slaves) in all of St. Peter's Parish. He was also an innovative planter, having installed the first steam-powered rice mill on the Carolina side of the Savannah River; Rowland, Moore, and Rogers, *History of Beaufort County,* 1:303, 322.

4. Rowland, Moore, and Rogers, *History of Beaufort County,* 1:308–9. Maner was also the long-serving state senator for St. Peter's Parish (Rowland, Moore, and Rogers 1:335).

5. George B. Davis et al., eds., *The Official Atlas of the Civil War* (Washington, D.C.: U.S. War Department, 1983), 76.2.

6. A map approximately identifying the locations of the major plantations of upper St Peter's in 1850 suggests that, of the names mentioned by Maria, the Taylors' nearest neighbors were the Martin, Bostick, Maner, and several Lawton families. See James Kilgo, *Pipe Creek to Matthew's Bluff: A Short History of Groton Plantation* (Privately printed for the Winthron Family, 1988), 63.

7. Rowland, Moore, and Rogers, *History of Beaufort County,* 1:308. Sweet potatoes and corn were provisioning crops for the large slave population of the coastal cotton and rice plantations.

8. Given the ages of the informants at the times they describe, their accounts must be based on childhood memories and the stories of older family members.

9. George P. Rawick, ed., *The American Slave: A Composite Autobiography* (Westport, Conn.: Greenwood, 1972), 3:153–54.

10. Benjamin Bostick, the Taylors' neighbor, was the third-largest slaveholder in the upper parish in 1840; Rowland, Moore, and Rogers, *History of Beaufort County,* 1:309. Bostick's wife, Jane, was a sister-in-law of John Taylor's aunt Catherine Maner (see Kilgo, *Short History of Groton Plantation,* 52).

11. Rawick, ed., *The American Slave,* 3:155–56.

12. Ibid., 3:266–69.

13. Ibid., 3:281–82.

14. Rowland, Moore, and Rogers, *History of Beaufort County,* 1:385–86.

Education of the Children

1. The Beaufort Female Seminary, which would have been much closer and which had several prominent Baptists as trustees, did not open until 1852; Rowland, Moore, and Rogers, *History of Beaufort County,* 1:382.

2. Walter Carroll Taylor, *History of Limestone College* (Gaffney, S.C.: Limestone College, 1937), 8.

3. Clyde N. Wilson, with Shirley Bright Cook and Alexander Moore, eds., *The Papers of John C. Calhoun* (Columbia: University of South Carolina Press, 1998), 24:329.

4. The passage is of course an extreme example of the periodic sentence, in which the main clause is delayed until the end, resolving a network of parallel phrases and subordinate clauses. In spite of the antiquated punctuation, the flawless complex structure comes through clearly.

5. The next two Taylor children, ages ten and seven.

6. That is, her twelfth birthday marks the completion of twelve years; hence Caroline has entered her thirteenth year, or first "teen" year.

7. Brackets indicate guesses at partially illegible words.

8. Caroline needed her "letter of dismission," a document indicating she was leaving in good standing, before she could be accepted by her church at home.

Church Life

1. Rowland, Moore, and Rogers, *History of Beaufort County,* 1:416.

2. Oak Grove, Maria's father's house.

3. That is, Josiah wants his sisters Maria and Ann Furman to write to Samuel, or perhaps to Mary, to add their disapproving voices. Samuel's brothers Josiah and James Clement felt so strongly about the situation that they conspired to see that Samuel was not reappointed to his position at the Furman Theological Institution.

4. Quoted in Klein, *Unification of a Slave State,* 280. The position was stated in reply to a query from the High Hills church, which Richard Furman had left for the Charleston Baptist church the previous year (1787); hence he may have had a hand in formulating it. The statement continues to the effect that age, circumstance, social position, means, and local customs should be considered in determining appropriate dress. Klein contends that the Baptist view of dress reveals "concern for the maintenance of social hierarchy" (280). While this statement may be true, Josiah's stated concerns are Mary's disordered mind, her family's purse, and the reputation of the church.

5. Klein, *Unification of a Slave State,* 43–44. The Furman sisters were evidently regarded by the whole family as repositories of "taste and judgment" (as Maria put it) in matters of dress.

6. Isaac Nicholes (1805–73) was pastor at the Lawtonville Pipe Creek Baptist Church, 1839–49; an obituary describes him as "unassuming, humble, conscientious, devout"; Coy K. Johnston, *Two Centuries of Lawtonville Baptists, 1775–1975* (Columbia, S.C.: State, 1974), 68–69. Nicholes was John Taylor's first cousin on the Morgandollar side.

7. Thomas Rambaut (1819–90) is discussed later in the text.

8. James Theophilus Sweat (1810–91) was pastor of the Lawtonville Pipe Creek Baptist Church, 1836–39, and served a number of other churches in the area; see Johnston, *Two Centuries of Lawtonville Baptists*, 66–67.

9. It may seem odd that children of the pastor needed to be converted; however, Baptists were admitted to the church as adults after a religious experience.

10. After presenting a similar (undated) account of a Methodist-sponsored revival in upper St. Peter's, James Kilgo comments that "some may find it surprising that planters of wealth and education would participate with such fervor in an event that sounds like backwoods revivalism . . . and here more clearly than anywhere else perhaps we see the difference between the planters of upper St. Peter's Parish and their more decorous Episcopalian counterparts along the coast" (see Kilgo, *Short History of Groton Plantation*, 56–57).

11. Maria's report designated $35 for foreign missions, $22.50 for missionaries to catechize colored people in St. Peter's Parish, and $35 to educate an Indian boy; Johnston, *Two Centuries of Lawtonville Baptists*, 146.

12. Rowland, Moore, and Rogers, *History of Beaufort County*, 1:408–13 passim.

13. Maria essentially accuses Fuller of perverting his calling, for he is destroying "faith" and taking the "[widow's] mite" away from the local church. His use of "flattery," one of Satan's well-known ploys, further allies him with evil forces.

14. The 1848 date of Maria's account of the question of building the new church in Lawtonville is at odds with the date of the new church given in Johnston, *Two Centuries of Lawtonville Baptists*, 54–56. According to Johnston, the new church was built in 1843 and survived the Civil War (photo Johnston 55). Maria refers again to the church in her letter of 4 September 1850 in terms that suggest it was built more recently than 1843. Also, it seems unlikely that a church built in 1843 would need to be replaced as soon as 1848.

15. Besides being a strong financial supporter, John was also an active church member; for example, in 1847 he served as the "messenger" from the Lawtonville church to the Baptist district meeting; see Johnston, *Two Centuries of Lawtonville Baptists*, 69. In Baptist parlance, the term "messenger" was preferred to "representative" or "delegate," because the messenger had no delegated authority to bind his church to anything and the local church could reject any action of the larger meeting; see Jack P. Dalton, "A History of Florida Baptists" (Ph.D. diss., University of Florida, 1952), 51–52.

16. Evidently Maria had her own money separate from John's, as apparently did other "sisters."

17. John obviously does not consider the in-laws Whitaker and Lawton to be "immediate family," and, because he too is an in-law, he enters the disclaimer that he is only "remotely" involved. The disclaimer is a rhetorical ploy, for John is obviously concerned about the situation; however, if he entered the fray on the basis of close family relationship, he would have to grant the same to Whitaker and Lawton, thus conceding them some right to produce their biography.

18. John never names the "friend" but "he" was probably Maria. If it had been anyone else, John would probably have identified him. James would no doubt recognize Maria's hand in the suggested solution and in the friend's attributes.

19. Probably Dr. Thomas Curtis of Limestone Springs Female High School. See pages 33–40.

20. Norman Fox, *Preacher and Teacher: A Sketch of the Life of Thomas Rambaut* (New York: Fords, 1892), 20–26.

21. Maria's diction suggests that the church was recently built (see note 14) and that her own fund-raising for it had been more successful than she expected it would in her letter of 29 September 1848.

22. The general dissatisfaction with Dr. Robert probably had at least in part to do with his abolitionist tendencies, discussed on pages 73–75.

23. John's aunt Catherine Morgandollar Maner, wife of Major John Seth Maner. The major was a Methodist.

24. Stephanie McCurry, *Masters of Small Worlds: Yeoman Households, Gender Relations, and the Political Culture of Antebellum South Carolina Low Country* (New York: Oxford University Press, 1995), 202.

25. Mrs. Bostick was a sister-in-law of John Taylor's aunt Catherine Maner. Such were the intricacies of relationship among the families of the area.

26. In a fragmentary newspaper obituary of Thomas Rambaut, source unidentified (Furman University).

27. This fact is not surprising given that, in Beaufort District as a whole, black people made up 85.5 percent of the population in 1850; see McCurry, *Masters of Small Worlds,* 306.

28. Richard Furman Whilden (no relation) to John S. Palmer, 10 August 1848, quoted in Louis P. Towles, ed., *A World Turned Upside Down: The Palmers of South Santee, 1818–1881* (Columbia: University of South Carolina Press, 1996), 139.

Family Deaths

1. Exact dates for the deaths of these children do not appear anywhere. However, a 20 April 1841 letter mentions them as living, and in "Home Memories" the stanza devoted to them immediately precedes a stanza about a death that occurred in December 1842.

2. The Euhaws Baptist Church, founded in 1737 or 1738, was in Coosawhatchie in neighboring St. Luke's Parish, the home of Mary's family of

origin. Euhaws was the mother church of the Baptist movement in Beaufort District; Rowland, Moore, and Rogers, *History of Beaufort County,* 1:121, 299.

3. Ann Eliza Furman, the addressee's sister.

4. See the Sumter County, S.C., Estate and Land Records for Rachel and Thomas Baker's wills.

Wife and Husband

1. Nell Irvin Painter, introduction to *The Secret Eye: The Journal of Ellen Gertrude Clanton Thomas, 1848–1889,* ed. Virginia Ingraham Burr (Chapel Hill: University of North Carolina Press, 1990), 60; Anne Firor Scott, *The Southern Lady: From Pedestal to Politics, 1830–1930* (Chicago: University of Chicago Press, 1970), 53.

2. The documents consist of forty-seven letters from a number of hands, twenty-two accountings of rice sales, and a lengthy legal opinion by W. F. Colcock.

3. Williamson was probably the J. P. Williamson who owned a rice plantation on the Savannah River, a few properties above Henry Taylor's Laurel Hill plantation; Rowland, Moore, and Rogers, *History of Beaufort County,* 1:309, 315. In his will Henry also named as executors two Englishmen in Liverpool who declined to serve.

4. Rowland, Moore, and Rogers, *History of Beaufort County,* 1:422–23.

5. A legal term meaning the waste of assets of the deceased by an executor, rendering him liable.

6. Colcock explains that the payment to the executor would be his 5 percent commission on estate transactions. John later claimed to have lost money in pursuing his duties.

7. The Taylor Estate was still operating the plantation in 1860; Rowland, Moore, and Rogers, *History of Beaufort County,* 1:327.

8. Rosengarten, *Tombee,* 170. Although Maria defers to John for the final decisions, she clearly has her own ideas on how things should be handled.

9. Probably the younger of the father-son educators encountered earlier.

10. Tom Wallace, John's brother-in-law.

11. The move took place in January 1853.

12. Phineas Behn of Savannah, the Taylors' cotton factor and general business agent in Savannah.

13. Perhaps David Levy Yulee, who earlier in his career did not use the last name he later adopted. Yulee is discussed in part 3.

14. W. F. Colcock served in the U.S. House of Representatives, 1848–52; hence he was being helpful to constituents and longtime acquaintances.

15. A neighbor, large landholder, and family connection of John's. He and John had earlier traveled to Florida together.

16. United States president, 1850–53.

Slavery and Plantation Affairs

1. "Upper St Peter's Parish was the only area in Beaufort District with a substantial number of free black farm families," the 1840 census revealing thirty free black farming families containing 147 people (see Rowland, Moore, and Rogers, *History of Beaufort County*, 1:305); Maria probably did not have the statistics, but she would have been aware that there was an unusual number of free blacks in her small area. See Rowland, Moore, and Rogers, 1:416, for the suggested interpretation of the size of this population.

2. Kilgo, *Short History of Groton Plantation*, 54.

3. William Sumner Jenkins, *Pro-Slavery Thought in the Old South* (Chapel Hill: University of North Carolina Press, 1935), 72; H. Shelton Smith, Robert T. Handy, and Lefferts A. Loetscher, *American Christianity: An Historical Interpretation with Representative Documents* (New York: Scribners, 1953), 2:183.

4. The quotations from Furman's letter are taken from James A. Rogers, *Richard Furman*, 277–79 and 283–84.

5. This is the same collection referred to in the conclusion to part 1. Maria's copy is inscribed "presented by her affectionate Sister Lydia Dick Baker" (her sister-in-law).

6. This euphemistic evasion was common southern usage; see Thomas Dyer, ed., *To Raise Myself a Little: The Diaries and Letters of Jennie, A Georgia Teacher, 1851–1886* (Athens: University of Georgia Press, 1982), 10. Perhaps evangelicals found it particularly congenial, for the scriptural passages on which they based their justification of slavery speak of "the servant," not "the slave."

7. Rosengarten, *Tombee*, 69.

8. Thomas Wallace, John's brother-in-law.

9. Glynn County, the second county north of Florida on the Georgia coast.

10. Summer resort villages had developed in several parts of Beaufort District but not in upper St. Peter's, where most of the planters could not afford a second residence; Rowland, Moore, and Rogers, *History of Beaufort County*, 1:386. Maria implies that this was the case with the Taylors at the time. In mentioning "the sickly season," Maria may have been thinking of the loss of two of her young children in 1842.

11. Johnston, *Two Centuries of Lawtonville Baptists*, 59–65; Stanley Harrold, *The Abolitionists and the South, 1831–1861* (Lexington: University Press of Kentucky, 1995), 144.

12. This may be Nathaniel Loughburrow, a correspondent of John Calhoun.

13. As slave driver, it would be Juss's job to see that those under him performed the work assigned.

14. Rachel, Sam, and Dublin are slaves.

15. It was common for slaves to own livestock over which they had complete control.

16. Rowland, Moore, and Rogers, *History of Beaufort County,* 1:376; Kilgo, *Short History of Groton Plantation,* 60.

17. Probably, "candling" means flaring up, and "a continual dropping" means nagging.

18. 1 Timothy 6:1–5 (KJV):

Let as many servants as are under the yoke count their own masters worthy of all honour, that the name of God and his doctrine be not blasphemed. And they that have believing masters, let them not despise them, because they are brethren; but rather do them service, because they are faithful and beloved, partakers of the benefit.

These things teach and exhort. If any man teach otherwise, and consent not to wholesome words, even the words of our Lord Jesus Christ, and to the doctrine which is according to godliness; he is proud, knowing nothing, but doting about questions and strifes of words, whereof cometh envy, strife, railings, evil surmisings, perverse disputings of men of corrupt minds, and destitute of the truth, supposing that gain is godliness; from such withdraw thyself.

19. The Reverend Joseph Thomas Robert, pastor of Maria's church. The attempts to get rid of him are presented on pages 48–51. The second mention of "Mrs R" seems to refer to the wife of "the Doctor" rather than to the wife of "Old Mr John Robert." James Kilgo refers to "the allegedly abolitionist views of the Rev. Joseph Thomas Robert and his wife, Adeline Lawton, who disposed of their slaves to members of their families and moved north"; see Kilgo, *Short History of Groton Plantation,* 54.

Conclusion

1. Wilson, ed., *Papers of John C. Calhoun,* 16:277, Dixon H. Lewis to Richard K. Crallé, 10 June 1842.

2. Wilson, ed., *Papers of John C. Calhoun,* 16:580, Dixon H. Lewis to Richard K. Crallé, 29 December 1842.

3. Wilson, ed., *Papers of John C. Calhoun,* 20:14, Thomas Wynns to John C. Calhoun, 1 October 1844.

4. Wilson, ed., *Papers of John C. Calhoun,* 20:639, Charles Augustus Davis to John C. Calhoun, 27 December 1844.

5. Wilson, ed., *Papers of John C. Calhoun,* 18:277, John C. Calhoun to Richard Pakenham, 18 April 1844.

6. Wilson, ed., *Papers of John C. Calhoun,* 22:127, James E. Broome to John C. Calhoun, 4 September 1845.

7. "Florida Crops of 1850," *Georgetown County (S.C.) Winyah Observer,* 8 January 1851, 2.

8. "Trade with Florida," *Georgetown County (S.C.) Winyah Observer,* 4 February 1852, 2. Reprinted from *Charleston Courier.*

9. "Florida," *Georgetown County (S.C.) Winyah Observer,* 28 July 1852, 2. Reprinted from *Columbia South Carolinian.*

10. This poetic conceit is based on the name of the river, after the New Testament evangelist.

Three

Introduction

1. Daniel L. Shafer, "U.S. Territory and State," in *The New History of Florida,* ed. Michael Gannon (Gainesville: University Press of Florida, 1996), 219; Julia Floyd Smith, *Slavery and Plantation Growth in Antebellum Florida: 1821–1860* (Gainesville: University of Florida Press, 1973), 11.

2. Larry E. Rivers, *Slavery in Florida: Territorial Days to Emancipation* (Gainesville: University Press of Florida, 2000), 66. The state as a whole increased in population by more than 60 percent between the 1850 and 1860 censuses.

3. Shafer, "U.S. Territory and State," 225; Canter Brown Jr., "The Civil War, 1861–1865," in *The New History of Florida,* ed. Michael Gannon (Gainesville: University Press of Florida, 1996), 232.

4. The choice of name suggests how remote the threat from the Seminole/escaped-slave coalition of the Second Seminole War, which had ended only fifteen years before, was now perceived to be.

5. Many antebellum southern families of Maria's class were very large, suggesting that birth control was unsuccessful if attempted at all; see Sally G. McMillen, *Motherhood in the Old South: Pregnancy, Childbirth, and Infant Rearing* (Baton Rouge: Louisiana State University Press, 1990), 107. It is unlikely that during this hiatus Maria had an unrecorded stillbirth or suddenly began having miscarriages.

6. McMillen, *Motherhood in the Old South,* 33n.

7. Exactly what words the letters stand for can only be guessed. Perhaps "on time on menstruation"? In any case, the regularly recurring notation and the often accompanying remark of not feeling well leave little doubt as to the subject.

8. McMillen, *Motherhood in the Old South,* 122. However, if Maria had nursed earlier children for this long, doing so had not delayed some of her pregnancies.

9. Carroll Smith-Rosenberg, "Hearing Women's Words: A Feminist Reconstruction of History," in *Disorderly Conduct: Visions of Gender in Victorian America* (New York: Knopf, 1985), 33–34.

10. Marion County Deed Books C, D.

11. For example, the Kanapaha plantation house of the Haile family near Gainesville, Fla., (the house still stands) is almost identical to the Osceola house. The Hailes, who became Taylor family in-laws, were also from South Carolina, so it was probably a transplanted style. Elizabeth Fox-Genovese speaks of "the modest nature of even a prosperous household's big house"; see Fox-Genovese, *Within the Plantation Household,* 105.

12. 1853 Marion County Tax Rolls; 1860 U.S. Census.

13. John E. Johns, *Florida during the Civil War* (Gainesville: University of Florida Press, 1963), 140.

14. Smith, *Slavery and Plantation Growth,* 27.

15. Rivers, *Slavery in Florida,* 34.

16. The value of slaves in Florida at the time can be estimated from the average price in sales of groups of slaves. Figures for three such sales in 1856 and 1857 yield an average price per slave of $677, $714, and $800 (see Smith, *Slavery and Plantation Growth,* 108–9). Valuation for county taxes was much lower; in 1856 John's sixty-two slaves were valued at $16,750, an average of only $280. Some of the difference may be accounted for by the age of the slaves, if those in the sales were only adult workers; plantation slave populations typically contained a large percentage of children.

17. Caroline was now eighteen years old.

18. Rivers, *Slavery in Florida,* 73.

19. Friedman, *The Enclosed Garden,* 21.

20. Dalton, "A History of Florida Baptists," 161.

21. Ibid., 160–61.

22. S. B. Rogers, *A Brief History of Florida Baptists, 1825–1925* (N.p.: Florida State Library, n.d.), 10.

23. Dalton, "A History of Florida Baptists," 39–41, 44–47.

Maria and Slavery

1. Shafer, "U.S. Territory and State," 224–25. For example, during the Spanish period slaves could own property, sue their owners, and gain their freedom fairly easily; see Rivers, *Slavery in Florida,* 66–67.

2. Discussed in "Slavery and Plantation Affairs" (pp. 66–75).

3. Maria's indignation here suggests that she was unfamiliar with "apology" in the sense of "defense."

4. See headnote to letter dated 29 September 1848 for identification of Richard Fuller. As a solution to slavery, Fuller advocated manumission with payment to the slaveholders and colonization back to Africa for the freed slaves, thus addressing the two deepest fears of the planter class: economic loss and social upheaval; Rowland, Moore, and Rogers, *History of Beaufort County,* 1:413–15.

5. An example is Maria's concern about Juss's hogs in her 26 February 1850 letter. The general practice is mentioned in Fox-Genovese, *Within the Plantation Household,* 95–96, and Rosengarten, *Tombee,* 80.

6. In testimony from slaves, a large percentage of those mentioning illness remembered being nursed by the mistress; see Catherine Clinton, *The Plantation Mistress: Woman's World in the Old South* (New York: Pantheon Books, 1982), 187.

7. Richard Furman, Maria's grandfather, was a leading Baptist exponent of this view. In Florida Baptist churches of Maria's time, black members were received into the regular fellowship and often were the majority of the members, as was the case in Ocala; see Dalton, "A History of Florida Baptists," 48.

8. There is no overlap in names between these two groups. The children's names, in the order of first mention, are Lydia, Richard, William, Susan, Caroline, Jane, Anne, and Mary.

9. Charles Haddon Spurgeon (1834–92) was the most acclaimed English Baptist divine of the century. Maria mentions him a number of times in her diaries.

10. Maria had paid him $2.50 for January preaching.

11. The moss was for making mattresses. In her memoir of antebellum times in Florida, Sarah Pamela Williams describes the process. The long, loose moss was pulled off trees with poles, gathered in piles, and hauled to scaffolds in the yard. There it was beaten, picked apart, and cleaned, then stuffed into ticks and sewed. The best moss had the consistency of horsehair (James M. Denham and Canter Brown Jr., eds., *Cracker Times and Pioneer Lives: The Florida Reminiscences of George Gillett Keen and Sarah Pamela Williams* [Columbia: University of South Carolina Press, 2000], 104–5). Maria bought her moss for 2.5 cents per pound.

12. This seems to mean that Maria handed Old John a document and hence that he could read. But "gave" may mean that she administered the catechism to him orally on the spot.

13. When Maria "makes" a servant do something, no resistance seems to be implied.

14. Daughter Mary's wedding cake. Other activities here are also in preparation for the wedding.

15. The term "complaining" is not a pejorative; Maria uses it for blacks and whites alike in the sense of a person announcing an illness.

16. "Mr B" is Maria's new son-in-law, Thomas Bauskett; Colonel Bauskett and John are his father and brother, visiting from South Carolina. The family was originally from Edgefield County, S.C., (known as "bloody Edgefield") and now lived in Columbia.

17. A pain killer containing opium.

18. For relatives in South Carolina. Tobacco was grown in Marion County at this time, but Maria never mentions her source.

19. An all-purpose remedy of indeterminate ingredients.

20. Abram is not mentioned again, so presumably he came in on his own. Because Maria expresses no indignation over the affair and because other slaves were left to bring in Sam, the absence was apparently not regarded as a serious escape attempt.

21. Daniel A. Vogt (1823–83), native of Orangeburg District, S.C., and graduate of the Medical College of the State of South Carolina, was a neighbor of the Taylors. He was also a small planter and politician, serving in the Florida House of Representatives, 1856–61, as a strong secessionist; see E. Ashby Hammond, *The Medical Profession in 19th Century Florida: A Biographical Register* (Gainesville: George A. Smathers Libraries of the University of Florida, 1996), 643–44. Vogt's nephew and foster son, Albertus, was a good friend of Richie Taylor. Vogt is mentioned many times in Maria's diaries.

22. Phillis was thus seriously ill. The 13 July entry explains Maria's accusation of deceit.

23. That is, her home-teaching of her own children.

24. Did arithmetic.

25. Probably A. C. Brown, a native of Georgia who practiced in Ocala in the1850s (Hammond, *Medical Profession in 19th Century Florida,* 89).

26. In Baptist organization, the association was the first level above the individual churches, the convention being statewide. Among the purposes of the association were to promote fellowship among neighboring churches, to advise on doctrine and discipline, and to aid in building new churches; see Dalton, "A History of Florida Baptists," 50–51.

27. Robin, already mentioned a number of times and obviously a highly versatile servant, was Maria's mainstay for many years.

28. Maria means the field hands, whose work was ordinarily not under her supervision.

29. Scott, *Southern Lady,* 46–47.

30. See note 4 of this chapter.

31. Loveland, *Southern Evangelicals,* 258–65.

32. Cook, *Life Work of James Clement Furman,* 194–202.

33. James M. Denham, *"A Rogue's Paradise": Crime and Punishment in Antebellum Florida, 1821–1861* (Tuscaloosa: University of Alabama Press, 1997), 199–200; Rowland, Moore, and Rogers, *History of Beaufort County,* 1:434–35.

Education of the Children, 1853–63

1. Dyer, *To Raise Myself a Little,* ix.

2. J. C. Furman was now chairman of the faculty at Furman Theological Institution, which had moved to Greenville, S.C.

3. Maria's use of "I" and "we" in the letter suggests that she had an equal voice in educational matters, a situation at variance with the finding that, in the southern evangelical community, "fathers made the ultimate decision concerning the children's education"; Friedman, *The Enclosed Garden,* 36.

4. Maria Baker, a cousin visiting from Beaufort, S.C., about the age of Maria's older daughters. Her father, John M. Baker, Maria's first cousin, was a banker and the tax collector in Beaufort.

5. By Mary Brien, resident Irish seamstress.

6. King's Mountain Military School in Yorkville, S.C.

7. John K. Mahon and Brent R. Weisman, "Florida's Seminole and Miccosukee Peoples," in *The New History of Florida,* ed. Michael Gannon (Gainesville: University Press of Florida, 1996), 200.

8. James W. Covington, *The Billy Bowlegs War, 1855–1858: The Final Stand of the Seminoles against the Whites* (Chuluota, Fla.: Mickler House, 1982), 71–80.

9. Maria's remarks, sympathetic to the Indians and mildly annoyed with the troops, indicate no alarm about the conflict. Although there had been a few Indian raids with white casualties, the closest the war had come to Osceola was Alachua County, which happened a year earlier (April–September 1846). Signs of Indians discovered by the infantry during that time showed that the Indians had already moved south, and some of the signs turned out to have been planted by whites (Covington, *Final Stand of the Seminoles,* 52–53). Maria's sympathy for the Indians seems to be unaffected by the well-known fact that runaway slaves had for decades joined the Seminoles.

10. A. C. Brown of Ocala. He was perhaps serving as physician to the regiment.

11. *Godey's Lady's Book,* a popular magazine.

12. This is the same Bauskett family discussed in Fox Butterfield, *All God's Children* (New York: Knopf, 1995), 19–21, 23–24, 26–32, 33.

13. That is, the Roman ecclesiastical tradition as opposed to scripture.

14. Carrie married James Baird Dawkins, discussed later in this chapter.

15. She is concerned about Caroline's impending marriage and Mary's sojourn among the Catholics.

16. The three-year-old had a toothache for the second day.

17. Probably the Arsenal; see pages 126–27.

18. Fox, *Preacher and Teacher,* 34.

19. It was Maria's lifelong habit to keep household accounts down to the half-penny.

20. Perhaps he also had to pay his school fees from the checks, although he does not record such transactions.

21. Willie's death is treated on pages 155–65.

22. Biographical data taken from James B. Dawkins's obituary in the *Gainesville Weekly Bee,* 16 February 1883.

23. The 1860 census recorded 223 whites and 86 blacks; the 1870 census recorded 679 whites and 765 blacks.

24. Charles H. Hildreth and Merlin G. Cox, *History of Gainesville, Florida: 1854–1979* (Gainesville: Alachua County Historical Society, 1981), 16.

Osceola and the Civil War, 1861–63

1. The 1860 U.S. Census puts the population of Florida (white and black) at about 140,500. Arkansas, the second least-populous southern state, had three times as many people.

2. David W. Hartman and David Coles, *Biographical Rosters of Florida's Confederate and Union Soldiers, 1861–1865* (Wilmington, N.C.: Broadfoot, 1995), 3:986, 1040. Johnny was described as "5'8", fair skin, grey eyes, dark hair."

3. Thomas does not appear on any army rolls, only on a ration list dated October 1862 (Hartman and Coles, *Biographical Rosters,* 5:2071). He is listed in Hartman and Coles under "Conscripts: Privates."

4. Johns, *Florida during the Civil War,* 40, 171.

5. Robert A. Taylor, *Rebel Storehouse: Florida in the Confederate Economy* (Tuscaloosa: University of Alabama Press, 1995), 78–79.

6. Rivers, *Slavery in Florida,* 246–47. For a nearby exception to this generalization, see Maria's diary entry of 10 April 1862.

7. Lydia, 20; Johnny, 19; Susan, 17; Willie, 15; Richie, 13; Fen, 12; Dore, 11; Janie, 7; and Anne, 5. Johnny, Susan, Willie, Richie, and Fen were away at school at various times during 1861–63 (pp. 109–25).

8. Mary had just had a baby.

9. Sister Lydia is Lydia Dick Baker, Maria's sister-in-law. Fanny is John Taylor's sister; Mr. Wallace is Fanny's husband, Tom; and Louise is their daughter. All were visiting from South Carolina.

10. A major Florida river, emptying into the Atlantic at Jacksonville.

11. Johns, *Florida during the Civil War,* 23–24, 42–55.

12. Maria's Bauskett granddaughter, age three.

13. That is, Maryland remained with the Union. The northwest counties of Virginia were overwhelmingly opposed to secession and broke away to form a new state, formally admitted as West Virginia in 1863.

14. Key West had been reinforced and firmly controlled by Union forces since 6 February (Johns, *Florida during the Civil War,* 26). Maria is referring to President Lincoln's 10 May suspension of habeas corpus at Key West; the president also authorized the removal of all suspicious persons from the area; see Frank Moore, ed., *The Rebellion Record: A Diary of American Events* (New York: Putnam, 1861–65; van Nostrand, 1866–67), 1:65–66.

15. Queen Victoria's proclamation was published on 14 May. Among many other provisions, it forbade privateering in contraband of war in support of either contending party (Moore, ed., *Rebellion Record,* 1:245–47, doc. 168).

16. The first battle of Bull Run, fought near Manassas, Va., on 21 July 1861, was a significant Confederate victory; see E. B. Long, with Barbara Long, *The Civil War Day by Day: An Almanac, 1861–1865* (New York: Da Capo, 1971), 99.

17. Fernandina, just south of the Georgia border, was the most important port on the Florida east coast.

18. The Taylors kept sheep on the Withlacoochee River and had their own wool.

19. James E. Broome, governor of Florida, 1852–56, lived nearby with his family, which included his niece Curran Broome, Johnny Taylor's fiancée and later wife.

20. That is, the letter she wrote on 10 September had been published and now brought results.

21. The mill was set up two miles from the house. John had been gathering machine parts for several weeks.

22. The principal town in the Taylors' former home district, situated on Port Royal Island in southeast South Carolina. Maria's first cousin John Baker and his numerous family still lived in the town, hence the emotive adjective "dreadful." On 9 November, Federal troops from their base at Port Royal a few miles away captured Beaufort without a fight (Long, *Civil War Day by Day,* 138) and without seeing anything to substantiate the report that Confederate batteries were concealed there (Moore, ed., *Rebellion Record,* 3:71–72). A little later, on 6–8 December, there was brief gunfire as Union forces took over all of Port Royal Island (Moore, ed., *Rebellion Record,* 3:107).

23. The first mention of Johnny's military service. He was still in the South Carolina home guard, not joining the Florida regular troops until February 1862.

24. Susan was attending Limestone Female High School in Gaffney, S.C.

25. That is, Johnny's being in the army.

26. In terms of volume, a barrel was usually about 32 gallons; a hogshead could be anywhere between 63 and 140 gallons. As for weight, in one specific case, 50,000 pounds was given as the weight of 64 hogsheads, about 780 pounds per hogshead (Taylor, *Florida in the Confederate Economy,* 78).

27. Benjamin Waldo (1816–71), a native of Edgefield District, S.C., and graduate of the South Carolina Medical College, moved to Marion County in the 1850s after having abandoned his medical practice in Madison County, Fla., because of ill health. He was now primarily a farmer and Osceola neighbor as well as a close friend and business associate of David Yulee (Hammond, *Medical Profession in 19th Century Florida,* 649–50). His wife appears earlier in this chapter, and his daughter Sally, apparently in her late teens, makes frequent appearances. Dr. Waldo, Sally, and Waldo's son Joseph, who volunteered for the Confederate Army in 1863 at age sixteen, are mentioned in chapter 5 of this section.

28. Johnny had been attending The Arsenal in Columbia, which, along with the Citadel in Charleston, formed the South Carolina Military Academy.

Administrative affairs for the Academy were handled at the Citadel, the senior branch. Like most cadets, Johnny served in the home guard before enlisting in a regular army unit.

29. The great Baptist allegorical poem (1678, 1684) by John Bunyan (1628–88). The work was a staple of the Taylors' religious life.

30. On 16 January Union forces attacked Cedar Key, a small town on the Cedar Keys off the northwest Florida coast that was the western terminus of the Florida Railroad and a center for blockade running. The Federals withdrew after destroying eight vessels, the wharf, the railroad depot, seven freight cars, and the Confederate defenses (Johns, *Florida during the Civil War,* 71–72).

31. The Dawkinses were going to Richmond, Va., where the Confederate Congress was convened.

32. A false rumor. Grant had prevented the Confederates from reinforcing Bowling Green, which they had occupied since September 1861. The Confederates began evacuating the town on 11 February, and on 14 February the Union forces occupied it (Long, *Civil War Day by Day,* 169–71).

33. These Confederate setbacks in the order Maria mentions them: Roanoke Island, off the North Carolina coast, was taken on 8 February (Moore, ed., *Rebellion Record,* 4:26); Fort Henry in Tennessee fell on 6 February (Moore, ed., *Rebellion Record,* 4:26); and Fort Donnelson, also in Tennessee, on 16 February, the latter being the first important Union victory of the war (Moore, ed., *Rebellion Record,* 4:43). At Florence, Ala., (not a fort) Union forces burned three steamboats and destroyed Confederate supplies (Moore, ed., *Rebellion Record,* 4:28).

34. This was Moses E. Levy, for whom Levy County, Fla., is named. The son resumed the name Yulee after his father had dropped it to assume his wife's family name, Levy.

35. Yulee had had legal dealings with Carrie's husband, James Dawkins, for a long time. In 1864, Yulee and Dawkins would be involved in a case that became quite a cause célèbre. As presiding judge in Alachua County, Dawkins granted Yulee an injunction against the Confederate Army when it confiscated twenty-four miles of tracks of Yulee's Florida Railroad for use elsewhere. Dawkins approved the military's purpose but opposed its failure to observe due process. In the end he was unable to enforce the injunction. The case is mentioned in William Watson Davis, *The Civil War and Reconstruction in Florida* (1913; reprint, Gainesville: University of Florida Press, 1964), 196, and Johns, *Florida during the Civil War,* 139. Johns misnames James Dawkins as "John Hawkins."

36. Fernandina was the eastern terminus of Yulee's Florida Railroad. Yulee was anticipating the Federal naval expedition that sailed from South Carolina that day to take this important port. Fernandina was taken on 2 March and evacuated 2–3 March (Johns, *Florida during the Civil War,* 62–63).

37. Apparently John had gone to see Johnny and to trade goods for syrup. Jacksonville, just a few miles south of Fernandina, was already in a panic.

38. Abandonment was a widespread fear after the taking of Fernandina by Union naval forces on 2 March and the anticipated taking of Jacksonville (which occurred that very day). The fear had some credibility inasmuch as on 24 February General Robert E. Lee had informed Florida Governor John Milton that Florida, even though its troops were insufficient, must defend itself, whereupon the coastal defenses withdrew to the interior (Taylor, *Florida in the Confederate Economy*, 30). On 19 April General Joseph Finegan, commander of the middle and east Florida Confederate forces, was officially notified not to defend the coasts because the Federals were not expected to attempt to move inland (Johns, *Florida during the Civil War*, 71).

39. New Smyrna Beach, just south of Daytona Beach and about seventy miles from Osceola, became prominent for blockade running, especially for arms. The shallow depth of the Mosquito Inlet harbor allowed small smuggling vessels to evade the large Federal warships fairly easily (Taylor, *Florida in the Confederate Economy*, 32).

40. On 11 March Confederate troops burned strategic sites in Jacksonville to render them useless to the Federals; these included sawmills, stored lumber, an iron foundry, and a Confederate gunboat under construction. Irregulars soon arrived and began burning buildings indiscriminately, including the Judson House, the city's largest hotel (Johns, *Florida during the Civil War*, 65).

41. The Florida east coast county in which New Smyrna is located.

42. On 22 March, forty-two Federals were killed in a skirmish with Confederate smugglers at New Smyrna (Johns, *Florida during the Civil War*, 73).

43. The Chattahoochee River forms part of the Florida-Georgia border and the Georgia-Alabama border. The Chattahoochee-Apalachicola River system, emptying into the Gulf of Mexico at the port city of Apalachicola, was an important outlet for cotton shipments for the three states (Taylor, *Florida in the Confederate Economy*, 29).

44. By Sir Walter Scott (1771–1832). *The Heart of Midlothian* (1818) is one of his Waverly novels.

45. Probably Hawkinsville in south-central Georgia.

46. Apparently the same prisoners referred to on 3 April. The gestures toward the enemy would be in the spirit of Maria's opening prayer for 1861.

47. The Federal forces retained control at the mouth of the river. General Joseph Finegan was holding the inland reaches to protect supplies received by blockade running (Johns, *Florida during the Civil War*, 71).

48. This may be Major Antonio Canova, Confederate supply officer with whom David Yulee tangled in 1863 over the impressment price for his sugar. The case made its way to the Florida Supreme Court, and Yulee won (Taylor, *Florida in the Confederate Economy*, 78).

49. The first mention of army service for Thomas Bauskett. He was conscripted as a private.

50. Caroline had had both scarlet fever and roseola in Richmond. She carried a serious spinal infection from the former for the rest of her life.

51. These and other medicines mentioned in this chapter will be identified in the next chapter, which focuses on illness.

52. The battle of Fair Oaks or Seven Pines occurred 31 May–1 June near Richmond. The Union forces hurled the Confederates back on the defenses of Richmond. Dawkins had just arrived at Osceola from Richmond.

53. Apparently, placed in chains. Maria gives little information about specific punishments for servants or children. Perhaps this one is specified because it is especially severe.

54. A hamlet on the Florida west coast a few miles south of Homosassa, and an important blockade runners' haven; for example, on 2 April seven blockade runners had managed to slip into port past Federal gunships; see George E. Buker, *Blockaders, Refugees, and Contrabands: Civil War on Florida's Gulf Coast, 1861–1865* (Tuscaloosa: University of Alabama Press, 1993), 64.

55. Nathaniel A. Pratt and Charles H. LaTrobe were in charge of locating nitre (saltpeter) caverns in the lower South, a search that included the many limestone caves in upper Florida. The mineral was crucial in the manufacture of ammunition and was scarce after the loss of nitre-producing caves in Kentucky, Tennessee, and Alabama earlier in 1862. The two agents had little success in Florida (Taylor, *Florida in the Confederate Economy,* 42). Maria does not mention the subject again.

56. Near Homosassa.

57. On 30 June 1862 a Union gunboat had lobbed between sixty and seventy shells into Tampa, Fla., but could not effect a landing (Moore, ed., *Rebellion Record,* 5:34).

58. Maria was caring for them during Mary's confinement.

59. In spite of the reflexive pronoun, Maria does not mean that Johnny brought the trouble on himself.

60. On 11 July a Union attack on Fort Wagner in Charleston harbor had been launched and repulsed.

61. Mary was going to Columbia, S.C., where her in-laws lived. Her husband remained at home.

62. Willie was attending the Georgia State Military Institute in Marietta.

63. The bombardment had reduced Fort Sumter to ruins by 22 August. When the Confederates refused the Union demand for surrender, Charleston itself was shelled on 23 August, an action Confederate General Beauregard termed "inhuman and unheard of" (Moore, ed., *Rebellion Record,* 7:43–44).

64. Probably Charles B. Jones, later appointed as home missionary by the Florida Baptist Convention (see Dalton, "A History of Florida Baptists," 308). His views on the black churches are unknown. Inasmuch as the Taylors had always attended churches with black members, they may have been opposed to the separate churches for black and white implied here.

65. A river a little southwest of Osceola.

66. Lieutenant Broome was Curran's brother; John Anderson was the son of an old Savannah friend of the Taylors.

67. Probably in payment for the spinning.

68. The subject of "determined" is unclear. Resistance to the low impressment prices was widespread (Taylor, *Florida in the Confederate Economy,* 79).

69. Confederate General Pierre G. T. Beauregard, now in charge of defending the Georgia–South Carolina coast.

70. By this time, Confederate General Braxton Bragg had been defeated by Grant at Chattanooga, was forced back into Georgia, and resigned command of the Army of Tennessee on 2 December. Perhaps Willie wrote before this last development or had not yet learned of it.

71. Daughters of Maria's sister in Sumter District, S.C., ages eighteen and twenty-two respectively. Willie was now on vacation from military school.

72. See note 6 on page 364.

73. These two teenagers were soon privates in the army, Dancy serving in the quartermaster department and Forward in the Second Florida Cavalry (Hartman and Coles, *Biographical Rosters,* 4:1517, 1533).

Sickness and Death, 1864

1. For example, the 1850 census reveals that in 1850 children under the age of five accounted for 29 percent of all deaths in South Carolina and 37 percent in Florida; statistics for 1860 were even worse (McMillen, *Motherhood in the Old South,* 195–96).

2. For reference, the servants' names in alphabetical order are Abram, Birch, Chloe, Cudjoe, Dinah, Eli, Eliza, Georgy, Isaac, Jack, Jim, Judy, Jupiter, Milton, Minty, Morgan, Peter, Phillis, Prince, Rachel, Robin, Sam, Sary, Scipio, Sukey, Tamar, Walter, and "the two little children." After Lincoln's Emancipation Proclamation of January 1863, they were no longer slaves from the Union point of view. However, black-white relations at Osceola seem unchanged.

3. Hammond, *Medical Profession in 19th Century Florida,* 92–93. Dr. Butt has already appeared several times in the previous chapter.

4. James E. Broome, governor of Florida, 1852–56, and Osceola neighbor.

5. Per pound. This was considerably more than the one dollar per pound David Yulee had sued the Confederate government to obtain for his sugar in July 1863 (Taylor, *Florida in the Confederate Economy,* 79).

6. In addition to Richie and Fen Taylor, these were their friends Wickliffe Yulee, Yulee Dancy, and Willie Forward. They were headed for the Yulees' plantation at Homosassa, on the Florida west coast.

7. The standard and effective remedy for malaria, which Willie no doubt had as a chronic condition. Most of the Taylors seem to have contracted malaria in Beaufort District; the mosquito-borne disease was prevalent in the South Carolina coastal regions.

8. The treatments for Georgy: Cupping was the practice of pressing a cup to the skin to form a vacuum that would bring blood to that spot. In "wet cupping" the skin was scratched, or scarified, so that the vacuum drew blood. This practice was, of course, harmful, as were most of the violently assaultive, even poisonous, medicines the Taylors used. For a full account of the "heroic medicine" common at the time (and practiced by the Taylors), see Rosengarten, *Tombee*, 185–88. Castor oil and turpentine were used internally as purgatives and externally as skin lubricants. A blister was a poultice spread with a heat-producing agent, such as mustard paste.

9. This effort at maintaining a cultivated home is noteworthy in the midst of the dire events.

10. Just six months earlier, the government impressment price for syrup had been six dollars per gallon (Taylor, *Florida in the Confederate Economy,* 77). Evidently John Taylor had to deliver the syrup to the railroad, which may account for part of the higher price he was being paid.

11. Stramonium, made from dried leaves of jimson weed, was used as a painkiller and narcotic, especially in cases of breathing difficulties.

12. "Spirits" probably means hard liquor. Wine was also frequently given medicinally.

13. Calomel was a corrosive mercury compound used as a harsh purgative; John is wet-cupping Willie.

14. The quantities of wine and beer Willie was allowed indicate their extensive medicinal use.

15. C. W. Lesesne (1810–80), native of South Carolina and graduate of the Medical College of South Carolina, Charleston, probably arrived in Marion County in the mid-1850s; "there appears to be no evidence that Dr. Lesesne ever practiced medicine beyond the bounds of his own estate" (Hammond, *Medical Profession in 19th Century Florida,* 360). John's sending for Lesesne thus seems to be a desperation move. He is not mentioned again.

16. George Baxter Hunter (1830–65), a native of Virginia and graduate of Jefferson Medical College in Philadelphia, settled in northwest Marion County in 1853, having coming south because of his tuberculosis (Hammond, *Medical Profession in 19th Century Florida,* 397).

17. One of the many children of Maria's first cousin John M. Baker in Beaufort, S.C. John was a banker and the Beaufort tax collector. Other of his daughters mentioned in the diaries include Maria, Eliza, and Julia.

18. A total of twenty people were gathered at this "last supper": John and Maria Taylor; their children Carrie, Mary, Lydia, Johnny, Susan, Willie, Richie, Fen, Dore, Jane, and Anne; their son-in-law Thomas Bauskett; Johnny's fiancée Curran Broome; nieces Mary and Nellie Jackson, and cousin Anne Baker Maxcy with her two children. (Anne and her children stayed with the Bausketts for some months while her husband was away in the army.)

19. This is the last mention of Jane's state of health. She remained sickly and died at the end of the year, at age ten.

20. A calmative made from the herb valeriana.

21. The situation with the quinine seems confused. That is, on the 29th Maria has no more quinine, but now on the 31st John gives Willie some—but then it might not have been quinine after all.

22. Hard liquor. He drank a good deal of beer and wine.

Confusions of War, 1864

1. The Union forces landed on 7 February and on 8 February began the march into the interior. On 9 February they took over Baldwin, about twenty miles west of Jacksonville (11 February entry). The Union line of march was roughly along the railroad from Jacksonville toward Lake City, about sixty-five miles west of Jacksonville.

2. Instead, Johnny's battalion, the First Florida, remained in Florida and fought in the Battle of Olustee on 20 February (Johns, *Florida during the Civil War,* 196).

3. John Taylor was now almost fifty-five, and the terrible illnesses at Osceola were continuing.

4. The Union forces were making diversionary raids south of the main line of march, the largest being at Gainesville on 14 February (Johns, *Florida during the Civil War,* 196).

5. Probably to protest or to negotiate a better price.

6. Dr. Patrick H. Todd (1810–80), a native of South Carolina who settled in Marion County in 1858, was listed as a "planter-doctor" in the 1860 U.S. Census.

7. This was the Battle of Olustee, fought on 20 February. General Joseph Finegan, the Confederate commander, made a stand a few miles east of Lake City. Fought by about 5,500 troops on each side, the battle was a Confederate victory and the most important Civil War battle in Florida. The victory occasioned great celebration throughout the Confederacy (Johns, *Florida during the Civil War,* 197–99). Given Maria's loss of Willie shortly before, some expression of thankfulness over Johnny's deliverance might be expected. However, she may have felt that such expressions would be unseemly in light of the casualties and Johnny's continued endangerment. Or perhaps she had exhausted that vein in the letters she had just written.

8. Names in this entry include Nellie, visiting South Carolina niece; Anne Baker Maxcy, the cousin from Savannah who with her children was staying out the war with the Bausketts; and Tommy, a Bauskett baby. Lyd, "the boys" Richie and Fen, and Mary are of course Taylor children.

9. Actually, to be tutored at the Yulees' house.

10. On the St. John's River, about forty-five miles northeast of Osceola. Skirmishes occurred at Palatka on 16 and 31 March.

11. John too was suffering, as David Yulee wrote to his wife on 19 March upon seeing Carrie in Gainesville: "Her mother will not visit you at present. I presume they do not like to leave Mr Taylor in his desolate spirit."

12. The governor of Florida had the authority to impress slaves for war-related construction work, and an order for 700 slaves from east of the Suwannee River was issued in the spring of 1864. This is probably the order relayed to the Taylors by Edward Haile, a plantation owner from near Gainesville whom the Taylors had known for some time. Of course, the Emancipation Proclamation of 1 January 1863, freeing all the slaves in the Confederate states, was not recognized in Florida.

13. This figure helps to put in perspective the $77,000+ that the Taylors were paid for the sugar.

14. Dora was now almost fourteen. Sending her to Gainesville to be educated by her sister was apparently the wartime equivalent of sending the older girls to school in South Carolina.

15. Johnny was now encamped near Baldwin, Fla., about twenty miles east of the Olustee Battle site.

16. Dr. Todd's son Patrick P. L. Todd, an 1858 graduate of the Georgia Medical College, enlisted in the Confederate Army and was killed at Mine Run, Va., in November 1863 (Hammond, *Medical Profession in 19th Century Florida,* 622).

17. That is, sent on from Gainesville.

18. Cudjoe's escaping back to Osceola rather than on to freedom illustrates Rivers' finding that "Middle Florida's slaveholders should have been pleased with the overall behavior of their bond servants" (*Slavery in Florida,* 246). Also, the Union lines were too far north to reach easily, and, after the Third Seminole War, the southern part of the state was no longer the refuge for runaways (in the eyes of Florida, which did not accept the Emancipation Proclamation) that it had been.

19. Emanuel Swedenborg (1688–1772), Swedish scientist and mystic.

20. An alkaloid mixture usually given for neuralgia and arthritis. It is an intense local irritant and a powerful muscle and nerve poison.

21. Probably Colonel Edward Hopkins. Governor Milton had questioned his military ability shortly before war broke out, relieving him of command of the Apalachicola River area. Hopkins was then transferred to the coast (Johns, *Florida during the Civil War,* 84).

22. General Patton Anderson was the Confederate commander for all of Florida (Johns, *Florida during the Civil War,* 109), and General Finegan was the commander of Middle and Eastern Florida, under whom Johnny served in the First Florida battalion. No doubt some advantage was being sought for Johnny.

23. An example of the kind of religious debate Maria enjoyed.

24. Apparently John Taylor sent Cudjoe back to work on the fortifications.

25. "Crane, Edward Payson," Index of Presbyterian Biography, Presbyterian Department of History. Philadelphia, Pa.

26. Johnny was on his way to Petersburg, Va., where the war's longest engagement would be fought. Petersburg guarded the southern approaches to Richmond, the Confederate capital, and was under siege by Union forces from 15 June 1864 to 3 April 1865, when it fell to Grant (Long, *Civil War Day by Day,* 522, 665). Johnny had arrived at Petersburg by 19 June.

27. Minty, Rachel, Phillis, Sara, Silvia, and Dinah. Mary Bauskett was also sick.

28. Entries for the next two weeks mention many comings and goings of Yulee between Homosassa, Osceola, and Gainesville, while he assessed his situation and decided where to move his family.

29. Mary Bauskett and Anne Maxcy (the Baker cousin staying out the war with the Bausketts) had a least five children between them. Counting these children, the young Yulees and Taylors, and the younger South Carolina niece, there were fourteen children and teenagers about the place at this time.

30. The tutor must have left Osceola temporarily.

31. The Yulee family had been at Osceola for a month. They would now take up residence in Gainesville.

32. Dr. Sloman William Moody (1834–98), a native of Sumter District, S.C., (Maria's family home) and 1857 honors graduate of the Medical College of South Carolina, moved to Ocala in 1857; although a popular and successful practitioner, he apparently never treated the Taylors or their servants (Hammond, *Medical Profession in 19th Century Florida,* 532). Maria's nieces Nellie and Mary Jackson had been at Osceola for six months, and their father was now sending for them. The crowd at Osceola was rapidly thinning out.

33. Maria's younger brother Thomas McD. Baker, who died about the same time as Willie. Apparently Tom had seen Willie when Willie went to Sumter District in December 1863 to pick up the Jackson girls.

34. The letters and goods mentioned in this entry are being prepared to go with the Jackson girls to relatives in South Carolina.

35. Sue fell in age between Johnny and Willie. Hence the endangered and deceased brothers had been her closest companions in the family.

36. The Weldon railroad near Petersburg. Grant's drive against this important target had been halted on 22 June (Long, *Civil War Day by Day,* 527).

37. That is, Johnny at age twenty-two has not yet made his confession of faith and been baptized.

38. The first of these reports was an exaggeration; on 9 July Union General George G. Mead had ordered increased pressure along the siege lines (Long, *Civil War Day by Day,* 536). As for the other reports, on 7–9 July Confederate General Joseph E. Johnston retreated to the gates of Atlanta; Confederate Jubal A. Early entered Maryland on 5 July and the Washington suburbs on 9 July, but

meeting strong resistance, he withdrew by 13 July (Long, *Civil War Day by Day,* 533, 535–36).

39. The events leading up to this mustering had developed following the Battle of Olustee on 20 February. Both sides had withdrawn and considerably diminished their forces in north Florida. However, anticipating another Federal advance from the east coast, Confederate General Beauregard came up with a plan for defending Florida that included gathering troops in the interior to engage the Federals in battle once they had dangerously extended their supply lines (Johns, *Florida during the Civil War,* 202).

40. That is, in heaven.

41. Hildreth and Cox, *History of Gainesville,* 36.

42. Richie does not appear on any militia rolls but received a pension from the state of Florida for his service in Howse's unit (Hartman and Coles, *Biographical Rosters,* 6:2346).

43. Harry G. Cutler, *History of Florida: Past and Present* (Chicago: Lewis, 1923), 3:184–85; Walter W. Manley II, E. Canter Brown Jr., and Eric W. Rise, *The Supreme Court of Florida and Its Successor Courts, 1821–1917* (Gainesville: University Press of Florida, 1997), 291.

44. Hartman and Coles, *Biographical Rosters,* 3:1040.

Education of the Children, 1864–73

1. Cutler, *History of Florida,* 3:184–85; Manley, Brown, and Rise, *Supreme Court of Florida,* 291.

2. Johns, *Florida during the Civil War,* 178, 180.

3. No explanation for the change can be found. The boys may not have been academically prepared for the college.

4. Perhaps the Taylors could not afford to continue this schooling, because in 1866 they had a great deal of labor trouble and went heavily into debt. Or perhaps that was all the institutional education they aspired to.

5. John Taylor perhaps had the contact through his friend David Yulee, also a railroad man. Johns Hopkins (1795–1873) is now best known as the founder of the university that bears his name.

6. Hildreth and Cox, *History of Gainesville,* 60.

7. Wallace is identified on page 242.

8. This whole outburst is uncharacteristic in its vehemence and incoherence. The gist appears to be that Maria had refused to attract Johnny to religion by diluting the true faith.

9. At this time, the Reverend P. P. Bishop was pastor of Bethel Baptist Church in Jacksonville, president of the Florida Baptist Convention, and general missionary for the Florida Baptist Mission Board.

10. Albertus Vogt, son of neighbor Dr. Vogt.

11. Sophie Bauskett, Maria's ten-year-old granddaughter who was on a prolonged visit with the Dawkinses.

12. Thomas Bauskett had died in 1868, and Mary, now married to William Ansley, was living in St. Augustine, Fla.

13. Julius's story is based on Citadel Conduct Rolls; Rawick, ed., *The American Slave*, 2:48–71; Jeannette May Christopher, *Glenn and Kin* (Franklin, N.C.: Genealogy Publishing Service, 1994), 111–16; John S. Reynolds, *Reconstruction in South Carolina* (Columbia, S.C.: State, 1905), 184–215; and family oral history. James Dawkins would have been especially sympathetic to Julius because his nephew Ben Dawkins was still in the Union jail.

14. John Taylor's final illness and death are treated on pages 227–37 of this section.

15. Hildreth and Cox, *History of Gainesville,* 61.

The Taylors and the Freedmen

1. Bostick, a former neighbor in upper St. Peter's Parish, had been one of the great planters of the area and a leading figure in the Taylors' church there.

2. The first extant after the war, the 1867 diary stands somewhat isolated because the diaries for 1865–66 and 1868–69 are missing. It is also the only diary that exists solely as a typescript.

3. The 1860 U.S. Census, the last under slavery, shows sixty-four slaves for the Taylors.

4. The Bausketts had moved to Palatka, Fla.

5. The Freedmen's Bureau, as passed in revised form on 16 July 1866, was organized under the War Department and was backed by military force. Except for its educational work, it was discontinued 1 July 1869. Considering that the bureau was generally hated by white southerners, the Taylors' relationship with Remley must have been unusual.

6. Maria so seldom uses the term "darkies" that it seems to express special exasperation when she does.

7. See note 21 on page 355.

8. Apparently Maria at age fifty-three is getting a full taste of "the cookpot" for the first time in her life.

9. See headnote to entry of 2 January 1864.

10. Wallace D. Dawkins (1843–90), born in South Carolina, later served as Ocala councilman, 1882–83; see Canter Brown Jr., *Florida's Black Public Officials, 1867–1924* (Tuscaloosa: University of Alabama Press, 1998), 83–84. His name suggests ties to two of the Taylor in-law families.

11. Whorden's and John Taylor's economic interests were of course at odds here. Whorden's share would be lessened by the outside labor while John Taylor's share would decrease if the crops were not worked.

12. That is, Maria was having her eleven-year-old daughter assist in the wine-making.

13. In the sense of "compelling obedience."

14. There was much talk around this time of bringing in Irish labor.

15. The purpose of the election was to approve the calling of a constitutional convention for Florida, preparatory to readmission to the Union, and to elect delegates to it. This was the first election in which Florida freedmen could vote.

Financial and Emotional Crises

1. Charlton W. Tebeau, *A History of Florida* (Miami: University of Miami Press, 1971), 257.

2. Marion County Deed Book H.

3. Dower right was the one-third interest in the husband's property that would automatically go to a married woman upon the husband's death and in which she had a vested interest during his lifetime. A husband could not sell a property unless the wife renounced her dower right in it, in effect giving her veto power over a sale or mortgage.

4. Lydia Taylor had married Edward Crane in 1869. They now lived in Pittsburgh, Pa.

5. Rosengarten, *Tombee*, 83.

6. These 185 acres were only a small part of the 1,000 acres of improved acreage listed for Osceola in the 1870 U.S. Agricultural Census (2,500 acres unimproved). Apparently John is not counting the land under cultivation by the sharecroppers.

7. That is, provide credit for seeds, equipment, and so on.

8. Marion County Deed Book I.

9. Florida legislator and later governor Ossian Bingley Hart pushed strongly for the bill, fighting efforts to weaken its provisions or prevent its passage. Hart considered the act as "one of the best . . . to be found on our statute books"; see Canter Brown Jr., *Ossian Bingley Hart, Florida's Loyalist Reconstruction Governor* (Baton Rouge: Louisiana State University Press, 1997), 62.

10. Maud Gary of Ocala was a leading Baptist in the area and a close friend of Maria's. She was president of the Baptist Missionary Society and she founded a school for girls, securing as principal the daughter of a celebrated Baptist theologian, Dr. Basil Manly Jr. (see Dalton, "A History of Florida Baptists," 377–78). Her husband, D. H. G. Gary, was a lawyer.

11. Apparently some of John's debt was held in South Carolina, perhaps through Behn's dealings.

12. Sarah and Henry Buzhart, a black couple. Henry, an important man on the place, was probably the overseer. He had some connection to Major Behn. Sarah is mentioned already in the 1867 diary.

13. "Exciting" is not used in the modern positive sense, but more in the vein of "agitating."

14. Apparently a creditor of John's had died and the executor had turned John's debt over to someone else.

15. No doubt there was a psychosomatic component in John's illness (as in Maria's spells), but he was mostly suffering from the effects of decades of malaria, an endemic disease in the South Carolina lowcountry.

16. On bringing over Irish labor to replace black workers, at this point a straw-clutching solution to his plantation problems.

17. The Old Testament book in which God tries Job's faith by inflicting disasters upon him.

18. Intermittent fever with no well-defined spasms of chill.

19. Here begins a barrage of assaultive medicines common at the time, some already familiar from the account of Willie's final illness. Alphabetized for easy reference, those mentioned here and later include: blue pill, a mercury compound and mild laxative; calomel, another mercury compound given as a purgative and specifically to kill intestinal worms; Dover's powder, a compound of ipecac and opium to kill pain and induce perspiration; hydrage, a diuretic; ipecac, an expectorant and specifically for amoebic dysentery; magnesia, a mild laxative; and quinine, the standard remedy for malaria. At least John was not wet-cupped.

20. Although over the years the diaries frequently mention John holding family services, attending church, and taking a hand in church affairs, Maria's first comment about his personal spirituality appears during this trying period.

21. From Palatka, where Dr. Moody now had "a handsome and well-appointed Drug Store" (Hammond, *Medical Profession in 19th Century Florida*, 439).

22. It must have been quite a blow to have Dr. Vogt sue and to hear about it second-hand. For years he had been neighbor and friend, and members of the two families socialized frequently. But everyone was having a hard time of it.

23. Maria is reminding herself of these Biblical maxims for her own guidance in difficult times.

24. John Keble (1792–1866), English clergyman and poet. His important and popular poetical work, *The Christian Year* (1827), was based on the Book of Common Prayer.

25. A daughter of James Clement Furman.

A Time of Transition

1. The 1872 diary is missing.

2. Fen helped a great deal, but it was Richie who bore the brunt of managing and working on the plantation.

3. These figures are still further reduced from the already low figure that John Taylor had given for 1870.

4. A Gainesville resident. Dawkins appears to have been her attorney.

5. James E Broome, former governor of Florida, a neighbor, and uncle of Johnny Taylor's wife.

6. Richard, twenty-five, and John, thirty, were both working for mercantile firms in New York City. Richie was able to live at Osceola for a good part of the year, using it as home base for his travels and doing some of his business by mail.

7. Grant took the photo of the Osceola plantation house in this volume, probably for prospective buyers. He seems to have been around still (or again) a year later. A notice in the *Ocala Banner* of 4 July 1874 (4:6) announces the Article of Incorporation of the Florida Agricultural, Immigration, and Improvement Company, with the purpose of establishing model farms and bringing in improved machinery, stock, seeds, skilled laborers, farmers, and gardeners; the signatories are J. B. Dawkins (Maria's son-in-law), Alonzo G. Grant, and R. F. Taylor (her son).

8. John was living in New York City with his wife, Curran, and two children.

9. By her own place, Maria means the eighty-acre homestead; Richie must have been assigned another parcel as his own.

10. From now on, Maria usually calls Anne "Nan."

11. The Reverend John Henry Tomkies, a native of Hanover County, Va., was the pastor of the Gainesville church and an editor of the newly founded *Florida Baptist* newspaper that later published some of Maria's pieces; see Dalton, "A History of Florida Baptists," 458.

12. The engine was one of Jackman's main responsibilities, so the housing for the family is being set up close by. The engine ran on a boiler, and equipment for sawing, ginning, grinding, and so on could be attached.

13. An attachment for the Osceola engine.

14. Although Maria always refers to Dore's husband as "Dr. Wallace," he is not listed in Hammond, *Medical Profession in 19th Century Florida,* a comprehensive account of nineteenth-century Florida physicians, nor is there any evidence in the MBT documents that he ever practiced as a physician. He may have practiced earlier in Kentucky, or the title may have been honorific considering his profession of druggist.

15. Her daughter, formerly Mary Bauskett.

16. That is, discouraged by the difficulties with the equipment. Maria was losing money by this decrease in customers.

17. Carrie was by now a confirmed semi-invalid.

18. Stowe (1811–96) was an almost exact contemporary of Maria's, and Maria surely knew that since 1867 Stowe had owned a Florida plantation on the St. John's River a little south of Jacksonville, where she wintered for years. Stowe was roundly attacked from many quarters for writing *Lady Byron Vindicated,* which accused Lord Byron of incest. For a discussion of the furor, see Joan D. Hedrick, *Harriet Beecher Stowe: A Life* (New York: Oxford University Press, 1994), 362–69.

19. As she often mentions doing, Maria took several days to finish this letter. Toward the end she talks about things that happened after the 30 September date of the letter.

20. "Darkies," a term very rare in Maria's writings, is here apparently confined to children.

21. That is, her own children, now all adults.

22. The reference is to Beecher and Elizabeth Tilton, his alleged lover. Frank Moulton, a mutual friend of Beecher and Theodore Tilton, the plaintiff, was a go-between and witness for the plaintiff. For a full discussion of the scandal and its social significance, see Clifford E. Clark Jr., *Henry Ward Beecher: Spokesman for a Middle-Class America* (Urbana: University of Illinois Press, 1978), 197–232.

23. Maria's grandchild Louise Bauskett, age six. Lydia had kept her for almost a year in Pittsburgh, then sent her to Osceola for another prolonged stay. She was now being sent back to her mother. Willie and Tommy Bauskett also spent much of 1871–75 at Osceola, cared for primarily by Sue. It never becomes clear why these children were not living with their mother and stepfather in St. Augustine.

24. An ironically understated criticism of Jackman, specifics unknown.

25. "Our Pittsburgh Letter, August 5th, 1875," *Ocala East Florida Banner,* 21 August 1875.

26. Thomas Rambaut now held the pulpit at the Tabernacle Baptist Church in Brooklyn.

Conclusion

1. Scott, *Southern Lady,* 67–73. An inveterate reader of a wide range of the religious press, Maria must have been acquainted with such arguments.

2. A. W. Yulee to D. L. Yulee, 11 July 1864.

3. *DeBow's Review,* Feb. 1856, quoted in Rosengarten, *Tombee,* 176. Whether Maria had the psychological sophistication to see a connection between this kind of character formation and the qualities needed to enforce the slavery system can only be conjectured.

4. L. T. Crane to D. T. Wallace, 13 March 1896.

5. Information on Robert Fenwick Taylor as justice is based on Manley, Brown, and Rise, *Supreme Court of Florida,* 290–92. "The longest-serving justice of his era," Fen was chief justice for twelve of his thirty-five years on the court. Manley, Brown, and Rise add that he participated in 76 percent of all cases decided by the Florida Supreme Court since its inception.

6. Manley, Brown, and Rise, *Supreme Court of Florida,* 291.

7. She probably had in mind the "local color" school of writing then coming into its own.

8. This view is discussed on pages 66–75.

9. See Stephen Jay Gould, *The Mismeasure of Man* (New York: Norton, 1981), 30–72, for discussion of these nineteenth-century attempts.

Four

Introduction

1. See Kathleen Woodward, "Simone de Beauvoir: Aging and Its Discontents," in *The Private Self: Theory and Practice of Women's Autobiographical Writings,* ed. Shari Benstock, (Chapel Hill: University of North Carolina Press, 1988), 93, for her presentation of these factors.

2. Carl Webber in *Eden of the South,* quoted in Jess G. Davis, *History of Gainesville Florida with Biographical Sketches of Families* (N.p., 1966), 35, 39.

Reading and Writing

1. Quoted by Ellen Sutton Wallace in her genealogical collection. Hocker was acquainted with Maria through her son Fen, whom he had probably known for years. A graduate of the University of Virginia law school, Hocker had a lucrative Florida law practice (ending up in Ocala), was an influential Democrat, and served in the state legislature. He was appointed Florida Fifth Circuit judge, a position earlier held by Maria's son-in-law James Dawkins, and joined Fen Taylor as a justice of the Florida Supreme Court after Maria's death; see Manley, Brown, and Rise, *Supreme Court of Florida,* 337–39.

2. In his obituary of Maria (see the epilogue). C. V. Waugh, a native of Virginia, had come to Gainesville to teach in the East Florida Seminary, established by the state of Florida. He then became pastor of the Gainesville Baptist Church and established a girls' school, advertising it as "the place to prepare your daughter for college." He was also active in promoting and editing Baptist newspapers (see Dalton, "A History of Florida Baptists," 378). He ended his career as professor at Florida Southern College in Lake City.

3. Edward E. Chielens, ed., *American Literary Magazines: The Eighteenth and Nineteenth Centuries* (New York: Greenwood, 1986), 168.

4. Hume (1711–76), Scottish philosopher and historian, was the greatest of the British empiricists. Macaulay (1800–59) was the most-read British historian of his time.

5. Admiral Matthew Calbraith Perry (1794–1858), whose 1853–54 expedition opened Japan to American trade; Sir Henry Morton Stanley (1841–1904), British journalist and explorer in Africa.

6. Lina Mainiero, ed., *American Women Writers* (New York: Ungar, 1979), 1:499.

7. Scott, *Southern Lady,* 118–21.

8. Chaudoin, for years Florida's most outstanding Baptist leader, served as secretary of the Florida Baptist Board of Domestic Missions, tirelessly promoting Baptist educational institutions and journalistic endeavors (see Dalton, "A History of Florida Baptists," 170, 313–19, 378). He was also president of

the Florida Baptist Convention, 1880–92 (Rogers, *A Brief History of Florida Baptists,* 9).

Serving the Family

1. A small island off the Florida west coast, directly west of Ocala.

2. Kate had died on 13 September 1876 at age nineteen months.

3. Fen was on a trip to Tampa to campaign for the Democratic party.

4. "Mr C" is Julius Carlisle. His sisters Susan and Thompson Carlisle were visiting from South Carolina.

5. However, Maria insisted on giving Fen "a pair of my oxen" in return for the fifty dollars he gave her.

6. James Fletcher McKinstry Sr. (1842–1926). His family moved from South Carolina to Florida when he was a small child. A graduate of the Long Island Hospital Medical School in New York, he opened practice in 1866 in Gainesville, where for many years he enjoyed "a splendid reputation as physician and concerned citizen" (Hammond, *Medical Profession in 19th Century Florida,* 408–9). His son married Maria's granddaughter Amelia Carlisle.

7. A poultice made from heat-producing ingredients.

8. A form of quinine, given for malaria.

9. A sedative.

10. Richie's brother-in-law George Ansley. George and Richie's wife, Kate, were stepchildren of Richie's sister Mary Ansley, formerly Bauskett.

11. Dore's husband, William Wallace. He was a pharmacist, not a physician.

12. The family group now includes two Carries and two Millies as well as two Marias.

13. Julius Jr. had died in 1887 as a small child.

14. The poem "Thanatopsis" (1813), a meditation on death, is one of the earliest and best-known works of William Cullen Bryant (1794–1878), American poet and newspaper editor.

15. Susan Hill Carlisle, Julius's younger sister. She remained with the Carlisles for at least twelve years.

Teaching the Grandchildren

1. This treatment is similar to that employed for items of a similar nature in part 2, dealing with the education of Maria's own children in 1859–63.

2. Maria's giving whiskey to eighteen-month-old John Carlisle, and evidently being pleased that he liked it, is a good example of the famous "medicinal purposes" to which hard liquor was put.

3. Evans Haile, a brother of Millie Taylor. The Haile plantation was just outside Gainesville.

4. Perhaps "so far" in Gainesville. A remark in her 9 January 1892 letter to Ann Furman indicates that Maria did not spare the rod. Describing a family

gathering at which her adult grandson Willie Bauskett was present, Maria writes, "They discussed some of the peach switches used in his behalf, & Willie asserted 'that we need never suppose he had gotten off from a whipping Grandma promised even if a week had passed.'" Willie had lived at Osceola under Maria and Sue's care from ages four to nine years in 1870–75. The remark seems to fall into the "fond family memories" category.

5. Meaning that the gaslight was too dim for her to see by.

Memorializing a Friend

1. Samuel Macauley Jackson, ed., *The New Schaff-Herzog Encyclopedia of Religious Knowledge* (New York: Funk and Wagnalls, 1910), 101–2.

2. Friedman, *The Enclosed Garden,* 113–18.

3. Dalton, "A History of Florida Baptists," 319.

4. Mr. Newel was a McAll worker, and the Record was the mission publication.

5. Mr. Curry can hardly have been enthusiastic about a diversion of his parishioners' charitable monies to Paris.

6. Apparently, Maria's letter is making a formal commitment to the mission and she wants to check out the legal implications for herself and the family with her lawyer son.

7. Maria's letter has not survived.

8. Translated by Susanne Bellocq.

9. A daughter of James Clement Furman.

10. That is, the national association, to which she was the Florida representative.

11. She means being finished with these wind-up chores.

Approaching Death

1. That is, Richard at age forty-six had still not had a conversion experience and been baptized.

2. Maria's daughter Carrie Dawkins. Her granddaughter Carrie Carlisle had died on 27 January 1894 of typhoid fever at age sixteen.

3. Her daughter Dore Wallace.

4. Those mentioned in this entry not earlier identified: Millie and Ena, Fen's wife and daughter Serena; Miss Sue, Thomas, John, and Kitty are Julius Carlisle's sister and his children (Maria's grandchildren); Richie and Kate are Maria's son and his wife.

5. Maria's poem on Carl's death was published in the *Gainesville Sun* and the *Baptist Witness.*

6. Kate and Curran are Maria's daughters-in-law, married respectively to Richard and John.

7. Her twelve-year-old granddaughter Ellen Wallace.

8. Serena was closely related to the husband of Mary Boykin Chesnut, the famed Civil War diarist, and more distantly to Mary Chesnut herself. Two of the Haile children married into the Taylor family: Millie to Fen Taylor, and Lawrence Whitaker Haile to Mary Louise Bauskett, Maria's granddaughter, in 1896.

9. That is, Sue's spiritual state was satisfactory.

10. Carrie's husband James Baird Dawkins had died in 1883.

11. Sue's husband, a contentious schoolmaster who had a hard time holding a job, was also personally trying.

Epilogue

1. These and other virtues are discussed in Personal Narratives Group, *Interpreting Women's Lives: Feminist Theory and Personal Narratives* (Blooming-ton: Indiana University Press, 1989), 140, 262–64.

2. Ellen Sutton Wallace (1883–1969) of Gainesville, who preserved much of the MBT material and read through it several times as an adult.

3. *Gainesville Sun,* 1 January 1896.

Bibliography

Bibliographical Note. The writings of Maria Baker Taylor and the family letters listed under Primary Documents constitute a small selection of the material available. The quantity of the largest categories of the total material is:

Writings of MBT

22 diaries: 576,000 words

81 letters: 70,200 words

16 prose pieces: 9,650 words

32 poems: 1,320 lines

miscellaneous juvenalia: 11,000 words

Associated letters

86 letters: 22,580 words

Sources

Family Personal Papers in Manuscript

Abbreviations of sources:

FFP = Furman Family Papers, Baptist Historical Collection, James B. Duke Library, Furman University, Greenville, S.C.

Wl = Ellen Sutton Wallace Collection (private), Gainesville, Fla. (copies of many items deposited in South Caroliniana Library, University of South Carolina, Columbia, S.C.)

Ws = Paul John Weiss Jr. Collection (private), Greensboro, N.C.

YP = David Levy Yulee Papers, P. J. Yonge Library of Florida History, University of Florida Libraries, Gainesville, Fla.

Anderson, John W. to John Morgandollar Taylor Sr. 11 April 1864.

Baker, Mary Louise. Letter to Maria Dorothea Furman. 15 September 1843. FFP.

Baker, Sarah Maria [MBT]. School Papers. Wl.

———. Letter to Harriet Davis Furman. 3 March 1834. FFP.

Baker, Thomas. Letter to Sarah Maria Baker. 5 March 1829. Wl.

———. Letter to James Clement Furman. 28 October 1836. FFP.

Bauskett, Mary Taylor. 1858 and 1859 Diaries. Ws.

Bauskett, Thomas Creyon. 1860 Diary. Ws.

Beard, Susan Taylor. Letter to Lydia Taylor Crane. 23 June 1884. Wl.

Behn, Phineas H. Letter to James Baird Dawkins. 20 March 1872. Wl.

Bracq, Emma W. Letter to Maria Baker Taylor. 5 March 1891. Wl.

Crane, Lydia Taylor. Letter to Maria Baker Taylor. 26 November 1870. Wl.

———. Seven letters to Dore Taylor Wallace. 1892–99. Wl.

Dalencourt, Justine. Letter to Emma W. Bracq. 5 March 1891. Wl.

Furman, Ann Eliza. Letter to James Clement Furman. 22 June 1855. FFP.

———. Two letters to Maria Dorothea Furman. 1833–34. FFP.

Furman, Henry Hart. Four letters to James Clement Furman. 1829–32. FFP.

Furman, James Clement. Letter to Harriet Davis Furman. 5 March 1834. FFP.

Furman, Josiah B. Letter to Maria Dorothea Furman. 10 June 1836. FFP.

Furman, Maria Dorothea. Four letters to Ann Eliza Furman. 1833. FFP.

———. Letter to Henrietta D. Furman. 8 October 1832. FFP.

Furman [Baker], Rachel. Letter to Rachel Brodhead Furman. 17 August 1793. FFP.

Furman, Richard. Letter to Sarah Furman Haynsworth. 4 March 1799. FFP.

Furman, Sara Susannah. Letter to Henrietta D Furman. 5 March 1833. FFP.

———. Three letters to Maria Dorothea Furman. 1823–30. FFP.

McAll, Robert Whitaker. Letter to David Levy Yulee. 1 October 1885. YP.

———. Letter to Maria Baker Taylor. 4 March 1891. Wl.

Taylor, Henry. Estate Papers. Forty-seven letters (various hands), twenty-two rice-sale accountings, W. F. Colcock legal opinion. Wl.

Taylor, John M., Jr. Letter to John M. Taylor Sr. 22 November 1870. Wl.

Taylor, John Morgandollar, Sr. Letter to L. Dozier. 7 May 1870. Wl.

———. Letter to Sarah Maria Baker. ca.1833. Wl.

———. Letter to James Clement Furman. 3 June 1849. FFP.

———. Two letters to Maria Baker Taylor. 1845, 1851. Wl.

Taylor, Maria Baker. Diaries. Ws: 1857–58, 1860–63. Wl: 1864, 1867, 1870–71, 1873–75, 1879. Ws: 1882. Wl: 1883, 1885. Ws: 1888. Tatom: 1889. Ws: 1890–91. Wl: 1895.

———. Thirty-five letters to Ann Eliza Furman. 1846–95. FFP.

———. Ten letters to James Clement Furman. 1841–78. FFP.

———. Letter to Dora Furman Hutson. 31 March 1891. FFP.

———. Letter to John Morgandollar Taylor Jr. 6 May 1859. Wl.

———. Two letters to John Morgandollar Taylor Sr. 1850, 1852. Wl.

———. Letter to Mrs. Tucker. 27 January 1887. Wl.

———. Letter to David Levy Yulee. 3 June 1886. YP.

———. Miscellaneous Prose and Poetry. 1847–94. Wl.

———. Memorandum Book. 1857–63. Wl.

Taylor, Maria Dorothea. Letter to Maria Baker Taylor. 11 June 1873. Wl.

Taylor, Richard Baker. Letter to Maria Baker Taylor. 23 April 1866. Wl.

Taylor, Robert Fenwick. Letter to Maria Baker Taylor. n.d. [1892].

Taylor, William Baker. School Papers. 1863–64. Wl.

Wallace, Ellen Sutton. Letter to Thomas deSaussure Furman. 14 March 1951. Wl.

Yulee, Anne Wickliffe. Three letters to David Levy Yulee. 1862–64. YP.

Yulee, David Levy. Letter to Maria Baker Taylor. 25 August 1885. YP.

———. Letter to Anne Wickliffe Yulee. 19 March 1864. YP.

Unpublished Genealogical and Biographical Sources

Furman, James Lyons. "Reminiscences of an Octagenarian." 1905. Thomas deSaussure Furman Collection.

Furman, Thomas deSaussure. "The Descendants of Wood Furman."

Lord, Mills M. "David Levy Yulee, Statesman and Railroad Builder." Master's Thesis, University of Florida, 1940.

Owens, Loulie Latimer. "The Family of Richard Furman." 1983. Furman University.

Wallace, Ellen Sutton. Morgandollar/Taylor Genealogical Collection.

Weiss, Paul John, Jr. Morgandollar/Taylor Genealogical Collection.

State, County, and Institutional Records

Baker, Rachel, and Thomas Baker. Estate and Land Records. Sumter County, S.C.

Carlisle, J. A. Confederate Army Records. South Carolina Department of Archives and History. Columbia, S.C.

The Citadel. 1863 Conduct Roll of All Cadets. Charleston, S.C.

"Crane, Edward Payson." Index of Presbyterian Biography. Presbyterian Department of History. Philadelphia, Pa.

Morgandollar, John. Land Records. South Carolina Historical Society. Charleston, S.C.

Taylor, John M., and Maria B. Taylor. Land Records. Marion County, Fla.

Maria Baker Taylor Estate Paper. Alachua County, Fla.

Newspapers

"Article of Incorporation of the Florida Agricultural, Immigration and Improvement Co." Ocala, Fla., *Ocala Banner,* 4 July 1874, 4.

"Florida." *Georgetown County (S.C.) Winyah Observer,* 28 July 1852, 2. Reprinted from *Charleston Courier.*

"Florida Crops of 1850." *Georgetown County (S.C.) Winyah Observer,* 8 January 1851, 2.

"James B. Dawkins." Obituary. *Gainesville Weekly Bee,* 16 February 1883, 2.

"Mary Morgandollar Taylor." Unidentified newspaper clipping. 1842. Ws.

Taylor, Maria Baker. "Anne W. Yulee." Obituary. *Fernandina Florida Mirror,* 18 July 1885.

———. "Economy." *Christian Index,* 28 May 1885, 2.

———. "The Evil Power." *Christian Index,* 13 December 1883, 7.

————. "Fagots from an Old Stick." *Florida Baptist,* 5 February 1878, 2.

————. "A Fragment." *Christian Index,* 16 October 1884, 6.

————. "A Letter from Grandma." *Christian Index,* 29 May 1880, 8.

————. "In Memory of Mrs. Anne Carlisle." *Christian Inquirer,* 10 August 1890.

————. "Oh, Can this Earth." *Religious Herald,* 4 June 1874, 1.

————. "Patience under Injury." *Christian Index,* 17 December 1885, 4.

————. "Thomas Willingham." Obituary. *Christian Index,* 7 August 1873.

————. "Truth, Light, and Love." *Christian Index,* 1 November 1883, 7.

"Trade with Florida." *Winyah Observer,* 4 February 1852, 2. Reprinted from *Charleston Courier.*

Waugh, C. V. "Maria Baker Taylor." Obituary. *Gainesville Sun,* 1 January 1896.

Books and Articles

Bailey, Rufus William. *The Family Preacher.* New York: Taylor, 1837.

Beauchamp, Virginia Walcott. *A Private War: Letters and Diaries of Madge Preston, 1862–1867.* New Brunswick, N.J.: Rutgers University Press, 1987.

Brown, Canter, Jr. "The Civil War, 1861–1865." In *The New History of Florida,* edited by Michael Gannon, 231–48. Gainesville: University Press of Florida, 1996.

————. *Florida's Black Public Officials, 1867–1924.* Tuscaloosa: University of Alabama Press, 1998.

————. *Ossian Bingley Hart, Florida's Loyalist Reconstruction Governor.* Baton Rouge: Louisiana State University Press, 1997.

Buker, George E. *Blockaders, Refugees, and Contrabands: Civil War on Florida's Gulf Coast, 1861–1865.* Tuscaloosa: University of Alabama Press, 1993.

Burr, Virginia Ingraham, ed. *The Secret Eye: The Journal of Ellen Gertrude Clanton Thomas, 1848–1889.* Chapel Hill: University of North Carolina Press, 1990.

Butterfield, Fox. *All God's Children.* New York: Knopf, 1995.

Chielens, Edward E., ed. *American Literary Magazines: The Eighteenth and Nineteenth Centuries.* New York: Greenwood, 1986.

Christopher, Jeannette May. *Glenn and Kin.* Franklin, N.C.: Genealogy Publishing Service, 1994.

Clark, Clifford E., Jr. *Henry Ward Beecher: Spokesman for a Middle-Class America.* Urbana: University of Illinois Press, 1978.

Clinton, Catherine. *The Plantation Mistress: Woman's World in the Old South.* New York: Pantheon Books, 1982.

Cook, Harvey Toliver. *The Life Work of James Clement Furman.* Greenville, S.C.: Furman University, 1926.

Covington, James W. *The Billy Bowlegs War, 1855–1858: The Final Stand of the Seminoles against the Whites.* Chuluota, Fla.: Mickler House, 1982.

Cutler, Harry G. *History of Florida: Past and Present.* Vol. 3. Chicago: Lewis, 1923.

Dalton, Jack P. "A History of Florida Baptists." Ph.D. Diss., University of Florida, 1952.

Davis, George B., et al., eds. *The Official Atlas of the Civil War.* Washington, D.C.: U.S. War Department, 1983.

Davis, Jess G. *History of Gainesville Florida with Biographical Sketches of Families.* N.p., 1966.

Davis, William Watson. *The Civil War and Reconstruction in Florida.* 1913. Reprint, Gainesville: University of Florida Press, 1964.

Denham, James M. *"A Rogue's Paradise": Crime and Punishment in Antebellum Florida, 1821–1861.* Tuscaloosa: University of Alabama Press, 1997.

Denham, James M., and Canter Brown Jr., eds. *Cracker Times and Pioneer Lives: The Florida Reminiscences of George Gillett Keen and Sarah Pamela Williams.* Columbia: University of South Carolina Press, 2000.

Dyer, Thomas, ed. *To Raise Myself a Little: The Diaries and Letters of Jennie, A Georgia Teacher, 1851–1886.* Athens: University of Georgia Press, 1982.

Fox, Norman. *Preacher and Teacher: A Sketch of the Life of Thomas Rambaut.* New York: Fords, 1892.

Fox-Genovese, Elizabeth. *Within the Plantation Household: Black and White Women of the Old South.* Chapel Hill: University of North Carolina Press, 1988.

Friedman, Jean E. *The Enclosed Garden: Women and Community in the Evangelical South, 1830–1900.* Chapel Hill: University of North Carolina Press, 1985.

Friedman, Susan Stanford. "Women's Autobiographical Selves." In *The Private Self: Theory and Practice of Women's Autobiographical Writings,* edited by Shari Benstock, 34–62. Chapel Hill: University of North Carolina Press, 1988.

Genovese, Eugene D. *The Slaveholders' Dilemma: Freedom and Progress in Southern Conservative Thought, 1820–1860.* Columbia: University of South Carolina Press, 1992.

Gibbes, Robert Wilson. *Documentary History of the American Revolution.* New York: New York Times, 1971.

Gould, Stephen Jay. *The Mismeasure of Man.* New York: Norton, 1981.

Gwin, Minrose C., ed. *Cornelia Peake McDonald: A Woman's Civil War. A Diary, with Reminiscences of the War from 1862.* Madison: University of Wisconsin Press, 1992.

Hammond, E. Ashby. *The Medical Profession in 19th Century Florida: A Biographical Register.* Gainesville: George A. Smathers Libraries of the University of Florida, 1996.

Hampsten, Elizabeth. *Read This Only to Yourself: The Private Writings of Midwestern Women, 1880–1910.* Bloomington: Indiana University Press, 1982.

Harrold, Stanley. *The Abolitionists and the South, 1831–1861.* Lexington: University Press of Kentucky, 1995.

Hartman, David W., and David Coles. *Biographical Rosters of Florida's Confederate and Union Soldiers, 1861–1865*. 6 vols. Wilmington, N.C.: Broadfoot, 1995.

Haynsworth, Hugh Charles. *Haynsworth-Furman and Allied Families*. Sumter, S.C.: Osteen, 1942.

Hedrick, Joan D. *Harriet Beecher Stowe: A Life*. New York: Oxford University Press, 1994.

Hildreth, Charles H., and Merlin G. Cox. *History of Gainesville, Florida: 1854–1979*. Gainesville: Alachua County Historical Society, 1981.

Jackson, Samuel Macauley, ed. *The New Schaff-Herzog Encyclopedia of Religious Knowledge*. New York: Funk and Wagnalls, 1910.

Jenkins, William Sumner. *Pro-Slavery Thought in the Old South*. Chapel Hill: University of North Carolina Press, 1935.

Johns, John E. *Florida during the Civil War*. Gainesville: University of Florida Press, 1963.

Johnson, Michael P., and James L. Roark. *Black Masters: A Free Family of Color in the Old South*. New York: Norton, 1984.

Johnston, Coy K. *Two Centuries of Lawtonville Baptists, 1775–1975*. Columbia, S.C.: State, 1974.

Kilgo, James. *Pipe Creek to Matthew's Bluff: A Short History of Groton Plantation*. Privately printed for the Winthron Family, 1988.

Klein, Rachel N. *Unification of a Slave State: The Rise of the Planter Class in the South Carolina Backcountry, 1760–1808*. Chapel Hill: University of North Carolina Press, 1990.

Koger, Larry. *Black Slaveowners: Free Black Slave Masters in South Carolina, 1790–1860*. Jefferson, N.C.: McFarland, 1985.

Lensink, Judy Nolte. *"A Secret to Be Burried": The Diary and Life of Emily Hawley Gillespie, 1858–1888*. Iowa City: University of Iowa Press, 1989.

Long, E. B., with Barbara Long. *The Civil War Day by Day: An Almanac, 1861–1865*. New York: Da Capo, 1971.

Loveland, Anne C. *Southern Evangelicals and the Social Order*. Baton Rouge: Louisiana State University Press, 1980.

Mahon, John K., and Brent R. Weisman. "Florida's Seminole and Miccosukee Peoples." In *The New History of Florida*, edited by Michael Gannon, 183–206. Gainesville: University Press of Florida, 1996.

Mainiero, Lina, ed. *American Women Writers*. 4 vols. New York: Ungar, 1979.

Manley, Walter W., II, E. Canter Brown Jr., and Eric W. Rise. *The Supreme Court of Florida and Its Successor Courts, 1821–1917*. Gainesville: University Press of Florida, 1997.

Mathews, Donald G. *Religion in the Old South*. Chicago: University of Chicago Press, 1977.

McCurry, Stephanie. *Masters of Small Worlds: Yeoman Households, Gender Relations, and the Political Culture of Antebellum South Carolina Low Country*. New York: Oxford University Press, 1995.

McMillen, Sally G. *Motherhood in the Old South: Pregnancy, Childbirth, and Infant Rearing*. Baton Rouge: Louisiana State University Press, 1990.

Mills, Robert. *Atlas of South Carolina*. Facsimile edition of 1825 original edition. Columbia, S.C.: Bostick and Thornley, 1838.

Moore, Frank, ed. *The Rebellion Record: A Diary of American Events*. 10 vols. New York: Putnam, 1861–65; van Nostrand, 1866–67.

Motz, Marilyn Ferris. *True Sisterhood: Michigan Women and Their Kin, 1820–1920*. Albany: State University of New York Press, 1983.

Myers, Robert Manson, ed. *The Children of Pride: A True Story of Georgia and the Civil War*. New Haven: Yale University Press, 1972.

Nicholes, Cassie. *Historical Sketches of Sumter County*. Sumter, S.C.: Sumter County Historical Commission, 1975.

Painter, Nell Irvin. Introduction to *The Secret Eye: The Journal of Ellen Gertrude Clanton Thomas, 1848–1889*, edited by Virginia Ingraham Burr, 1–67. Chapel Hill: University of North Carolina Press, 1990.

Palmer, Benjamin Morgan. *The Life and Letters of James Henley Thornwell*. Richmond, Va.: Whittet and Shepperson, 1875.

Pease, William H., and Jane H. Pease. *Private Values and Public Styles in Boston and Charleston, 1828–1843*. New York: Oxford University Press, 1985.

Personal Narratives Group. *Interpreting Women's Lives: Feminist Theory and Personal Narratives*. Bloomington: Indiana University Press, 1989.

Rawick, George P., ed. *The American Slave: A Composite Autobiography*. Vols. 2–3, *South Carolina Narratives*. Westport, Conn.: Greenwood, 1972.

Remini, Robert V. *Henry Clay: Statesman for the Union*. New York: Norton, 1991.

Reynolds, John S. *Reconstruction in South Carolina*. Columbia, S.C.: State, 1905.

Rivers, Larry E. *Slavery in Florida: Territorial Days to Emancipation*. Gainesville: University Press of Florida, 2000.

Rogers, James A. *Richard Furman: Life and Legacy*. Macon, Ga.: Mercer University Press, 1985.

Rogers, S. B. *A Brief History of Florida Baptists, 1825–1925*. N.p.: Florida State Library, n.d.

Rosengarten, Theodore. *Tombee: Portrait of a Cotton Planter with the Journal of Thomas B. Chaplin (1822–1890)*. New York: Morrow, 1986.

Rowland, Lawrence S., Alexander Moore, and George C. Rogers Jr. *The History of Beaufort County, South Carolina*. Vol. 1, *1514–1861*. Columbia: University of South Carolina Press, 1996.

Schleuter, Paul, and Jane Schleuter, eds. *An Encyclopedia of British Women Writers*. New York: Garland, 1988.

Scott, Anne Firor. *The Southern Lady: From Pedestal to Politics, 1830–1930*. Chicago: University of Chicago Press, 1970.

Shafer, Daniel L. "U.S. Territory and State." In *The New History of Florida*, edited by Michael Gannon, 207–30. Gainesville: University Press of Florida, 1996.

Sims, J. Marion. *The Story of My Life.* New York: Appleton, 1884.

Smith, H. Shelton, Robert T. Handy, and Lefferts A. Loetscher. *American Christianity: An Historical Interpretation with Representative Documents.* 2 vols. New York: Scribners, 1953.

Smith, Julia Floyd. *Slavery and Plantation Growth in Antebellum Florida: 1821–1860.* Gainesville: University of Florida Press, 1973.

Smith-Rosenberg, Carroll. "Hearing Women's Words: A Feminist Reconstruction of History." In *Disorderly Conduct: Visions of Gender in Victorian America,* 11–52. New York: Knopf, 1985.

Sutherland, Daniel E. *The Expansion of Everyday Life, 1860–1876.* New York: Harper and Row, 1989.

Taylor, Robert A. *Rebel Storehouse: Florida in the Confederate Economy.* Tuscaloosa: University of Alabama Press, 1995.

Taylor, Walter Carroll. *History of Limestone College.* Gaffney, S.C.: Limestone College, 1937.

Tebeau, Charlton W. *A History of Florida.* Miami: University of Miami Press, 1971.

Towles, Louis P., ed. *A World Turned Upside Down: The Palmers of South Santee, 1818–1881.* Columbia: University of South Carolina Press, 1996.

Ulrich, Laurel Thatcher. *A Midwife's Tale: The Life of Martha Ballard, Based on Her Diary, 1785–1812.* New York: Vintage Books, 1991.

Virkus, Frederick A., ed. *First Families of America: The Abridged Compendium of American Genealogy.* 7 vols. Chicago: F. A. Virkus, 1925.

Wilson, Clyde N., with Shirley Bright Cook and Alexander Moore, eds. *The Papers of John C. Calhoun.* 26 vols to date. Vols. 16, 18, 20, 22, 24. Columbia: University of South Carolina Press, 1984, 1988, 1991, 1995, 1998.

Woodward, Kathleen. "Simone de Beauvoir: Aging and Its Discontents." In *The Private Self: Theory and Practice of Women's Autobiographical Writings,* edited by Shari Benstock, 90–113. Chapel Hill: University of North Carolina Press, 1988.

Index